9/29/01
$30.00
B&T

AS
14 day
10/01

Withdrawn

DATE DUE	

The

Great

War

& the

Twentieth

Century

THE

GREAT

WAR

AND THE

TWENTIETH

CENTURY

EDITED BY

Jay Winter, Geoffrey Parker, and Mary R. Habeck

Yale University Press *New Haven & London*

Published with assistance from the Louis Stern Memorial Fund.

Designed by James J. Johnson and set in Minion Roman types.
Printed in the United States of America.

Library of Congress Cataloging-in-Publication Data

The Great War and the twentieth century / edited by Jay Winter,
Geoffrey Parker, and Mary R. Habeck.
    p. cm.
  Includes bibliographical references and index.
  ISBN 0-300-08154-5 (alk. paper)

  1. World War, 1914–1918.   I. Title. Great War and the 20th century.
II. Winter, J. M   III. Parker, Geoffrey, 1943–   .   IV. Habeck, Mary R.
D521 .G72 2000
940.3—dc21   00-028212

A catalogue record for this book is available from the British Library.

The paper in this book meets the guidelines for permanence and durability
of the Committee on Production Guidelines for Book Longevity of the
Council on Library Resources.

10 9 8 7 6 5 4 3 2 1

Contents

Part III *The Shadow of War*

Acknowledgments

Most of the essays in this volume originated in a series of lectures organized by the editors and delivered in 1994 at Yale University to commemorate the eightieth anniversary of the outbreak of World War I. The contributions were then revised, and a few others were added. We are grateful to those without whose support neither the lectures nor the book would have seen the light of day. A generous grant from the Lynde and Harry Bradley Foundation funded the lecture series, and another from the International Security Studies Program of Yale allowed its development into a book. Yale's history department provided a congenial home for sustained discussions between the speakers and their audiences. Essential help in organizing the project was provided by George Andreopoulos, Sir Michael Howard, Donald Kagan, Mark Shulman, and, above all, Paul Kennedy. Ann Carter-Drier provided vital logistical assistance throughout. We thank them all.

The

Great

War

& the

Twentieth

Century

Introduction

To this day the First World War remains contested territory: people still care passionately about it and hotly dispute its causes, its character, and its legacies. Studies of the war have therefore grown exponentially. Part of the fascination arises from a general sense of fin-de-siècle: the events of the early twentieth century are close enough for us to touch, both through our family histories and in a host of more public ways. Moreover, the great ideological and national conflicts ignited in 1914–18 dominated the rest of the century. It is hardly surprising, therefore, that the war itself seems both strangely familiar and curiously archaic: the whole conflict has acquired a sepia tint. To contemplate the Great War is to approach something at one and the same time familiar, unreachable, and terribly important.

This sense of significance derives from two sources. The first is the richness of the cultural artifacts and of the echoes of the war all around us. Our language bears the scars of the war in a host of mundane ways: in "going over the top," "no man's land," "fighting it out in the trenches," even in the medical category "shell shock." Enduring cultural references to 1914–18 retain their iconic power for another reason, however. They beckon us back to something the

world had never seen before: armed conflict on a world stage between industrialized powers, the first total war in history.

The phrase "total war" is shorthand for a process—an unfolding
set of events, not an outcome. It resembles a mathematical asymp-
tote, or Xeno's paradox, always approaching a limit but never getting
there. Rather, as the war spread, it sucked in more and more of the
world's manpower and resources. Each of the elements mobilized in
1914–18 had existed separately, but their combination was new, and
it soon acquired a deadly multiplicative character. Each element
tended to amplify the others so that the whole became far more
terrible than the sum of its parts.

Consider, for example, the war's unprecedented demographic
impact. Of the male population between the ages of fifteen and
forty-nine on the eve of the war, a huge proportion became soldiers:
about 80 percent in France and Germany, 75 percent in Austria-
Hungary, between 50 and 60 percent in Britain, Serbia, and the
Ottoman Empire, and 40 percent in Russia. Of these men—some
nine million in all—half were killed, wounded, or taken prisoner.
The losses, however, were not equal: one in three of all Serbs who
served in the war perished, compared with one in four Romanians,
Turks, and Bulgarians, one in six Frenchmen, and one in eight Brit-
ons. Casualties on this scale caused severe repercussions at home. As
many recent studies have emphasized, the removal from the labor
force of so many workers affected the war economies, welfare, and
women; less studied is the mass mourning that the mass deaths
produced. Although the civilian population may never have been
able to imagine the terrible killing fields where their loved ones fell,
the people at home certainly knew how murderous the war was,
despite the attempts of many soldiers and journalists to mislead
them. From 1914 they saw millions of refugees streaming from the
fighting in Belgium, France, Serbia, and Russia; soon they saw the
mutilated, and then they mourned the dead. By 1916 more than a

million French soldiers had died, as had almost as many Germans; by 1918 virtually every household in Europe had been hit by the pain of loss, although newspapers seldom reported or even acknowledged its ubiquity.

This silence was no accident. To maintain the commitment to the war effort, and to justify the massive slaughter, each combatant country organized an elaborate cultural campaign to steel the will of participants and to stifle dissent, thereby making it impossible for one to consider anything other than total victory or total defeat. By and large this campaign worked. Anti-war sentiment certainly grew as the conflict dragged on, but (with the notable exception of Russia) anti-war activists were unable to shorten the war by even one hour. This was largely because state-directed propaganda played only a part—often a minor part—in this cultural mobilization. Although political and social elites tried to manipulate opinion by using censorship and imprisonment, neither group did much to formulate public opinion in wartime. Their messages succeeded only in combination with those coming from below. The Great War revealed the propensity for populations to generate a commitment to a policy that involved unprecedented carnage. Kitsch, "thrillers," and the press disseminated direct messages with mass appeal about the virtues of one side and the villainy of the other. Music halls, movies, and the gramophone industry all expanded rapidly during the war, presenting anodyne or uplifting images to an increasingly tired and irritable population. The importance of this multimedia effort was clearly demonstrated in fall 1918, when the morale of both the German army and the German home front collapsed at the same time, when both "populations" came to realize that further sacrifices had become pointless. A ceasefire became inevitable.[1]

This cultural mobilization permitted what Peter Gay has called the "cultivation of hatred," which provided the context for war crimes of a revolutionary scale and character. Total war entailed the brutalization of millions and thereby raised radically the tolerance of violence in some of the societies caught up in armed conflict. Total war resembles an infection: it has the capacity to contaminate many populations, although most—through their legal systems, education, religious beliefs, military traditions, or other convictions and practices—possess some immunity. Those not so fortunate, those (so to speak) lacking the antibodies, succumb to the infection, and then the innocent suffer. In the first weeks of the war the streams of refugees and the widespread reprisals showed that massive forced migrations and systematic brutality were accepted as inevitable; then came the ruthless exploitation of Oberost (the territories conquered by the German army in the east) and the 1915 slaughter of the Armenian population by Turkish troops—a genocidal act committed under conditions of total war, a terrible harbinger of things to come. It was in Armenia that the darkest meaning of total war emerged. Its consequences are with us still.

*   *   *

The chapters in this book reveal some of the ways that historians have tried to interpret the causes, conduct, and consequences of the first total war. The authors draw on a wide body of scholarship about the 1914–18 conflict, the volume of which threatens to overwhelm anyone who attempts to keep up with it, let alone to add to it. Trench warfare on the Western front dominates this volume, as it did strategic discussions during the war itself. We have tried to present as much material as possible on the Eastern Front, but much of the history of the war in southeastern Europe—in Serbia, Romania, Bulgaria, and the Ottoman Empire—where casualty rates were even higher than in the West, has still to be written. Inevitably, many gaps remain. Readers should look elsewhere for recent accounts of the impact of the Great War on women's history, on medical history, on the economic aftermath of the war, and on veterans' associations.

Some historians have urged us to see 1914–45 as a second Thirty Years' War, with two major conflicts between the Great Powers separated by a temporary and fragile truce.[2] Although this view draws attention to important continuities, the Great War was also a watershed: it marked the end of one world and the beginning of another. In military terms, much changed from the start of the war to its end. Although the duke of Wellington would have recognized many tactical aspects of the war of 1914, just four years later even veterans of the early campaigns would have discovered a new and entirely unfamiliar world had they returned to the Western Front. Beyond the battlefield, to study the Great War is to encounter the demolition of far more than the four defeated empires—Russia, Germany, Austria-Hungary, and Turkey. It is to face the unraveling of a set of assumptions among both the victors and the vanquished about hope, progress, and the possibilities of a better future. In sum, it is to provide an essential framework for understanding the entire twentieth century.

Because no single volume can approach comprehensive coverage of a subject so vast and a literature so varied as that of the Great War, this book instead offers a summary of the current state of historical knowledge and debate—eight decades later—about the first total war of the twentieth century. The essays span the origins, conduct, and consequences of the conflict. In Part I, Michael Howard, William C. Fuller, Jr., and David Stevenson all bypass the "war as accident" school of thought, popularized by A. J. P. Taylor thirty years ago, and address the deeper sources of the collision of power between Britain and Germany over control of northwest Europe, and among Germany and Austria on the one hand and Russia on the other for hegemony in Eastern Europe. These clashes, although triggered by the conflict between Austria-Hungary and Serbia, with Russia behind Serbia, were hardly superficial events. "Pills to cure an earthquake!" the French historian Elie Halévy scoffed at those who saw one diplomatic move here or there as sufficient to have averted the war. "My subject," he wrote in 1930, "is the earthquake itself."[3] So, seventy years later, is ours.

The chapters in Parts II and III trace aspects of the first total war in comparative perspective. Mary R. Habeck and Leonard V. Smith address many issues in both military and cultural history raised by the gigantic mobilization of men and materiel in the field and their deployment on land, sea, and air. Gerald Feldman and John Horne analyze the "totalizing" effects of this unprecedented war effort with respect to industry and labor. The profound consequences of the war to the imperial system and to international relations are considered by A. S. Kanya-Forstner and Zara Steiner, and two concluding essays examine the cultural aftermath of the conflict: Holger H. Herwig considers how historians in the 1920s and 1930s helped create myths to allow their political leaders to evade accusations of war guilt, and Modris Eksteins argues that in the cultural domain, at least, Germany may be said to have won the war. Germany, the carrier of all the contradictions of "modernism"—understood as the detonation of the nineteenth-century belief in progress, conventional virtues, and values—had to sign the Armistice and admit defeat. By contrast, Britain and France, the victors who wanted to preserve the nineteenth-century order, became, Eksteins claims, the ultimate losers. They could not stem the tide of the modern; instead, it swept them under.

Although the authors of these chapters deploy archival material unexploited or unavailable until a few years ago, they still present only points of view, elements of an overall argument, rather than final resolutions of the conundrums raised by the Great War. The conflict seems to have raised so many issues of historical importance that, even eighty years later, the best service we can offer is to unpack the ways that today's historians have struggled to understand them.

Yet this book is also a collective endeavor in another, less direct way. In four respects the contributions are linked with the cataclysmic events of the 1990s. First, the collapse of the Soviet Union and its satellites has led to the waning of interest among historians of the war in the Russian Revolutions of 1917, and the waxing of interest in Russia and Eastern Europe in the first three years of the conflict. Until very recently this has constituted the greatest lacuna in First World War historiography, and our volume points to some of the ways that historians have begun to fill the gap.

Second, the unification of Germany has highlighted again the character of the conflict as (in Howard's words) a "war for the dominance of Europe," a struggle separated from but interlinked with the wars of German unification in 1866–71 and with the war in Western Europe in 1939–40 and in Eastern Europe thereafter. Anyone writing history in the 1990s can see how much of the debate over the "German problem" at the beginning of the twentieth century was still alive at its end.

Third, the breakup of Yugoslavia and the brushfire wars in parts of the old Soviet empire have reminded historians and their readers (if they needed any reminding) of the imperial character of the war and its outcome. This was as true within Europe as it was in Africa and Asia. Multinational cooperation and coalitions for war did not produce alliances for peace; instead, the outcome was an unstable (and probably doomed) reordering of imperial holdings, and a rekindling of imperial and anti-imperial conflicts.

Finally, the ambiguous position of the United States in world affairs, so clearly launched by the Great War, stands out in this volume: a major international force yet not a permanent part of the diplomatic system. As we struggle today to define the limits and principles underlying the role of the United States in the international system, it may be sobering to consider how similar were the debates on the same subject nine decades ago, first when the world went to war without the United States, and then after the United States joined the world at war in 1917.

Upheaval in Russia and Eastern Europe, the German question, the problem of ethnic conflict and national self-determination, the oscillations of American participation in European and world affairs: these issues have dominated what Eric Hobsbawm has dubbed the "short twentieth century": 1914–89. Not surprisingly, these themes inform historical debate today and are likely to do so for some years to come. The chapters in this volume, therefore, may be termed—in a very broad sense—present-minded. The same may be said for the mixture of approaches adopted in them. The contributors have sketched out a field in which, over the past two decades, military history, international history, and cultural history have come together; they realize the impossibility of segregating or privileging any one of these essential currents of study to the exclusion of the others. Instead, they present here a broader and more inclusive historical literature on the Great War than was available twenty years ago—one that relates ideas and public opinion to logistics and to the political and strategic aims for which millions of men and women were prepared to sacrifice so much.

This more comprehensive approach to the study of war may also reflect the world in which this scholarship was formed. Many of the contributors (and two of the editors) started their careers while the Cold War was at its height, yet by the mid-1970s the whole subject of military affairs was under the shadow of the Vietnam conflict. Whatever one's personal views, that war clearly demonstrated the need to study military history from a multiplicity of viewpoints. Focusing solely on strategic considerations, technology, logistics, ideology, or mass psychology would not do; only with a more inclusive approach could one begin to analyze the contours and character of military affairs. This challenge has been met by scholars in a number of fields, and their work has enriched our understanding of this critical interplay of elements. First World War studies, in particular, have become a house of many mansions, and we need to work toward what some French scholars call "l'histoire totale de guerre"—best understood not as the total history of total war but as the comparative history of armies and societies at war in this century. If this collection serves as a step in this direction, our volume will have realized part of its purpose.

NOTES

1. The fact that they crumbled together is hardly surprising, though the linkage has been obscured by the claim (generated during the war itself and widely disseminated in 1919) that the soldiers at the front had to surrender only because they were betrayed by cowards at home—the "stab-in-the-back" legend. Almost exactly the reverse happened: there was indeed a stab in the back, but the knife was wielded by a military leadership that led the country into a war it could not win and then brilliantly shifted responsibility for the disaster onto all shoulders except those who really bore the blame.

2. P. H. M. Bell, *The Origins of the Second World War in Europe* (London, 1986); and Michael Howard, "A Thirty Years' War? The Two World Wars in Historical Perspective," *Transactions of the Royal Historical Society,* 6th ser., 3 (1993): 171–84.

3. Elie Halévy, *The World Crisis of 1914–1918: An Interpretation; Being the Rhodes Memorial Lectures* (Oxford, 1930), 4.

Part

I

The

Framework

CHAPTER 1

The First World War Reconsidered

MICHAEL HOWARD

Outside Woolsey Hall at Yale University there stands a cenotaph, an empty tomb, bearing the inscription:

> In Memory of the Men of Yale
> Who, True to Her Traditions,
> Gave Their Lives That Freedom
> Might Not Perish from the Earth
> 1914–1918

In a nearby corridor the names of the hundreds of young men who gave their lives are inscribed on the walls. Most of them died within a space of three months: September, October, and November 1918. It is as if they had been lining up to get killed, much as their British contemporaries two years earlier had lined up to die in the Battle of the Somme.

This book does not deal with American participation in the First World War. We would need a different type of study to explain why so many of the most intelligent and courageous young men in the United States came to believe that unless their country took part in the war freedom would indeed perish from the earth. Rather, we are concerned with that war as a crisis in the history of Europe. But because Europe was then the fulcrum of world history—as it had never quite been before nor has been since—the war was also a critical event in the history of the world.

The name "First World War" was coined a few years after the event by a sardonic and farsighted journalist.[1] It is inaccurate. The Seven Years' War of 1756–63, whose decisive battles were fought as much in North America and in the Indian Ocean as they were on the plains of Europe, has a far better claim to that title. Most of those who took part in it—certainly the British—called it simply the Great War, and this somber spondee, like a tolling bell, seems a far more appropriate description of that huge tragedy. For the French it was *la Grande Guerre,* for the Italians *la Grande Guerra.* But to this general consensus there was a significant exception—the Germans. In spite of their minimal military and naval commitments outside Europe, the war was for them, from the very beginning, *das Weltkrieg,* the World War. Perhaps that in itself tells us something about German aspirations in 1914.

The "First World War" is appropriate in that it suggests, as was intended, that the war had left unfinished business and that further wars were bound to follow. This apprehension was generally shared in 1919. Immediately after the signature of the Treaty of Versailles, the *Daily Herald* published a cartoon showing Wilson, Clemenceau, and Lloyd George leaving the conference chamber and saying to each other, "Curious! I seem to hear a child weeping"; and sure enough, behind a pillar, there is a little boy crying his heart out, with "1940 class" above his head.

There are indeed those who would see the two world wars as a single Thirty Years' War interrupted by a long truce. There is much to be said for this view. I myself have suggested that the campaigns of 1939–40 be seen as a continuation of the First World War; a war for the dominance of Europe that Germany ultimately won—which had to be won before Hitler could begin the war that he really wanted, to conquer his *Lebensraum* in the East and create his Thousand-Year

Reich.[2] But more appropriate would be Raymond Aron's description of those years as *Guerres en Chaine,* wars separated but interlinked; a title that seemed all the more significant at the time that he published his book in the 1950s, when the Second World War seemed likely to precipitate a third.[3]

But once we put aside the naming of the war the historian is faced with a mass of questions about it. These questions fall under three main headings. First, of course, and most difficult of all: What was the war about? And—not necessarily the same thing—What did the belligerents think that it was about? Second (the concern primarily for military historians), Why did it take the form that it did? And finally, What were its consequences, for those taking part and for the world as a whole?

For the young men of Yale, as for most Americans, it was like all American wars, a war of ideology to protect and defend Freedom. Cynics have pointed out that the principal freedom these young men were defending was that of American businessmen to trade and make money. But for those who hold the values of the Enlightenment, freedom was and is indissoluble, whether it be freedom to trade or to travel, to speak one's mind or to change one's government. It must be said that these values were not generally accepted in the Germany of 1914, nor would the German government have promoted them generally if Germany had won. For Liberals in Britain the cause was much the same, though the emphasis was laid not so much on abstract Freedom as on upholding the Rule of Law, the sanctity of treaties and the rights of small nations. Again, cynics can point out that at the time the Rule of Law upheld the global supremacy of the British Empire, and that for the British the rights of small nations had not included those of the former Boer Republics or indeed the nascent Irish nation. But it can be said that in 1914 these matters lay heavy on the conscience of the Liberal administrators who took the country into war to defend the independence of

Belgium; and these leaders could legitimately claim that they had restored self-government to the Boers and were attempting in good faith to reach an equally generous settlement with the Irish—so generous indeed that in 1914 they had brought their own country to the brink of civil war.

On the war memorials that one finds in even the smallest villages throughout the United Kingdom there are not, in fact, many high-sounding statements about Freedom and the Rule of Law, but one phrase is carved on nearly all of them: God, King, and Country. It is the same on the more old-fashioned memorials in Germany—*Gott, König und Vaterland;* although under the Weimar Republic the first two words tended to disappear, as they had long since in postrevolutionary France. There they mourned simply the millions who had died *pour la Patrie.* Country, *Patrie, Vaterland*—these were the "causes" in defense of which the young men of Europe enlisted, rather than Freedom, Democracy, or the Rule of Law; and these were the communities that mourned them—and still mourn them—long after they were gone.

These monuments, rather than any purely documentary material, should be the starting point for new generations studying the First World War. They tell us a number of things. First, they are monuments of mourning, not of triumph: all of them, even those of the victors, depict the war as a tragedy, rather than—as is often the case with the Second World War—a triumphant crusade. They emphasize sacrifice rather than achievement. Second, their presence in nearly every settlement, however small, throughout Western Europe bears witness to the total involvement of those communities in the war. (And if they are less common in Eastern Europe, it is only because of the political confusion that developed in the region after 1918 rather than because the losses were any less severe or any less keenly felt.) The names on those memorials—many, tragically, from the same small number of families—give the measure of the loss;

those on the walls of elite universities and colleges show the extent to which entire classes were decimated.

Finally, and perhaps most important, the memorials reveal the solidarity of European society at the beginning of the twentieth century, a solidarity that did not survive the war. Only tiny minorities in any of the belligerent countries questioned their duty to serve or the legitimacy of the call made on them. "King and Country" or its equivalent was enough. The most successful recruiting poster of the war, and perhaps of any war, consisted simply of a picture of a uniformed general, Britain's premier war hero Herbert Horatio Kitchener, pointing his finger and saying "Your King and Country need YOU!"; a poster later to be imitated innumerable times, however sardonically, in the United States and elsewhere. After a few years, as sacrifices grew and enthusiasm ebbed, that call had to be reinforced by massive propaganda, but in 1914 it tapped deep resources of patriotic sentiment throughout Europe, sentiment that rose to frenzied enthusiasm in the great cities.

France was an exception. Within the previous few years a revival of nationalism had led many French intellectuals to greet war with the enthusiasm of their British and German counterparts, but that response found little echo in the countryside, *la France profonde*. There the memory of the war and invasion forty years earlier was still fresh to the older generation, and their children responded to the call to colors in a mood of stoical resignation rather than patriotic enthusiasm. But respond they did.[4] For the French, more perhaps than for any other of the great powers, there was clear *casus belli*. Once again their territory had been invaded, this time without the shadow of an excuse. On the eve of the war the socialist leader Jean Jaurès was assassinated by a right-wing fanatic in the belief that he was a pacifist. He was not. He had spent his life fighting for international understanding and for the abolition of war, but no one supported more strongly the necessity for national defense. The working classes as a whole took the same line, and France entered war united in a *union sacrée* hardly known since the Revolution.

The charge that in 1914 the peoples of Europe were being manipulated by warmongering elites was scornfully rejected by at least one witness in Germany. "The struggle of the year 1914 was not forced on the masses—no, by the living God—it was desired by the whole people," he wrote. "People wanted at length to put an end to the general uncertainty. Only thus can it be understood that more than two million German men and boys thronged to the colors for this hardest of all struggles, prepared to defend the flag with the last drop of their blood."[5] The fact that this witness was Adolf Hitler does not make him any less reliable: there is plenty of evidence to bear him out.

It cannot be said that this patriotic enthusiasm—the famous "mood of 1914" that appeared as strongly in the dynastic states of Russia and Austria-Hungary as it did in the "mature" nations of Western Europe—in itself created the war. Indeed, it took the leaders themselves by surprise: it had been only a few years since massive "peace" demonstrations had been held in all major European cities, including Berlin. The French authorities were in genuine doubt as to how many of their conscripts would answer the call to the colors, and police stood ready to intern left-wing political leaders. The more farsighted European statesmen realized that, however great the popular enthusiasm, the long-term consequences of the war were incalculable, and that it might, in the words of the German Chancellor Bethmann Hollweg, "topple many a throne." But in no country was policymaking crippled, as it was to be so disastrously in France and Britain in 1938, by a public profoundly reluctant to face the need for war. If there were groups critical of their government's brinksmanship, they were outshouted if not outnumbered, especially in Germany, by powerful and equally popular forces on the Right. Those forces preached that war was necessary as an instrument not simply of policy but of legitimate self-assertion, and they would make considerable trouble if it were not so used. The crowds that surged around the royal palace in Berlin on those hot July nights while issues of peace or war were being debated inside were not urging peace.[6]

So the peoples of Europe—including the intellectuals—fought because their governments told them to in causes that, insofar as they understood them, they entirely approved. So what were the causes, or the "Causes," of the First World War?

It is important to realize that not just one war broke out in 1914 but rather two, interlinked yet distinct. Each was fought over issues about which war would have been very difficult to avoid, assuming there had been any great desire to avoid it.

The first of the conflicts might be termed the Third Balkan War, or the War of the Austrian Succession; it was fought to determine who was to be master in the Balkans, Austria-Hungary, or the Russian Empire. This war had been threatening ever since the Congress of Berlin in 1878, and an entire generation of European diplomats had successfully devoted their careers to preventing it. The second conflict might be called the First German War; it was fought to expand or contain the immense latent power of the recently united Germany. Within the same framework of conflict are other equally distinct minor wars. The Italian war was the final act—or the intended final act—of the Risorgimento, the struggle to expel the Austrians from the peninsula. For Britain there was an opportunity to consolidate the empire's possessions in a great arc around the Indian Ocean, from South Africa to Singapore. Japan likewise gained an opportunity for some limited imperial expansion. But none of those opportunities would have arisen except in the context of the great general conflagration ignited by the pistol-shot fired by Gavril Princip on June 28, 1914.

That pistol-shot precipitated what was at first seen as merely the latest in a six-year succession of Balkan crises—ever since Austria-

Hungary annexed Bosnia-Herzegovina in 1908 and upset the balance established thirty years earlier at the Congress of Berlin. This new eruption did not at first cause any general concern. All the previous crises had been managed, so why not this one? Indeed, historians might well wonder why war had not broken out at any point during the previous six years.

Probably no few days in the history of the world have been subjected to such scrutiny as those between June 28, when the Archduke Franz Ferdinand was assassinated, and August 4, when Britain declared war: scrutiny not only by historians but by political scientists, who saw in the Balkan confrontation a sinister but useful paradigm for the problems of crisis-management in the Cold War. In that confrontation they found the situation with which their generation was so familiar: two major powers contesting dominance of a region through satellites they controlled imperfectly; neither willing to risk war, but neither ready to abandon their stakes and admit defeat at the hands of a dangerous adversary. As long as both major powers understood the situation—and could when necessary be reminded of it by their allies—peace could be kept and crises could be surmounted. So what went wrong?

One new factor in 1914 was that Austria-Hungary had ceased to be part of the solution and instead became a major part of the problem. Two developments had come together in an explosive critical mass. The first was the internal disintegration of Austria-Hungary, with the national minorities in both parts of the monarchy becoming increasingly unmanageable. The other was the march of a triumphalist Serbia, increasingly perceived as a magnet for the South Slavs within the Dual Monarchy, whose territory and military powers had doubled between 1912 and 1914 as a result of the two Balkan Wars. Each of these problems might have been managed on its own. Without an external threat, Vienna and Budapest might have coasted along indefinitely, managing their minorities with a mixture of repression and concession. Even if they could not, the disintegration of the monarchy, so widely foreseen on the death of the aged Emperor Franz-Joseph, need not have in itself caused a European war. On the other hand, a united and confident monarchy might have regarded the rise of Serbia more calmly and taken more effective steps to deal with it. As it was, the existence of each problem made the other lethal. A war that would destroy Serbian power and unite the monarchy seemed to the statesmen in Vienna the only way to postpone the ultimate and inevitable disaster.

Certainly the declaration of war was immensely popular in Vienna, not least among its formidable circle of intellectuals. Those young enough—Kokoschka, Musil, von Hoffmansthal, Wittgenstein, to name only a few—enlisted in the Royal and Imperial Army. Sigmund Freud, too old to enlist, nonetheless dedicated his libido, as he put it, to the service of the monarchy.[7] Despite the monarchy's inadequacies and inequities, none of its subject peoples—with the possible exception of the Czechs and perhaps a growing number of Croats—wished to see it humiliated and destroyed. They sang the anthem *Gott erhalten Franz den Kaiser* probably with greater enthusiasm than ever before in their lives.

Nor did literate citizens of the Russian Empire wish to see their country humiliated. Those optimistic thinkers who believe that the spread of democratic institutions necessarily guarantees international peace should ponder the example of Russia in the late nineteenth and early twentieth centuries. There the growth of representative institutions only increased internal pressures for a "forward" policy in the Balkans to rescue brother Slavs, first from Ottoman and then from Magyar and German oppression. The record over the past eight years had not been good: Russia had repeatedly encouraged the Serbs and then, conscious of its own military weakness, retreated under German pressure. There may not have been the same enthusiasm for the Serbs in Moscow and St. Petersburg as there had been for the Bulgarians in 1877, but Russian "honour" (a quality perhaps better known today as "credibility") was as integral to their support as that of Britain would be in supporting the Belgians a few weeks later. With Austria determined effectively to destroy Serbia, the Russian government confronted the alternatives of fighting or suffering a further massive humiliation; and that "public opinion," as expressed through the press and in the Duma, was not prepared to tolerate.

Whether Austria would have pressed on to the destruction of Serbia without its blank check from Germany is still a matter of controversy; but to my mind those historians (nowadays primarily German) who locate responsibility for the war entirely in Berlin and see the Austrians as mere puppets of the Germans take too little account of the situation in Vienna. The Austrians needed no urging from Berlin; they might indeed have ignored an attempt to veto their action. But Berlin made no such attempt, and that brings us to the German Question.

Analysis of the German Question has been confused, first by the accusation that Germany was solely responsible for the war—a charge first made by the victorious allies at Versailles and later revived by Fritz Fischer and his associates[8]—and then by the rebuttal, so popular in the 1930s, that Germany had no greater responsibility than anybody else. But the question is not whether Germany planned and then provoked a world war, as Fischer and his colleagues suggest. The questions are, rather, Was Germany set on a course that was bound to lead to armed conflict with its neighbors? And did German leaders act in a way that they *knew* carried a high risk of escalation into a European and—since Britain would almost certainly be involved—a world war?

The answer to both questions seems to be affirmative. Before 1914 the German government had been behaving in a manner that made war highly probable. In German leaders' eyes—and in those of a large proportion of the German political classes—what we would now term war-avoidance enjoyed a low priority indeed. Over the Sarajevo crisis the German leaders pursued a policy that they must have known carried a very high risk not only of European but of world war. They did this on the assumption that war was inevitable and that, given the growing power of the Russian Empire, the balance of military power was as favorable at that moment as it was ever likely to be. Statesmen like Bethmann Hollweg could thus regard it as a justifiable preemptive war and depict it to the Reichstag as entirely defensive. By so doing Bethmann Hollweg was able to enlist the support of all parties and create a degree of national unity unknown since 1870. The emotion that this engendered was so intense that even the level-headed minister for war, General von Falkenhayn, made the amazing declaration that "even if everything turns out disastrously, it will have been worth it."[9]

But for many influential German thinkers and political leaders it was not a preemptive war at all. It was the dawn of the long-awaited day when Germany could make evident the full measure of its greatness as a world power. As Germany had asserted its status as a European power only by defeating France, so could it break into the ranks of the world powers only by defeating and humiliating England. This view was held by many German publicists and journalists, and a significant number of people, not least in England, had come to believe them.

In his definitive study *The Anglo-German Antagonism,* Paul Kennedy makes it clear that in 1914 Germany had nothing specific to fight Britain about.[10] Each was the other's best customer commercially, and there were no territorial disputes overseas that had not been peacefully settled. But Germany had nothing specific to fight *anyone* about. Germany needed and desired no more territory; economically it was becoming dominant throughout Central Europe, a dominance that was ripening into a hegemony; and it was peacefully and skillfully penetrating the Middle East with the acquiescence (if not the explicit consent) of a Britain that saw German influence there as a useful counterbalance to that of Russia.

But that was exactly the trouble. Germany was both a satisfied yet deeply *dissatisfied* power. It is difficult to assess how far the profound need for expansion and self-assertion so typical of German writing before 1914 was the result of internal social tensions. Also difficult to assess is the influence of such thinkers as Nietzsche and such intellectual trends as Social Darwinism, with their emphasis on the inevitability and indeed the glory of conflict. These ideas were common throughout Europe and the United States, but in Germany they combined in a uniquely explosive way. Further, they had no legitimate outlet within the existing political framework. The British, the Russians, the Americans, and even the French and the Italians could pursue their "manifest destinies" within the framework of their own territories or empires without disturbing the international system. But landlocked Germany could expand only at the expense of its neighbors, and in so doing destroy a European order that had been peacefully established for a hundred years. Germany could not, as could a later generation of German statesmen, make understandable, limited, and negotiable claims for frontier revision. The war-aims that emerged within a few weeks of the outbreak of war in the notorious September Programme—with its claims for mastery over the Low Countries and the Channel coast, the perpetual subordination of France, and the massive redrawing of frontiers in the Baltic—was a program not for limited revisions based on principles of ethnic consolidation but for a New European Order designed to perpetuate German mastery.

The British were bound to react to such a challenge. Even if the Germans had not invaded Belgium, which they very conveniently did, and even if their troops there had behaved impeccably, which it has to be said they did not, it would not have been difficult to convince even the most liberal and peace-loving Englishman that German power and explicit intentions constituted a threat to international justice and the rule of law. British Conservatives believed with equally good reason that Germany's target was nothing less than the British Empire itself, or at the very least the oceanic supremacy on which the very survival of the British Isles depended.

There is today a tendency to think that whereas the Second World War was necessary and fought for serious causes that justified the sacrifices needed to win it, the First World War was not: that it began and continued as a result of mutual misunderstandings and that all who died in it laid down their lives in vain. That was certainly not the understanding of the generation that fought the war. The threat posed both to core democratic values and to national survival by the Germany personified by the grotesque figure of the Kaiser and the philosophy rather misleadingly labeled as "Prussian militarism" appeared to them quite as total and as dangerous as that which was to confront their children a generation later, and one that no sacrifice seemed too great to avert.

Moreover, with time the threat became ever more real. The September Programme makes clear the peace that Germany would have imposed on Europe in 1914 had the Schlieffen plan worked, as it very nearly did. During the ensuing years, as Germany became more desperate and the right wing tightened its grip on the government, the country's objectives became so extreme that Bethmann Hollweg did not dare to state them when challenged to do so by President Wilson in the winter of 1916. The treaties of Brest-Litovsk, with their sweeping annexations to the east and the virtual destruction of the Russian Empire, were a preliminary blueprint for the objectives to be pursued by the Third Reich. There is no reason to suppose that the terms imposed by a victorious Ludendorff in the West would have been any more moderate. And it was in the shadow of the treaties of Brest-Litovsk, we must remember, that the victorious allies drafted the punitive Treaty of Versailles.

Let us not forget that the Schlieffen plan nearly did succeed, and had the German generalship been more enterprising and the French less phlegmatic it might well have done so. If the French army had been defeated, Russia would almost certainly have hurried to make peace. Austria would have had its will with Serbia and gained at least a stay of execution. Germany would have emerged triumphant on the Continent and the right wing triumphant within Germany. Not a pretty prospect; but would it have been peace? Hardly. Britain would have been beaten off the continent, as it had been during the Napoleonic Wars and would be again in 1940. But it would not have been defeated. That could have been achieved only by such extreme measures of naval warfare as those that brought the United States into the war. It is significant that the German political and military leadership had never thought through the implications of the war with England that had been so widely expected before 1914. The army and navy had never discussed it together, and neither had raised the matter with the politicians. The Prussian military tradition—and the Germans had no other—was rigorously ethnocentric. In their book, wars were won by military victory in the field, and that was it. The book in question was Clausewitz' *On War*. In that immensely influential treatise, naval and economic warfare are not even mentioned.

So Germany's successes in the field could not have defeated Britain any more than did Napoleon's. But more to the point, they could not in themselves—unlike Napoleon's great victories—even defeat Britain's continental allies, France and Russia. After a year the Germans realized this and set out to wear down their adversaries by attrition. This technique was effective enough against the Russians, but it was equally disastrous for Germany's allies the Austrians, whose collapse followed that of the Russians within a matter of months. As for the Western allies, such a strategy was playing to their strength. France and Britain admittedly made matters worse for themselves by continuing with their costly and clumsy attacks on the Western Front, but with American resources behind them they could exhaust Germany long before they themselves collapsed; and those resources could be cut off only by measures that were almost certain to bring the United States into the war as a full belligerent. Unrestricted submarine warfare was for the Germans a desperate gamble revealing the bankruptcy of their strategy. "It is Germany's last card," said one of her statesmen. "If it is not trumps, we are lost for centuries." It was not trumps. As a result, Germany found itself fighting against impossible odds.

In its defeat Germany dragged down the whole of Europe. Within the tightly integrated nexus of interdependent industrial societies, the strategy of attrition is almost as mutually destructive as a strategy of nuclear war. The German general staff consciously destroyed the political system of the Russian Empire by subventing the Bolshevik Party and facilitating Lenin's return from exile at a crucial moment during the Russian Revolution; and having sown the wind, they lived in dread of reaping the whirlwind—which they did almost exactly a year later. The Habsburg Empire disintegrated—despite its faults it had been the major element of stability in Central Europe—and the Western allies probably could not have saved it had they wanted to. In Germany itself civil war was averted only by an unholy alliance between the revolutionary government and the conservative military leadership. The decade of instability that followed prepared many Germans of all classes to welcome Hitler as a rescuer and leader, not caring very much where he led them. As for the victorious powers, France and Britain—they were left wondering whether victory at such a cost had really been worth it, and determined to avoid ever having to endure such an ordeal again.

*   *   *

Had it been worth it? If Germany had won, would freedom really have perished from the earth? We must allow for natural hyperbole, and nobody writing such an epitaph is on oath. But if the United States had stood back and allowed Germany to win the First World War—and without American intervention, it is hard to see how this could have been prevented—both Germany and Europe as a whole would have been a much nastier place. Ludendorff and his followers of the extreme right wing would have been solidly in power; and though not all shared Adolf Hitler's fanatical anti-Semitism, their philosophy was intrinsically racist and explicitly anti-democratic. The methods they would have used to suppress liberal and socialist opposition might not have been so brutal as those employed by the Nazi regime, but they would have been ugly and probably effective. The protofascist ideas that were germinating throughout Europe would have flowered sooner and more prolifically than they did. The defeat of Germany at least gave the cause of democracy in Europe another chance.

NOTES

1. Charles A'Court Repington, *The First World War, 1914–1918,* 2 vols. (London 1921). Colonel Repington was the military correspondent of the London *Times.*

2. Michael Howard, "A Thirty Years' War? The Two World Wars in Historical Perspective," *Transactions of the Royal Historical Society,* 6th ser., vol. 3 (1993): 171–84.

3. Raymond Aron, *Les guerres en chaine* (Paris, 1951).

4. See J. J. Becker, 1914: *Comment les Français sont entrés dans la guerre* (Paris, 1977).

5. Adolf Hitler, *Mein Kampf* (London, 1969), 148.

6. See the vivid account in Modris Eksteins, *The Rites of Spring: The Great War and the Birth of the Modern Age* (London, 1989), 55–64.

7. E. Jones, *The Life and Works of Sigmund Freud*, 3 vols. (London, 1953–57), 1: 192.

8. See Fritz Fischer, *Griff nach der Weltmacht* (Dusseldorf, 1961), and the long controversy precipitated by that work.

9. Fritz Stern, "Bethmann Hollweg and the War," in G. L. Krieger and Fritz Stern, eds., *The Responsibility of Power* (London, 1968), 268.

10. Paul Kennedy, *The Rise of the Anglo-German Antagonism, 1860–1914* (London, 1980). See also Chapter 10 in this volume.

CHAPTER 2

The Eastern Front

WILLIAM C. FULLER, JR.

The past twenty years or so have seen an explosion in historical writing about the First World War. In addition to studies of strategy, operations, tactics, and technology there have been examinations of the experience of front-line soldiers, drawing on insights from social psychology and anthropology. There have been investigations of the pressures that war placed on civilians at home and of the social transformations it provoked. And there have been studies of how the war was understood, remembered, and invested with significance. Yet there is a curious feature of much of this distinguished literature: most of it has concentrated on the war on the Western Front. The Eastern Front has been comparatively neglected.

In one sense this is understandable. The outcome of the Great War was decided on the Western Front, after the Russo-German Treaty of Brest-Litovsk had put an end to the fighting in the East. Then too, there is nothing strange about Western scholars being attracted to historical topics involving their own societies and military experiences. It did not help that Russian archival materials relating to the war became, by and large, off limits to foreign researchers.

But the relative silence about the Eastern Front was a feature not only of Western but of *Soviet* historiography. According to the official ideology that guided the writing of history in the Soviet Union, World War I was an "imperialist" war, caused by the rivalry of bourgeois powers for colonies and markets. The Bolsheviks at the time demanded the "transformation of the imperialist war into civil war," a transformation over which they eventually presided with stunning success. The Russian Civil War (1918–21) validated the Communist claim to rule and became an integral part of the Soviet foundation myth. As such, it was allotted a historical significance that considerably overshadowed the events of 1914–17. Indeed, it is not too much to say that memory of the civil war virtually buried the memory of the world war in the popular mind.

To be sure, former imperial officers in exile wrote many volumes of wartime reminiscences. A handful of Soviet officers, veterans of the tsarist army, also included material about the Great War in their memoirs. Soviet writers created a voluminous technical military literature principally concerned with operational issues, which treated the war like a mine from which useful military lessons could be quarried for the present and the future.[1] Typical of the prevailing Soviet attitude toward the historical record was the fact that in the 1930s, shortly after Hitler's accession to power, the operational planning documents prepared by the tsarist general staff from 1906–14 were removed from the military historical archives and turned over to the staff of the Red Army for it to use in crafting its plans for war with Germany. There the documents remained until 1989.

Yet with a few honorable exceptions, both Russian popular and historical writers disregarded the subject of the war.[2] In the previous chapter, Michael Howard refers to the numerous World War I memorials and statues found in France, Britain, Germany, and the United States. But to date there exists no such monument on the territory of the Russian Federation that commemorates the war or honors the 1.3 million tsarist troops, at a bare minimum, who lost their lives in the effort.[3] There could probably be no better illustration of the neglect of the war than this.

The collapse of communism, however, is changing this situation, as it has changed so much else. For many Russian citizens, the end of communism has provided opportunities for the recovery (or exhumation) of memory; the appearance of popular works devoted to the war testifies to a growing interest in it.[4]

But for trained historians of Russia, the disintegration of the Soviet regime has meant an emancipation from the old periodization of the Russian past, in which the events of 1917 were perceived as the inevitable, natural culmination of tsarist history, and in which the revolution stood as a sharp dividing line between backwardness and modernity. The discrediting of this particular interpretive paradigm has brought the issue of contingency once more to the fore. It is an appreciation of contingency that must inform any reassessment of the Eastern Front in the First World War.[5]

In considering the First World War with a particular emphasis on Russia and the Eastern Front, I will address four sets of questions. First, what were the war's political stakes? What did the governments of the belligerent states think that they would accomplish by waging war? In short, what was the war for? Second, why (and how) did Russia lose the First World War? Third, did Russia ever have a chance to win? If so, how might such a victory have been achieved? Finally, what was the meaning of the outcome? Were there potentially better outcomes?

I begin with the political purposes behind the war in the East. The chief players on the Eastern Front were of course Austria-Hungary, Germany, and Russia. Vienna's principal war aim was simple and consistent: perceiving nationalism (particularly south Slavic nationalism) as the greatest threat to the continued existence of her multi-ethnic empire, Austria-Hungary sought the dismemberment of Serbia—in effect, its elimination as a factor in Central European politics. Although there were disagreements among Austrian and Hungarian statesmen about the best method for achieving this (that is, the best mix of annexations and partitions), the military operations of the Habsburg monarchy supported this objective from the beginning: Austria took the field planning to deliver the heaviest blow against Belgrade, not Petrograd. Germany's goals were more ambitious. Although they underwent considerable evolution during the war, Germany's positive war aims in the East came to include the annexation of Courland, as well as sections of Lithuania and Belorussia, and the union of much of Russia's Polish territory into a "self-ruling" Polish state, which would actually be an Austro-German dependency. These aims (and others) were technically if impermanently achieved by the German empire in the treaty it signed at Brest-Litovsk with Bolshevik Russia in March 1918.

For Russia, there was of course always a negative or defensive political aim connected with the war. Although the Empire nominally fought in defense of Serbia, her deeper motivation was to avoid defeat and remain in the ranks of the Great Powers. Indeed, it was the perceived need to defend Russia's status and credibility as a Great Power that had been the primary consideration behind the imperial government's mobilization in August 1914, despite the obvious risk of general European war that this entailed.[6] Once hostilities had broken out, this negative political aim was refined: in order to eliminate the menace of resurgent German power in the aftermath of allied victory, it might be necessary to undo the unification of Germany—by restoring the Hanoverian monarchy, for example.[7]

But Russia had considerably greater problems developing a lucid agenda of positive war aims. Unlike some of the other belligerents, Russia never developed a formalized, coherent statement of them.[8] It was only in late 1916 that Nicholas II ordered former chairman of the council of ministers Count V. N. Kokovtsov to prepare a document that spelled them out. Kokovtsov had not even completed a first draft when the February revolution swept the monarchy from power.[9]

The reason for this was not so much incompetence or sloth as the inherent difficulty of conceiving of territorial gains that could realistically be both acquired and retained. Take the question of the annexation of German or Austro-Hungarian territory. Although various officers, both active and retired, proposed Russian absorption of East Prussia and Silesia, such schemes never won the approval of the highest military or civil leadership of the empire.[10] There were serious reservations about the wisdom of attempting to digest large populations of disgruntled Germans, not to mention doubts about allied reception of so extreme a claim. As for Austria-Hungary, Galicia, a territory inhabited by Poles and Ruthenes, had some attractiveness as a candidate for incorporation into the Russian empire. Russia in fact treated the province as conquered territory after occupying it in 1915. In 1916, Russia impulsively proclaimed its formal annexation. However, the indigenous Polish population was implacably hostile to Russian rule, an attitude intensified by the brutality and religious persecution meted out by the Russian occupiers. In short, plans to exact territorial gains from either Germany or Austria-Hungary had considerable drawbacks, not least because the costs of maintaining such holdings could easily outweigh any benefits that Russia could derive from them.

There was, however, another territorial objective that many Russian statesmen contemplated with enthusiasm: the Turkish straits. To control the Bosphorus and Dardanelles was to command the entrance and egress of the Black Sea, and gaining such control was consequently a matter of the highest strategic and economic importance. Russia was reminded of the dual significance of the straits in the decade prior to 1914. The closure of the straits to Russia's warships during the Russo-Japanese war (1904–5) had rendered the Black Sea fleet useless, and the closure of the straits to commercial shipping during the Italo-Turkish war (1911–12) had deprived her of foreign trade revenues to the tune of 20 million rubles a month. In November 1913 the imperial government adopted the findings of a secret study which concluded that Russia had to prepare to take Constantinople and the straits "in the event of a European conflagration."[11]

Although that conflagration broke out in August 1914, it was only after Turkey entered the war on the side of the central powers in October that the straits became a viable political objective. There were, however, substantive problems with the attainment of this Russian ambition. First, Russia's allies had to acquiesce in it. This was no simple matter, as for a century London had adamantly opposed any Russian encroachments on Constantinople, the Bosphorus, and the Dardanelles. In March 1915, however, the British repudiated their traditional policy in an aide-memoire that promised Russia both Constantinople and the straits after the war had been won. On April 10, 1915, the government of France also approved this arrangement, at least in principle.

Yet the spoils of war had to be seized before they could be enjoyed. Could Russia or her allies take the straits? It was beyond Russia's capabilities to march on Constantinople overland as long as she had the German and Austrian armies to contend with. Clearly some sort of amphibious operation would be necessary. The British invasion of the Gallipoli peninsula (April 1915) seemed to fit the bill, for its goal was to capture Constantinople in one swift stroke, thus knocking Turkey out of the war and opening a year-round sea lane to Russia. Although it was Russia's own request for military assistance against the Turks that elicited the Gallipoli landings, the expedition provoked considerable anxiety in Petrograd. In the words of the British ambassador the straits were the "richest prize of the entire war."[12] If the British Empire took this prize by force of arms was it *truly* likely to transfer possession to Russia?[13] After all, Russia could at that moment detach no forces of her own to participate, since she was anticipating a major Austro-German offensive in Poland and was also hard pressed on the Caucasian front, where Turkish troops outnumbered hers by two to one.[14] As it turned out, Britain would never be in a position to redeem her pledge to Russia: the Gallipoli operation proved a sanguinary catastrophe. But its failure was secretly welcomed by at least some Russians. General Ia. G. Zhilinskii, who represented the Russian army in Paris, expressed his relief at Britain's impending evacuation of the Gallipoli peninsula in December 1915, saying he had no desire to see the "creation of a permanent British post, a new Gibraltar, at the exit to the Mediterranean."[15]

The logic of Zhilinskii's position implied that Russia had to take the straits on her own. The difficulty was that scarcely any senior Russian army officials believed in the feasibility of this mission. General Iu. Danilov, Quartermaster General at Russian Headquarters (Stavka), insisted that the "conquest of the Bosphorus would require an entirely separate war."[16] Danilov was apparently of the view that domination of the straits would not be secure without the pacification of at least part of the Anatolian hinterland, a task that would require a military effort as great as the one Russia was mounting against Austria-Hungary and Germany. Russia's first supreme commander, Grand Duke Nikolai Nikolaevich, regarded the war with Turkey as a noisome distraction from the essential job of defeating Vienna and Berlin; Russia could neither take nor hold the straits until that had been done.[17] Still more pessimistic was general M. V. Alekseev, who served as Chief of Staff of Russia's armies after the tsar took personal command. In 1916 he argued for a separate peace with the Ottoman empire because, in his opinion, it was an "illusion" that Russia could gain the straits as a result of victory in the First World War.[18]

With regard to the most important element of her positive agenda—possession of Constantinople and the straits—there was thus a gap, if not a chasm, between Russia's political ends and military means. By the admission of her own most highly placed generals, even the most wildly successful military operations in Central and Eastern Europe could not produce the desired result. It is breathtakingly obvious that Russia could not possibly control the straits if she made no effort to seize them. But the reason for the lack of effort was Stavka's fixation on the land war against Germany and Austria, a fixation explained by the fact that Russia was fighting a war to defend her Great Power status, with the annexationist objective an afterthought. Of course in the end Russia signally failed to accomplish even her negative purpose.

On the most fundamental level, Russia lost the war because of the coming of the revolutions of 1917. There were clearly backward and forward linkages between the phenomena of war and revolution. Lenin himself described the war as a "gigantic accelerator" of the revolutionary process in Russia.[19] For example, combat casualty rates among front-line officers were so enormous that by January 1917 the percentage of officers whose commissions antedated the war was minuscule.[20] According to one estimate, by that point no more than 10 percent of the officers in the army were prewar regulars, and many of them held jobs on the staffs rather than in the line.[21] In effect, Russia had exchanged professional military officers for a corps of amateurs who commanded less respect and exerted less authority than the men they had replaced. One consequence was a deterioration of discipline among the troops that helped to diffuse revolutionary sentiments throughout the army. And in civil society, Russia's bad performance on the battlefield convinced tens of thousands of people that the tsarist government was either too incompetent to conduct the war, too corrupt to win it, or both. When the provisional government came to power after the collapse of the monarchy in February 1917, it was, however, committed to continuing the war as an ally of Britain and France.

It took the October revolution to put Russia on the road to peace. Lenin's Bolshevik government had pledged itself to end the war and soon opened negotiations with representatives of the central powers. But when the Germans demanded large territorial concessions the Russian government overruled Lenin, broke off the talks, and adopted Trotsky's ridiculous "neither war nor peace" policy. The upshot was a renewal of the German advance, which the remnants of the Russian army were in no condition to resist. The Bolsheviks simply had nothing with which to fight. In January 1918 the chief of staff of the First Army had reported that, because of desertions, there were companies mustering as few as seven men. "The soldiers demand peace at any price and an immediate return home. They are completely indifferent to calls for a holy war against Germany and the bourgeoisie."[22] Eventually, as Lenin had been urging from the beginning, the Bolsheviks gave in to the Germans and signed the Treaty of Brest-Litovsk in March, thus taking Russia out of the war.

Although it is difficult to imagine how Russia might have averted something akin to the February revolution once the war had dragged on for more than two years, February did not foreordain October. Even the Bolsheviks admitted at the time that their revolution was a very close-run thing. If the Provisional Government or *any* Russian government had managed to hang on until November 1918—that is, slightly more than eight months—Russia would, ipso facto, have been numbered among the victorious allies. Without February, however, there could have been no October. And as I suggested above, the mass perception that Russia was losing the war helped to bring on February.

How do we account for Russia's poor combat performance from August 1914 to February 1917? The explanation preferred by many ex-tsarist officers in emigration was Russia's technological backwardness: that is, that Russia lacked the technology to manufacture the arms and matériel needed to prosecute the struggle.[23] Although she possessed a burgeoning industrial sector, Russia was inferior to her Western neighbors in the output of such commodities as electrical equipment, chemicals, and machine tools. Prior to the war, for instance, Russia's total production of machinery of all kinds met less than 50 percent of the empire's internal demand.[24] When Russia had exhausted her stockpiles of rifles, bullets, and shells, she could not replace them as rapidly as Germany could. The deleterious result was the great "shell hunger" of 1915, the German conquest of Poland, Livonia, and much of the Baltic coast, and the demoralization of front and rear alike.

In the early 1970s Norman Stone rejected the view that Russia's Eastern defeats were largely explicable in terms of industrial underdevelopment. He noted that all other belligerent countries had problems with munitions; he pointed to examples of nations that have prevailed in war despite relative quantitative or qualitative industrial inadequacy; and he further demonstrated that Russia had experienced a considerable industrial upsurge by 1916—which led to substantial improvements in the army supply picture.[25] In his opinion, Russia's generals "discovered" material shortages retroactively and then used them to excuse their own military failures, in a variation of the game of wooden leg.

Some of Stone's points are valid, but his attempt to dismiss the effects of industrial backwardness on Russia's war effort is misconceived. First, the munitions shortage experienced by Russia's army in the war was a reality, not a myth. The lack of rifles was particularly burdensome in the early months and years of the war. The rifle crisis was considerably exacerbated by episodes of mass surrender of Russian troops and the propensity of thousands of others to fling their rifles aside while in retreat or flight.

The Russian high command evinced an awareness of the gravity of the rifle problem from the beginning of the war. As early as

August 26, 1914, Stavka was ordering the collection of the rifles of the dead and wounded. Two months later the commander of the Northwest Front began to pay bounties to civilians who brought in even Austrian or German rifles discarded on the battlefield.[26] Frantic attempts were made to replenish Russia's arsenals through foreign purchases, but contracting procedures were slow and deliveries tardy and sporadic. In May 1915, 150,000 men on the Southwest Front still had no rifles, and 286,000 soldiers on the West Front were without them in January 1916.[27] In all, Russia's armies in Europe were by then short some 666,000 rifles—a full third of the total number needed.[28] As a result, wrote one high War Ministry official, "our army is drowning in its own blood."[29]

The shell crisis was as real as the rifle crisis, and its consequences proved more dire. German superiority in quantities of shells (if not in gunnery) began to make itself felt early in 1915.[30] By the spring of that year Russia's reserve of artillery ammunition was so depleted that, as one officer recalled, shells were doled out "as in a pharmacy, by the teaspoon."[31] On March 7, 1915, the Germans lobbed more than 1,200 shells into positions held by the First Guards Infantry Division (near Lomzha). The Guards had but thirty rounds with which to reply.[32] The Germans prepared their Gorlice/Tarnow breakthrough with an annihilating artillery barrage conducted by the greatest concentration of guns ever assembled in the war to that point. On May 2, 1915, 400,000 shells rained down on the Russian Third Army in the space of four hours.[33] During the campaign which began that day and continued until August, 300,000 of the outgunned (and outshelled) Russians were killed or wounded per month.[34] The Germans took 2 million prisoners and occupied a quarter of the European part of the Russian Empire.[35] Dispatch after dispatch from the front emphasized that the enemy's superiority in heavy artillery was responsible for this stunning military reverse. As the commander of the Eighth Army reported, "The enemy is not frightening face to face but whole units are deranged almost to a man by his numerous heavy guns."[36] Confronted by this terrible imbalance in ordnance, the Russian high command usually chose to expend men to compensate for its lack of steel.[37] In the absence of heavy artillery, noted one general in his diary, "we are fighting with human bodies."[38] Eventually even this dreadful option became unavailable. Far from having an inexhaustible supply of troops, Russia had actually used up almost all of her trained reserves before the end of 1914; thereafter she would experience chronic shortages of trained military manpower.[39]

Second, even if Russia's industrial output soared in 1916, as indeed it did (Stone goes so far as to write of a crisis of economic modernization), this does not mean that Russia could produce everything she needed.[40] For example, Stone correctly observes that Russia's output of three-inch field guns had increased dramatically by 1916. The three-inch field gun was an anti-personnel weapon, firing shrapnel that could be devastating against concentrations of troops in the open. But this weapon, the workhorse of the Russian artillery, was virtually useless against an entrenched army. To kill soldiers in trenches, let alone concrete bunkers, it was necessary to employ heavy artillery with high-caliber, high-explosive shells ("suitcases" in Russian soldiers' slang). And Russian industry proved incapable of ever manufacturing enough heavy guns of HE shell to satisfy the army's demands. For example, by summer 1916 (the time at which Stone pronounces the shell crisis over) the Russian army's monthly requirement for artillery ammunition came to 1.5 million shells. Included in this figure were 300,000 forty-eight-line howitzer shells and 225,000 rounds for the six-inch heavy gun. Actual deliveries, however, amounted to a mere 100,000 howitzer shells and 40,000 six-inch projectiles.[41] In fact, throughout the war, Russia was constantly short of large-caliber artillery, machine guns, high explosives, poison gases, air-burst fuses, and rifles.[42]

Third, industrial backwardness in areas other than armament production had devastating effects on the war effort. The most important of these was transport. Russia's railway net was less dense than that of its Western neighbors. This disadvantage, and the lack of lines paralleling the front in particular, was one reason why the Russian High Command was so often incapable of stemming the German onslaught in spring and summer 1915. Since reserves could not be rushed by train to a threatened sector, Stavka often responded to a localized German breakthrough by retracting its entire front.[43] Later in the war the inability of Russia's factories to turn out locomotives, signals, switching devices, and rails in adequate quantities led to a systemic breakdown in the transportation system that crippled the manufacture and distribution of supplies to the army. In the summer of 1916, for instance, Alekseev estimated that defense factories disposed of only 50 to 60 percent of the railway transport they really required.[44] As time passed the transportation system decayed still further: fewer than half of the 20,000 locomotives that Russia possessed of in 1914 were still operational twenty-seven months into the war.[45] It was because of transportation bottlenecks, not lack of foodstuffs, that the army had only a twelve-day reserve of comestibles at the end of 1916.[46] The consequences were even worse for urban Russia, where the food and fuel crises that ensued were the proximate causes of the February revolution. After February, the Provisional Government proved as incapable of solving Russia's transport problem as its imperial predecessor: by July 1917 food deliveries to the front-line troops amounted to only one-third of the prescribed norm.[47]

Could Russia have overcome her material disadvantages by organizing her war economy more quickly and more rationally? Some historians say "yes." With respect to the economy, a view long standard in Western historical literature holds that tsarist Russia's sluggish response to the demands of total war stemmed from its historic mistrust of educated society. The argument goes roughly as follows. The regime initially refused to mobilize society, industry, and labor for the war effort, a refusal for which it eventually paid a heavy price. Left to its own devices, the bureaucratic-autocratic state was incapable of alleviating the crises of munitions and matériel. It was only after much balking, and as a result of much public pressure, that the regime fired its unpopular reactionary ministers, empowered the Zemgor (union of rural and town councils) to engage in war work, set up the war industry committees (with representatives from both labor and capital), and established a system of four Special Conferences (August 1915) to manage the war economy. The labors of these civic and semi-civic institutions came to fruition only in 1916.[48] But by then it was too late: the government had already squandered hundreds of thousands of lives as well as any claim on public trust. If the imperial government had only embraced "society" earlier, then the war might have been won and tsarist Russia saved.[49]

This argument is, however, conspicuously weak in several respects. It certainly is true that the imperial government was relatively slow in appealing to society for help. But was this really the solution to the problem of the war economy? Turning to society involved chartering or establishing numerous committees, commissions, and quasi-public, quasi-private organizations. Some of these, particularly those sponsored by the Union of Zemstvos and Towns, performed valuable work in furnishing food, clothing, and medical services to the troops.[50] Yet others, particularly the war industry committees, were far less efficient: they often failed to complete orders, engaged in subversive political activity, and openly competed with official state organizations for technical personnel and scarce raw materials.[51] Mobilizing society therefore did not mean rationalizing, centralizing, or militarizing the economy. Rather it meant anarchy, redundancy, and waste. Optimal industrial performance in World War I would have required imposing an economic dictatorship, something Russia never did. The Special Conference system compartmentalized rather than coordinated the output of food, fuel, transportation, and munitions and therefore fell far short of the mark.[52] The lack of rational central planning led to numerous absurdities: at one point in 1915 most railroad repair shops in the country were dragooned into shell production; the consequences for the empire's transportation network were ignored.[53]

Unlike the argument made by Stone, material insufficiency was not a flimsy ex-post-facto apology for military defeat. It did cause Russia to lose numerous battles—and not just in 1915, despite the subsequent improvements in the war economy. An internal Stavka memorandum of January 1917 described the rout of elements of the Fourth and Sixth Armies (Romanian front) as an "understandable and natural phenomenon," given the enemy's preponderance of heavy artillery.[54] Yet even if Russia had better organized her economy for war, taking into consideration her lack of many basic industries essential for the manufacture of complex modern arms, there were real limits to what Russia could have achieved alone. Entire industries, after all, could not be conjured up out of thin air. Nonetheless, although relative technical inferiority made a powerful contribution to Russia's failure in the Great War, it did not *decide* it: it was a necessary but not sufficient condition for defeat.

Another popular explanation for Russia's wartime failure concerns the inadequacy of military leadership. According to this interpretation, Russia, although blessed with hundreds of thousands of brave soldiers, was cursed with an inept and incompetent high command. Some have blamed the autocratic system itself for this state of affairs, noting that nepotism, favoritism, and dynastic considerations tainted the process of military promotions and led to the elevation of numerous mediocrities. Russia's generals have been accused of almost every sin, from spiteful ambition to excessive timidity to crude recklessness. Writing of Russia's field generals after the

East Prussian disaster of August 1914, War Minister Sukhomlinov (who later became a scapegoat for Russian defeat) acidly observed that "it would be better if several of them were on the side of our enemies."[55] Certainly the catalogue of Russian defeats that stemmed from bad command decisions is both extensive and depressing: Tannenberg (1914), the Carpathian campaign (winter 1914–15), Augustow Forest (1915), and Riga (1917), to mention just a few.

What accounts for the mistakes of the Russian high command? Leaving aside those attributable to defects of character and psychology, and others too technical for discussion here, three broad explanations recommend themselves: intellectual failings, institutional obstacles, and interallied relations.

The intellectual explanation emphasizes the conceptual weakness of Russian strategy. In reviewing the protocols of the Russian front conferences one notices a general lack of strategic reasoning, a tendency to think of the war as a set of operational puzzles decoupled from a broader strategic purpose. For example, those attending the meeting of front commanders on November 30, 1914, assigned each of Russia's armies a geographical goal (holding a particular line, advancing to a particular town) without discussing how these operations would advance the overall goal of winning the war.[56] It is clear that by spring 1916 most of the key figures at Stavka had embraced the "attritional" approach to the defeat of Germany then favored by the staffs of its allies. Presupposing that rapid decision and breakthroughs were unlikely, if not impossible, the attritional strategy concentrated on killing as many German soldiers as possible in the hope that Germany would eventually be compelled to surrender due to debility or despair. Unfortunately, attrition ground down both sides: the Russians discovered, as did the French and the British, that in seeking to exhaust the enemy it was all too easy to exhaust oneself.

By contrast, the institutional explanation centers on Russia's bizarre apportionment of forces in what was after all a multi-front war. Before any campaign Russia had to set priorities and decide how many troops to deploy against Germany, Austria-Hungary, and Turkey. She also had to choose whether to target Germany or Austria for the main blow in the principal theater of war. Although all of the allies (including Russia) formally agreed that Germany was the primary enemy, Russia's anti-German offensives were often weak, owing to Stavka's insistence on mounting a simultaneous attack on the Austrians. In the winter of 1914–15, for instance, Russia attempted to invade both East Prussia and Hungary. After Russia adopted an Austria-first strategy in December 1916 (in the belief that "the road to Berlin lies through [Austrian] Galicia") the situation did not improve: excessively large anti-German deployments are said to have consistently blunted Russia's offensives against the Austro-Hungarian army.[57] During all phases of the war this division of forces diluted both offensives and diminished chances for the success of either.[58]

This state of affairs is usually ascribed to institutional failure, itself rooted in the tradition of prewar planning in the military districts. Stavka permitted excessive independence for the front commanders—each was allowed to fight virtually his own separate war. After Nicholas II replaced Nikolai Nikolaevich and took over supreme command himself, the front commanders reportedly became still more obstreperous because the tsar lacked the force of will to bring them to heel.[59]

The third explanation identifies Stavka's excessive servility toward the Western allies as a source of defeat. Throughout the war France and Britain badgered Russia to launch operations in support of their own offensives and defensives on the Western Front.[60] Russia frequently acceded to these requests, either by starting a planned offensive prematurely or by improvising an assault on German positions. In August 1914, for example, Russia invaded East Prussia before the logistical apparatus for such an attack was in place in order to fulfill her treaty obligations to the French. In March 1916, Stavka initiated an attack at Lake Naroch to relieve the pressure on the French at Verdun. Other examples could be adduced. The point is that most operations of this sort were costly, wasteful, and indecisive; some were unmitigated catastrophes. In the Naroch operation, for example, Russia lost almost 80,000 men—a full third of those committed—within ten days. According to the (mostly Russian) historians who have propounded this explanation, Russia martyred herself in the interests of her allies, sacrificing thousands of men to save the French at the Marne in 1914 and the Italians in 1916, and so forth.[61]

But were Russia's generals really that much less competent than those of any other belligerent? First, it is important not to forget that generalship and military performance are of course relative. Russia may have committed many egregious military blunders, but so too did France (the Nivelle offensive), Britain (the Somme) and Germany (Verdun). An obsession with tactics and operations to the detriment of strategy was not unique to the Russian generals and was in fact to be encountered at the GHQ of every belligerent power.

Second, although it is true that Stavka probably should have concentrated on only one axis of advance—that is, either against Germany or against Austria-Hungary—the problem of allocating forces among the fronts was in fact very complex. There were ferocious debates at the time about which of her two Central European enemies Russia should seek to defeat first. If Germany surrendered the war would be over, because Austria-Hungary could scarcely continue to fight in isolation. On the other hand, a solid case could be made that Germany's war effort would falter if Austria collapsed. Might it be possible to win the war more quickly and with fewer casualties by forcing a beaten Austria-Hungary to sign a separate peace? Russian generals could not agree about this matter during the war, and there has emerged no consensus among historians to this day about the choice Russia should have made.[62] Whichever enemy Russia elected to concentrate on, it was of course impossible to strip the inactive front bare. No invasion of Germany, whether into East Prussia or Silesia, had a prayer of success if the Austrian forces on the Russian left were not pinned down. In the same way, Russia would still have had to deploy a sizable contingent of troops to hold the Germans in place for a movement against Galicia or Hungary to have been effective. While none of this excuses Russia's pattern of double offensives, it does make it somewhat more understandable.

Penultimately, there is the issue of the allies. Although many of the military operations that Russia undertook at her allies' behest were fiascoes, in large measure Russia's accommodation of Britain and France was in her own best interest. Russia depended on her allies not only for munitions and matériel but also for loans to defray the costs of the war. Russia borrowed a fifth of the money used to finance the war and obtained almost 90 percent of that amount from Paris and London.[63] Allied good will was essential for Russia's access to Western capital and to the continuing deliveries of the output of British and French factories. Russia was by no means a puppet, however; on many occasions she declined to act in her allies' support, as in spring 1917.

Finally, almost all discussions of Russian command ineptitude fail to emphasize the Russian generals' great successes, such as their victories at Gumbinnen, Gnila Lipa, Lodzinsk, and Przemysl. The most striking of Russia's operational triumphs was achieved by General A. A. Brusilov in the summer of 1916. Before it sputtered to a standstill, the offensive of his Southwest Front inflicted a million enemy casualties, took more than 450,000 prisoners, captured 496 guns, and conquered 575,000 square kilometers—a territory larger than France.[64]

Ironically, the Brusilov offensive was never intended to succeed: it was supposed to simply distract the Central Powers from the main Russian strike, which was to be in the north. Brusilov, however, was both aggressive and imaginative: in seeking to surprise the enemy he constructed *place d'armes* in some twenty locations along his front, limited his preliminary artillery barrage, and employed shock units to bypass enemy strong points and thus widen the rupture in his lines. Yet, although it was an operational triumph, the Brusilov offensive was a strategic disaster. Romania was emboldened to enter the war on the side of the entente, but she promptly collapsed, thus delivering large resources of oil and wheat to German control. At the same time, Russian casualties were enormous, and the army became thoroughly demoralized. Between June 3 and 13 alone Brusilov lost more than 490,000 men.[65] The horrific costs and feeble results of the Brusilov campaign left even the officers wondering whether victory could *ever* be achieved, regardless of how well supplied the army was.[66] By January 1917—the third winter of the war—fighting spirit had all but collapsed along the front line.

The military elite came to the absolutely erroneous conclusion that the best medicine for Russia's ailing field forces would be a new offensive. What those forces needed, of course, was not an offensive but a defensive that would permit reinforcement, regrouping, and recuperation; but the provisional government launched its offensive anyway in the summer of 1917. The eminently predictable failure of that operation resulted in two hundred thousand casualties and a further degradation of morale.[67] The Russian high command itself estimated in August 1917 that it would take months to restore the army to combat readiness, and even then only through the restoration of draconian military discipline.[68] This, however, was not a course that the Provisional Government in Petrograd could stomach. A telling index of military disintegration was the fact that by

September 1917 at least a million military deserters were wandering throughout Russia, clogging the railroad stations, swelling the urban mobs, and engaging in mendicancy, vagabondage, and crime.[69]

Clearly many factors contributed to Russia's defeat in the First World War. On the most elementary level, Russia lost the war because of the decomposition of both her political system, which led to the February and then the October revolutions. Russia's poor conduct of the war powerfully contributed to that decomposition. Although technological insufficiency and command ineptitude led to military defeats that discredited the regime and alienated the population, the offensive spirit and military success embodied in the Brusilov offensive *also* played a critical role in demoralizing the army and preparing the way for ultimate defeat. In a not too dissimilar fashion, the great offensives that Germany conducted in France in the spring of 1918, although tactically brilliant, actually accelerated her collapse.[70]

Russia's defeat, however, was not inevitable. If the October revolution had been averted or reversed, Russian survival—and therefore victory—would have been possible. That aside, might other realistic alternatives have improved Russia's odds of prevailing in the war? I shall briefly examine three hypothetical options, one tactical (breaking the front), one operational (launching peripheral and combined operations), and one strategic (effecting greater strategic coordination with the allies).

It is a cliché to state that the problem of the Western Front in the First World War was the tactical impasse. After the "race to the sea" and the stabilization of the front in December 1914 both sides were locked into a pattern of protracted, bloody, and inconclusive trench warfare in which virtually every attempt to break through enemy lines was thwarted. The conventional explanation of this is the temporary superiority of defensive to offensive military technologies. Newer and more sophisticated interpretations deemphasize the "technological fix," arguing that the correct sort of tactical and doctrinal innovations were the antidote to the stalemate on the Western Front.[71]

During the trench warfare phases on the Eastern Front, Russia certainly acquired the same bitter knowledge as her Western allies: that frontal assaults against fortified enemy positions were typically costly, if not hopeless. Moreover, even if an enemy position could be taken, the Russia army usually could not hold it since reinforcements and extra ammunition could rarely be brought up before the enemy counterattacked.[72] It was exactly the same story in the West.

Certainly Russia's military leadership was alive to the special tactical requirements of trench warfare and expended enormous quantities of mental energy in studying them. Nor did Russia's generals operate in an intellectual vacuum, for they exchanged considerable information and ideas with their counterparts in Belgium and France.[73]

But the Eastern Front was by no means identical to the Western Front because there was more to that conflict than two masses of entrenched soldiers battering away at each other. Whereas the Western Front was relatively static, the Eastern Front was dynamic; on numerous occasions attackers ruptured the opposing front and threw it back scores of miles. Consider Russia's two invasions of East Prussia, the German movement on Warsaw, the Russian thrust into Galicia, the Gorlice-Tarnow operation, the Brusilov offensive and the Riga breakthrough. The contrast with the Western Front, where advance and retreat were all too often measured in yards, could not be more striking.

The relative mobility of operations in the East was the result of the vast size of of the theater and the enormous distances involved. The Western Front extended 700 kilometers, from Nieuport on the English Channel to the Swiss frontier. But the Eastern Front stretched across more than 1,600 kilometers and, after Romania's entry into the war in 1916, ran from the Black Sea to the Baltic. This meant that the Eastern Front could not be held with anything like the density of troops deployed in the West. Whereas in the winter of 1915–16 the Western allies deployed 2,134 soldiers per kilometer of front, Russia had but 1,200.[74] The Eastern Front was therefore never continuous in precisely the sense that the Western Front was. As Churchill wrote, "In the West the armies were too big for the country; in the East the country was too big for the armies."[75]

Given the low ratio of men to length of front it was possible for each side in the East to attempt outflanking maneuvers—an expedient that had all but vanished from the repertory of armies in the West after the first few months of the war. The most promising areas for these attacks were the junctions between armies or groups of armies. If contact between the wings of these abutting enemy forces was weak or nonexistent, it might be possible to punch a hole through the front and get into the enemy's rear. Because this was so, cavalry (uselessly pent up behind the lines in the West) acquired a distinctive value on the Eastern Front. In September 1915, for instance, Hindenberg dispatched several cavalry divisions to drive a wedge between the Russian North and West Fronts—and might have succeeded if the Russian army had not hastily improvised a counterattack with cavalry formations of its own.[76]

In view of the special characteristics of war in the East, might Russia have employed novel infiltration tactics to smash the front of either of its two principal enemies, thus marching on to decisive victory in Vienna or Berlin? In more concrete terms, perhaps the Brusilov offensive could have been made to work, or, failing that, perhaps other Brusilov-style offensives could have been mounted until one of them finally produced the desired result. Certainly the advance of Russia's Southwest Front in the summer of 1916 revived the hope that the breakthrough, rather than attrition, would be the key to victory.[77]

In my view, this hope was extremely remote. If the huge scale of the Eastern Front provided tactical opportunities undreamed of in the West, it simultaneously reduced the chances of extracting any strategic advantage from them. As we have already seen, breakthroughs were possible on the Eastern Front. But for a breakthrough to resolve the war it had to be exploited, which involved passing large forces through the gap or gaps created in the enemy's front and driving them deep into his hinterland, perhaps even to his capital. Yet in view of the rudimentary development of motorized transportation at the time, there were two virtually insurmountable obstacles to accomplishing this. In the first place, the difficulty of supplying attack columns behind enemy lines was enormous and multiplied with every kilometer of advance until it was almost guaranteed to produce a total logistical collapse. The second limit to the strategic success of offensive operations in the East was the human body itself. Troops required to fight and march continuously over a period of a month or more would eventually be rendered worthless through simple exhaustion. Russia's campaign against Austria in 1914 began with a flourish but bogged down not only because of bad weather and a shortage of munitions but also because many of the soldiers were exhausted, having been engaged in combat for fifty straight days without relief.[78] Brusilov's offensive stalled in large measure for the same reasons. Despite their own operational triumphs against Russia, the more sensible of the Germans eventually realized that the geography and scale of the Eastern Front were sturdy barriers to decisive *military* victory there.[79] What was true for Germany was no less true for Russia.

Another military option available to Russia was the peripheral operation. This involved employing a combination of land and sea forces to deliver a blow in a secondary theater that, in theory, would fundamentally alter the course of the war. In Britain, during the early stages of the war, there was open conflict between the "Westerners" (who believed that the war could be won only in France) and the "Easterners" (who maintained that the peripheral operation was the alternative to the messy carnage of frontal attack that could turn the war around). The best-known attempt to realize the ideas of the Easterners was, of course, the Anglo-French Gallipoli expedition. In some quarters today it is popular to dismiss the Gallipoli campaign as a costly sideshow that had little prospect for success and that, even if it had somehow succeeded, would have had little strategic result.[80] But the Germans were frightened by this expedition, believed its defeat to have been a stroke of great luck, and did not doubt that a British victory on the Gallipoli peninsula would have had the most dramatic consequences for the course of the war.[81] Perhaps unfortunately, the failure of Gallipoli dampened any enthusiasm for amphibious operations on the part of the French and British.

The Russian high command had its own version of the Easterner-Westerner dispute. Both before and after Gallipoli some Russian naval officers at Stavka strongly advocated peripheral operations and drafted numerous plans for their execution. In general, these men evinced a keen appreciation of the connections between the war on land and the war at sea, as well as considerable imagination. In September 1914, Captain A. D. Bubnov, a leading figure in the group, suggested landing an expeditionary force on the Jutland peninsula to threaten the Kiel canal. In Bubnov's opinion, the costs of this operation (the probability of failure, the international opprobrium connected with the violation of Danish neutrality) were outweighed by its benefits. Indeed, merely signaling that such an expedition was imminent would compel Germany to take one of two steps beneficial to the Allies: either the Germans would have to subtract troops from the fighting fronts for the defense of the Canal, or, alternatively, they might be forced to send their High Seas Fleet out into the North Sea (where the Royal Navy would doubtless defeat it in a new Trafalgar).

Either way the allies were winners. Any reduction in German fighting on the Western or Eastern Fronts could only improve the allies' odds in land battles, while the destruction of Germany's seagoing navy would permit amphibious landings on the North German coast and the insertion of sizable allied forces behind the enemy's front.[82] Leaving aside the question of feasibility for a moment, Bubnov's memorandum at the very least proves that some officers at Stavka could think creatively about using joint operations to shape the war.

Bubnov and his colleagues remained adherents of the amphibious attack throughout the war. The Russian navy developed various plans to move against the Bosphorus in 1915 and continued to draft them even after the British withdrawal from Gallipoli.[83] In 1916 naval officers at Stavka proposed earmarking three corps (i.e., 86,400 men) for a descent on Constantinople. In March 1917, Bubnov made a last pitch for a Bosphorus expedition. Arguing that the Turks were distracted by campaigns in Mesopotamia, the Balkans, and Transcaucasia, he outlined an economy of force operation in which three highly trained Russian divisions would make a surprise landing within the Bosphorus fortified region, supported by the entire Black Sea fleet.[84]

None of these proposals was ever carried out. One reason was that the Russian army mistrusted the Russian navy, largely because of its disastrous record in the Japanese war. Another was the a priori insistence by the generals on husbanding assets for the all-important ground war; they rejected out of hand the idea that any amphibious operations could affect the military balance on land. Alekseev, for instance, managed to block the 1916 naval plan by persistently denying that the army could spare the three corps required.[85] The same objection lay behind the rejection of Bubnov's plan for 1917, even though Russia had three divisions based near Odessa that had trained for just this operation for months.

Were any of these peripheral operations feasible? The Kiel canal plan gets low marks on this score, for Germany could at that time deploy sixteen battleships in the Baltic to Russia's two. It is likewise the case that the prospects for an attack on the straits in 1915 would not have been good, for the Gallipoli expedition had alerted the Turks to the vulnerability of their capital. They had consequently strengthened their defenses at the Bosphorus; by the spring of 1915 they had increased the number of soldiers positioned there to 100,000 and had installed additional batteries of shore guns at likely landing sites. As if this were not bad enough, Russia calculated that it would require at least fifteen days to ferry even one corps from Batum to the Bosphorus, owing to the small number of troop ships available.[86]

But the plans developed for 1916 and 1917 are a different matter and require more serious consideration. By spring 1916, Turkey had withdrawn many units based in Constantinople to reinforce her armies operating in the Caucasus and Middle East. At the same time, an aggressive construction program had significantly altered the naval balance in the Black Sea in Russia's favor. In addition, Russia's Black Sea Fleet had built enough transport vessels to move an entire army corps at once, and had acquired experience in successful amphibious warfare during its operations against the Turkish port of Trebizond.[87] In certain respects, conditions for an attack were even more propitious in 1917. Turkey was by then so hard pressed in the other theaters of war that she had but two divisions available for service in the Bosphorus.

If either of these operations had been attempted and had succeeded, they might have produced interesting results. Naval-minded strategists in both Britain and Russia made expansive claims about the potential rewards of a successful attack on the straits: Turkey's withdrawal from the war; the acquisition of new Balkan allies; the capitulation of Austria-Hungary; and the consequent surrender of an isolated Germany. Both their contemporary critiques and subsequent historians have derided these claims as unrealistic fantasies. Yet the point is that an amphibious operation against Turkey did not have to realize the entire list of *desiderata* in order to confer benefits on the allies. In the first place, if the straits could not have been taken it did not matter whether Turkey abandoned the war immediately, for European and Asiatic Turkey would have been split asunder. Since all of Turkey's armament factories were in Europe and her principal agricultural territories in Asia, it is difficult to see how the Turks could have continued to fight effectively for long on either continent. Second, a sea lane of communication between Russia and her Western allies would have been opened. This might have led to increased allied deliveries of war matériel. Even if it did not, the allies would definitely have received larger shipments of Russian grain, which, inter alia, would have scotched Germany's strategy for submarine warfare. Finally, one should not discount the psychological impact of a victory at the Bosphorus on the public mood in the belligerent countries.

The risks connected with any operation of this type were, of course, immense. Russia's troop convoys would have been vulnerable to submarines, mines, and shore batteries. The best port for supplying the expedition was Bugas, in hostile Bulgaria, and an attempt to take it in advance would have telegraphed Russia's intentions. It would be easy to expand on this list of objections. Yet what did Russia have to lose by trying? Even if a Bosphorus operation had resulted in high casualties and the destruction of naval assets, Russia's war effort would not have been badly damaged. Considering even the minimum benefits that might have accrued from success, Russia might have done well to accept the gamble.

A third possible avenue to Russian victory in the Great War entailed improvements in strategic coordination. This obviously was beyond Russia's powers to accomplish without the cooperation of her allies. Hitler once described Germany's situation in World

War I—caught between enemies on each side—as a nightmare. Yet what is amazing about the history of the war is the degree to which the allies ceded the strategic initiative to Germany by failing to exploit the disadvantages of her military encirclement. Coordination meant seeing the war as the *whole* it actually was. This implied that the allies should pool their resources, and implied as well that they should seek to pressure their enemies everywhere and at once.

Although many allied leaders had an abstract grasp of the value of strategic coordination, they were slow to take steps necessary to make it a reality. The first allied conference devoted to this subject did not convene until December 1915, in Chantilly. Nor were the results of the meeting satisfactory. Alekseev, for one, was chagrined that the conference produced no unified or coherent plans. This failure, he wrote, "illustrated the lack in our alliance of any general strategic concept . . . the absence of a willingness to see the general goal of the struggle rather than one's own interests."[88] Other Chantilly conferences ensued in February–March 1916 and November 1916. The last of the big interallied conferences in which imperial Russia would participate met in Petrograd on the eve of the revolution, in January 1917.[89]

Even after the conference system came into being, true strategic coordination proved elusive. All of the conferences discussed coordinating operations among European fronts. There were also fiery declarations of principle: those attending the February–March 1916 conference proclaimed that henceforth there would exist only a "unified army and a unified front."[90] Rhetoric about the importance of cooperation was, however, no substitute for concrete deeds. Probably the closest the allies even came to approximating true coordination was the coincidence of timing between the Brusilov offensive and the battle of the Somme in 1916. But Brusilov's forces had been fighting for a month before the British started their attack, evoking Falkenhayn's comment that "in Galicia the most dangerous moment of the Russian [Brusilov] offensive had passed before the first shot on the Somme was fired."[91]

With regard to pooling resources, which in practical terms meant supplying Russia, the entente performed somewhat better. Although the Russians grumbled bitterly about the low quality of aid they obtained from London and Paris, it is hard to imagine how the allies could have provided military supplies in greater amounts. France and Britain had munitions crises of their own that persisted at least until the end of 1915. The number of British merchant ships that could be set aside for Russian service was limited, and there were obvious navigational problems with transporting goods to Russia via the White Sea, the most practical route owing to enemy closure of the Black and Baltic Seas. Since Russia lacked efficient transportation links to its White Sea ports until the Murmansk railway was completed at the end of 1916, she had difficulty digesting even such supplies as she received. In December 1915, for instance, there were 468,000 tons of military equipment uselessly piled on the docks of Archangel.[92] Despite the transportation bottleneck, large quantities of allied supplies did in fact reach the Russian front. It has been estimated that until the end of 1916 more than half of the artillery shells fired from Russian guns were the product of Western factories.[93] But if Russia was not on firm ground complaining about gross tonnage of allied aid, she had a better case with regard to the actual inventory of equipment received. The most important category of arms in which Russia was deficient was heavy artillery; Russia looked to allies for help in rectifying this weakness in her arsenal. But the allies furnished Russia with only 745 heavy artillery pieces during the war, less than one-quarter of those requested.[94] It might be said that heavy ordinance was too useful on the Western Front for the allies to part with more than they did. But it might have been still more useful to the allied case overall if France and Britain had been more generous in dispatching large-caliber artillery to their Eastern ally. It clearly availed the Western powers nothing if Russia made little military progress, or even suffered defeat, as a result of having too little heavy ordnance.

What impeded coordination? Russia's proverbial secretiveness—her reluctance to share information with allies—obviously played a part. The representatives that Russia sent to Western strategic conferences were never empowered to make authoritative comments binding on their government at home. Sometimes they were not even adequately briefed on the true military situation on the Eastern Front, on the capabilities of the Russian army or the intentions of the Russian High Command. Unless this situation were rectified, Lloyd George observed in August 1917, "full and constant coordination" would never be achieved.[95] Of course on occasion the allies repaid Russia in her own coin, as in November 1915, when they attempted to strike a deal about the Salonika front behind Russia's back.[96]

Sometimes the elements—climate and weather—ruled out successful coordination. The British wanted Russia to start an offensive in April 1915 without considering that the dreaded spring thaw (or *rasputitsa*), making Russian roads virtually impassable, would be well under way by then.[97] So when on the Russian Second and Fifth Armies advanced between the Disenka River and Lake Vishenevskoe on April 16 they bogged down almost immediately.

On other occasions coordination failed because of the extreme variations in the preparedness of the allied armies engaged in East and West. The Chantilly conference of November 1916 called for a general allied offensive to commence the following February. But Russia's forces, exhausted by the Brusilov offensive, were not physically or morally capable of playing the part they had been assigned.[98] There was also something at work that might be called the tyranny of dissynchronous production cycles: no allied army wanted to start an attack until it was fully munitioned, yet because national war industries produced armaments at different speeds and levels of efficiency, it was hard for the allies to agree on when each army would be equally ready.

Finally, it is necessary to point to the centripetal effects of the self-interest of the allied powers. Self-interest was a source of disunion among the partners in the entente, as it has always been in any military coalition. There was tendency, albeit shortsighted, for each member of the alliance to attempt to minimize its own casualties and maximize its own political influence within the alliance by transferring as much of the burden as possible to the others. There are many examples of this sort of thing: Britain versus France in 1915, France versus Britain in 1916, Alekseev's demand for the expansion of operations in Salonika, and so forth.

Although the obstacles to strategic coordination were both profound and numerous, enhancing it would have offered Russia the best chance of winning the First World War. Britain and France would have also been beneficiaries: authentic strategic coordination might have brought about victory sooner, and at lower cost. In the end the allies won the war without Russia; the belated entry of the United States into the conflict more than compensated for Russia's absence. But it would have been best for the entente powers if they had won the war while Russia was still included in their number.

In the preceding chapter Michael Howard argues eloquently that World War I was necessary, that the allied cause was just, and that an allied victory was essential. From the standpoint of the information available to the combatants at the time, he is doubtless correct. The allied soldiers of the Great War, and the civilian populations who supported them, could not imagine a bleaker future than one in which Imperial Germany dominated Europe. We, however, have the advantage of hindsight and know better. In retrospect, was allied victory *without* Russia the optimal outcome of the First World War? Under the circumstances, might not German victory have been better for civilization and humanity? If the Imperial German government had prevailed in the war it would have made short shrift of the Bolshevik regime. In that event we would have had a twentieth century in which neither Stalin nor Hitler ever came to power. Our hypothetical twentieth century would surely have been replete with other horrors, but could any of these have equaled or exceeded the ones that actually ensued?

NOTES

1. For some examples, see A. Beloi, *Galitsiiskaia bitva* (Moscow, 1929); *Vostochno-prusskaia operatsiia: Sbornik dokumentov ob mirovoi imperialisticheskoi voiny na russkom fronte* (Moscow, 1939); General'nyi Shtab RKKA, *Lodzinskaia operatsiia: Sbornik dokumentov* (Moscow, 1936); General'nyi Shtab RKKA, *Varshavsko-ivangorodskaia operatsiia: Sbornik dokumentov* (Moscow, 1938).

2. Among these must be numbered I. I. Rostunov, *Ruskii front pervoi mirovoi voiny* (Moscow, 1976), V. A. Emets, *Ocherki vneshnei politiki Rossii v period pervoi mirovoi voiny: Vzaimootnosheniia Rossii s soiuznikami po voprosam vedeniia voiny* (Moscow, 1977), and L. G. Beskrovnyi, *Armiia i flot Rossii v nachale xxv: Ocherki voenno-ekonomicheskogo potentsiala* (Moscow, 1986). Rostunov's work focuses on operations and offers a qualified defense of the competence of the Russian high command. Emets provides a sophisticated analysis of interallied relations during the war. Beskrovnyi's posthumous work, a quantitative study of the tsarist Russian military establishment, was edited by Emets and Rostunov. Also note M. Frenkin, *Russkaia armiia i revoliutsiia* (Munich, 1978), a work finished by the author in exile but based on years of archival research in the Soviet Union. Useful information (if not persuasive interpretation) can also be found in A. L. Sidorov, *Finansovoe polozhenie Rossii v gody pervoi mirovoi voiny* (Moscow, 1960), and Sidorov, *Ekonomicheskoe polozhenie Rossii v gody pervoi mirovoi voiny* (Moscow, 1973). Among foreign studies: Norman Stone, *The Eastern Front, 1914–1917* (New York, 1975), Horst Günther Linke, *Das Zarische Russland und der erste Weltkrieg: Diplomatie und Kriegsziele, 1914–1917* (Munich, 1982), Lewis H. Siegelbaum, *The Politics of Industrial Mobilization in Russia, 1914–1917: A Study of the War-Industries Committees* (New York, 1983), Keith Neilson, *Strategy and Supply: The Anglo-Russian Alliance, 1914–1917* (London, 1984), W. Bruce Lincoln, *Passage Through Armageddon: The Russians in War and Revolution, 1914–1918* (New York, 1986), David R. Jones, "Imperial Russia's Forces at War," in Allan R. Millett and Williamson Murray, eds., *Military Effectiveness*, vol. 1: *The First World War* (Boston, 1988), 249–328; Dennis Showalter, *Tannenberg: Clash of Empires* (Hamden, Conn., 1991), and Hubertus F. Jahn, *Patriotic Culture in Russia During World War I* (Ithaca, N.Y., 1995).

3. The statistic on war deaths comes from N. N. Golovin, *The Russian Army in the World War* (New Haven, 1931), 94. Much higher figures are occasionally encountered in the literature: N. M. Iakupov, *Revoliutsiia i mir (soldatskie massy protiv imperialisticheskoi voiny 1917–mart 1918 gg.)* (Moscow, 1980), 16, estimates that 2.5 million tsarist troops died in the war. On the other hand, *Rossiia v mirovoi voine 1914–1918 goda (v tsifrakh)* (Moscow, 1925), 31, offers a figure of about 650,000 war deaths.

4. For an example, see R. M. Portugal'skii, P. D. Alekseev, and V. A. Runov, *Pervaia mirovaia v zhizneopisaniiakh russkikh voenachalnikov* (Moscow, 1994). On a more sinister note, the third edition of Nikolai Iakolev's *1 avgusta 1914* was issued in Moscow in 1993. This ultra-nationalist work, originally published in 1974 with the connivance of the KGB, argues that Russia lost the war because of the treachery of bourgeois liberals, masons, and others who sabotaged the war effort in their quest for power.

5. For a sense of where postcommunist Russian historiography may be headed, see Iu. A. Pisarev, "Novye pokhody k izucheniiu istorii pervoi mirovoi voiny," *Novaia i noveishaia istoriia*, no. 3, 1993, pp. 46–57, and "Kruglyi stol. Pervaia mirovaia voina i ee vozdeistvie na isotriiu xx v.," *Novaia i noveishaia istoriia*, nos. 4–5, 1994.

6. D. C. B. Lieven, *Russia and the Origins of the First World War* (New York, 1983), 141–50. See also the note prepared at Stavka by Captain A. v. Nemitts in December 1914, which defined Russia's negative political goal as "ridding herself of the constant attempts of Germany and Austria to wound and shake Russia's prestige as a great power." Arkhiv Vneshnei Politiki Rossiskoi Imperii (hereafter AVPRI), f. 133, op. 467, d. 491/513a, 1. 4. (I follow the standard Russian practice in citing archival materials: fond, abbreviated f., means collection; opis', abbreviated op., means catalogue; delo, abbreviated d., means file; while list' and listi, abbreviated l. and ll., mean page, pages.)

7. Sir Alfred Knox, *With the Russian Army, 1914–1917: Being Chiefly Extracts from the Diary of a Military Attaché*,vol. 1 (London, 1921), 43. As early as November 1913 the Russian foreign minister had drafted a list of thirteen principles that called for the fragmentation of Germany into independent kingdoms and principalities based on principles of "national self-determination"—e.g., Hanover for the Hanoverians, etc. Linke, *Das Zarische Russland*, 39, 235.

8. Nicholas's proclamation of 12/25 December 1916, which spoke of Russian absorption of Constantinople and the Straits, as well as the creation of an independent Poland through the unification of all of Russia's, Germany's, and Austria's Polish territories, was neither comprehensive nor coherent (*Vospominaniia Lukomskago*, 114–15).

9. AVPRI, f. 138 (secret archive of the minister), op. 467, d. 705/748, ll. 1, 8–9.

10. Rossiskii Gosudarstvennyi Voenno-Istoricheskii Arkhiv (hereafter RGVIA), f. 2000 (General Staff), op. 1, d. 7203 for a proposal by A. N. Kuropatkin.

11. RGVIA, f. 2000, op. 1, d. 1835, l. 8.

12. AVPRI, f. 138 (secret archive of the minister), op. 467, d. 469/488, l. 60.

13. Foreign Minister Sazonov had strong doubts on this score. See AVPRI, f. 138, op. 467, d. 472/492, l. 50.

14. RGVIA, f. 2003, op. 1, d. 1113, l. 291.

15. RGVIA, f. 2003 (Stavka), op. 1, d. 1165, l. 31.

16. "Stavka i ministerstvo inostrannykh del," *Krasnyi arkhiv,* vol. 1 (20), 1928, 45.

17. Gosudarstvennyi Arkhiv Rossiskoi Federatsii (hereafter GARF) f. 601 (Nicholas II), op. 1, d. 549, l. 195.

18. "Stavka i ministerstvo inostrannykh del," vii.

19. N. G. Dumova, *Kadetskaia partiia v period pervoi mirovoi voiny i Fevral'skoi revoliutsii* (Moscow, 1988), 222.

20. RGVIA, f. 2000 (General Staff), op. 1, d. 1894, l. 2.

21. Jones, "Imperial Russia's Forces," 282.

22. RGVIA, f. 2003, op. 1, d. 534, l. 87.

23. For an example, see General Aleksei Alekseivich Brussilov, *A Soldier's Notebook, 1914–1918* (London, 1930), 324.

24. *Doklad soveta s'ezdov o merakh k razvitiiu proizvoditel'nykh sil Rossii* (Petrograd, 1915), 176.

25. Stone, *Eastern Front,* 13–14.

26. Mikhail Lemke, *250 dnei v tsarskoi stavke (25 sent. 1915–2 juliia 1916)* (Petersburg, 1920), 97.

27. "Perepiska V. A. Sukhomlinova s N. N. Ianushkevichem," *Krasnvi arkhiv,* vol. 3 (Moscow/Petrograd, 1923), 70; Lemke, *250 dnei,* 459.

28. RGVIA, f. 2003, op. 1, d. 1165, l. 105.

29. Beliaev, quoted in Lincoln, *Passage Through Armageddon,* 145.

30. In fact, Russian gunners, who had profited from the experience of the Japanese War, were superior to their Austrian and German counterparts in the initial phases of the world war. Showalter, *Tannenberg,* 161; Beloi, *Galitsiiskaia bitva,* 199.

31. Erast Giatsintov, *Zapiski belogo ofitsera* (St. Petersburg, 1992), 54.

32. Knox, *With the Russian Army,* vol. 1, 259.

33. Knox, *With the Russian Army,* vol. 1, 282.

34. P. P. Petrov, *Rokovye gody 1914–1920* (California [*sic*], 1965), 31.

35. Brussilov, *Notebook,* 219–20.

36. RGVIA, f. 2003, op. 1, d. 120, l. 71.

37. Brussilov, *Notebook,* 18, observes that the technical inferiority of the Russian army to the German was so great that it "could be counterbalanced only by an additional sacrifice of life."

38. F. F. Palitsyn, "V shtabe severno-zapadnogo fronta (s kontsa apreliia

1915 goda po 30 avgusta togo zhe goda," *Voennyi sbornik obshchestva revnitelei voennykh znanii,* vol. 3 (Belgrade, 1922), 164.

39. In his circular to the military districts of August 1915, acting War Minister Polivanov referred to a shortage of 600,000 men in the active army, adding that the new replacements being sent out to the front from the interior of the country "are completely unsuitable, both in terms of their military training, and more importantly, in terms . . . of the development in them of feelings of military duty. It is necessary to say openly that the latter circumstance explains the considerable number of our men taken prisoner by the Germans." RGVIA, f. 2003, op. 1, d. 1767, l. 73.

40. Stone, *Eastern Front,* 285–86.

41. GARF, f. 601 (Nicholas II), op. 1, d. 657, l. 2.

42. *Vospominaniia Generala A. S. Lukomskago,* vol. 1 (Berlin, 1922), 68. In May 1917, the Russian High Command was still appealing in vain to its French allies for deliveries of heavy artillery; Denikin stated that "we are so weak in heavy artillery that any pieces with calibers larger than 6″ would be highly desirable for us." RGVIA, f. 2003, op. 1, d. 1767, l. 73.

43. Gourko, *War and Revolution,* 130.

44. GARF, f. 601, op. 1, d. 657, l. 4.

45. Daniel Graf, "The Reign of the Generals: Military Government in Western Russia, 1914–1915," Ph.D. diss., University of Nebraska, 1972, 70.

46. T. M. Kitanina, *Voina, khleb i revoliutsiia (prodovol'stvennyi vopros v Rossii 1914-Oktiabr' 1917 g.)* (Leningrad, 1985), 218.

47. Iakupov, *Revoliutsiia i mir,* 20–21.

48. For works praising the activities of the civic organizations, see, among others, Brussilov, *Notebook,* 198.

49. K. A. Krivoshein, *A. V. Krivoshein: Ego zhachenie v istorii Rossii nachala xx veka* (Paris, 1973), 239.

50. Tikhon Polner, Vladimir Obolensky and Sergius P. Turin, *Russian Local Government During the War* (New Haven, 1930), 241, 279; Paul P. Gronsky, *The War and the Russian Government* (New Haven, 1929), 221, 257; General Basil Gourko, *War and Revolution in Russia, 1914–1917* (New York, 1919), 154–57.

51. Sidorov, *Ekonomicheskoe polozhenic,* 193–201; Siegelbaum, *Politics of Industrial Mobilization,* 104, 118, 156, 158, 192. Siegelbaum is nonetheless more inclined to find favor with the work of at least some of the military-industrial committees than are other authors. He notes (p. 95) that the committees furnished the army with almost 48 percent of all the hand grenades it received in 1915 and 1916. However, this accomplishment may not be all that it seems: field trials in 1916 indicated that up to 65 percent of the grenades dispatched to the army were duds. See: L. G. Beskrovnyi et al., eds., *Zhurnal osobogo soveshchaniia po oborone gosudarstva 1916 god* (Moscow, 1977), 252.

52. A. N. Naumov, *Iz utselevshikh vospominanii 1868–1917 gg.* (New York, 1955), 377.

53. Vladimir N. Ipatieff, *The Life of a Chemist: Memoirs of Vladimir N. Ipatieff,* Xenia Joufkoff Evdin, Helen Dwight Fisher, and Harold H. Fisher, eds., Vladimir Haensel and Mrs. Ralph H. Lusher, trans. (Palo Alto, Calif., 1946), 192.

54. RGVIA, f. 2003, op. 1, d. 63, l. 81.

55. "Perepiska V. A. Sukhomlinova s N. N. Ianushkevichem," *Krasnvi arkhiv,* vol. 1 (Moscow/Petrograd, 1922), 225.

56. RGVIA, f. 2003, op. 1, d. 40, l. 178.

57. See Alekseev's note to Ivanov of October 21, 1914: *Lodzinskaia operatsiia,* 63.

58. Brussilov noted that Stavka invariably hesitated after adopting a particular plan of operations and always tried to skimp on the number of forces assigned to it. Brussilov, *Notebook,* 117.

59. A. I. Denikin, *Put' russkogo ofitsera* (New York, 1953), 377.

60. See, for example, Joffre's letter to Alekseev of April 2/15, 1915, in RGVIA, f. 2003, op. 1, d. 54, l. 360.

61. Iu. N. Danilov, *Rossiia v mirovoi voine 1914–1915 gg.* (Berlin, 1924), 392, 397; Ipatieff, *Life of a Chemist,* 247; Emets, *Ocherki vneshnei politiki,* 107.

62. See, for example, Stone, *Eastern Front,* 35, which argues for Germany as the top priority enemy. Richard Pipes, *The Russian Revolution* (New York, 1990), 199, argues for an offensive against Austria.

63. Alexander M. Michelson, Paul N. Apostol, and Michael W. Bernatzky, *Russian Public Finance During the War* (New Haven, 1928), 320–22.

64. Brussilov, *Notebook,* 256, 266.

65. A. Zaionchkovskii, *Mirovaia voina 1914–1918 g.g.,* vol. 2 (Moscow, 1938), 66.

66. *Vospominaniia Lukomskago,* vol. 2, 105.

67. Iakupov, *Revoliutsiia i mir,* 91.

68. RGVIA, f. 2003, op. 1, d. 1242, l. 24.

69. Frenkin, *Russkaia armiia,* 197.

70. Avner Offer, *The First World War: An Agrarian Interpretation* (Oxford, 1989), 76.

71. I have in mind Millet and Williamson, *The First World War.* See particularly the essay by Paul Kennedy, "Military Effectiveness in the First World War," 329–50.

72. Lemke, *250 dnei,* 73.

73. See, for example, RGVIA, f. 2003, op. 1, d. 518, l. 1; RGVIA, f. 2003, op. 1, d. 112, ll. 10–11; RGVIA, f. 2003, op. 1, d. 58, l. 138; RGVIA, f. 2003, op. 1, d. 512, ll. 128 ff.

74. Emets, *Ocherki vneshnei politiki,* 99.

75. Winston S. Churchill, *The Unknown War: The Eastern Front* (New York, 1931), 76.

76. Rostunov, *Ruskii front*, 260–72. In effect, Stavka created an independent cavalry army on this occasion. This military innovation, like so many others claimed by the Soviets as their own, should actually be credited to the tsarist army. There is even a precedent for Stalin's evacuation of industry to the East in World War II. Beginning in the summer of 1915 a variety of industrial plants were dismantled and shipped to the Volga provinces of Samara and Saratov, and reconstituted. See E. D. Rumiantsev, *Rabochii klass povolzhia v gody pervoi mirovoi voiny i fevral'skoi revoliutsii (1914–1917 gg.)* (Kazan, 1989), 51.

77. RGVIA, f. 2003, op. 1, d. 112, l. 168 (instructions from the commander of the Russian Seventh army to his corps commanders, March 11, 1917).

78. RGVIA, f. 2003, op. 1, d. 39, l. 173g.

79. Erich von Falkenhayn was one of those who understood that even the most successful breakthrough would scarcely translate into the total military defeat of the enemy, given the conditions on the ground on the Eastern Front. In the late summer of 1915 he wrote, "It is impossible to try to annihilate an enemy who is far superior in numbers, must be attacked frontally, and has excellent lines of communication, any amount of time and space at his disposal." General von Falkenhayn, *The German General Staff and Its Decisions, 1914–1916* (New York, 1920), 142. On the other hand, General von Hoffman, *The War of Lost Opportunities* (New York, 1925), 121, maintains that only command errors prevented destruction of the Russian army by the Central Powers in the spring of 1915.

80. See, for example, Trevor Wilson, *The Myriad Faces of War* (Cambridge, 1986), 117–21, 130–40, 269, 275. See also J. M. Bourne, *Britain and the Great War, 1914–1918* (New York, 1989), 40–41, 47–48.

81. See the remarks of Ludendorff. General Ludendorff, *My War Memories*, vol. 1 (London, n.d.), 174. See also Liman von Sanders, *Five Years in Turkey* (Annapolis, Md., 1927), 87–89.

82. RGVIA, f. 2003, op. 1, d. 40, ll. 196–97, 200, 203.

83. RGVIA, f. 2003, op. 1, d. 51, ll. 256–68.

84. RGVIA, f. 2003, op. 1, d. 1133, ll. 358–60.

85. A. Bubnov, *V tsarskoi stavke* (New York, 1955), 279.

86. AVPRI, f. 138, op. 467, d. 472/492, l. 13.

87. Bubnov, *V tsarskoi stavke*, 215; Paul Halpern, *A Naval History of World War I* (Annapolis, Md., 1994), 238–45.

88. RGVIA, f. 2003, op. 1, 1165, l. 53.

89. GARF, f. 601, op. 1, 797, l. 13.

90. Emets, *Ocherki vneshnei politiki*, 353.

91. Falkenhayn, *German General Staff*, 304.

92. RGVIA, f. 2003, op. 1, d. 512, l. 4.

93. Lincoln, *Passage Through Armageddon*, 61.

94. Calculated on the basis of Golovin, *Russian Army*, 142.

95. RGVIA, f. 2003, op. 1, d. 1242, l. 17. Note also Nabokov's letter of August 7/20, 1917, imploring the Provisional Government to give a complete briefing to General Dessino, its military representative in London. Ibid., l. 33.

96. AVPRI, f. 134., op. 473, d. 118:106, l. 27.

97. RGVIA, f. 2003, op. 1, d. 1165, l. 101.

98. RGVIA, f. 2003, op. 1, d. 63, l. 87.

CHAPTER 3

The Politics of the Two Alliances

DAVID STEVENSON

The First World War was not over by Christmas. If, as in 1870, the war had lasted months rather than in years, 1914 would still have been a benchmark date. But it is hardly likely that it would have signified "the end of the European era."[1] Despite the German chancellor's prediction of a "violent, but short storm," the storm was violent and long. It grew into the first general war, involving all the strongest countries of the day since the fall of Napoleon, and the first ever such war to be fought between industrialized powers. It came closer than any predecessor to Clausewitz's conception of an "absolute" or total conflict, and its destructiveness was unprecedented. In short, it was a disaster, and a drum-roll for disasters to follow. Stalinism in Russia, the rise of Fascism, the 1929 Depression, and the Second World War can all be seen as more or less direct consequences of World War I. Only after the Soviet collapse of 1989–91 could it plausibly be argued that what E. J. Hobsbawm has christened the Age of Extremes inaugurated at Sarajevo had finally closed.[2]

All of the global repercussions of the war in Europe arose from its development, between 1914 and 1917, into an intractable stalemate between evenly matched adversaries. The first and most familiar element in this stalemate was military, and it is still the imagery of deadlock on the Western Front that mention of the war most vividly recaptures: that of trenches, machine guns, and corpses on the barbed wire. Neither side could surmount the tactical challenges created by high force-to-space ratios and the prevailing weapons technology, which on the Gallipoli peninsula and the Isonzo plateau produced even more atrocious battlefield conditions than in Flanders and France. At sea the allied surface blockade was countered by the German submarine one, and neither worked fast. Yet even in Eastern Europe, where the campaigning was much more mobile, no Great Power was eliminated during the first three years. The military decision took so long not merely because of the invulnerability of field fortifications but also because both sides controlled enormous resources and because until 1918 neither enjoyed a commanding lead.

Nonetheless, the operational deadlock was only one of three mutually reinforcing elements in the impasse. The second was the extraordinary resilience of the combatants and of the home fronts, reflecting the survival in all the major belligerents of a consensus in support of governments that were committed to keep fighting rather than settling on unfavorable terms. The roots of this consensus have formed one of the fastest-growing topics of scholarly research in recent years. The circumstances in which war broke out contributed to it by allowing the authorities on both sides to claim that they were acting in self-defense against provocation, and that only victory would cripple an unscrupulous foe. In addition, the "short-war illusion," to use Lancelot Farrar's phrase, did not end in August or even in November 1914.[3] The conflict continued, as it had begun, by incremental steps. For governments and publics alike the operative choice was not whether to hold on for another three years but whether to do so for another six months. It was easier to bear the strain if a push in the next spring or autumn might end it, and compromise would be repugnant if it meant that the dead had lost their lives in vain. Even so, morale was tested to the limit, and it was no accident that it broke earlier in the multinational Eastern European monarchies than in France, Germany, and Britain. In the words of F. Scott Fitzgerald's anti-hero Dick Diver, revisiting the French battlegrounds in the 1920s, "the Russians and Italians weren't any good on this front. You had to have a whole-souled sentimental equipment going back further than you could remember. You had to remember Christmas and postcards of the Crown Prince and his fianceé and little cafés in Unter den Linden, and going to the Derby and your grandfather's whiskers. . . . This was a love battle—there was a century of middle-class love spent here."[4]

War was the ultimate test of nationhood, and of subliminal processes molding national consciousness that were still at work. French soldiers may have been sustained by a visceral attachment to their own and to their comrades' soil. Probably of greater relevance for the British, however, is Denis Winter's comment that prewar England remained a deferential society in which industrial workers were outnumbered by domestic servants and agricultural laborers, and life for most was hard, regimented, and sometimes dangerous even in time of peace.[5]

The third element in the impasse concerned diplomacy. If the conflict could not be ended by an operational breakthrough, or by mutiny and insurrection behind the lines, neither could it be ended by negotiation. The first and most obvious reason was the opposition between the two sides' war aims, which since the opening of the relevant archives have been examined in depth. The documentation is copious but difficult to interpret. What was publicly acknowledged differed from what was privately planned, and even in confidential discussion war aims were often in flux. They were hypothetical statements of the desirable, not necessarily adhered to regardless of the military prospects. Nonetheless, the imperial German government, having barely considered its war aims in July 1914, subsequently gave them great attention. In addition to a worldwide chain of naval bases and a consolidated belt of territory in Africa running from coast to coast, German leaders wanted a customs union in Central Europe and small but significant annexations on the country's eastern and western borders, including Liège, Luxembourg, the Longwy-Briey iron-ore basin, and a Polish "frontier strip" that would be cleared of Jews and Slavs and resettled. The rest of Belgium, Russian Poland, and the Baltic provinces would remain nominally independent but would enter into customs and monetary union with the Reich, which would garrison them and manage their railways. If implemented, such proposals would give Berlin de facto continental hegemony, and by 1918 a swathe of buffer states in the east had already extended its *imperium* through the Ukraine and as far as the Caucasus.[6]

German policy conflicted with Britain's (less clearly formulated) objectives not only in its general threat to the balance of power in Europe but more specifically in its challenge to the London government's goals of restoring Belgian independence and neutrality, destroying Germany's overseas empire, and confiscating its fleet. The French authorities, in contrast, wished not simply to liberate Belgium from German domination but also to bring it and Luxembourg into their own sphere of influence, as well as to regain the provinces of Alsace-Lorraine, which had been lost in 1871, and to incorporate Togoland and Kamerun. By 1917 they also planned to annex the Saar coal field and to separate the left bank of the Rhine from the remainder of Germany, permanently occupying the region and absorbing it into the French monetary and customs zone. To some extent the German project of expansion via buffer states was mirrored by a French one, and in the east, German and Austrian designs for a Polish satellite kingdom were counterpoised by tsarist ones to reunite the Polish-speaking regions of Germany, Austria-Hungary, and Russia into a single entity linked by personal union with the Romanov empire and with its defense and foreign policy under Russian control.[7]

To these direct contradictions between German objectives and those of Britain, France, and Russia, the two sides' commitments to their partners added indirect ones. In the Balkans, Austro-German and Bulgarian plans to partition and subordinate Serbia, Montenegro, and Romania conflicted with British, French, and Russian pledges to support expansion by their protégés. In the Ottoman Empire, starting with the undertaking in the Straits Agreement of March–April 1915 that Russia could annex Constantinople and the Bosporus, the allies carved out their intended zones of dominance. Italy was brought into the war by the April 1915 Treaty of London, which promised it Austrian territory in the Trentino and along the eastern shore of the Adriatic; Japan was encouraged to stay in by agreements to back its demands on Germany's Chinese and Pacific possessions. Both in the traditional European marchlands along the Rhine and Vistula, and outside the Continent in Asia and Africa, the list of territorial disputes was long. To the list should be added the potential for antagonism contained between Germany's design for a Central European customs union, into which its buffer states would be incorporated, and that of the allies to form a self-sufficient bloc, barring the Central Powers from trading with the outside world.[8]

Too close a scrutiny of the belligerents' economic and territorial objectives may obscure rather than illuminate what the struggle was about. In public both sides preferred to portray the issues as moral and ideological: the allies by reference to the Anglo-Saxon and the French Republican traditions of political liberalism, the Germans by invoking the martial values known as the "ideas of 1914" against a materialist and decadent bourgeois order.[9] It is easy to expose the elements of hypocrisy in such pretensions, but they had a resonance in and beyond the policymaking elites, and they cannot be discounted as mere verbiage. In contrast, many war aims were neither openly avowed nor unanimously supported in the bureaucracies, and in public, statesmen referred to them in coded language as "security guarantees." All the same, war aims were a major obstacle to attempts at compromise. The demands for strategic frontiers and for raw materials stemmed from apprehension that the relatively benign and open international order of the later nineteenth century was dead, and that a new age of iron was impending. In his portrayal of Georges Clemenceau, the French prime minister at the Paris Peace Conference, J. M. Keynes satirized this view as one of European history as a "perpetual prize-fight": Germany's Field Marshal Paul von Hindenburg exemplified it when in 1917 he demanded the Baltic provinces as a maneuvering ground for his left flank in the next war.[10] It was critical in accounting for the most tragic and arresting paradox of 1914–18: that of a total war fought for limited ends. Battles unprecedented in their scale and casualties were fought by powers that were separated by no such ideological gulf as in the Second World War, and none of which, if they sued for peace, would face annihilation. Such objectives as Belgium and Alsace-Lorraine seemed in retrospect utterly disproportionate to their cost. It was partly for this reason—the inability to discern for what compelling reason the war had been fought—that by the 1930s it was widely attributed in the democracies to the machinations of bankers, diplomats, and arms firms. At best it was seen as a monument to futility.

The paradox of the disproportion between ends and means can partially be resolved by remembering that World War I was a coalition conflict. Wars between two single powers may also bog down if the opponents are far enough apart, as in the American Civil War and in the 1980–88 Iran-Iraq conflict. But during World War I both sides were alliances with no single power clearly dominant, and this lent the struggle a peculiar dynamic. Although the coalition factor was not the only relevant variable, it strengthened all three elements of the stalemate.

It may seem excessive to invest the coalitions with such significance, but in their memoirs the wartime leaders acknowledge that alliance management had often been intensely frustrating. This experience helps explain the relief expressed by some in Britain after France fell in 1940. At least from now on they would be on their own,[11] even if Winston Churchill himself remarked that the only thing worse than fighting with allies is fighting without them.[12] Recent research on 1914–18 has stripped away the surface pieties of comradeship in arms to expose the underlying divergences of style and perception, and the continuing pursuit of national interest vis-à-vis allies as well as enemies. In the case of the Central Powers, Georges-Henri Soutou has underlined that Germany's project for a Central European customs union, or Mitteleuropa, had power-political rather than commercial goals.[13] In the words of the September 1914 program of the chancellor, Theobald von Bethmann Hollweg, its objective was "to stabilize Germany's economic dominance over Central Europe," which meant principally over Austria-Hungary, the partner Germany had so energetically championed in July.[14] The authorities in Vienna were well aware of such designs, and they did their best to frustrate them. Werner Conze, Fritz Fischer, and Gerhard Ritter, among others, have analyzed the wrangling between the two powers over the future of Poland.[15] Gerald Silberstein has highlighted the distrust that impeded Austro-German military cooperation to the extent that no unified command was created until Russia's General Brusilov routed the Habsburg forces in 1916.[16] Even the Ottoman Empire, despite its seeming economic and military vulnerability, upheld its independence and wrested from Berlin a string of diplomatic concessions. For much of the war Germany was unable to dictate to its weaker partners, and it created little institutional machinery to facilitate coordination.[17]

It is unsurprising that on the allied side, where no one capital could rival Berlin's claim to dominance, internecine rivalries were still more evident. No more than in 1941–45 were East and West comfortable partners, and tsarist officials were almost as suspicious of the British as would be their Soviet successors.[18] As in the 1940s, too, there was Anglo-American competition, elements in the Woodrow Wilson administration seeking to build up U.S. merchant shipping, trade with Latin America, and Wall Street's role as a financial center, all at London's expense.[19] The French government alleged that an independent American Expeditionary Force would be militarily ineffective, but for Washington the AEF was essential to its diplomatic leverage. Tension over the issue exploded in the quarrel in the winter of 1917–18 over the proposed amalgamation of French and American units, which the American commander, John J. Pershing, was determined to resist.[20] It is true that by the end of the conflict there existed a superstructure of international institutions prefiguring the inter-allied boards and committees of 1939–45 and the Cold War. The Interallied Maritime Transport Council (IMTC), for shipping, and the Supreme War Council (SWC), for strategy, are the best known.[21] It is open to question, however, how far the SWC and Ferdinand Foch, generalissimo on the Western Front in 1918, succeeded in harmonizing the national war efforts and contributed to the eventual victory. The basic reason for that victory, as Paul Kennedy reminds us, was the immense allied superiority in material resources resulting from the United States' entry into the war. Once American intervention was secured, the outcome became largely a matter of what Churchill described, in reference to the Second World War, as the "proper application of overwhelming force."[22]

The foregoing may suggest that coalition warfare was a struggle of all against all, as much within as between the opposing camps. Given this divisiveness, perhaps the alliances should be written out of the history of the conflict altogether. Yet to do so would be misleading, especially if their role is viewed from the perspective of diplomacy rather than that of strategy or logistics. From this vantage point what stands out is not their fragility but their cohesion. On one level, what was at stake in the war was the future pattern of international alignments.

To clarify this point it is necessary to reconsider the origins of the two coalitions. The prewar generation had witnessed the first extended division of Europe during peacetime between armed blocs. The armies of the Austro-German alliance, concluded in 1879, and the Franco-Russian one, concluded in 1891–94, had grown accustomed to regarding the opposing combination as the most likely potential enemy for purposes of mobilization and concentration planning, intelligence gathering and assessment, and decisions on manpower and weaponry deployments. Admittedly there was friction within the blocs, and the degree of polarization between them fluctuated. At the turn of the century Austria-Hungary and Russia had agreed to freeze their competition in the Balkans and respect the status quo, while France, Germany, and Russia felt a common hostility to British policy in southern Africa. Nonetheless, in the run-up to war the alliances were becoming more solid. Military staff liaison between their members, which had been in abeyance at the turn of the century, revived. Between about 1905 and 1911 the most dynamic and dangerous European arms races pitted Germany against Britain in the North Sea, and two supposed allies, Austria-Hungary and Italy, against each other in the Adriatic. But by 1912–14 both of these contests were overshadowed by the competition in armaments between the Austro-German and the Franco-Russian blocs.[23] Diplomatically, the Balkan upheavals of 1912–13 drew France closer to Russia and Germany to Austria-Hungary, while the entente agreements of 1904 and 1907, followed by the first Moroccan and the Bosnian annexation crises, drew London into habitual cooperation with Paris and St. Petersburg. All of these developments aggravated the Central Powers' phobia of encirclement, and the Germans' frustration at their inability to break out. When Bethmann Hollweg became chancellor in 1909 he saw his primary task in foreign policy as being to "split up the coalition directed against us."[24] But his attempts to detach the British in 1909–12, through armaments and neutrality negotiations, and the Russians in 1910–11, through agreements on Asian spheres of influence, failed. German diplomacy could not shake the solidarity of the Anglo-Franco-Russian combination, and inter-bloc rivalry was increasingly militarized. Among the consequences was the paralysis of the rudimentary conciliation machinery known as the Concert of Europe, and the growing desperation in Berlin and Vienna that culminated in decisions to fight.[25]

Strictly speaking it is not true that in July–August 1914 the provisions of the alliance treaties drew Europe into war. Germany was not required to support Austria-Hungary's attack on Serbia, and by ordering general mobilization without prior discussion the Russians violated their 1891 political agreement with Paris.[26] Britain had undertaken to the French merely to consult them in the event of a threat to the peace, and the Cabinet considered that a decision to uphold the guarantee of Belgium in the 1839 London Treaty would be "rather one of policy than legal obligation."[27] All the same, without the existence of the alliances it is impossible to explain the powers' decisions. Bethmann Hollweg faced an entente bloc that, if present trends continued, would in two to three years gain military superiority. He saw the opportunity, if France withheld support from Russia, to fracture the entente by a localized operation in the Balkans; or, if Paris and St. Petersburg opted for a Continental conflict, to overwhelm them before it was too late. Conversely, he may have feared that if he failed to back up Austria-Hungary after the Sarajevo assassinations he would estrange his one reliable Great Power ally. From the beginning of the crisis he and Wilhelm II accepted the military argument that if Russia mobilized, Germany must do likewise and strike out as rapidly as possible in the west; but German strategic planning rested on the political assumption that a war with Russia could not be isolated, which turned out to be entirely justified. When the French government was presented with an ultimatum to repudiate the Russian alliance or face war, it scarcely hesitated before opting for the latter. President Poincaré commented in retrospect on the government's duty "not to break up an alliance on which French policy had been based for a quarter of a century and the break-up of which would leave us in isolation and at the mercy of our rivals."[28] In contrast, Bethmann Hollweg was over-optimistic about the possibility of securing British neutrality, but when on July 29 he bid precisely for this, in return for offering not to annex French and Belgian territory in Europe, the response in Whitehall was indignant. The Russian foreign minister had already warned that if the British stayed aloof they would sacrifice tsarist friendship and endanger India, which may have helped to tilt the Foreign Office toward intervention. For the key figures in the British government, however, the decisive consideration was their security imperative (though neither legal nor moral obligation) to protect France against Germany. As the prime minister, Herbert Asquith, wrote on August 2, "It is against British interests that France shd. be wiped out as a Great Power."[29]

In 1914 as previously, then, the Germans hoped to break the opposing encirclement, and the French and British stood by their entente partners. For the underlying structure of international alignments the outbreak of war was not a turning point. On the contrary, the pattern established by the diplomatic revolution of 1904–7 survived until 1917. From now on Germany and Austria-Hungary used military force to try to breach their enemies' solidarity, as well as continuing political inducements. But neither method succeeded, any more than did allied efforts to split the Central Powers.

The historian who has analyzed the resulting stalemate most incisively is Lancelot Farrar. His work helps us to conceptualize the differences between a coalition conflict and a bilateral one.[30] In the opening weeks the German leaders hoped to defeat France and Russia in quick succession, thus forcing Britain to come to terms. Bethmann Hollweg's celebrated—or notorious—war aims program of September 5, 1914, reflects this optimism. But within two months both he and the commander-in-chief, General Erich von Falkenhayn, had accepted that the chance to sweep the board was lost, and that they risked being ground down in a war of attrition unless they could extricate themselves by dividing their antagonists. Hence the chancellor reverted to his peacetime refrain, writing in December that "for us everything depends on shattering the coalition, i.e., on a separate peace with one of our enemies." In August 1916 he advocated an agreement with the Russians in order to "blow up the Entente," and in April 1917 he advised the Kaiser that in the eventual peace negotiations "our objective will then as now have to be to achieve a separate peace with one or other of our enemies. . . . The main consideration will be to shatter the present coalition of our opponents and to bring one or several of them over to our side." Similar remarks were made by Falkenhayn and by the state secretary for foreign affairs, Gottlieb von Jagow, as well as by Jagow's successor, Richard von Kühlmann, the principal director of German diplomacy in 1917–18. According to Kühlmann in December 1917, "the disruption of the Entente and the subsequent creation of coalitions agreeable to us constitute the most important war aims of our diplomacy." Thus the Austro-German advance into Poland in 1915 was accompanied by abortive feelers to the Russians, and equally abortive feelers to the French paralleled Falkenhayn's efforts to "bleed white" their army at Verdun.[31]

Yet in spite of the appalling damage inflicted on both sides, by the end of 1916 the Germans seemed no nearer to escaping their predicament than they had been two years earlier.

One reason was that they had little to offer. Against France, if it was willing to detach itself from its allies, the German Foreign Ministry was willing in June 1916 to settle for the border iron-ore field around Longwy-Briey (which was France's main source of supply) and a large war indemnity, but if the country fought on alongside Britain, Germany must seek its "complete overthrow."[32] Bethmann Hollweg's successor, Georg Michaelis, was prepared to waive the annexation of Longwy-Briey if Germany were guaranteed access to the ore.[33] But at no point were the Germans willing to yield to French objectives in the Rhineland, the Saarland, or Belgium, and in Alsace-Lorraine they would contemplate surrendering only a few border villages. To Russia, in early 1915, Germany was willing to grant peace in return for a revised trade treaty and for small frontier annexations, principally the Polish frontier strip.[34] But when Petrograd refused to cooperate, German objectives grew, and in November 1916, Bethmann Hollweg took what he considered an irreversible step by committing himself to nominal independence for the Russian portion of Poland, which would become a German buffer zone.[35] The Polish declaration, moreover, was a first sign of the new extremism that resulted from Falkenhayn's replacement by Hindenburg, assisted by General Erich Ludendorff, in the High Command. From 1915 on, as Fischer and Hans Gatzke have shown, wide sections of German society, including businessmen, agrarians, intellectuals, and most of the centrist and right-wing political parties, supported sweeping claims for annexations and buffer states within Europe and for colonies overseas. In contrast, although clashing with Bethmann Hollweg over such questions as submarine warfare, Falkenhayn broadly agreed with him over war aims and the priority of splitting Germany's enemies. Hindenburg and Ludendorff, however, refused to compromise in their quest for total victory and were more resolved to pin down the chancellor, and Wilhelm feared confronting them. In war-aims discussions in November 1916 and the spring of 1917 they pushed Berlin toward intransigence.[36]

All the same, in 1915 and 1916 Russia and France could probably have escaped with small territorial losses if they had deserted the alliance and accepted German terms. Even though the war had taken on a shape and was demanding sacrifices undreamt of before its outbreak, they opted not to do so. On the contrary, the second reason for Germany's failure to divide the allies was their determination not to be split. In the September 1914 Pact of London, Britain, France, and Russia bound themselves neither to negotiate nor to make peace separately. Their commitment stemmed in part from the distrust and fear of Germany that had built up before the war. In addition, the imperative of preserving unity was a constant priority of coalition management that critically influenced allied diplomacy and strategy. The French government probably felt the imperative most keenly, and it was acutely suspicious of peace feelers either from the Central Powers or from neutrals, which it suspected of being "snares." The French foreign minister in 1914–15, Théophile Delcassé, vetoed feelers to Austria-Hungary for fear of weakening the pro-allied forces in Petrograd.[37] But the British Foreign Office had similar concerns, and neither London nor Paris would have been likely to concede the 1915 Straits Agreement had it not been for their fears of a Russo-German deal. David French has argued that at first the British leaders hoped that France and Russia would take the brunt of the fighting until a new British army was ready to play the decisive role in achieving victory, thereby giving London the principal voice in the peace settlement. It soon became clear that such a program was untenable. Instead, in 1915–16 the British took enormous casualties on the Western Front by launching offensives intended to relieve the pressure on their allies, and diverted forces to Salonika to appease French domestic political pressures.[38] The allies arranged their diplomacy and strategy in order to reduce the danger that any coalition member would be tempted by a separate peace, and the larger the coalition grew, the more complex this task became. To some extent the same applied for their enemies. Whereas in August 1914, Germany failed to deliver on a prewar promise to Austria-Hungary to launch an opening offensive against Russia, in the following spring additional German troops went to the Eastern Front in part because of fear that Vienna might seek to break away.[39]

Between 1914 and 1917 the coalition factor impinged on all aspects of the stalemate. Militarily, had either France or Russia faced Germany alone, it would certainly have been beaten, as would Austria-Hungary had it faced Russia. Both coalitions disposed of economic and manpower resources much greater than even their strongest member did alone. On the home fronts, confidence in their partners' support played a probably indispensable role in rallying French politicians and generals after their early disasters, and in steeling the Russians to keep fighting after their 1915 debacle in Poland. Diplomatically, there was a standoff not only between the two sides' opposing war aims but also between the Germans' determination to split their enemies and realign the European political constellation, and allied determination to resist. If military breakthrough, pacifist or socialist revolution, and negotiated compromises were all excluded, every exit from the carnage was blocked.

Thus the role of coalition dynamics in creating the stalemate. We must now examine the persistence of the established pattern through the crises of 1917, and its eventual supersession. The outstanding development in 1917 was the erosion of the second element in the impasse, that of civilian and combatant morale. It was in the east that war weariness was greatest, and within each grouping Austria-Hungary and Russia made analogous efforts to scale down their partners' objectives. The new Habsburg Emperor, Karl, and his foreign minister, Count Ottokar Czernin, made overtures to the opposition in the German Reichstag. The Russian Provisional Government, formed in Petrograd after Nicholas II abdicated, sympathized with the appeal from the Bureau of the Second International for a conference at Stockholm of neutral and belligerent socialist parties.

Resurgent national separatism in Austria-Hungary and revolution in Russia were accompanied by mutinies in the French army, the Italian collapse at the battle of Caporetto, and industrial unrest in Germany and Britain. All the warring governments, except the American, were more willing at least to talk, and most of the major peace initiatives took place during 1917.

Early assessments of such episodes as the attempted mediation between Austria-Hungary and the allies by Prince Sixte de Bourbon, or the Franco-German contact known as the Briand-Lancken affair, blamed their failure on the incompetence of amateur intermediaries or on individual intrigues.[40] In reality the belligerents remained far apart, and the obstacles to peace were formidable. Russia and Austria-Hungary won changes in the presentation of the two sides' war aims but little moderation in the substance. Yet advocates of separate peace prevailed in neither country until Lenin and the Bolsheviks seized power. Arguably both Karl and the Petrograd Provisional Government destroyed themselves by their inability or unwillingness to detach themselves from their partners. Outside Russia civilian and combatant morale was shaken, but it recovered, and the coalition dynamic continued to operate. Britain and Germany were divided over colonies and Belgium; France and Germany over the Rhineland and Alsace-Lorraine; Russia and Germany over Poland and the Baltic provinces; Austria-Hungary and Italy over the Trentino and Trieste. Peace feelers were still intended to divide the enemy as much as hasten reconciliation.

Most of the feelers came from Germany and Austria-Hungary, sometimes profiting from interventions by such neutral parties as the Socialist International and the pope. The Central Powers already occupied most of the territory that concerned them, and although Germany had lost its overseas colonies its interest was in a ceasefire along the existing fronts. The Sixte de Bourbon episode made the German leaders (who learned of it only indirectly) highly uncomfortable, and when France, in the so-called Armand-Revertera conversations, offered the Habsburgs German territory Berlin launched a counteroffer in the hope of splitting off Britain. Although by the autumn of 1917 the Germans were ready to suspend their demands for U-boat bases on the Belgian coast, as well as that for the annexation of Longwy-Briey, their other Western war aims were not much changed and their eastern objectives were more ambitious than ever.[41] Pressure from Vienna and from the domestic opposition had made little substantive difference, and the Austrians themselves were still unwilling to settle for the prewar status quo.

Within the allied camp the position was similar. French war aims during 1917 changed more in appearance than in substance; in London, the Lloyd George Cabinet espoused the League of Nations while expanding Britain's Middle Eastern objectives. The Russian Provisional Government was willing to abandon most of the tsarist war aims, but it could neither persuade France and Britain to jettison ballast nor itself resolve to part company with them, especially given its knowledge of the scale of Germany's demands. Similarly, although the French and British pursued the Sixte de Bourbon mediation in the hope of detaching Karl, they remained loyal to their undertakings to Italy. In contrast, by September 1917, Lloyd George and possibly the French Premier, Paul Painlevé, were willing to contemplate a "peace on Russia's back" that would sanction German expansion in the east. But most of the British Cabinet opposed this idea, as did the American president and Painlevé's successor, Clemenceau.[42] When Germany's feelers reached France and Britain that autumn, both decided to refuse discussions until they had consulted their partners. Both still feared that almost any contact with the enemy might begin to unravel the alliance.

Whereas Germany's interest lay in a speedy armistice, it was for the allies to decide whether to prolong hostilities in the hope that the war, if fought to a conclusion, would turn their way. The chances of its doing so, and of exhausted publics continuing to support it, rested largely on American intervention. The judgment facing London and Paris was complex. America's resources vastly outweighed Russia's, and after April 1917 the North Atlantic states were potentially far stronger than their adversaries. Ideologically, the two sides had become more sharply demarcated, and there was greater justification for the allies' claim to be a muster of the democracies against autocratic rule. These may be grounds for saying that 1917–18, rather than 1914, heralded the end of the European era and the emergence of a combination "whose nerve centre was the ocean," foreshadowing the World War II Grand Alliance and NATO.[43] Yet in many ways American entry made Germany's enemies less cohesive, not more so. Woodrow Wilson was hostile in public and in private to the European diplomatic tradition. By placing his faith in collective security and the rule of law he repudiated the principle of the balance of power and sought to avoid long-term alliance commitments. The United States distanced itself from the intra-allied secret treaties and fought alongside its partners as an Associated Power, retaining the option of negotiating separately. It had never immersed itself in European politics so deeply, yet it remained self-consciously aloof.

Wilson did not believe that Lloyd George and Clemenceau were fighting for his objectives, and his cooperation with them was tactical. Both leaders were aware of his distrust, but they viewed him as naive and inexperienced, and believed that they could harness American power to their own ends. The upshot was that the entry of the United States prolonged the war. It failed to frighten Berlin into submission, because American military assistance—and to an extent even logistical assistance—to the allies was slow to materialize. But U.S. Treasury credits enabled Britain and France to continue to finance their war efforts after they had teetered on the brink of insolvency. Whereas Germany gambled that Russia's disintegration would allow it to overwhelm the Western allies before American resources could be brought to bear, Britain and France gambled that with Wilson's aid they could still achieve their objectives. "Until the United States has made the decisive effort it is preparing," cabled the French foreign minister, "we shall not be in a favourable position to negotiate," and Lloyd George in his memoirs justified his actions on similar lines.[44] Both countries adopted Fabian strategies, looking to a defensive war in 1918 and a decisive effort thereafter. But this timetable harmonized with Wilson's own. In July 1917 he made the often quoted comment on his allies (in a letter to his adviser, Colonel House), that "when the war is over we can force them to our way of thinking because by that time they will, among other things, be financially in our hands."[45] He too was playing a waiting game, increasing his leverage over his partners while Germany was ground down—but the first part of the quotation should be emphasized. The showdown with London and Paris would come *after* Germany had been beaten and its militarists humbled. For the time being, the United States opposed attempts by neutral forces to mediate peace.

This analysis provides the groundwork for understanding the events that ended the war. The processes that led to them in Eastern and in Western Europe differed radically. In the east the Soviet-German peace treaty signed at Brest-Litovsk in March 1918 was followed by supplementary agreements in August, which came close to reversing the 1914 alignments and reduced the former tsarist empire to a chain of German-dominated satellites. The root cause of this first major breach in the impasse was the Russian masses' insistence on peace at any price, leading to the greatest army mutiny in history and their leaders' inability to sustain resistance even to the most draconian demands, as was demonstrated by the failure of Leon Trotsky's "No war, no peace" tactics. The collapse of the pro-war domestic consensus settled the military issue, and diplomacy merely ratified the outcome.[46]

In the west, in contrast, Germany's request on October 4, 1918, for an armistice was precipitated by Bulgaria's application for a ceasefire. This does not mean that the collapse of the smallest Central Power caused that of the greatest. Bulgaria's defection was only the latest in a run of reverses, and the loss since July of the initiative on the Western Front was the principal reason for the German overture. Ludendorff's army was outnumbered, poorly equipped, and being driven back in a campaign that resembled the tank- and air-supported operations of World War II rather than the battles of the Somme or Ypres.[47] Although German forces still stood on foreign territory, their leaders had lost hope of winning.

Yet not only the military variable in the stalemate had altered. Instead of approaching the allies collectively, Berlin appealed to Woodrow Wilson alone. In addition to an armistice, the Germans requested a peace based on the president's war aims, as set out in his Fourteen Points address of January 1918 and in his subsequent speeches. A simultaneous reshuffle made the German Cabinet more representative of the majority in the Reichstag, thus gesturing toward American denunciations of Prussian autocracy. In short, this was another attempt to divide the opposition and to cash in on Germany's remaining strength in order to get the best possible deal. It is true that it was much more urgent than had been its predecessors, and it elicited a very different response. In contrast to the British and French in 1917, Wilson decided neither to reject the approach nor to consult his partners, but to beat down his enemy in a public exchange of notes. Once the Germans had promised to accept ceasefire terms that would effectively disarm them, Wilson turned formally to the allies at the Paris conference of October 29–November 4, 1918, during which his representative, Colonel House, warned that the United States might make a separate peace. In the so-called Lansing Note of November 4, London, Paris, and Rome accepted an "armistice contract," agreeing, with two reservations, to the Fourteen Points, even though Wilson had intended that the

Points should distance him from his partners' more far-reaching goals. Seven days later the guns fell silent. Although the precondition for the break in the diplomatic stalemate was the break in the military one, therefore, the armistice came about as it did because the United States moved to occupy in some degree the role of arbiter, hustling both sides into a settlement on its conditions. It might seem that Germany had finally succeeded in dividing its enemies.

Such an interpretation would be misleading. Wilson had indeed acquired a dominance that enabled him to act as no allied power could have previously. But we should still not conclude that the European era was over and that the American century had dawned. On the contrary, it suited both the British and the French to liquidate the war when they did. Both governments calculated that if the fighting continued, American ascendancy would grow even greater whereas now the Central Powers were weakened enough to allow the victors to impose their terms. The collapse of Germany's home front, culminating in Wilhelm II's abdication on November 9 and the formation of a socialist Provisional Government, was the consequence rather than the cause of the military defeat. But by destroying the Reich's ability to resist it reduced allied dependence on Washington and undermined Wilson's bargaining position. In any case, Lloyd George and Clemenceau had decided that the Fourteen Points were vague enough not seriously to restrict them, and that the *military* terms of the ceasefire gave them much of what they wanted. France occupied Alsace-Lorraine, the Saar, and southern Rhineland; Britain interned the German fleet, expelled Germany from Belgium, and kept control of Germany's colonies. Italy occupied the territory it wanted in Dalmatia. On balance, the November 1918 armistice weakened America's ability to impose its views, and instead of forcing his partners to his way of thinking Wilson had only modest success in scaling down their war aims at the peace conference. On the contrary, in the negotiation of the Versailles treaty he as much as they found it necessary to make concessions in order to preserve a semblance of unity and to keep a faltering coalition in being.[48]

To recapitulate. What I have presented here is a political inter-pretation of the nature of international conflict. It is one possible approach among many, but it offers powerful insights. For all that recent research has revealed about the stresses and strains behind the public facades of unity, what was most impressive, at least until 1918, was the durability of the alliance bonds on both sides. Neither the stalemate of the first three years nor the peace feelers of 1917 restruc-tured the international alignments established between 1879 and 1907. And new entrants, such as Japan, the Ottoman Empire, and Italy, added their forces to the groupings that had coalesced around the Austro-German and Franco-Russian blocs. In 1918, by contrast, the Bolshevik Revolution and Wilson's new assertiveness brought more significant changes, which partly account for the timing and character of the ceasefire. The overriding conclusion is that the Great Powers in the opposing blocs retained much of their diplo-matic independence. If the outbreak of the war required a willing-ness to fight on all sides, its conclusion required a general willingness for peace. In November 1918, Britain and France, as well as the United States and Germany, were convinced that an armistice would serve their interests, all parties fearing that a prolongation of the fighting would reduce their influence on the postwar settlement. Even in Washington any further stimulus to American nationalism might hamper Wilson's ability to gain the sort of treaty that he wished for, whatever the growth of America's material preponder-ance. In 1917, in contrast, the greater dispersion of power within the allied coalition, as well as its members' dread of being divided, rein-forced the other obstacles to a settlement.

To focus on the coalition dynamics of international politics in 1914–18 also sheds light on what followed. There is a remarkable contrast between the robustness of the allied coalition while the war was in progress and the speed of its subsequent break-up. Already at the Paris peace conference (in contrast with Vienna a hundred years before), consensus proved so difficult to establish that the victors preferred to dictate conditions to their defeated enemies rather than jeopardize their solidarity by negotiating.[49] After the Senate withheld treaty ratification the Anglo-American guarantee of France offered at the conference fell through, and during the 1920s British strategic planners regarded both France and the United States as potential, if not very probable, enemies. It is true that more informal vestiges of an Atlantic community of interest persisted, as was shown, for example, in intermittent cooperation between central banks and in the Anglo-French diplomatic rapprochement of the Locarno period. But the onset of economic crisis after 1929 strengthened the forces making for disintegration, and Western disunity in the early 1930s helped create conditions in which German, Japanese, and Italian challenges to the postwar order could become formidable.[50] Earlier international settlements had all also been revised with time. What is remarkable about that of 1919–20, however, is the speed with which it fell to pieces, and that in 1939 Britain and France found themselves at war with Germany again, and in less favorable circumstances. The new research on the allied coalition in World War I helps to account for these developments by underlining its fragility even in the hour of victory. The implication is that geopolitical considerations and not much else held its members together, and that once Germany had been beaten they lacked the foresight or the willingness to maintain concerted action in order to promote lasting stability.

All of this may have a bearing on more recent events. If cultural, ideological, and economic solidarity was feeble in the allied coalition of 1914–19, it was still weaker in its successor of 1941–45 and in the Gulf War coalition of 1991. The Western-Arab combination against Saddam Hussein held together for as long as it did in large measure because the Gulf ceasefire, resembling that of November 1918, failed to eliminate the Iraqi threat. By comparison with the Gulf coalition, the alliance of North Atlantic and Pacific powers that "won" the Cold War against the Soviet Union was culturally and ideologically more uniform and economically more interdependent, and had behind it four decades of cooperation. Yet it remains uncertain, even in a much more integrated and homogeneous Western world than that of the 1920s, how long these considerations will avert a breakdown comparable to the one that squandered the fruits of victory after 1918.

NOTES

This chapter is based on a lecture given at Yale University on October 24, 1994. I am grateful to Geoffrey Parker, Paul Kennedy, and Jay Winter for the invitation, and for their hospitality at New Haven.

1. "The End of the European Era?" was the subtitle of the Yale lecture series.

2. Eric J. Hobsbawm, *Age of Extremes: The Short Twentieth Century, 1914–1991* (London: Michael Joseph, 1994).

3. Lancelot L. Farrar, Jr., *The Short-War Illusion: German Policy, Strategy, and Domestic Affairs, August–December 1914* (Santa Barbara: ABC-Clio, 1973).

4. F. Scott Fitzgerald, *Tender Is the Night* (Harmondsworth: Penguin, 1985), 66–67.

5. Stéphane Audoin-Rouzeau, "The National Sentiment of Soldiers During the Great War," in *Nationhood and Nationalism in France: From Boulangism to the Great War, 1889–1918*, ed. R. S. Tombs (London: Harper Collins, 1991), 95. Denis Winter, *Death's Men: Soldiers of the Great War* (Harmondsworth: Penguin, 1978), ch. 14.

6. On German war aims, see inter alia Hans W. Gatzke, *Germany's Drive to the West: A Study of Western War Aims During the First World War* (Baltimore: Johns Hopkins University Press, 1950); Immanuel Geiss, *Der Polnische Grenzstreifen, 1914–1918: Ein Beitrag zur Deutschen Kriegszielpolitik im Ersten Weltkrieg* (Lübeck: Matthiesen Verlag, 1960); Fritz Fischer, *Germany's Aims in the First World War*, trans. (London: Chatto and Windus, 1967); Gerhard Ritter, *The Sword and the Sceptre: The Problem of Militarism in Germany*, trans. Heinz Norden, 4 vols. (London: Allen Lane, 1969–73); Georges-Henri Soutou, *L'Or et le sang: Les buts de guerre économiques de la Première Guerre mondiale* (Paris: Fayard, 1989).

7. On Britain, see Victor Howard Rothwell, *British War Aims and Peace*

Diplomacy, 1914–1918 (Oxford: Oxford University Press, 1971); on France, David Stevenson, *French War Aims Against Germany, 1914–1919* (Oxford: Oxford University Press, 1982); Georges-Henri Soutou, "La France et les marches de l'est, 1914–1919," *Revue historique* 528 (1978): 341–88; on Russia, Clarence J. Smith, *The Russian Struggle for Power, 1914–1917: A Study of Russian Foreign Policy During the First World War* (New York: Philosophical Library, 1956); Horst G. Linke, *Das Zarische Russland und der Erste Weltkrieg: Diplomatie und Kriegsziele, 1914–1917* (Munich: Wilhelm Fink, 1982). On extra-European war aims, see ch. 8 of this volume.

8. See generally David Stevenson, *The First World War and International Politics* (Oxford: Oxford University Press, 1988), chs. 2–3; and Soutou, *L'Or et le sang,* for economic war aims.

9. Modris Eksteins, *Rites of Spring: The Great War and the Birth of the Modern Age* (London: Black Swan, 1989), is illuminating on this point.

10. John Maynard Keynes, *The Economic Consequences of the Peace* (London, 1920), 31. John Wheeler-Bennett, *Brest-Litovsk: The Forgotten Peace, March 1918* (New York: Norton, 1938), 109.

11. Eleanor M. Gates, *End of the Affair: The Collapse of the Anglo-French Alliance, 1939–1940* (Berkeley: University of California Press, 1981), 566n.

12. David J. Reynolds, *Britannia Overruled: British Policy and World Power in the Twentieth Century* (London: Longman, 1991), 150.

13. Soutou, *L'Or et le sang,* ch. 1.

14. Fischer, *Germany's Aims,* 104.

15. Ibid., e.g., 113–17, 236–44, 271–73; Ritter, *Sword,* vol. 3, chs. 4, 7; Werner Conze, *Polnische Nation und Deutsche Politik* (Cologne, 1958). On the relationship as a whole, see Holger Herwig, *The First World War: Germany and Austria-Hungary, 1914–1918* (London: Arnold, 1997).

16. Gerard E. Silberstein, *The Troubled Alliance: German-Austrian Relations, 1914 to 1917* (Lexington: University Press of Kentucky, 1970), 317–19.

17. Ulrich Trumpener, *Germany and the Ottoman Empire, 1914–1918* (Princeton: Princeton University Press, 1968).

18. Keith Neilson, *Strategy and Supply: The Anglo-Russian Alliance, 1914–1917* (London: Allen and Unwin, 1984), 315.

19. See Carl P. Parrini, *Heir to Empire: United States Economic Diplomacy, 1916–1923* (Pittsburgh: University of Pittsburgh Press, 1969); Burton I. Kaufman, *Efficiency and Expansion: Foreign Trade Organization in the Wilson Administration* (Westport, Conn.: Greenwood, 1974); Edward B. Parsons, *Wilsonian Diplomacy: Allied-American Rivalries in War and Peace* (St. Louis: Forum, 1978); Jeffrey J. Safford, *Wilsonian Maritime Diplomacy, 1913–1921* (New Brunswick: Rutgers University Press, 1978); David M. Kennedy, *Over Here: The First World War and American Society* (London: Oxford University Press, 1980), ch. 6; Kathleen Burk, *Britain, America, and the Sinews of War, 1914–1918* (Boston: Allen and Unwin, 1985).

20. André Kaspi, *Le Temps des Américains: Le concours américain à la France en 1917–1918* (Paris: University of Paris-I, 1976), ch. 8.

21. J. A. Salter, *Allied Shipping Control: An Experiment in International Administration* (Oxford: Oxford University Press, 1921); Etienne Clémentel, *La France et la politique interalliée* (Paris: PUF, 1931); David F. Trask, *The United States in the Supreme War Council: American War Aims and Inter-Allied Strategy, 1917–1918* (Westport, Conn.: Greenwood, 1961).

22. Paul M. Kennedy, *The Rise and Fall of the Great Powers: Economic Change and Military Conflict from 1500 to 2000* (London: Fontana, 1989), 350, 447.

23. These topics are examined in David Stevenson, *Armaments and the Coming of War: Europe, 1904–1914* (Oxford: Oxford University Press, 1996), and David G. Herrmann, *The Arming of Europe and the Making of the First World War* (Princeton: Princeton University Press, 1996).

24. Fritz Fischer, *War of Illusions: German Policies from 1911 to 1914*, trans. Marion Jackson (London: Chatto and Windus, 1975), 63.

25. Konrad H. Jarausch, *The Enigmatic Chancellor: Bethmann Hollweg and the Hubris of Imperial Germany* (New Haven: Yale University Press, 1973), ch. 5. Richard Langhorne, *The Collapse of the Concert of Europe: International Politics, 1890–1914* (London: Macmillan, 1981).

26. For the texts of the alliance treaties, see Michael Hurst, ed., *Key Treaties for the Great Powers, 1814–1914* (Newton Abbot: David and Charles, 1972), 2: docs. 117, 139, 141.

27. On France, see Trevor Wilson, "Britain's 'Moral Commitment' to France in August 1914," *History* 64, no. 212 (1979): 80–90. On Belgium, see Daniel H. Thomas, *The Guarantee of Belgian Independence and Neutrality in European Diplomacy, 1830s–1930s* (Kingston, R.I.: D. H. Thomas, 1983), 511.

28. Raymond N. L. Poincaré, *Au service de la France: neuf années de souvenirs* (Paris: Plon, 1927), 4: 412.

29. K. M. Wilson, ed., *Decisions for War, 1914* (New York: St. Martin's, 1995), essay on Britain. M. and E. Brock, eds., H. H. Asquith, *Letters to Venetia Stanley* (Oxford: Oxford University Press, 1982), 146. On 1914, see D. Stevenson, *The Outbreak of the First World War: 1914 in Perspective* (London: Macmillan 1996).

30. L. L. Farrar, Jr., *Divide and Conquer: German Efforts to Conclude a Separate Peace, 1914–1918* (New York: Columbia University Press, 1978).

31. Farrar, *Divide and Conquer*, 5–7, 105, chs. 2, 4.

32. Jagow to Romberg, June 8, 1916, in A. Scherer and J. Grünewald, eds., *L'Allemagne et les problèmes de la paix pendant la Première Guerre Mondiale*, 4 vols. (Paris: Presses Universitaires de France, 1966–78), i, doc. 268.

33. Michaelis to Czernin, August 17, 1917; Minutes of Prussian Crown Council, September 4, 1917, ibid., ii, docs. 211, 236.

34. Bethmann Hollweg to Copenhagen Legation, March 6, 1915, ibid., i, doc. 52.

35. Bethmann Hollweg to Hertling, January 26, 1918, in G. D. Feldman, ed.,

German Imperialism, 1914–1918: The Development of a Historical Debate (New York: Wiley, 1972), doc. 28.

36. Gatzke, *Drive to the West;* Fischer, *Germany's Aims,* chs., 5, 10, 12.

37. Stevenson, *French War Aims,* 13–15, 28.

38. D. French, *The British Way in Warfare, 1688–2000* (London: Unwin Hyman, 1990), 168–73, and more fully in the same author's *British Strategy and War Aims, 1914–1916* (London: Allen & Unwin, 1986). See also P. Guinn, *British Strategy and Politics, 1914–1918* (Oxford: Oxford University Press, 1965). Concern for French morale also motivated the Third Ypres offensive: D. French, *The Strategy of the Lloyd George Coalition, 1916–1918* (Oxford: Oxford University Press, 1995), ch. 4.

39. N. Stone, *The Eastern Front, 1914–1917* (London: Jonathan Cape, 1975), 128.

40. On morale in 1917 see the chapters in this volume by L. V. Smith and J. Horne. On the peace feelers, G. Pedroncini, *Les Négociations secrètes pendant la Grande Guerre* (Paris: PUF, 1969); Stevenson, *First World War,* ch. 4; and D. Stevenson, "The Failure of Peace by Negotiation in 1917," *Historical Journal* 34, no. 1 (1992): 65–86.

41. Kühlmann memorandum, September 3, Michaelis to Hindenburg, September 12, Hindenburg to Michaelis, September 15, 1917, Scherer and Grünewald, eds., *L'Allemagne,* docs., 235, 247, 251. This German initiative is usually known as the "Villalobar kite," after the Spanish diplomat who acted as intermediary.

42. D. R. Woodward, "David Lloyd George, a Negotiated Peace with Germany, and the Kühlmann Peace Kite of September 1917," *Canadian Journal of History* 6, no. 1 (1971): 75–93. Stevenson, *French War Aims,* 105.

43. Kaspi, *Temps des Américains,* 340.

44. Ribot to Jusserand, September 30, 1917, Archives du Ministère des Affaires Etrangères, Paris, Papiers Jules Jusserand (32). David Lloyd George, *War Memoirs,* 6 vols. (Boston: Little, Brown, 1933–36), iv, 2104.

45. L. W. Martin, *Peace Without Victory: Woodrow Wilson and the British Liberals* (New Haven: Yale University Press, 1958), 141.

46. On Brest-Litovsk, see Wheeler-Bennett, *Forgotten Peace;* W. Baumgart, *Deutsche Ostpolitik, 1918: von Brest-Litovsk bis zum Ende des Ersten Weltkrieges* (Vienna: Oldenbourg, 1966); R. K. Debo, *Revolution and Survival: The Foreign Policy of Soviet Russia, 1917–1918* (Toronto: University of Toronto Press, 1979).

47. However, T. Travers, *How the War Was Won: Command and Technology in the British Army on the Western Front, 1917–1918* (London: Routledge, 1992), points out that the tank attacks of July and August 1918 were followed by more conventional operations.

48. On the armistice, see P. Renouvin, *L'Armistice de Rethondes, 11 novembre 1918* (Paris: Hachette, 1968); I. Floto, *Colonel House in Paris: A Study of American Policy at the Paris Peace Conference, 1919* (Aarhus: Universitetsforlaget i Aarhus, 1973); A. Walworth, *America's Moment, 1918: American Diplomacy at*

the End of World War I (New York: Norton, 1977); Stevenson, *French War Aims,* ch. 5. K. Schwabe, *Woodrow Wilson, Revolutionary Germany, and peacemaking, 1918–1919* (Chapel Hill: University of North Carolina Press, 1985); B. Lowry, *Armistice 1918* (Kent, Ohio: Kent State University Press, 1996).

49. On the peace settlement, see ch. 9 of this volume.

50. R. W. D. Boyce, "World War, World Depression: Some Economic Origins of the Second World War," in R. W. D. Boyce and E. M. Robertson, eds., *Paths to War: New Essays on the Origins of the Second World War* (Basingstoke: Macmillan, 1989), 55–95.

Part

II

The

Waging

of

War

CHAPTER 4

Technology in the First World War
The View from Below

MARY R. HABECK

The First World War has entered our collective imagination as the *Materielschlacht*, the war of machines, a conflict in which the individual soldier was dwarfed by a technology of unparalleled destructiveness. The exponential growth in the lethality of combat came directly from the application of smokeless gunpowder, the machine gun, TNT and other high explosives, heavy artillery, the quick-firing breech-loaded infantry rifle, the submarine, and, not least, the airplane. During the war itself grenades, trench mortars, poison gases, flamethrowers, and tanks were added to this long list of technical "achievements."[1] Whereas horses and men required the bulk of supplies in nineteenth-century warfare, now, after 1914, supplying machines became infinitely more costly and more difficult than supplying soldiers.

Almost every student of the era has noted the repercussions of this industrialization of warfare, not only on how war was waged but on its costs to the societies waging it.[2] Perhaps most important, the new weapons gave the tactical defensive an overwhelming advantage that led directly to the stalemate on the Western Front and to terrible slaughter wherever combatants attempted to assault well-armed defenders.

This outcome may seem obvious to us now, but it was not so at the time. Military leaders had argued that technology might favor the offensive, or that superior morale was what truly mattered. Only after the war began did the heads of the armies of Europe discover how futile it had been to increase firepower without finding a way to maintain mobility under the new conditions of industrialized warfare. A scramble for an answer to the problem created by technology began in 1915 and continued with relatively little success until the end of the war.

In the meantime, the ordinary men caught up in the maelstrom of the Great War were obliged, for their physical and psychological survival, to deal with technology on a more direct and intimate level. Their struggle to make sense of the matériel of war is a dominant motif in their memoirs, diaries, and letters, creating the image of frail men against overwhelming fire that would become a potent myth of the Great War and shape what Samuel Hynes calls the "war-in-the-head" for later generations.[3] From their descriptions it is clear that it was on the Western Front, where military technology immobilized the armies of three empires, that the struggle to live with the new weapons took on its most extreme form. As Eric Leed has pointed out, many soldiers on that front failed to deal positively with the war of matériel, seeing technology as monstrous.[4] Yet not every soldier saw technology as demonic, and a few even learned to deal with the material character of modern war with a modicum of affection—even, at times, of love.

Anyone who surveys the mountains of correspondence and memoirs produced by front-line soldiers will be struck by the nearly universal references to the hardware of the war, to the material texture of everyday life. But can we speak of a common language employed by soldiers of different armies, drawn from societies of very different levels of economic and social development? On balance, I believe the answer is yes. Here I am following the lead of

Hynes, who has gone beyond this one category of soldiers' reactions to war—its material character—to posit a genre of soldiers' writing that distinguishes it from all other narratives. He calls this genre the "soldiers' tale."[5] This chapter is about what the French call *l'imaginaire* of industrialized war, the metaphors and signifying practices through which soldiers tried to make sense of a world both familiar and very, very strange.

Where did these metaphors come from? It is of course necessary to offer a plural answer. Because most of the men who fought had lived on the land, it is difficult to treat as fully representative the memoirs of urban, highly educated officers. And yet there is much that links the language of city dwellers turned soldiers with the cadences of thought and expression of their rural comrades. On the one hand is the fascination with the new machinery of war; on the other hand is the fear that it simply has spiraled out of control. The soldiers' tale is of a war in which machines have developed much more rapidly than have the minds of the men controlling them. That discordant pace of development is a critical aspect of responses to the technology of warfare among very different kinds of men.

Industrialized combat brought them all down to earth, as it were. Some felt the thud more than others. The romantic dreamers in the Italian futurist movement discovered that machines dedicated to killing were not as beautiful as their prewar reveries had suggested. Even the legendary storm trooper Ernst Jünger broke under the terrifying weight of bombardment. Others who broke down made less of a fuss about it. They had simply faced forces beyond them.

* * *

This sense of stoicism, of facing powers that can be managed but not overcome, is what gives soldiers' narratives about the Materielschlacht their rough unity. This laconic acceptance of the way war had changed is hardly surprising. The soldiers who wrote about the war were not the professionals who began the fighting in August

1914. They were instead the volunteers and draftees called up to supplement or replace the small professional armies decimated during the first few months of fighting. The officers of these new armies were young, educated, middle-class men with little or no experience in the military before the outbreak of fighting. Sharing a common educational and class background, and a common innocence about war, explains some of the similarities in the writing produced by these novices.[6] The men they led may have experienced military life through prewar conscription, which made soldiering a commonplace experience in France and Germany in 1914. But no one had any idea what soldiering was to become after the failure of the Schlieffen plan and the stabilization of trench warfare. By Christmas 1914 all of these men had entered a war no one had volunteered to fight. And once in that war, there was no way out.

Machinery did not liberate soldiers from the task to be done; it imprisoned them in that inescapable environment. Far from protecting the foot soldier from the tasks of combat, or freeing him from the need to wrench enemy trenches from their occupants, the machinery of warfare turned cold. It froze armies into immobility and allowed the systematic industrialization of killing.

Faced with this immense contradiction, the men in the trenches were forced to adapt to the battlefield, to radically transform themselves and their views of technology in order to survive. As Leonard Smith shows in Chapter 5, there was much more to adaptation than a simple process whereby men accepted the defensive pose as their fate.[7] To keep from becoming victims of the war and of their own technology, they would have to become hardened, nerveless, able "to stand without trembling," as Marc Bloch puts it.[8] Jünger realized this early on: "What was a man's life in this wilderness whose vapour was laden with the stench of thousands upon thousands of decaying bodies? Death lay in ambush for each one in every shell-hole, merciless, and making one merciless in turn. Chivalry here took a final farewell. It had to yield to the heightened intensity of war, just as all fine and personal feeling has to yield when machinery gets the upper hand."[9]

*   *   *

How did soldiers come to an understanding of this process of machinery getting the upper hand? There were basically three ways that they viewed technology: as superhuman or supernatural (monstrous and demonic); as subhuman (either machinelike or a force of nature); and as human or connected with the human world. The soldiers of the Great War used all three of these metaphors, and a multiplicity of variations on them. At times during their stay on the front they acknowledged that it was nothing but unfeeling metal that killed, and at other moments they chose to believe that artillery, tanks, and bombs could have (usually malignant) intentions and emotions. Men felt most in control, the masters of technology, when they compared it to ordinary objects and entities (animal or human) from their prewar lives. Use of subhuman metaphors showed that they saw technology as more difficult to cope with, but they were still seeking some way to manage it within the scope of their previous lives. If, however, men perceived the weapons of war as supernatural or monstrous, they saw technology as uncontrollable and their own lives as unmanageable. It was under these circumstances that soldiers entered the limbo of "no-man's-land," in Eric Leed's terminology, a terrible environment from which many never escaped.

Leed's work has shown that at some point soldiers had to decide whether they could live with the material of the conflict, or whether they fundamentally rejected the weapons and the impersonal combat that these represented. The decision to accept or reject technology was, of course, not always a conscious one. Some soldiers simply could not stand the strain that accompanied lengthy bombardments, constant machine-gun fire, bombs, and mortars. Yet it is clear that there were times when technology could demoralize soldiers and others when it encouraged them. There were distinct circumstances that governed which outcome would prevail, and again the metaphors that soldiers used when describing technology help us see the fluctuations of their mood, the oscillations between those moments when they tolerated the weapons of war and the times when they were repelled and frightened by them.

The first thing that struck these new warriors was the sheer strangeness of modern battle and of the weapons used to fight it.[10] Jünger, writing just two years after the fighting ended, remembered how innocent he was when first exposed to the "multiple din of the war": "I was still without experience of the fighting, and saw it as a recruit. The battle seemed to proceed as strangely and disconnectedly as though it went on upon another planet. At the same time I had no fear. For I felt that I was not seen, and I could not believe that any one aimed at me or that I should be hit. Indeed, when I rejoined my section I surveyed our front with complete calm. It was the courage of ignorance."[11]

Beyond the simple strangeness of their new world, the element most commented on by men as they entered the front was the sound that the new matériel created, the noise of artillery, rifle, and machine-gun fire.[12] For many it was overpowering, a cacophony of crashes, bangs, and booms that stunned the ears and boggled the mind. Almost every memoirist describes the bombardments, the shells hurtling, whizzing, shrieking, and singing overhead.[13] When looking back at his introduction to the war, the German soldier Hans Zöberlein remembered only the "hoarse, threatening roar of the eternal battle of Verdun."[14] Others were so overwhelmed that they could only record the sounds as they heard them.[15] One of the most troubling aspects of the sounds of technology was that the new recruit had no idea what they meant, nor how he should react to them.[16] Lack of knowledge created a confusion that kept the novice's nerves continually on edge and prevented him from dealing with his surroundings in a positive way. Paul Lintier, who took part in the retreat toward Paris in August 1914, wrote that the noise and smoke were so overpowering that "death seems inevitable. The danger is unknown, and is magnified a thousandfold by the imagination. One makes no attempt to analyse it."[17] In fact, as Leed has pointed out, the new and overwhelming sounds encouraged men to become more superstitious, to see themselves as not in control but at the mercy of fate and the machines.[18]

Men also had to learn how to act under fire. The natural reaction was to duck, but as Jack Campbell, a young American, wrote, "One soon learns that he can't do that. Life would be just one long 'duck.' "[19] "Rifle-fire at short range is comparatively child's-play," another new soldier wrote, "though last night I found myself continually ducking as they pinged overhead. We ought to get out of that habit soon, as it serves no purpose, except to make the neck muscles ache."[20] Bernard Adams, a young Welsh officer, was completely bewildered by his first serious artillery shelling, writing later that "I hadn't the least idea what to do. The textbooks, I believe, said 'Throw yourself on the ground.' I therefore looked at my orderly; but he was ducking behind his bicycle, which I am sure is not recommended by any manual of military training! I ducked behind nothing, copying him."[21]

During the next few weeks at the front, soldiers had their initial lessons on how to cope with technological war. In general this followed two paths: first, they became experts at identifying the different sounds, and second, they imitated men who were more accustomed to living under fire. The most urgent requirement was to learn to hear all over again, mastering the noise of technology so that one could understand which sounds were life-threatening and which were merely annoying.[22] Wilfred Brenton Kerr thought of becoming accustomed to the sounds as "reasoned confidence," which he defined as "knowing when there was danger and when not. One was able to judge where the shell would fall by the pitch of its shriek.

A noise like a train overhead meant a destination miles in the rear; a sharp shriek or a deep growl meant imminent danger; and between the two there lay a wide variety of pitches, which one soon learned to interpret properly."[23] The result, Lintier wrote, was that "one no longer crouches down unnecessarily, and only seeks shelter knowingly, when it is imperative to do so. Danger no longer masters but is mastered."[24] The older and more experienced occupants of the front, especially those who exhibited the most "coolness" under fire, provided the best examples for young soldiers to imitate.[25] One could also look to the natives of the area, for they generally had been exposed to modern military technology longer than anyone else. Thus, when he saw women standing in front of their houses calmly watching the shells burst, Adams was shamed into leaving his "duck behind nothing."[26]

Once past his introduction to warfare the new soldier still had far to go before he could adapt successfully to technology. Knowing which sounds were potentially harmful did not guarantee that one would be able to avoid death and injury from flying steel. And when men learned to live with the danger posed by heavy artillery, rifle fire, and mortars, the enemy discovered fresh ways to disrupt life, with gas, tanks, and bombs. The continually changing metaphors that men chose to describe the technology that they encountered, demonic, subhuman, or somehow connected to the world of men, showed how they viewed technology and thus how well they were adjusting to the war. As Leed has argued, at some point in their war experience most soldiers believed that "demons" and "monsters" reigned at the front, showing that they found the matériel used in war almost incomprehensible, certainly beyond their control, and eminently threatening. This is most obvious in the accounts that they gave of the sounds of technology. Unlike the newest soldiers, these men emphasized that shells and other matériel produced "diabolical" and "demoniacal" screams, even the shrieks of "a Fury."[27]

When combined into a complete bombardment they could make a "demoniac uproar that sundered air particles and spun them into everlasting reverberations" or an "all-destroying, flaming, raging Moloch."[28] French and German descriptions, especially, emphasized the inhuman character of modern technology in war, at times identifying specific weapon systems as particularly fiendish.[29] One German soldier, Rudolf Binding, who had been consistently optimistic about the chances for his country winning the war, finally gave in on July 29, 1917, writing, "I am scared. For the first time in this war I have doubts whether we shall be able to hold out against the odds. Thirty new four-gun batteries have appeared on the enemy's front in a single day, not counting those which may not have been spotted; on the Fourth Army front alone there are 160 of those monsters which belch the most enormous shells at us from twenty-five miles away. . . . Verdun, the Somme, and Arras are mere purgatories compared with this concentrated hell, which one of these days will be stoked up to white-heat."[30]

The intensity of the bombardments could even make one almost sympathize with the enemy. Hervey Allen, who fought only during the final days of the war, thought that the shelling of the retreating Germans "must have been truly infernal. Over the edge of the world, uttering their *banshee* like screams of vengeance, and roaring like express trains, came the messengers of the outraged republics. There would be a frightful red flare, the bellow of an explosion, arms, legs, trunks of men, death-dealing fragments of jagged steel and whirling wreckage falling for miles along the grey-helmeted, rearward-plodding columns. . . . It must have been during those nights of horror when our shells ate him up like cannibalistic devils that 'Fritz' at last came to realize that 'the jig was up.' "[31]

* * *

If some technology was fiendish, other weapons systems were monstrous or grotesque. Again the emphasis was usually on the unnatural, incomprehensible, and menacing qualities of these machines that placed them beyond human control and management. The concept of monster could have two sides, however: if fighting for the enemy, it was comparable to "hellish" or "demoniacal" technology; if working for your side, it was more awesome or grotesque than threatening. This is clear in descriptions of the huge artillery pieces that bombarded the enemy's rear. Hans Zöberlein, cowering under an attack by one such cannon, saw it as monstrous and evil, while Harold Baldwin, a Canadian, ran eagerly with his mates to witness the arrival of a "monster gun" that would be fighting for them. Other responses to the "monsters" reflected the positive opinion of modernity generally associated with the Germans. A German gunner could write with great feeling after the war of his longing to hear once again the "symphony of fiery spirits" and to see the chaos of the battle carried on by his beloved artillery.[32] The destruction of nature that artillery wrought was, on the other hand, always seen as grotesque and beyond understanding. Kerr, viewing the scene after a battle, thought that it had become "a wilderness of desolation and devastation . . . a whole countryside mangled and murdered as if by some frightful monsters," a haunt "of dragons breathing fire and tearing flesh much more ferociously than those of fable."[33]

The contrast between adversarial and friendly monsters is also obvious in the one technology that soldiers usually described as grotesque: the tank. Its size, shape, weapons, and way of moving combined to create an image of a ponderously crawling steel beast that crushed anything in its path as it spewed fire and death from its mouth. Everyone who witnessed an assault with tanks agreed that they were living things rather than simply armored vehicles. They crawled, waddled, or crept, could be injured or even "mortally wounded," and certainly had intentions like any other animal. Philip Gibbs, a journalist who spent a great deal of the war on the front, wrote of seeing the tanks as "queer, low-squatting things moving slowly in the creeping mists" while others were "crawling about the battlefield or resting under cover like herds of prehistoric animals."[34] Later in the war a Frenchman described derelict tanks that were "sticking out of holes like lame monsters, their noses pointing defiantly towards the ridge."[35] The affectionate names that the Commonwealth soldiers gave to their tanks also showed this tendency to see the machines as alive.[36]

Since the allied forces were the first to use the tank, they generally imagined the machines as fantastic and awe-inspiring rather than diabolical. Trying to describe his experiences in the Tank Corps for the home audience, Richard Haigh noted that the name "tank" brings to mind "a picture of an iron monster, breathing fire and exhaling bullets and shells, hurling itself against the enemy, unassailable by men and impervious to the most deadly engines of war; sublime, indeed, in its expression of indomitable power and resolution."[37] The reaction of allied soldiers on seeing a tank for the first time was surprise and great interest, but rarely fear. Thus a Canadian soldier, while lying low in a shell hole during the concluding days of the Somme, trying to decide whether to go forward or back, saw a tank moving relentlessly forward over the shell-stricken battlefield as merely a "strange and curious sight."[38]

German soldiers, on the other hand, emphasized the inhuman and menacing qualities of the tank. This was only natural—the German high command had decided to develop gas and other technologies of war but not an armored vehicle with caterpillar treads. When the British first used the tank, therefore, not only were German soldiers and officers taken completely by surprise, they also had no way to counter an armor assault. The result was that they saw the tank not only as a "steel monster" but also as "apparently indestructible," an "elephant" that trampled men to death.[39] The Germans, in stark contrast to the Allies, described the tanks as mechanical monstrosities out of control, as destructive beasts unfeelingly mangling human bodies. One soldier explained how four steel monsters rolled up to his company from the edge of the forest with "unnatural slowness, steadiness and infallibility—fate and disaster given form."[40] Zöberlein provides a vivid word-picture of the German reaction to this unknown and frightening technology:

> Hey—listen! What is that? A droning, popping pounding and a squealing rattle. "Tank!" horrified I scream the word into the mute company of my comrades. . . . Then I see him as well, how the shaking Box with a roar races towards us on the street from the village. It seems to me that he's trying to escape. . . . Lying across the street are the dead Scots from a short time ago, there— now the Box rolls across them like a monster feeding and crushes and tears them into shapeless lumps—ice-cold, brutal."[41]

*   *   *

If the characterization of technology as supernatural showed that soldiers of the Great War had difficulty adapting themselves to the new matériel, the fact that many imagined artillery, machine guns, and other weapons as subhuman (like nature or a machine) indicated that they were trying to find a way to integrate technology into their "normal" (prewar) lives. They saw themselves threatened by large impersonal forces outside their control, but these were not as alien to their experience as the monsters and demons. How they chose to report the sights and sounds that they witnessed reflected this unconscious desire to make what was strange and threatening somehow more familiar by comparing it to elements from their everyday existence. The noises made by large-caliber shells, for instance, were often likened to the sounds of trains—more specifically, express trains (because of their extra speed and louder sound) or subway trains (because of the heightened noise experienced inside the underground tunnels).[42] While capturing the sound, speed, and size of the shells, the train metaphor also made this deadly technology into an everyday object and therefore less threatening.

In the same way, when exposed to modern battle with thousands of shell, machine gun, and rifle projectiles flying through the air, men thought of storms, hurricanes, avalanches, or blizzards, natural phenomena that made the bombardment more manageable.[43] It was not just Jünger who thought of the Great War as a "storm of steel": almost every soldier who experienced a shelling thought of himself as caught in a tempest, a sudden thunderstorm or shower of metal.[44] When an actual rain or snowstorm interrupted the battle, which seemed to occur fairly frequently, the comparison between the two seemed all the more apt.[45] Within the storm itself men imagined themselves menaced not by steel but by rain, hail, or thunderbolt.[46] To be caught in a sudden downpour was to experience the raging of a storm larger and more deadly than anything the soldiers had witnessed before, and yet, like the trains, made less alien by the comparison.

Other metaphors from nature placed more emphasis on the irresistible character of the technology that men faced. The most common of these portrayed men advancing into defensive fire as "ripe corn" before the scythe or as snow melted by the sun.[47] The dangers here were very real. Jünger described one particular shelling in which "the power of logical thought and the force of gravity seemed alike to be suspended. One had the sense of something as unescapable and as unconditionally fated as a catastrophe of nature. An N.C.O. of No. 3 platoon went mad."[48] As with the storm and machine comparisons, these descriptions suggested that there was little that soldiers could do to affect their fates, and perhaps took the helplessness of men caught in the war even further; men had to learn to be calm and fatalistic, since time and chance alone would decide who was ready for the grim harvest and who would survive.

It is no coincidence that, having seen the resemblance between technology and destructive natural forces, men would also remark on how the artillery and other matériel affected nature itself. Shells, one French soldier wrote, "destroy the earth," and other observers agreed.[49] Many men described the devastation of forests, such as the

Trône Wood that, as a British officer wrote, remained "a wood only in name. It had been swept with shell-fire until there was not a tree that had not been stripped of leaf and branch."[50] An anonymous casualty of the war described the beginnings of a shelling in which the "ferns of the forest shivered, as if awakened from a sunny dream to face terrible calamities. The trees seemed to shake with a delicate fear of what was in store for them."[51] "Once seen," Jünger wrote, "the landscape is an unforgettable one."

> In this neighbourhood of villages, meadows, woods, and fields there was literally not a bush or a tiniest blade of grass to be seen. Every hand's-breadth of ground had been churned up again and again; trees had been uprooted, smashed, and ground to touchwood, the houses blown to bits and turned to dust; hills had been levelled and the arable land made a desert. . . . and there, where lately there had been the idyllic picture of rural peace, there was as faithful a picture of the soul of scientific war. In earlier wars, certainly, towns and villages had been burned, but what was that compared with this sea of craters dug out by machines.[52]

An early account of one man's experience in the war showed that this destructive interaction with nature could change one's perception of the immediate world. When the author looked at the surrounding terrain he no longer saw hills and gullies, woods and fields but rather the "machine-gun possibilities of the land." Later he admitted that he now thought that "a tree was the sort of thing the gunners took to range on; a sunset indicated a quantity of light in which it was unsafe to walk abroad."[53] The war had made soldiers revisualize both weapons and the natural world, transforming technology into a force of nature and nature into a part of the battle of matériel.

The final method through which men dealt with the technology of the Great War was perhaps the most rational. To counteract the immensely impersonal character of modern warfare they came to perceive weapons not as inhuman but as connected to the world of men. This could be either directly, through personification, or indirectly, as animals or objects from their normal, prewar lives. Such a view of technology not only gave it a human face but, as with the metaphors from nature, allowed men to take what was an incomprehensible and uncontrolled experience and connect it to the familiar and everyday. Again the reported sounds of battle showed this difference in perception and interpretation. Shells flying overhead, for some people, whistled, sang, sighed, moaned, and groaned.[54] Mussolini commented on an "exceptional rain of bombs" that arrived with a "curious hissing sound—almost human."[55] Machine guns, too, had their own voices: they spoke, chattered, rattled away, and stuttered.[56] Connected to this perception was a view of technological noise not as demonic or a force of nature but as a concert, a chorus, or an orchestra of curiously harmonious sounds.[57] Not everyone who heard the sounds of battle in the Great War thought of symphonies. When Lintier described a shelling in which shrapnel "whistled by like an angry wind," he was not alone.[58] Other soldiers agreed, emphasizing the evil yet human intent of the shells and bullets that hissed, snarled, and barked at them or, as an officer wrote, were like "vicious personal spits."[59] The result, however, was the same for those who heard evil and those who heard concerts: such men could imagine themselves in battle with something that had a mind and will of its own and could, therefore, deal with their lives in the trenches more positively.

Giving names to particular weapons furthered the process of anthropomorphism, although this was a path taken mostly by allied forces.[60] Almost all large cannon had feminine names (Fat Bertha and Mother, the British 9.2 howitzer), but anti-aircraft artillery was known as Archie. The British treated tanks almost like ships, giving each a (generally) whimsical name. But it is significant that the first three machines had human designations: Mother and Big and Little Willie.[61] Other nicknames for technology usually had a connection to the world of men.[62] This was not purely a Commonwealth view of technology. The Italians called shells "telegrams" (because of the message they sent?), and French soldiers thought of machine guns as "coffee mills."[63] The Germans followed the same practice, calling shells with black smoke "Americans" or "coalboxes," mortars "toffee-apples," and lemon-shaped bombs "duck's eggs." In one of the more picturesque images of a bombardment, Jünger wrote that German soldiers named cylinder-shaped missiles "clothes-baskets," and "it often looked as though the sky was raining baskets."[64]

Some participants in the war ascribed other human characteristics to weapons, including intentions and emotions. Not surprisingly, it was to shells and artillery, the technology most likely to wound or kill by sheer chance, that many soldiers felt compelled to assign the attributes of a sentient being. Generally soldiers chose particularly "evil" types of artillery for this kind of treatment: Little Willie, which was a "nasty little fellow," or the Jack Johnson shell, which came over "searching for human food."[65] Ian Hay, who shipped over with the first of the civilian volunteers and wanted to put life at the front in its best possible light, still had nothing good to say about trench mortars. The Minnie, as the British named it, was the "most unpleasant of her sex"; it had a tendency to discharge exploding offspring.[66] Pilots at times also personified the anti-aircraft artillery (Archie), with one writing that "he" might get "roused," and calling him a "dirty dog" for trying to blow the pilot's head off.[67] Meanwhile, shells that did not explode were called "blind" by both Germans and some British soldiers, while stray bullets could get "tired."[68] To these almost light-hearted depictions of enemy technology must be added the terms which showed that soldiers were well aware of the lethal nature of the bits of steel heading their way. Shells, for instance, could be "vicious" or "venomous," "hiss" and "snarl."[69]

The types of technology that attracted the most attempts at anthropomorphism were the two that were the most alien to the human experience: the tank and the airplane. British soldiers not only named their tanks but also attributed the characteristics of humans or familiar animals to the vehicles. This began very early on. The designers of the vehicles produced two machines, one "male" and the other "female," based on weaponry (the "female" had only machine guns, while the "male" also had light field guns). Ernest Swinton, the tank's inventor, explained that the "male" vehicles had to have a "consort, or 'man-killing' Tank" to protect them from the enemy infantry.[70] The idea of sexes for the tank caught on, and the official course for new recruits to the British Tank Corps taught that there was no "it" for tanks, only "he" or "she."[71] Soldiers even extended the concept to parts of the machine, calling the cannons, for instance, "noses."[72]

Men also often likened airplanes to living things, in this case, naturally enough, to birds. In their battles with each other, a German Fokker might "pounce" on a British plane like "a hawk on a bird," or an airplane could be "winged" and brought down to earth.[73] A British pilot placed dogfighting with German aircraft in the same realm as a day spent hunting game. He thought of his accomplishment in shooting down thirteen "Huns" in one day as "a pretty good bag."[74] For those without any real defense against the enemy's aircraft, being threatened by a strafing from above made soldiers feel like "a flock of frightened sparrows beneath the shadow of the hawk."[75] As with the tank, the airplane was often treated as a living thing, especially by the pilots. They complained of the aircraft's difficult moods (planes were almost always known as "she") or praised her for her game attempts to hold together in the face of trouble.[76] In contrast to tanks, however, aircraft, even that of the enemy, rarely evoked horror. Trench warriors and pilots on both sides of no-man's-land greeted the concept of men flying through the air as a sign of freedom and escape. They usually treated air battles as an excuse to forget their own misery and rejoice in the spectacle of an individual making a difference in the war.[77]

If the metaphors that men at the front used to describe technology show how they were reacting to technology, and to their new lives as soldiers, they also allow us to see their reaction to the reality of industrialized death. In the end, soldiers had to decide whether the new weapons were something that they could adapt to or even learn to like, or whether they rejected this "resituation" of technology. When weapons did their job—that is, helped to defeat the enemy, and saved lives in doing so—soldiers were naturally more willing to accept technology. Grateful troops cheered a good artillery shelling by their own batteries, fully aware that they were giving back to the enemy what they themselves had suffered.[78] It was during such bombardments that men were most likely to compare technology to the human world in some way. When Harold Baldwin heard the ear-splitting report of his guns replying to the Germans, he thought that "of all the music I ever heard that was the sweetest."[79] And as an American gunner heard the sound of the supporting artillery at Gallipoli, he compared his relief and joy to that of "hearing an old friend's voice over the telephone, and everybody in our shell-hole cheered."[80] Jünger wrote that German soldiers reacted to the opening of the great March Offensive, one of the largest bombardments of the war, by "running along the trench and shouting delightedly into each other's ears. Infantry and artillery, engineers and signallers, Prussians and Bavarians, officers and men, were all alike in transports over this elemental expression of German power."[81]

It was even better for one's view of technology if your side was the first to develop a lifesaving (and possibly war-shortening) weapon. The British invention of the tank was a good example, because, as an observer noted, it gave new life and vigor to the men. When the very first tank went out on the Somme battlefield, "men from the ground looked up, rose as if from the dead, and running from the flanks to behind it, followed in the rear as if to be in on the kill."[82] A French lieutenant could write that the appearance of friendly aircraft intoxicated his men with enthusiasm, since, as everyone knew, the French had invented this "marvellous little thing."[83] Soldiers also felt better about technology when their army managed to equal or counter an advance made by the enemy. German forces soon got over the fear that they felt at the appearance of the tank when defensive measures were found (directed artillery fire) and when their officers proved to them that the machines were not invulnerable.[84] Similarly, gas, bombs, and mortars were all terrifying for the Entente forces until they learned how to deal with each of these new menaces.[85] To find a flaw in the adversary's weapons was also encouraging for troops, as when Wilfred Brenton Kerr realized that the new sensitive fuses of the Germans, which gave their shells greater range, had a compensating weakness.[86]

A few men even embraced their weaponry as not only effective for combating the enemy but awesome or beautiful in and of itself. These men were among that small minority who accepted modernity's transformation of warfare into a part of the industrialization process.[87] Soldiers expressed this view of technology in two ways: through enjoying the "show" put on by bombardments and aircraft, and by appreciating the beauty of material or technical expertise, even when it was that of the enemy.[88] During major offensives, and especially at night, when the sights and sounds of a shelling could be enjoyed to the maximum, many combatants forgot the terror that they might have felt and, in fact, the point of the battle, to stop and stare in wonder.[89] A mine "going up" was a thrilling sight for Bernard Adams, until he remembered the death and destruction that it was causing among the enemy.[90] The other important spectacle for men in the trenches was the airplane fight. This provided an excuse for soldiers to forget the mud and death around them, bask in the

sun, and concentrate on the supposedly more chivalrous battle between "knights" in the air.[91]

A more intense expression of this attitude was the love of technology for technology's sake. Some men simply found fascinating
the technical capabilities of the cannons, machine guns, airplanes,
and tanks. The Handley Page struck a pilot as a "colossal machine";
the 9.2 was the "especial object of our admiration"; the appearance
of a tank was "one of the rare occasions when the war has been
dramatic and exciting"; watching a howitzer battery was "fascinating"; and a "75" was a "fine piece" and a "little beauty," according
to various soldiers.[92] The men who felt this way about technology
praised the enemy's weaponry as much as their own. "We rather
admired the technical efficiency of the Germans, even if we suffered
from it," Kerr admitted, "and we were most proud of ourselves when
we surpassed it."[93]

Probably the majority of those who ended up in the separate
technical specialties of the various armies belonged to this category
of soldier. They tended, at least at first, to find new technology
exciting and interesting rather than frightening, and they dedicated
themselves to becoming experts at its use.[94] The range of specialization was immense and grew larger as the war progressed. By mid-
war, air pilots, machine-gunners, bombers, snipers, gunners, tank
"pilots," and mortar crews each had a sense of separate existence as a
privileged band.[95] The air pilots in particular were treated with respect and even awe by foot soldiers, who saw them as fearless (and
perhaps just a little insane) for their mastery of the air and the
airplane and their willingness to take extraordinary risks.[96] Pilots
themselves saw their part in the war as a game or as a strong reaffir-
mation that their individual effort made a difference. They, unlike so
many others caught up in the Great War, had control over their own
fates and fought the enemy face to face.[97] It is not surprising, then,

that pilots and ordinary soldiers loved their planes and thought of them as human beings or as fierce, independent hawks and eagles.

Other men in the special services were more ambiguous about their weapons, about their part in the war, and about the other troops. Tank crews, for instance, were shut up inside slow-moving machines and exposed to temperatures of 120 degrees. The exhaust and noise from the engines were pumped into the cabin, and the crews suffered the "blind helplessness of being cooped up . . . entirely at the mercy of the big shells." They soon decided that they did not have a enviable life.[98] Snipers and machine-gunners, especially in the French army, had a sense of elite status and privilege, but this was not always true for their British counterparts.[99] In fact, as will be shown later, the ordinary soldiers had uncomfortable relationships with all of the specialty groups. The technology that they used was not seen as particularly helpful for the prosecution of the war, at least by trench soldiers, and it usually provoked nothing but the enemy's wrath and retaliation.

The encouraging side of technology was, in fact, only half of the story. There were many more times when artillery, gas, mortars, and the other weapons of the Great War discouraged and demoralized the men at the front. Under these circumstances, soldiers learned to fear and hate the new matériel of war. One of the worst aspects of the conflict was that men were killed from a distance by an "infernal" machine, shell, or grenade; they never even saw the enemy that was attacking them.[100] "We preferred honest man-to-man fighting to being blown into the air," Rommel wrote of the French "love" for mines.[101] Mussolini thought that trench warfare, with its demands for resignation, patience, tenacity, and dependence on bombs and the "murderous hand grenade," was particularly unsuited for the Italian temperament.[102] But in fact none of the combatants in this war wanted to sit in a trench and be felled by an invisible enemy.[103] As an anonymous officer wrote: "It would not be so bad if one could see the thing whistling through the air, or even when it bursts; but one cannot. After the crash a man may scream or moan, totter and fall, but for all one can see he might have been struck down by the wrath of God."[104]

Here was death uncontrolled and uncontrollable. And it was in these situations that soldiers most often referred to technology as demonic, monstrous, or a force of nature.[105] In fact, of those weapons that were given human characteristics, only the trench mortars were consistently hated by troops on all sides, although at first the men had thought that "she" would be easier to live with than the artillery. The deciding factor here was the unpredictability of its flight, and therefore of the destruction that it caused. "There's something rending about them," Jünger agreed, "and treacherous, and something personally malignant."[106]

It was even worse to face an enemy that was better or more amply armed than one's own forces. The invention of a technology gave the innovator the upper hand for at least a short while and caused soldiers to hate not only the enemy but also the terrible new weapons that he was using. The Germans were the first to produce gas, flame-throwers, and bombs, and allied troops were unable to cope with this "frightfulness."[107] It is worth noting that the British had no nicknames for gas and flame-throwers, and only after they developed their own bombs did they come up with familiar terms for them.[108] In the same way, the Germans were initially terrified by tanks, and did not think of the vehicles as "friendly monsters."[109] Only when the German high command had developed artillery tactics to neutralize the threat could Jünger smile at their whimsical names and pity the men caught inside when they were hit by shells. Even then, he still thought them grotesque: "gigantic helpless cockchafers," crawling about the battlefield.[110]

Local superiority was the other way that men attained technical dominance, and it affected their views of technology as much as the complete absence of a weapon type. Soldiers felt helpless and out of control when they saw that the enemy had the upper hand in maté-riel and could therefore bomb, shell, or gas without fear of retalia-tion. At various points during the war the allied forces believed that the Germans had better shells, artillery, rifles, airplanes, and ma-chine guns. The result was to throw ordinary soldiers into despair as they watched, for instance, while the Germans in better and faster airplanes easily shot down their airmen.[111] Others took to denigrat-ing their own technology in the face of the enemy's more effective weapons.[112]

Finally, men learned to hate even their own weapons when they thought that this technology made their lives in the trenches more hellish. This eventually affected even the specializations that men at first held in high regard. In September 1917, wrote a British in-fantry officer, dissatisfaction with the air forces came to a head. "The complaint was that our fliers were going in too much for solo ribbon-hunting stunts, to the neglect of contact, spotting, and help-ing counter-battery."[113] A French soldier's view of the first Saint-Chamond tanks led him to admit that they "don't much inspire confidence." His misgivings were later confirmed when the French used the large vehicles in a battle and met almost total destruction, leaving him and his fellow soldiers open to attack.[114] Tanks disheart-ened allied forces even more when soldiers realized how vulnerable the vehicles were to enemy artillery shells and how they attracted this fire onto any infantry that happened to be nearby. By September 1917 the joy at a tank's arrival was long gone, and a machine that showed up late to support British foot soldiers "was cursed heartily for turning up then, 'only to draw fire.' "[115] As for the special formations that were already not as well-respected (artillery, mortars, and ma-chine guns), men at the front frequently became angry or discour-aged if they provoked retaliation.[116]

The result of these negative views of technology, combined with the deadly action of the enemy's weaponry, could be the ultimate rejection of matériel and the ultimate failure to adapt to the war: "shell" and "gun-shock," or an all-pervasive fatalism. Even gun crews suffered from the "deafening voices of their own pets," as Baldwin put it, let alone those who were on the receiving end of their missiles.[117] The soldiers who did not succumb immediately to the effects of the noise and fire of technology, and yet were unable to find a positive way to view such technology (seeing it as demonic, monstrous, or an irresistible force of nature), might think of war as a game of chance, with bullets and shells that had one's name on them: only luck and fate decided who would survive and who would die.[118] Many men who survived the war could remember instances when a shell had fallen at their feet, only to fail to explode, as well as the sudden step, chance move, or other trivial incident that had meant the difference between life and death.[119] To believe that one had such little control over one's own life could be an unbearable thought, that "without warning, death like an avalanche falls from the sky, and in a moment horror and death assume control. . . . Fate descends suddenly from nowhere, and its sweeping scythe brings death, agony and terror. There is nothing to hit back at, all man can do is to grit his teeth, wait in suspense and curse impotently."[120] To ward off death from blind chance and unfeeling technology, soldiers depended on amulets and good luck charms, and many went into battle with a cross, images of the saints, or a lucky stone around their necks.[121] Other men actually took comfort in the thought that there was nothing that they could do to control their own fate, that it did not matter which path one took or how one ducked and ran. By the end of his stay at the front Lintier believed that fatalism was the beginning of courage: "The enemy was firing without seeing us, and his shells seemed like the blows of Fate descending from heaven. Why here rather than there? We did not know, and the enemy assuredly did not know either. In that case, what was the good of hurrying? Death might as easily overtake us a little farther on. Useless to hurry, then; absolutely useless."[122] Many other soldiers would agree, writing that they no longer had any control over their lives: it was all in the hands of God or up to the whims of fate.[123]

As should be clear from the preceding discussion, men went through many phases during their stay at the front, accepting and rejecting technology based on the expectations they brought to the war and their personal experiences during combat. The preliminary encounters with unknown terrors were transformed by soldiers into the familiar sounds of animals and men only to change into demonic monstrosities when the enemy used new weapons or friends fell victim to the matériel of the war. When soldiers and officers saw technology as threatening and outside of their control, they were least able to comprehend the alien place in which they found themselves, and were most likely to believe that they no longer controlled their own fates, that they were indeed "victims" of the war. Yet it was possible to deal with the extreme conditions of the front if soldiers could find a way to imagine the technology threatening them in a bizarrely benign way. By placing the Materielschlacht in familiar and manageable contexts, or even by learning to appreciate the beauty of weapons and warfare, men found that they could live with the new technology of war and survive their experience at the front.

The domestication of industrialized warfare was never easy and never complete. Elements of trench warfare remained as uncanny and unpalatable at the end of the conflict as they were at the beginning. But what many soldiers managed to do was construct a kind of language that enabled them to talk about these gigantic weapons systems, and what they did to the human body, without, as Marc Bloch put it so eloquently, trembling too much. Many of their accounts describe a private language, a kind of conversation that only old soldiers could understand. But some of their words have come down to us, and retain an aura of meaning at the heart of our understanding of the war. Machines did indeed outstrip the capacity of men to control them in 1914–18, but they did not outstrip the capacity of men to try to give meaning to the world of warfare into which they had been so unceremoniously thrust. In a collection of essays on the Great War eighty years after the Armistice, their achievement commands our attention and respect.

NOTES

1. For a complete look at the technological changes in warfare at this time, see Hubert C. Johnson, *Breakthrough! Tactics, Technology, and the Search for Victory on the Western Front* (Novato: Presidio, 1994), especially pp. 3–7, 88–89, 113–39. The improvement and use of artillery (and other firepower) before and during World War I are discussed in Shelford Bidwell and Dominick Graham, *Fire-Power: British Army Weapons and Theories of War, 1904–1945* (Boston: George Allen & Unwin, 1982), 7–146.

2. A list of the authors who have examined the effects of technology in the war would include every scholar who has looked at the Great War. Here are just a few of those who have studied at least some aspect of this question: every chapter in Allan R. Millett and Williamson Murray, *Military Effectiveness,* vol. 1: *The First World War* (Boston: Allen & Unwin, 1988); Bidwell and Graham, *Fire-Power;* Tim Travers, *The Killing Ground: The British Army, the Western Front, and the Emergence of Modern Warfare, 1900–1918* (London: Allen & Unwin, 1987); Tim Travers, *How the War Was Won: Command and Technology in the British Army on the Western Front, 1917–1918* (London: Routledge, 1992); Tony Ashworth, *Trench Warfare, 1914–1918: The Live and Let Live System* (London: Macmillan, 1980); Eric J. Leed, *No Man's Land: Combat and Identity in World War I* (Cambridge: Cambridge University Press, 1979); Bruce I. Gudmundsson, *Stormtroop Tactics: Innovation in the German Army, 1914–1918* (New York: Praeger, 1989); J. F. C. Fuller, *Tanks in the Great War* (London: John Murray, 1920). Even works that are primarily concerned with other issues, such as the cultural consequences of the war, mutinies, morale at the front, and so on, generally take into consideration the effect that the new technology had on these questions.

3. Samuel Hynes, *The Soldiers' Tale: Bearing Witness to Modern War* (New York: Penguin, 1997), xiii, 52.

4. Leed, *No Man's Land,* 31.

5. Hynes, *Soldiers' Tale.*

6. See Hynes, *Soldiers' Tale,* 32, 43.

7. See Chapter 5.

8. Leed, *No Man's Land*, 105–14; Samuel Hynes, *Soldiers' Tale*, 57–58. See also Ernst Jünger, *The Storm of Steel* (New York: Howard Fertig, 1966 [1929]), 86.

9. Jünger, *Storm of Steel*, 109–10.

10. For an exploration of the theme of strangeness in war see Samuel Hynes, *Soldiers' Tale*, 18, 19, 52, 53.

11. Jünger, *Storm of Steel*, 24–25.

12. Leed has argued that "hearing became much more important than vision as an index of what was real and threatening" at the front. Leed, *No Man's Land*, 124.

13. "Casualty" [pseud.], *Contemptible* (London: William Heinemann, 1916), 24–25.

14. Hans Zöberlein, *Der Glaube an Deutschland* (Munich: Zentralverlag der NSDAP, 1936 [1931]), 45.

15. Giles E. M. Eyre, *Somme Harvest: Memories of a P. B. I. in the Summer of 1916* (London: London Stamp Exchange, 1991 [1938]), 15; Zöberlein, *Der Glaube*, 22–23. Even seasoned warriors continually faced sounds that they had never before experienced. See Henry Page Croft, *Twenty-Two Months Under Fire* (London: John Murray, 1917), 84. During the great offensive on the Somme, another hardened soldier was impressed anew by the increased noise of battle, almost as if hearing the "roar that deafened" for the first time. R. Hugh Knyvett, *Over There with the Australians* (New York: Charles Scribner's Sons, 1918), 216–17.

16. Bernard Adams, *Nothing of Importance: Eight Months at the Front with a Welsh Battalion* (New York: Robert M. McBride, 1918), 13. Looking back at his younger self three years later, the same man addressed himself as "dear innocence" for his lack of comprehension of the different sounds of artillery (16). A general noticed how tiring it was for soldiers to sit still all day in poor shelters under heavy shelling, and especially for the new troops "who can hardly distinguish the noise of the burst of an enemy shell from that of their own guns." Croft, *Twenty-Two Months*, 45.

17. Paul Lintier, *My .75* [*Ma pièce*] (New York: George H. Doran, 1917), 161.

18. Leed, *No Man's Land*, 126–28.

19. Charles W. Turner, ed., *Jack Campbell's War Diary (1918–1919)* (Verona, Va.: McClure, 1982), 9.

20. V. F. Eberle, *My Sapper Venture* (London: Pitman, 1973), 9–10.

21. Adams, *Nothing of Importance*, 16–17.

22. Eberle, *My Sapper Venture*, 9–10.

23. Wilfred Brenton Kerr, *Shrieks and Crashes: Being Memories of Canada's Corps, 1917* (Toronto: Hunter Rose, 1929), 131.

24. Lintier, *My .75*, 162.

25. Richard Haigh, *Life in a Tank* (Boston: Houghton Mifflin, 1918), 4.

26. Adams, *Nothing of Importance*, 16–17, 36. He also found that watching the new draft get the "wind up" helped him to steady himself and lose his nervousness under fire.

27. Kerr, *Shrieks and Crashes*, 36, 74, 78.

28. Carroll Carstairs, *A Generation Missing* (Stevenage, Eng.: Strong Oak, 1989 [1930]), 101; Eyre, *Somme Harvest*, 148.

29. See also Zöberlein, *Der Glaube*, 85; Wilhelm Hartung, *Grosskampf, Männer und Granaten!* (Berlin: Verlag Tradition Wilhelm Kolk, 1930), 244; Georges Lafond, *Covered with Mud and Glory* (Boston: Small, Maynard, 1918), 168; Henri Desagneaux, *A French Soldier's War Diary, 1914–1918* (Morley, England: Elmfield, 1975), 22.

30. Rudolf Binding, *A Fatalist at War* (Boston: Houghton Mifflin, 1929), 177, 178.

31. Hervey Allen, *Toward the Flame* (New York: George H. Doran, 1926), 152.

32. Zöberlein, *Der Glaube*, 22–23; Harold Baldwin, *Holding the Line* (Chicago: A. C. McClurg, 1918), 113; Hartung, *Grosskampf!* 621. See also Brusilov's use of the term "monster gun" to describe the artillery that took him and the rest of the Russian army by surprise in 1914. A. A. Brusilov, *A Soldier's Notebook, 1914–1918* (Westport, Conn.: Greenwood, 1971 [1930]), 168.

33. Kerr, *Shrieks and Crashes*, 173, 112.

34. Philip Gibbs, *Open Warfare: The Way to Victory* (London: William Heinemann, 1919), 99. See p. 57 for his description of a "mortally wounded" tank.

35. Paul Maze, *A Frenchman in Khaki* (London: William Heinemann, 1934), 186.

36. For examples, see Ernest D. Swinton, *Eyewitness: Being Personal Reminiscences of Certain Phases of the Great War, Including the Genesis of the Tank* (London: Hodder and Stoughton, 1932), 290–91.

37. Haigh, *Life in a Tank*, 1–2.

38. Reginald H. Roy, ed., *The Journal of Private Fraser, 1914–1918: Canadian Expeditionary Force* (Victoria, B.C.: Sono Nis, 1985), 207–8. On almost the same day another Canadian wrote in his diary that he got his first look at a tank and thought that he was drunk after seeing the "old buckets of bolts lumbering along the road, snorting and shooting fire from their nostrils like blooming dragons." Peter G. Rogers, ed., *Gunner Ferguson's Diary* (Hantsport, Nova Scotia: Lancelot, 1985), 50.

39. Walter Friedrich, "Tankschlacht," in Friedrich Felger, ed., *Was Wir vom Weltkrieg nicht wissen* (Berlin: Wilhelm Andermann Verlag, 1929), 317; Ferdinand Bringolf, "Tanks," in Ernst Jünger, ed., *Das Antlitz des Weltkrieges: Fronterlebnisse deutscher Soldaten* (Berlin: Neufeld & Henius Verlag, 1930), 36–37; Friedrich v. Bernhardi, *Vom Kriege der Zukunft: Nach dem Erfahrungen des Weltkrieges* (Berlin: Ernst Siegfried Mittler und Sohn, 1920), 37. The German words most often used to describe the tank in the Great War were *Ungetum* and *Ungeheuer*, both stressing the unnatural character of the machines.

40. Bringolf, "Tanks," 52.

41. Zöberlein, *Der Glaube*, 404.

42. See, e.g., David Fraser, ed., *In Good Company: The First World War Diaries of the Hon. William Fraser Gordon Highlanders* (Salisbury: Michael Russel, 1990), 16; F. C. Hitchcock, *Stand To: A Diary of the Trenches, 1915–18* (Norwich: Gliddon, 1988 [1937]), 46; Rogers, *Gunner Ferguson's Diary*, 37; John Glubb, *Into Battle: A Soldier's Diary of the Great War* (London: Cassell, 1978), 93. Hitchcock, *Stand To*, 46. The common British idea of shell as train was paralleled by the Italian naming of a certain large shell the "omnibus." Benito Mussolini, *My Diary, 1915–17* (Boston: Small, Maynard, 1925), 55.

43. [Donald Hankey], *A Student in Arms* (London: Andrew Melrose, 1916), 259; Zöberlein, *Der Glaube*, 33; Edwin Campion Vaughan, *Some Desperate Glory: The Diary of a Young Officer, 1917* (London: Macmillan, 1985), 40.

44. See Rogers, *Gunner Ferguson's Diary*, 75; Erwin Rommel, *Infantry Attacks* (Washington, D.C.: Infantry Journal, 1944 [1937]), 16; Binding, *Fatalist at War*, 89.

45. For two examples see A. Lobanov-Rostovsky, *The Grinding Mill: Reminiscences of War and Revolution in Russia, 1913–1920* (New York: Macmillan, 1935), 91; Fraser, *In Good Company*, 291–92.

46. Christian Mallet, *Impressions and Experiences of a French Trooper, 1914–1915* (London: Constable, 1916), 92; Pierre Loti, *War* (Philadelphia: Lippincott, 1917), 241; R. Hugh Knyvett, *Over There with the Australians*, 177; Hankey, *Student in Arms*, 252; Vaughan, *Some Desperate Glory*, 17; Hitchcock, *Stand To*, 142; Carstairs, *Generation Missing*, 47.

47. Rommel, *Infantry Attacks*, 152; Vaughan, *Some Desperate Glory*, 202; Hitchcock, *Stand To*, 64; Knyvett, *Over There with the Australians*, 214.

48. Jünger, *Storm of Steel*, 96.

49. As cited in Johnson, *Breakthrough!* 73.

50. Carstairs, *Generation Missing*, 63. Marc Bloch was amazed at the appearance of another "forest," where "the shells and even more the machine gun fire had mowed down the branches and even the trunks of trees." Bloch, *Memoirs of War, 1914–15* (Ithaca: Cornell University Press, 1980), 137.

51. "Casualty," *Contemptible*, 67. It was not just trees that suffered in this way. During one particularly unimaginable shelling in the summer of 1917, a French soldier described how even the terrified rats fled the scene "in an army of their own." Maze, *Frenchman in Khaki*, 242.

52. Jünger, *Storm of Steel*, 108–9.

53. Bruce Bairnsfather, *Bullets & Billets* (London: Grant Richards, 1916), 205, 236.

54. Almost every depiction of battle in the Great War includes some variation of these descriptions. For two good examples, see Carstairs, *Generation Missing*, 127, and Vaughan, *Some Desperate Glory*, 43–44, 209. One officer even gave the various types of artillery different voices: 9-inch and 15-inch shells moaned, the 60-pounders gave tongue, and the field howitzers, "with unassuming voice," joined in the chorus. Croft, *Twenty-Two Months*, 84.

55. Mussolini, *My Diary*, 28.

56. Once again, common to many descriptions of battle. See Maze, *Frenchman in Khaki*, 163; Hitchcock, *Stand To*, 249, 293; Eyre, *Somme Harvest*, 152.

57. See, e.g., Adams, *Nothing of Importance*, 198; Mussolini, *My Diary*, 59, 125. Carroll Carstairs took the analogy one step further, writing that "the air seemed alive with invisible wires being twanged, while the earth was thumped and beaten." Carstairs, *Generation Missing*, 127.

58. Lintier, *My .75*, 81.

59. Adams, *Nothing of Importance*, 62, 169; Vaughan, *Some Desperate Glory*, 92.

60. The range of designations was truly impressive. Among the shells and mortars there were females—Black Maria, Minnie, and Silent Susan (the last so named because it arrived without a warning noise), but there were also males, like Silver King. One British company called the silent mortars the "lads with the rubber heels." Hitchcock, *Stand To*, 210.

61. Travers, *How the War Was Won*, 7; Eberle, *My Sapper Venture*, 130. The earliest conception of the tank and its role, provided by Churchill, envisioned a "Landship" that would sail the plains of the Western Front as untroubled by enemy fire as were the dreadnoughts on the North Sea.

62. The types of grenades, for instance, were known variously as the Jam Tin, Potato Masher, and Hair-Brush. Ian Hay, *The First Hundred Thousand: Being an Unofficial Chronicle of a Unit of "K(1)"* (Edinburgh: William Blackwood and Sons, 1915), 233; F. C. Hitchcock, *Stand To*, 61. One kind of British mortar was the "rum jar," and 5.9 shells were "coalboxes." Ashworth, *Trench Warfare*, 64, 124; Vaughan, *Some Desperate Glory*, 72.

63. Bloch, *Memoirs of War*, 131.

64. Mussolini, *My Diary*, 161; Jünger, *Storm of Steel*, 25, 70, 75, 194. Comparisons to familiar animals or assigning to technology the anatomical features of a human or animal further aided the soldier in his adjustment to the matériel of war. There were mortars known as the flying or blind pig; a bombardment was described as a "covey of Hun shells"; bombs from a passing airplane were "eggs"; and the bullets from an airplane machine gun went whistling over soldiers' heads like "partridges." Hitchcock, *Stand To*, 291; Eyre, *Somme Harvest*, 127; Paolo Monelli, *Toes Up [Le Scarpe al Sole]* (London: Duckworth, 1930), 46.

65. Eberle, *My Sapper Venture*, 9–10; Croft, *Twenty-Two Months*, 20.

66. Hay, *First Hundred Thousand*, 259. Mussolini gave each of four different artillery pieces in the Italian arsenal its own personality: the Italian 75 had a "furious" explosion; the 849 was imposing and had an "almost jovial" detonation; the 210 barked dully; and the 305 traveled over the mountains like a pilgrim, slowly and "solemnly." Mussolini, *My Diary*, 53–54.

67. Gwilym H. Lewis, *Wings Over the Somme, 1916–1918* (London: William Kimber, 1976), 73, 82–83, 132.

68. Eberle, *My Sapper Venture*, 19, 27. The normal German term for "dud" is *Blindgänger*.

69. Kerr, *Shrieks and Crashes*, 36; Adams, *Nothing of Importance*, 62.

70. Swinton, *Eyewitness*, 226–27.

71. Haigh, *Life in a Tank*, 28. When a pilot got his first look at the "brutes," he decided that, "as expected, the 'Female' looks the most dangerous." Lewis, *Wings Over the Somme*, 88–89. J. F. C. Fuller would later add to the analogy of tank as living thing, calling the tank an "armoured mechanical horse" and comparing it with knights in armor. Johnson, *Breakthrough!* 250; Fuller, *Tanks in the Great War*, 2.

72. Travers, *How the War Was Won*, 7.

73. Franz Wallenborn, *1000 Tage Westfront: Der Erlebnisse eines einfachen Soldaten* (Leipzig: Hesse & Becker Verlag, 1929), 32, 221; Fraser, *In Good Company*, 291; Allen, *Toward the Flame*, 145; Anon., *The War the Infantry Knew, 1914–1919* (London: P. S. King & Son, 1938); Hitchcock, *Stand To*, 97.

74. Lewis, *Wings Over the Somme*, 82. A less common metaphor likened a German Taube ("dove"), to a "huge insect with a buzz of whirring wings." "Casualty," *Contemptible*, 67.

75. Lintier, *My .75*, 158.

76. See especially C. P. O. Bartlett, *In the Teeth of the Wind: The Story of a Naval Pilot on the Western Front, 1916–1918* (Annapolis, Md.: Naval Institute Press, 1994), 11, 24, 118.

77. As Hynes notes, the air war was romantic from the beginning because flying was. Hynes, *Soldiers' Tale*, 81.

78. See, e.g., Hitchcock, *Stand To*, 69.

79. Baldwin, *Holding the Line*, 191.

80. Albert N. Depew, *Gunner Depew* (London: Cassell, 1918), 160. Cheering at the sound of one's own artillery seems to have been fairly common. See Mussolini, *My Diary*, 53–54.

81. Jünger, *Storm of Steel*, 250, 251.

82. Roy, *Journal of Private Fraser*, 207–8.

83. Antoine Redier, *Comrades in Courage* [*Méditations dans la tranchée*] (Garden City, N.Y.: Doubleday, Page, 1918), 255.

84. Bernhardi, *Vom Kriege der Zukunft*, 37; Bringolf, "Tanks," 36–37; Alfred Volckheim, *Der Kampfwagen in der heutigen Kriegführung: Organization, Verwendung und Bekämpfung. Ein Handbuch für alle Waffen* (Berlin: E. S. Mittler & Sohn, 1924), 2; Bundesarchiv/Militärarchiv, Freiburg. PH3/294, *Abwehrmaßnamen gegen Tanks*, dated 24.11.1917, p. 47.

85. Maze, *Frenchman in Khaki*, 100; Vaughan, *Some Desperate Glory*, 33; Croft, *Twenty-Two Months*, 142–43; Kerr, *Shrieks and Crashes*, 130.

86. Kerr, *Shrieks and Crashes*, 132.

87. As Philip Lawrence has also pointed out, some people simply consider

airplanes, tanks, and artillery to be "aesthetically attractive." Philip K. Lawrence, *Modernity and War: The Creed of Absolute Violence* (London: Macmillan, 1997), 37.

88. Leed, *No Man's Land,* 100.

89. There are numerous examples of this attitude toward technology on display, and from every arena of the war. A few instances are Loti, *War,* 51; Depew, *Gunner Depew,* 161; Fraser, *In Good Company,* 176; Vaughan, *Some Desperate Glory,* 160; Glubb, *Into Battle,* 63; Carstairs, *Generation Missing,* 104, 179; Roy, *Journal of Private Fraser,* 134; Pál Kelemen, *Hussar's Picture Book: From the Diary of a Hungarian Cavalry Officer in World War I* (Bloomington: Indiana University Press, 1972), 11; Lobanov-Rostovsky, *Grinding Mill,* 29, 77.

90. Adams, *Nothing of Importance,* 197–98, 232, 283.

91. See Eberle, *My Sapper Venture,* 10–11; Hitchcock, *Stand To,* 119; Fraser, *In Good Company,* 291; Gilbert Mant, ed., *Soldier Boy: The Letters of Gunner W. J. Duffell, 1915–18* (Kenthurst: Kangaroo Press, 1992), 40; Turner, *Jack Campbell's War Diary,* 17; Kerr, *Shrieks and Crashes,* 124–25; Eyre, *Somme Harvest,* 201–2, 224; Carstairs, *Generation Missing,* 47; *War the Infantry Knew,* 240, 250; Zöberlein, *Der Glaube,* 14; Wallenborn, *1000 Tage Westfront,* 32, 221.

92. Bartlett, *In the Teeth of the Wind,* 34; Kerr, *Shrieks and Crashes,* 123; Glubb, *Into Battle,* 62; Haigh, *Life in a Tank,* 93; Depew, *Gunner Depew,* 46. For an example of this attitude taken further, see Georges Lafond, *Covered with Mud and Glory* (Boston: Small, Maynard, 1918), 36–38.

93. Kerr, *Shrieks and Crashes,* 133. See also Roy, *Journal of Private Fraser,* 271–72; Rogers, *Gunner Ferguson's Diary,* 99; Haigh, *Life in a Tank,* 56–57.

94. This was not true of all those in the specialist groups: there were men who simply wanted to differentiate themselves from the regular troops or to get out of the trenches to avoid a more certain death.

95. Ashworth, *Trench Warfare,* 57–60, 65, 69; David R. Jones, "Imperial Russia's Forces at War," in Millett and Murray, *The First World War,* 310.

96. Lewis, *Wings Over the Somme,* 42, 73; Rogers, *Gunner Ferguson's Diary,* 41, 84; Roy, *Journal of Private Fraser,* 82; Vaughan, *Some Desperate Glory,* 140.

97. Lewis, *Wings Over the Somme,* 46; Hermann Fricke, "Wie der Flieger den Krieg sah," in Ernst Jünger, ed., *Das Antlitz des Weltkrieges: Fronterlebnisse deutscher Soldaten* (Berlin: Neufeld & Henius Verlag, 1930), 145.

98. Haigh, *Life in a Tank,* 110. For the elite status of the French tank corps, see Desagneaux, *French Soldier's War Diary,* 52.

99. Depew, *Gunner Depew,* 38; Lafond, *Covered with Mud and Glory,* 38–39; Bairnsfather, *Bullets & Billets,* 246.

100. See J. G. Fuller, *Troop Morale and Popular Culture in the British and Dominion Armies, 1914–1918* (Oxford: Clarendon, 1990), 28.

101. Rommel, *Infantry Attacks,* 71.

102. Mussolini, *My Diary,* 59.

103. See Hitchcock, *Stand To*, 168; Vaughan, *Some Desperate Glory*, 199; *War the Infantry Knew*, 432.

104. "Casualty," *Contemptible*, 31.

105. The "pet enemy" of one group of Canadian soldiers, the 5.9 howitzer, was described as having the "shriek of a Fury" and as being a "huge black monster" that created an "inferno." Kerr, *Shrieks and Crashes*, 128.

106. Jünger, *The Storm of Steel*, 40. See also Roy, *Journal of Private Fraser*, 53; Adams, *Nothing of Importance*, 120–21; Knyvett, *Over There with the Australians*, 192–93; Croft, *Twenty-Two Months*, 142–43; Rommel, *Infantry Attacks*, 62–63.

107. Baldwin, *Holding the Line*, 168; Hitchcock, *Stand To*, 56–57.

108. A French officer compared the sound made by gas shells to the deadly call of the sirens. Loti, *War*, 201.

109. They even had to invent a new word, *Tankschrecken*, to describe the panic that the machines provoked. Gibbs, *Open Warfare*, 29, 34–35; Major Walther Nehring, *Kampfwagen an die Front! Geschichtliche und neuzeitliche Entwicklung des Kampfwagens ("Tanks") im Ausland* (Leipzig: Verlag Johannes Detke, Kommanditgesellschaft, 1934), 7–8; Fr. v. Taysen, *Material oder Moral? Ein Beitrag zur Beurteilung der im französischen Heere Herrschenden Kampfgrundsätze* (Charlottenburg: Verlag "Offene Wort," 1923), 28.

110. Jünger, *Storm of Steel*, 286–87.

111. Roy, *Journal of Private Fraser*, 69 104, 289; Baldwin, *Holding the Line*, 97–99; Desagneaux, *French Soldier's War Diary*, 41.

112. Kerr, *Shrieks and Crashes*, 132.

113. *War the Infantry Knew*, 382–83.

114. Desagneaux, *French Soldier's War Diary*, 52, 83.

115. *War the Infantry Knew*, 394.

116. Hay, *First Hundred Thousand*, 279–81.

117. Baldwin, *Holding the Line*, 112.

118. Eberle, *My Sapper Venture*, 17; Carstairs, *Generation Missing*, 119–20.

119. A common incident in the lives of many soldiers. See Haigh, *Life in a Tank*, 80; Croft, *Twenty-Two Months*, 107; Maze, *Frenchman in Khaki*, 129–30, 163.

120. Eyre, *Somme Harvest*, 25–26.

121. Hitchcock, *Stand To*, 76; Carstairs, *Generation Missing*, 93–94; Mussolini, *My Diary*, 69.

122. Lintier, *My .75*, 117.

123. Kerr, *Shrieks and Crashes*, 144; Allen, *Toward the Flame*, 50.

CHAPTER 5

Narrative and Identity at the Front
"Theory and the Poor Bloody Infantry"

LEONARD V. SMITH

A good fifteen years after its inception, the "literary turn" of historical analysis has succeeded to the extent that most historians will now agree that history is about narratives that structure the reality of the past. At the same time, most would agree that historical narratives contain within them an explicit or implicit statement about the makeup of the individuals whose lives history recounts. Historical narratives show what makes individuals function as such, and what they can and cannot do to shape history. It is my purpose here to explore the cultural history of battlefield experience in World War I through reflecting on the relationship between historical narratives and military identity in World War I.[1]

To keep my focus on the "poor bloody infantry" rather than on the theory, I will simply assert that there are two broad forms of narrative explanation operative among historians nowadays, "modern" and "postmodern."[2] Both present specific notions of the individual. Modernist narratives present themselves as "true," in the sense that they are verifiable through agreed-upon rules of evidence and argument. Most modernist narratives posit progress toward a positive teleology of history, either the present or somewhere in the future. The individual underpinning this narrative is rational and morally autonomous, able if not always willing to shape history toward that positive end. Postmodern narratives reject not just "truth" but even teleologies, in favor of analyzing endless and indeterminate games around relations of power. Hierarchies such as those of race, class, and gender can be forever reconfigured and transformed but never really overcome. The very concept of an individual is constructed through this sort of indeterminate narrative. To some postmodernists individuality itself is simply the product of language, which is the essential venue of games of power.

Yet in considering World War I and particularly soldiers' experiences in it, it is striking to think about how much common ground exists between modernist and postmodernist narratives, both concerning the war itself and the individual. Both narratives, I would suggest, partake of what Jean-François Lyotard called a "metanarrative," an unquestioned interpretive structure into which more specific disciplinary interpretive narratives fit.[3] This metanarrative represents World War I as the quintessential tragedy and the soldier as the quintessential victim of that tragedy. Scholars in myriad fields—history, literary criticism, sociology, psychology, even economics—could all fit their work into the metanarrative of World War I as tragedy.

Among historians, modernists could understand the war as the tragic calamity that for nearly a century stole away the promise of nineteenth-century positivism. The war proceeded from the fatal flaws of Western civilization, whether militarism, nationalism, or capitalism.[4] European societies were shattered by the experience of the war and were unable to prevent the calamities that followed in its wake. The victimization of the front soldier was extended to European societies as a whole. World War I set in motion a chain reaction of traumas, leading from war to economic depression, back to war and genocide in the Holocaust, then to a divided Europe in which Europeans had largely lost control over their own affairs.[5] Indeed, a modernist could argue that this chain of victimization was broken, and the promise of modernism fully restored, only with the Revolutions of 1989.

To postmodernists, World War I can be read as the moment when the grim power games of Western civilization showed themselves with unusual clarity.[6] The internal contradictions of nation, honor, and duty deconstructed on the bloodied bodies and battlefields. A war fought "to end all wars" put in place the even deadlier power game that became World War II. The genders remained unequal, and class conflict became ever more bitter—nowhere more so than in the newborn Soviet Union, which aspired to abolish it. Racial hatreds, whether based in ethnicity or in color, intensified in Europe, as well as in the ever more unstable European empires.

In short, despite completely opposite epistemological starting points, modernists and postmodernists have shown a shared interest in narrating the war as tragedy and the individual caught up in it in as victim. Perhaps this surprising concurrence of views even helps explain the renaissance in the study of World War I in the past fifteen years. The tragic metanarrative of World War I has created a tent big enough to include practically everyone.

Yet like any other narrative form, metanarrative achieves coherence by inclusion and exclusion. The tragic metanarrative of World War I is like an assembled watch that works well enough but that leaves many unincorporated pieces lying alongside on the table. In this chapter I look at the watch and examine the importance of some of the pieces left behind. The "pieces" suggest other narrative frameworks and other concepts of military identity that historians of World War I have barely begun to understand. My approach is eclectic, mixing both historical and literary sources, which I think is appropriate for a subject of this breadth. In any event, lines are not easily drawn between "fictional" and "nonfictional" texts from

World War I. And "fictional" texts came to play a major causal role in the formation of the tragic metanarrative.

World War I in the Tragic Mode, and the Soldier as Victim

I employ tragedy as narrative and metanarrative in a simple, classical sense. The pivotal character is the hero, a figure of great virtue but fatal flaws. He is, as Northrop Frye has noted, "somewhere between the divine and the 'all too human.'"[7] In time, the hero becomes aware the convergence of fate and his own flaws, but too late to avert the final calamity. These flaws set in motion the hero's destruction, inexorably brought about by fate. His destruction restores the moral order he disrupted. The hero's demise is foreordained; the moral of the story is strictly for consumption by survivors in the tragedy and for the audience. Complementary in the metanarrative of World War I as tragedy are the two most salient aspects of soldiers' experience in it—the enthusiasm that greeted the outbreak of war in 1914 and the disillusion amid the personal and social destruction that followed. Enthusiasm and despair are inextricably linked, for men had to give themselves over entirely to the war at the outset if they were to be so cruelly disillusioned with it thereafter.

The hero of August 1914 was the heir of Peter Pan, from J. M. Barrie's 1904 play of that name. Peter is the archetype of the "new man" of the late nineteenth century, paradoxically represented as a boy who refuses to grow up. He will not be taken in by the drab life of bourgeois commercialism bequeathed to him by his forefathers. He will forever seek new challenge and excitement in a century all his own. He cannot even fathom real fear. "To die," he proclaims, "will be an awfully big adventure."[8] His real life counterpart in August 1914 was the poet Rupert Brooke, the intelligent and handsome red-blond Cambridge man who penned perhaps the most famous words in the English language about the outbreak of the war:

> Now God be thanked Who has matched us with His hour,
>   And caught our youth, and wakened us from sleeping,
> With hand made sure, clear eye, and sharpened power,
>   To turn, as swimmers into cleanness leaping,
> Glad from a world grown old and cold and weary,
>   Leave the sick hearts that honour could not move,
> And half-men, and their dirty songs and dreary,
>   And all the little emptiness of love![9]

The war offered the hero nothing less than what Eric Leed called the "escape from modernity,"[10] from the "old and cold and weary" nineteenth-century world that liberalism and capitalism had made, with its mundane comforts and tribulations. Battle for Brooke was supposed to be a clean, redemptive experience, and the battlefield a place "where there's no ill, no grief, but sleep has mending." Indeed, battle is nothing more than a painful stop in the path to apotheosis, "in some corner of a foreign field / That is forever England." Brooke himself would not live to test his prediction of the experience of battle and its transformation of the self. He suffered a variety of illnesses en route to Gallipoli, and he died in April 1915. Speaking simply in terms of his literary reputation, his death was a timely one.

Yet the heroic soldier of August 1914 had his darker side, which spoke to his fatal flaws. One of the most troubling and foreboding images of August 1914 is a famous photograph of a Munich crowd at the announcement of the declaration of war. In the foreground is a young man easily identifiable as Adolf Hitler, experiencing a moment of epiphany. The hero, according to the tragic metanarrative of World War I, embraced the outbreak of war in a spasm of atavistic fury.[11] As Modris Eksteins has explained so eloquently, that fury was long in the making in European culture. Its emblem was the famous ballet *Le Sacre de printemps* (The Rite of Spring), with music by Igor

Stravinsky, dancing by Vaslav Nijinksy, and staging by Sergei Diaghilev. The ballet premiered in Paris on May 29, 1913, just over a year before the outbreak of war. The ballet, originally titled by Stravinsky *The Victim,* portrayed a dance of death linking freedom to the powers of mass destruction as the supreme chance to follow Goethe's invocation to *stirb und werde,* to die and become. Peter Pan had been stripped of some of his illusions, even before the war.

As with other tragic heroes, the fatal flaws of the soldier of 1914 amounted to those of pride. To be sure, the sins of pride had originated with his elders. The exemplary prideful father was the aged emperor-king Francis Joseph of Austria-Hungary, who sent his sons off to fight a war he started in revenge over the assassination of his heir by Serbian nationalists. But the kaiser in Germany, the tsar in Russia, the king in England, even the guardians of the Republic in France, all shared the same hubris. In a famous poem entitled "The Parable of the Old Man and the Young," Wilfred Owen retells the story of Abraham and Isaac with a very different ending.[12] The angel appears to Abraham at the moment he is about to slay his son and offers him the Ram of Pride in his stead: "But the old man would not so, but slew his son,/And half the seed of Europe, one by one." Yet Owen was a poet of the last years of the war, when the tragedy was well along the path to its inescapable conclusion. Owen himself was a quintessentially tragic figure, killed just days before the Armistice in November 1918. The turning of the sons against the fathers occurred well after August 1914. At the outset, the soldier was proud of his nation, his government, his army, his uniform, his gender. Young man Hitler, born in Austria, could not contemplate serving in the multinational army of the Habsburgs, but he quickly found a home for his national pride in the army of Kaiser Wilhelm II.

The instrument of fate was the technology of industrialized "total" warfare. Of course, war by definition involves great physical danger. But the tragic metanarrative of combat in World War I rests in part on a technological transformation of war itself. As Mary R. Habeck shows in this volume, new instruments of carnage appeared and older ones were used to an extent hitherto not believed possible.[13] The vast capacity of industrial Europe turned itself toward mass killing. The British fired some 1.5 million shells in the seven days preceding their attack along the Somme in July 1916, or some 30 shells per thousand square yards of front—all for a strategically insignificant advance.[14] By the time the French were successfully advancing in the summer of 1918 they were firing some three shells per meter of front.[15] A soldier was not safe even between pitched battles. The proximity of the opposing lines, particularly on the Western Front, kept physical risk constant. A soldier in the trenches could be shot or blown up any hour of the day or night.

If war has a logic, that logic involves the application of physical force toward a rational political end. As World War I continued, that logic became perverse. The Germans had made huge gains in Belgium, France, and Eastern Europe in 1914 but lacked the means to defeat the alliance of French, British, Russians, and later Italians arrayed against them. Yet the military technology in place at the time so favored the defensive that this alliance could not drive back the Germans to a strategically significant extent. On the Eastern Front a stalemate of space ensued, in which the lines could move miles one way or the other at the expense of millions of lives but without threatening the position of either protagonist. On the Western Front a stalemate of force reached its nadir in the eight-month battle of Verdun in 1916. Nearly 1 million casualties were suffered between the French and the Germans, yet the lines ended up about where they were when the battle began. As A. J. P. Taylor put it: "To a detached view, the military deadlock ought to have produced a willingness to compromise. It did the opposite."[16] The tragic victim that was the poor bloody infantry paid the price.

By victim I mean a soldier who has experienced an annihilation of the self, independent of what happens to his body. Some of the soldier-victims of World War I were killed body and soul, and quickly. The young Carl Joseph von Trotta of Joseph Roth's novel *The Radetzky March* spent his childhood dreaming of a romantic death in the service of Emperor Francis Joseph, against the backdrop of the famous tune.[17] Yet the contradictions of the Dual Monarchy were so profound even before the war that, lacking a secure base for his identity, he sinks into a dissolute life of gambling and drink. In the opening battle against the Russian army in 1914, he endeavors to redeem himself through a suicide mission (unsuccessful at that) to bring water to his men. He achieves the dream of his youth; he dies with the Radetzky March ringing in his ears, projected there by his imagination. Yet "he" is scarcely there by that time; he is as hollow as the tune itself. Habeck has described the coping mechanisms developed by soldiers who survived the initial battles. Yet according to the tragic metanarrative, all of these efforts had to fail in the end. Total war required a total victim.

Elaine Showalter has posited an intriguing variation on the destroyed self of the trench soldier through a gender analysis of shell shock.[18] The stalemated war disrupted the power game of masculinity in the service of the nation by rendering conventional courage dysfunctional. The most "courageous" of men would simply get himself killed, to no military purpose. The result, according to Showalter, was acute male gender anxiety. Men were unable to fulfill the deepest expectations of their culture yet were equally unable to change them. Shell shock thus provided an emotional escape from an unlivable situation, a "disguised male protest not only against the war but against the concept of 'manliness' itself."[19] The malady constituted, in effect, a male appropriation of the nineteenth-century "female" condition of hysteria, and thus a particularly ironic example of the gender disorder invoked by World War I.

Psychiatry mobilized powerfully to respond to the phenomenon of shell shock, with a focus on behavior over causation. Psychiatrists took any measures deemed necessary to get men back into the trenches. At least in the British army, treatments had a stunning class bias. Common soldiers found themselves subjected to physical coercion. The common symptom of mutism, for example, could be treated by electric shocks to the neck and throat, and with lighted cigarette tips placed at the tip of the tongue.[20] Shell-shocked officers, in contrast, were more likely to be treated according to the latest Freudian techniques of talking therapy. Showalter illustrates the latter approach in the case of perhaps the most famous nonvictim of shell shock, the war poet Siegfried Sassoon.[21]

The psychiatric response proved not unsuccessful; shell shock remained a considerable but manageable problem in all the protagonist armies. But the soldier paid the price. As Showalter argues, his treatment reinscribed the very gender anxieties that had led to the crisis in the first place. The soldier, in a very real sense, "became" his therapy. In common soldiers subjected to disciplinary therapy, this process occurred through their bodies. The very objective was to make soldiers feel immediate therapeutic pain more acutely than the apprehension that would result from behaving as though their morale was intact. In Sassoon's case, Showalter argued, talking therapy worked more insidiously but even more effectively. His psychiatrist, W. H. R. Rivers, became to Sassoon a combination of all male ideals— father, confessor, even platonic lover. Rivers won the inherently unequal therapeutic duel, and Sassoon returned to the trenches.

But both varieties of therapy "worked" through alienating behavior from the self. Shell-shocked soldiers were not necessarily emotionally exterminated—though many soldiers supposedly "cured" died not-so-mysteriously shortly after they resumed their duties. But the conflict between self-expectations and the stalemated war was never resolved. The war thus became literally a traumatic experience from which soldiers could never recover. Whether through the unpredictable reemergence of the symptoms of shell shock or, as Showalter described Sassoon's case, through an "obsessive revisiting and rewriting of his experiences before and during the war,"[22] these men spent the rest of their lives reenacting the trauma of the male self destroyed.

The archetype of the self victimized and destroyed by the war is Paul Bäumer, the twenty-year-old protagonist from Erich Maria Remarque's 1929 novel *All Quiet on the Western Front*.[23] The components of the book had actually been in the literary mix for a good decade previously, yet virtually upon publication it became the definitive work of fiction about World War I, which it remains today. The book provided a capstone to the construction of World War I as tragedy. In the epigraph to the book, Remarque could scarcely have stated his intention more explicitly; he meant to tell "of a generation of men who, even though they may have escaped the shells, were destroyed by the war." He wrote of what became of the beautiful, idealistic young men who thanked God for matching them with his hour, but who did not die quick, clean deaths in August 1914.

All Quiet tells a tale that could have come out of Michel Foucault's *Discipline and Punish*.[24] Paul is seduced into joining the army at the age of nineteen by the mindless nationalism of his schoolmaster. Once at the front, his very soul is torn asunder and recast by the confinement and physical tortures inflicted by the war of the trenches. His comrades die horrific deaths one by one, all narrated in the gruesome detail for which World War I fiction is famous. In time, Paul loses all ability to connect to life beyond the war, even to his mother, who is dying of cancer. By the end of the book the war has reduced him to what Foucault might have called a "docile body," a perverse variation on the courageous soldier.[25] He obeys orders, shoots, and even kills when ordered to do so. And although he obeys, he no longer *wants* to obey—because by the end of the book there is no longer a Paul capable of conscious volition. Any life in him remains purely biological, as he laments near the end of the book: "Let the months and years come, they can take nothing from me, they can take nothing more. I am so alone, and so without hope that I can confront them without fear. The life that has borne me through these years in still in my hands and my eyes. Whether I have subdued it, I know not. But so long as it is there it will seek its own way out, heedless of the will that is within me."[26] Paul's physical death occurs as an afterthought, in October 1918, as the war is coming to a close, on a day reported as "all quiet on the Western Front." The cultural system of the victimized self has no spirituality; the annihilation of Paul's body merely completes the annihilation of his identity.

Perhaps the most troubling example of the victimized self would have described himself as anything but—Ernst Jünger. Yet Jünger symbolized the grim portents of the aftermath of World War I. He had already run off to join the French Foreign Legion in 1913, only to desert and be returned to his parents for being under age. In 1914 he took advantage of a special program to leave the *Gymnasium* one year early and train for the war.[27] But actual combat led Jünger to what at first seems a diametrically opposite response from Paul Bäumer's. To paraphrase Friedrich Nietzsche, the war did not kill him, therefore it made him strong. "He" became reborn through internalizing the twisted ethos of the war itself. As Jünger wrote in *War as an Inner Experience* (1922): "The war, father of all things, is also our father. It has hammered, cast and tempered us into what we are. And always, as the whirling wheel of life turns in us, the war will be the axis around which it turns."[28]

In this "new man" born of struggle, blood, and death, courage and idealism reemerged in unsettling ways. Stalemate rather than physical danger became the threat to the self. His identity was recast according to the principles of the doctrine of the offensive, as that doctrine was itself recast in the last years of the war. Jünger joined the stormtroopers, specially trained commandos formed by all the protagonist armies in an effort to restore the war of movement. Stormtroopers operated under conditions of completely devolved command authority and maximized personal initiative. Their success depended on internalized aggression. After a short but severe artillery barrage stormtroopers would infiltrate the broken enemy positions to keep them from re-forming.[29] Their objective was to penetrate ever more deeply into enemy positions and to leave behind islands of resistance for the regular army soldiers to absorb as they advanced. The word "penetrate" was chosen intentionally, as Jünger wrote about combat in highly sensual terms. Little affinity for feminist theory is necessary to read sexual aggression into this description of combat from *Fire and Blood* (1925): "But now we will rip away this veil instead of gingerly lifting its corner. We approach as conquerors, armed with all the means of power. We will force open the closed door and enter by force into the forbidden land. And for us who have, for so long, been forced to accumulate in desolate fields of shell holes, the idea of this thrust into the depths holds a compelling fascination."[30]

Jünger himself disdained National Socialism after the war, calling it a movement that pandered to the ignorant and unimprovable masses. But the image that he helped evoke of a self annihilated and re-created in violence, hatred, and desire rather than in reason and generosity proved one means through which the tragedy of World War I evolved into the even greater tragedy of World War II. Even though it enfranchised women, the Weimar Republic based itself on a male citizenry shattered by the war—on the brothers in arms of Paul Baümer and Ernst Jünger. Ex-soldiers mobilized themselves into the Freikorps, militias that guaranteed the survival of the Republic in its first days. But it was as though the maintaining of order in the streets had been entrusted to the Ku Klux Klan. The Republic was born in blood as the Freikorps continued the war after the Armistice against their fellow Germans on the political left. Weimar relied on a nursemaid who accentuated its birth trauma. The Paul Baümers of interwar Germany were in no position to fight back. The Ernst Jüngers did not want to.

Jay Winter and Blaine Baggett's *The Great War and the Shaping of the Twentieth Century,* published in 1996, concludes with a chapter entitled "War Without End," which traces connections between the two world wars by following people whose lives bring individualized versions of the tragic narrative to fruition. Rudolf Höss joined the German army in 1916 at the age of sixteen and one year later became its youngest noncommissioned officer. After service in the Middle East he joined the Freikorps and, not long thereafter, the Nazi Party. During World War II, Höss became commandant of Auschwitz, where by his own admission he oversaw the deaths of some 2 million people. The authors note that not all German veterans made war criminality a way of life. Rather, "what the 1914–1918 war did was to make those crimes possible. The war opened a doorway to brutality through which men like Höss willingly passed."[31]

Yet every tragedy has to have survivors. These survivors are principally witnesses to the tragedy, and by definition they cannot have played determinant roles in it. Among the survivors identified by Winter and Baggett are Albert Camus and Boris Pasternak. Neither fought in World War I—Camus was born in November 1913, and Pasternak had suffered a bad fall from a horse as a youth that had rendered him unfit for military service. Yet both suffered from the war. Camus's father was killed at the Battle of the Marne in 1914, and Pasternak lost a great number of friends in the Stalinist terror that followed the Russian Revolution, which itself proceeded from World War I. Winter and Baggett employ Camus and Pasternak as survivors to give closure to their tragic narrative: "They had much in common; victims of war and violence, they cried out against them both. They are among those who stood by art, who asserted human values even in the face of extinction, and in so doing stood by us all."[32]

Military Identity in the Comic Mode?

It is far from my intention to relativize—let alone trivialize—what happened to those caught in the maelstrom of World War I. Rather, my point is that the metanarrative of the war as tragedy is not the only framework for interpreting that conflict and how it altered soldiers' lives and identities. Tragedy allows for the inclusion of some stories but pointedly excludes others. I am arguing not that the tragic metanarrative of World War I is "untrue" but rather that it does not tell us everything we need to know. Lyotard himself argued that the decline of metanarrative has been a key component of post-modernity in its broadest cultural sense.[33]

But if at the end of the day all history is narrative, how then to replace tragedy? Carolyn Bynum and Lynn Hunt have posited the comic mode as a suggestive narrative form for historical writing.[34] They mean "comic" not in the sense of history written to evoke laughter, though it can sometimes do that in the most unlikely settings.[35] Rather, the comic mode is useful because it simply owns up to the basic contrivance of narrative itself. As Bynum put it, "Comedy tells many stories, achieves conclusion only by coincidence and wild improbability, and undergirds our sense of human limitation, even our cynicism about our motives and self-awareness."[36] There is no single version of the self that underpins the comic mode—it is dominated by neither the rational self of modernism nor the individual constituted through the linguistic power games of postmodernism. Rather, historical stories in the comic mode are as diverse as the stories individuals tell, and through which these individuals themselves are constituted. They emphasize process over outcome; they might have a moral, but more often they do not, at least not an explicit one.

Even literature, so crucial to the construction of the metanarrative of World War I as tragedy, partook of the comic mode. If the aged emperor-king Francis Joseph, the young Lieutenant Carl von Trotta, who died, and the young Hitler, who didn't, are all cultural actors in the history of the Habsburg Monarchy during World War I, so too is Good Soldier Svejk, from Jaroslav Hasek's episodic novel of that name from the 1920s.[37] Svejk is literally a comic character in a war seldom looked to as a source of humor. Obstinance seems to lie at the heart of his character. He wages war on his surroundings through passive aggression—which shows itself as circumvention, deception, and feigned (and real) stupidity. Svejk never met a digression he did not like, and he regularly confounds the reader as to just what he understands and what he does not. Along the way Svejk exposes the monarchy's many contradictions, confusing and ultimately thwarting capricious Habsburg officialdom at every turn.

In August 1914 he is lying in bed stricken with rheumatism, reading a newspaper account of the rout of the Royal and Imperial army in Galicia.[38] He announces to his charwoman friend that he must join the Habsburg forces immediately to save the realm and begins singing songs of dynastic loyalty. She panics and runs off to tell a doctor that Svejk is suffering from the mad delusion that Austria-Hungary is going to win the war. Nevertheless, she dutifully pushes the wheelchair-bound Svejk off to the recruiting station later that day. The incident appears in the Prague newspapers as proof of the loyalty of the Czech people. Yet the medical officer on duty is so keen to brand all Czechs malingerers that he has Svejk packed off to prison. And so begins Svejk's roller-coaster ride through the war.

Historians working within the narrative forms of social history have also raised questions about the tragic metanarrative of World War I. As might be expected, given the origins of the Annales paradigm, historians of France have played an important role in applying social history narratives to the study of the war.[39] Social historians have looked for deeper sources of structural continuity and long-term change beneath the calamitous but transitory *évènements* (events) taking place at the surface.

In France, social history entered the study of World War I through political history, mostly via two students of great political historian Pierre Renouvin. Both saw French nationalism as a site of reasoned discourse on the part of French soldiers, as something that called forth martial ardor but also restrained it. In a magisterial study of French public opinion among soldiers and civilians in August 1914, Jean-Jacques Becker effectively dismantled the idea of a vengeful and bloodthirsty France rushing off to war.[40] He concluded that the French in and out of uniform were neither bellicose nor pacifist in August 1914. Nationalism indeed pulled soldiers toward the conflict, but not toward a war of expansionist conquest. Rather, the French were characterized by a grim resolution first to expel the invader and then to reclaim Alsace and Lorraine in a war France did not initiate. In the first study of the 1917 French army mutinies using the complete archival record, Guy Pedroncini concluded that the French patriotism rendered the mutinies not a revolutionary movement but a rational and sophisticated protest against a particular military strategy.[41] Both Becker and Pedroncini recount chapters in the history of "eternal France" that survived the trauma of the war as a coherent national community.

Social historians have generally relied on some variation of the modernist self, a sane soldier endeavoring to impose order on an insane war. His survival lies at the heart of the narrative. Social historians have devoted considerable attention to the conditions of daily life in the trenches, and to the ways that soldiers mitigated and to some extent controlled the circumstances of their lives. In an important study of British and Dominion troops, J. G. Fuller pointed to the influence of civilian popular culture—whether through playing sports, singing songs, or producing and reading trench newspapers—in normalizing the dreadfulness of service in the front lines.[42] Sociologist Tony Ashworth posited a new model for understanding "trench warfare," which he defined simply as what happened in the front lines between pitched battles.[43] Ashworth argued that tacit truces prevailed along many sectors of the Western Front, as nominal enemies allowed each other to go about their business in peace so long as they returned the favor. It turned out that there existed many ways to regulate and limit violence in the trenches. Shelling and sniping could take place only at particular times of the day, or in a way so as to be sure to miss enemy soldiers. On exceptional occasions, such as Christmas 1914, command authority was flouted as British and German soldiers openly fraternized across no-man's-land.[44]

Much influenced by both Ashworth and Becker, I argued in a close examination of one infantry division in the French army that something had to be wrong with the generic literary representation of a World War I battle—in which unquestioning, innocent, and vulnerable young men leaped into no-man's-land like lambs to the slaughter.[45] If all World War I soldiers were Paul Bäumers, they should have died his death—or if they survived have lived Ernst Jünger's life. Although the story I told was distinctly postmodern in its structure as an indeterminate power game, it very much rested on a modernist identity of the soldier. I posited a "rational" or "utilitarian" model that made possible a reconsideration of relations between soldiers and commanders. Soldiers simply stopped advancing when they saw no additional military utility to their efforts. Those at physical risk thus determined an outcome in the field that the formal command structure was then obliged to accept as adequate.

Particularly since 1992, the study of World War I has been undergoing a transformation in Europe, with the establishment of the Historial de la Grande Guerre in Péronne, France, and its Centre de Recherche. Its objectives, according to Stéphane Audoin-Rouzeau and Annette Becker, directors of the center, has been to understand the unique *culture de guerre* of World War I, through "all of the representations that have been given to us of this immense ordeal, both during it and after."[46] The many colloquia sponsored by the Historial have been directed toward the comparative and international study of the war, and toward understanding the complex and close relationship between military and civilian society.[47] Although Audoin-Rouzeau and Becker have eschewed as such the thorny issues of theory and the poor bloody infantry, their work has helped set the stage for a fundamental rethinking of the relationship between narrative and military identity. Like Pedroncini and Jean-Jacques Becker, both look beyond the tragic metanarrative of the war, toward the components of the national community that sustained the French in and out of uniform through four horrible years. But in suggestive ways they both also look beyond the rational or utilitarian model of the soldier's identity that dominated my earlier work.

Audoin-Rouzeau has considered the reconstruction of military identity in the trenches in a study of trench newspapers.[48] Writing itself becomes an act of the will and of resistance to domination of the self by the war. Rather than a means to reenacting a permanent mutilation of the self, as writing is in Remarque, Sassoon, and Jünger, writing constitutes a defense of an embattled but in some sense still autonomous self. Gruesome description is not absent, but it speaks to an acute concern with the vulnerability of the body and a need to communicate that vulnerability. Confessing this vulnerability to themselves and each other led soldiers toward a special appreciation of the minute pleasures of simply living, as shown in a quote from a trench newspaper written in 1917. In this defense of life in opposition to the war, Audoin-Rouzeau argues, lies a defense of the self. "They" are still there, beneath the horrible things happening to them. "For us, living an animal life where only primitive feelings existed, for us, . . . threatened with annihilation or the most terrible sufferings, this was the only way to be happy: not to think of the past, to enjoy the present moment intensely and uniquely."[49]

Religion, according to Annette Becker, provided another way for soldiers to impose meaning on the war beyond rationality. To be sure, religion mobilized soldiers. "We make war because of a certain way of viewing the world," wrote Jacques Rivière from a prisoner-of-war camp in Germany. "All wars are wars of religion."[50] Yet soldiers also mobilized religion. For devout Catholics, for example, suffering could take on the meaning of *imitatio Christi*, of achieving personal redemption through imitating the suffering of Christ. As J. Bellouard put it, "Lord, my calvary is hard. But yours was harder still. . . . Therefore, I will mix my sweat with your sweat, my tears with your tears."[51] Soldiers used religion to explain what the rational calculus of military utility could not. They mobilized religion both to convey meaning to their suffering in this world and to guarantee their survival in the next. As with Jesus in Christian theology, suffering becomes a conduit to a higher plane of existence. Plainly, the soldier here is neither a simple victim nor an individual constituted purely through utilitarian calculation.

I argue that the next step in writing the cultural history of military identity in World War I involves more explicitly recognizing the influence of elements of postmodern theory. This long after the "literary turn" we can take for granted that World War I comprises any number of stories in the tragic and comic modes—none of which should assume the status of metanarrative. Likewise, we can take military identities within these narratives to be constructed rather than absolute. Individuals are at least in part the product of discourses, such as resistance or religion, that shape the narratives around them. I argue, then, for identifying issues of postmodern theory and exploring where they lead. Applied judiciously, issues of postmodern theory can help us answer the most basic and enduring questions about World War I, and respond to Michael Howard's exhortation to reconsider what the war was about.[52]

Perhaps the best way to do so is through a particular example: the composition and reconfiguration of political identity during the French and Russian army mutinies of 1917. In both countries the mutinous soldiers were neither victims nor completely "free," "rational," or autonomous actors. At stake in both cases was the affirmation or the construction of a political identity that authorized both resistance and obedience.

Historians have long considered 1917 as the year when what the war was about changed fundamentally.[53] As Arno Mayer argued in 1959, three years of "total" war made creak the basic prewar ideological equilibrium of Europe.[54] By 1917 a dichotomy emerged between the "forces of order," who advocated an international system based on traditional power politics, and the "forces of movement," who sought a new order based on idealistic principle. Exactly who was fighting whom had become remarkably unclear by the third year of war.

The crises of 1917 and 1918 form a continuum—from the microdramas of protest over capricious and immediate command authority to the macrodramas of mutiny and revolution with global implications. Situational protests occurred in all armies, such as the effective takeover by British and Anzac troops of the Etaples camp in September 1917 or the demobilization riots among Canadian troops after the armistice.[55] Military collapse in part attributable to soldierly despair occurred in the Italian army at Caporetto in November 1917, the British Army in March 1918, and in the German and Habsburg armies in the fall of 1918. Open mutiny occurred in the Imperial Russian army in February 1917, in the French army in May and June 1917, and in the German navy in the fall of 1918.

Plainly, much more than simple war weariness or what John Keegan called "survivability" was involved.[56] The British, French, and Italian armies not only survived their crises but won the war. In the Russian case, to cite the most dramatic example, soldiers had enough fight left in them after the Revolutions of February and October 1917 to embark on a hideous civil war that would last until 1921. Even elements of the Habsburg forces continued the fight, in the improbable setting of prisoner-of-war camps in Russia. A Czech Legion was formed to fight the Bolsheviks while as many as 100,000 Hungarians found their way into the Red Army.[57]

But just how the microdramas and macrodramas of the last years of the war intersected is poorly understood by historians. The politics of these crises is best understood through thinking about politics as a discourse—a system of understanding linking institutions and identities. Politics is about politicians, legislatures, bureaucracies, and armies. But it is also about what Michel Foucault called "governmentality," or the art of governing. Foucault argued that the art of governing proceeds not just through governing *over* individual subjects, but *within* those subjects themselves.[58] Governmentality shapes the frameworks that determine choice and motivation—what it means, in short, to be a political individual. Governmentality operated in very different ways in the crises of 1917 in France and Russia. In France, mutiny occurred among and within citizens of a well-established republic. In Russia, mutiny occurred among subjects of the tsar. Revolution turned these subjects into citizen-soldiers virtually overnight, in a volatile and unpredictable situation. But in both the French and Russian cases, understanding how political discourse shaped the identities of the discontented soldiers is essential to understanding two very different outcomes.

In May and June 1917, in the wake of the failed offensive along the Chemin des Dames, constituent units of about one-half of the divisions in the French army refused at one point or another to take up positions in the front lines. Guy Pedroncini argued that the mutinies were "military" rather than political, and he placed General Philippe

Pétain at the center of their resolution.[59] Pétain, according to this explanation, restored "reason" to the French military effort through particular reforms in leave and food policies and, most important, through tacitly agreeing not to initiate any more general offensives until tanks and American reinforcements gave France an unquestionable military superiority.

My explanation, on the other hand, focused on the political identity of French soldiers.[60] I argued that by the time the French army experienced its crisis of military identity, who was leading the French high command really was not the point at all. Rather, the mutinies of 1917 were the culmination of a long process in which soldiers wrenched power from the formal command structure.[61] After the Chemin des Dames offensive, soldiers saw two militarily pointless options—attacking for largely symbolic gains, and murderous trench warfare from vulnerable positions. The moment of explicit defiance of command authority came most often at railway depots or other embarkation points. Groups of soldiers would refuse point blank to advance into the front lines and would hold antiwar demonstrations instead. Initially, and from Pétain down, the French high command chose not to confront the demonstrators directly. In many cases generals literally retreated to their tents, leaving formal command temporarily in abeyance. This was the moment at which the French army mutinies went beyond a relatively straightforward crisis of military survivability. At no point did the command structure have enough reliable troops at its disposition to repress the mutinies by force, even if it had chosen to. In the absence of external suasion, only internal suasion kept the mutinies from going further than they did.

The French army mutinies are best understood in the context of soldiers working out two paradoxical components of their identity as citizen-soldiers—direct democracy and representative government. Direct democracy authorized resistance and wide-ranging political expression—as it had in the many French revolutions since 1789. Certainly at the outset, soldiers wanted far more than Pétain's solution of drafting reforms in the conditions of daily life and waiting for the tanks and the Americans. Relatively mundane demands for better food and a fairer leave policy existed alongside demands for an immediate peace and for "liberty." Soldiers' demands were riddled with curious inconsistencies, such as the fact that immediate peace would have made a better leave policy irrelevant. There were also important elements of conservatism in what soldiers wanted out of the mutinies. Many soldiers claimed, for example, that their struggles paralleled those of the *midinettes,* the female textile workers striking in Paris and other large cities. But at the same time the soldiers sought to reassert traditional male roles as protectors and providers. They wanted immediate peace, as one soldier put it, "to feed our wives and children and to be able to give bread to the orphans."[62]

Yet the demands of the soldiers also showed the importance to them of representative government, which in the end authorized obedience to formal command authority just when no external force could have compelled them to do so. Soldiers demanded that their commanders tell their representatives in the Chambers of Deputies of their plight. "We want the deputies to know of our demonstrations," one soldier was reported to have said. "It is the only means we have at our disposition to make them understand that we want peace."[63] The significance of soldiers asserting their identities as citizens of the French Third Republic can scarcely be exaggerated. In doing so they affirmed the basic legitimacy of republican institutions and of the deputies representing them. They recognized the legitimacy of the sovereign power that put them in uniform as emanating, ultimately, from themselves. The Third Republic as a representative democracy existed in each of them and informed their very conception of what power and politics were all about. The Third Republic demarcated the boundaries of their political imagination.

The drama of direct democracy versus representative government played itself out over the issue of war aims, which figured prominently in the late stages of the mutinies. At one point a police spy was sent to ask mutinous soldiers from the Fifth Division what they wanted from the situation. They responded that they sought immediate peace and a negotiated settlement with the Germans. The French position, as the spy reported it, was to be the following: "They demand Alsace, Lorraine, and the maintenance of the status quo (no indemnity, no annexations)."[64] This was an extraordinary demand. They expected the Germans to give up not only most of northeastern France, which they had taken in 1914, but also the two provinces that they had taken in the Franco-Prussian War of 1870–71. Their continued acceptance of the war aims of their commanders and their political leaders meant that they had two options—return to the trenches or lose the war. This helps explain their response to the police spy when he asked what they would do if the Germans took advantage of the mutinies to attack. They responded in the language of Verdun: "*Les Boches ne passeront pas* (the Germans shall not pass)." Another soldier wrote that "if the Boches do not want to accept a peace corresponding to the sacrifices that we have made and satisfactory to our honor, we will push them out ourselves."[65]

In the end, after substantial mediation on the part of junior officers, soldiers once again accepted formal command authority. What followed involved a complex reconfiguration of the moral economy of power within the French army. Real concessions to the dialogical nature of command authority were masked by highly selective punishment of a group of soldiers designated (not always convincingly) as "leaders." The mutinies concluded as an anguished, conditional affirmation of Third Republic France and of the responsibilities of citizenship underpinning it. Principles of representative government restrained those of direct democracy. The very notion of republican citizenship, reaffirmed in the crisis situation of the mutinies, had perpetuated soldiers' participation in the war. Power, as mediated by the idea of citizenship, infiltrated soldiers' very ways of thinking about freedom and responsibility. Republican identity carried within it the means of its own internal coercion. It authorized obedience as well as mutiny.

The Russian soldiers of August 1914 brought with them, more or less directly from the countryside, two ancient and often conflicting images of authority.[66] Obedience in the tsar's army was based on a notion of immediate authority vested in the officer as the counterpart of the landowner. This authority was as irresistible as it was capricious; the soldier could only submit and hope for a better life later, most probably in the next world. Against this image of authority lay that of the tsar, the very good but very mysterious, the "little father" whose will was constantly thwarted by those exercising immediate authority. Over the course of the nineteenth century little change occurred through reformist efforts to motivate soldiers along "modern" lines by giving them an otherwise unobtainable civil status. In the Revolution of 1905–6 soldiers mutinied one day and repressed workers' strikes the next, depending on whichever ancient image of authority they thought the stronger. Imperial Russian soldiers entered the war unincorporated into any national community as Westerners understood it.

In Russia the Old Regime conception of the political self proved ill suited to a protracted and "total" war of nation-states. Casualty figures remain open to considerable dispute. But no one doubts that Russian casualties were the highest in absolute numbers—by 1917 some 5.5 million killed, wounded or captured.[67] Tsar Nicholas II made a bad situation worse in 1916 when he assumed personal command of his armies. In so doing he nailed the flag of his autocracy to the tottering mast of Russian military performance. The little father became very real and very fallible, as Nicholas undercut the mysticism so important to his own legitimacy. External suasion ceased to exist as the tsar's regime, and ultimately the state collapsed. The issue became putting into place the means of internal suasion.

Despite a generally deteriorating military situation, the Russian crisis of morale was not connected to any particular calamity on the battlefield. Rather, it was provoked by a subsistence crisis in the large cities of the interior. Nicholas precipitated the disintegration of his own authority at the end of February 1917 when he ordered garrison units to fire on the civilian population to end food riots. He could scarcely have chosen a more volatile situation or a less reliable instrument. Urban garrisons comprised two varieties of soldiers—recuperating wounded veterans and semi-trained recruits. Both could be counted on to have more immediate links to the suffering people in the interior than to those ordering them to shoot. The garrisons refused wholesale to fire on the crowds, provoking a crisis that led, in a matter of days, to the tsar's abdication.

As the Revolution spread to the front in the days and weeks that followed, some similarities to the French mutinies were striking.[68] Soldiers expressed the same anguished concern for their families and for a renewed connection to life beyond the war. Russian officers were treated more roughly than were the French, perhaps in part because they understood less acutely the limits on their power. But as in France, soldiers were more restive behind the front lines than in them. Generally speaking, Russian soldiers would hold their positions along the front so long as they were not ordered to attack.

But of course the differences between the Russian and French cases proved far more significant than the similarities. With the demise of the tsar's regime and the systemic question of authority within the army that followed, soldiers ceased to have a clear notion of to what or to whom they were loyal. Whoever could remobilize their military and civilian identities would stand a good chance of gaining power in Russia. Alexander Kerensky, the leader of the Provisional Government, was a superbly educated "European" Russian.

As such, he had in mind the image of the French armies of the Year II of the French Revolution. In 1793–94, the Revolution had called into being the most impressive military machine the world had ever seen. Kerensky tried to make history repeat itself by transforming the soldier of the tsar into the citizen-soldier of an emerging Russian republic in a matter of months. His effort collapsed for two main reasons.

First, an alternative source of authority emerged within the army more or less simultaneously with that of the Provisional Government—the soldiers' councils, more commonly known as soviets. The soviets institutionalized the negotiation of military authority. They dealt with matters as diverse as food distribution, military justice, and whether and how to take up positions in the front lines. In this sense, the soviets constituted something of an institutionalized mutiny. But as such, and paradoxically, the soviets began the inculcation of the idea that sovereignty existed within the individual. The Provisional Government did everything it could to circumvent and undermine the soviets, as a direct institutional challenge to itself.

Second, Kerensky badly overplayed a weak hand by ordering, incredibly, another offensive in June 1917, just as the French army mutinies were calming down. Pétain and his political masters in the Third Republic would not have dared order such an attack at the time, even though they very much encouraged the Russians to do so. In the summer of 1917, Kerensky placed far greater demands on his newborn citizen-soldiers than the French on theirs, on a far more uncertain basis. By the fall the Provisional Republic had gone the way of the tsar's regime.

Only the Bolsheviks, led by another superbly educated European Russian, V. I. Lenin, understood the delicate interplay between the microdramas of military authority and the macrodramas of keeping and holding state power. To the majority of Russian soldiers in 1917, loyalty meant mostly loyalty to home and village. Land and peace meant more to them than whether "Russia" lost the war. Indeed, by the summer of 1917, Russia ceased to have much coherence at all. The Russia of the tsar had been swept away, and no new Russia existed yet—at least not one responsive to their profoundly local concerns. The Bolsheviks understood that by delivering land and peace they could gain state power immediately. They could mobilize soldiers to resist a return of the Old Regime and so could consolidate that power. This happened during the civil war. Later the Bolsheviks could proceed to the design and construction of the new citizen and the new citizen-soldier.

Kerensky, ostensibly the Western-style democrat, failed to grasp the complexities of constructing an obedient citizen-soldier grounded in an ideology of popular sovereignty. This identity could not be conjured up overnight, at least not in a country as vast and rural as Russia. Ironically, the Bolsheviks had a far more sophisticated understanding of popular sovereignty as an instrument of governmentality. The key lay not in repressing or circumventing the soviets but in coopting them. For in the soviets lay the means of constructing a soldier who would not just resist the old source of authority but obey the new one. As Mark von Hagen has persuasively argued, the Bolshevik state and the Red Army constructed each other over the course of the 1920s through what he called "militarized socialism."[69] Soldiers even more than workers became the vanguard of the proletarian dictatorship. By the time Josef Stalin turned to the Red Army to make war on his real and imagined internal enemies, the Bolshevik citizen-soldiers had their cues thoroughly internalized.

Conclusion

What one generation of historians might see as "myth" another might see as narrative. Some myths and narratives are constructed

with explicit intent and self-justification and deserve to be dismantled—such as the mythology of German innocence in World War I
taken on by Holger Herwig.[70] But all history partakes of narrative
convention, and all underlying assumptions and intentions of historians at least bear examination. I began this chapter with the broad
propositions that all history is narrative and that narrative has to rest
on particular assumptions about individual identity. I argued that in
considering narrative and identity at the front in World War I both
modernists and postmodernists have generally followed a metanarrative of tragedy, which rests on a construction of the soldier as
victim. Modernists have seen the war as a tragic assault on the
rational and morally autonomous individual, while postmodernists
read the war as a historical episode when the power games of Western civilization showed themselves with unusual clarity. The narrative or metanarrative of tragedy and victimization achieved the status of myth, in part through appealing to otherwise divergent points
of view.

Yet I have also suggested that elements of postmodern theory can
be applied in more than one way. They can take apart as well as
affirm the metanarrative of soldier as victim. Historical reality to
a postmodernist is changeable by definition. That which is constructed can be constructed differently.[71] Considering narrative and
identity as negotiable in almost any historical context opens up
possibilities that scholars of World War I have only barely begun to
understand—the possibilities of history in the comic as opposed to
the tragic mode. Narrative and identity in the comic mode certainly
need not be humorous and need not even be triumphalist. In France,
veterans and citizen-soldiers failed to save the Third Republic in
1940, while in Russia the Bolshevik citizen-soldier became virtually
from birth an instrument of dictatorship. Yet posing some of the
issues raised by postmodern theory can illuminate some of the deepest questions of just what World War I was about and the long-term

effects that proceeded from it. But the first step, I would argue, involves giving up closure, in the sense of versions neatly wrapped up in advance of the stories that historians tell and the individuals caught up in and constituted through them.

NOTES

1. The subtitle of this essay is borrowed from a quite cranky but not entirely unfavorable review of my earlier work: John Keegan, "An Army Downs Tools: Mutiny in the First World War: Theory and the Poor Bloody Infantry," *Times Literary Supplement,* May 15, 1994, 3–4.

The leave for writing the original version this chapter was funded by a Fellowship for College Teachers from the National Endowment for the Humanities, a Mellon Fellowship from the National Humanities Center, and an Andrew Delaney Fellowship and Research Status appointment from Oberlin College. Revised versions were presented before the Intellectual History Colloquium at the University of Michigan at Ann Arbor in December 1994, and as the keynote lecture at the Multidisciplinary Conference on World War I, Fort Hays State University, Fort Hays, Kan., in April 1996. I am grateful to the sources of support and to those who attended the presentations of this piece.

2. This broad distinction relies on the fine and accessible study by Joyce Appleby, Margaret Jacobs, and Lynn Hunt, *Telling the Truth About History* (New York: W. W. Norton, 1994).

3. See Jean-François Lyotard, *The Postmodern Condition: A Report on Knowledge,* Theory and History of Literature, vol. 10 (Minneapolis: University of Minnesota Press, 1993 [originally published in French in 1979]), 34, 37. Hayden White has played the pivotal role in incorporating metanarrative into historical analysis, particularly in *Metahistory: The Historical Imagination in Nineteenth-Century Europe* (Baltimore: Johns Hopkins University Press, 1973), and *The Content of the Form: Narrative Discourse and Historical Representation* (Baltimore: Johns Hopkins University Press, 1987).

4. Modris Eksteins pursues this theme, particularly with regard to Germany. See Chapter 11.

5. This is very much the thesis of a 1996 television documentary made by PBS and the BBC, and of the companion volume of the same title. See Jay Winter and Blaine Baggett, *The Great War and the Shaping of the Twentieth Century* (New York: Penguin, 1996).

6. It should be noted that postmodernists tend to blanch at the term "victim" because of the unfortunate and often inaccurate connections made between postmodern theory and academic struggles in the United States over "political correctness." Happily, these struggles, which always generated more

heat than light, seem to be fading in significance. Most postmodernists would probably choose a term like "decentered self," meaning personal identity based in desire and a culturally produced illusion of wholeness rather than in reason.

So far as I know, there is no self-consciously postmodern general history of World War I. But a great deal of recent work on World War I partakes of various aspects of postmodern theory, including my own *Between Mutiny and Obedience: The Case of the French Fifth Infantry Division during World War I* (Princeton: Princeton University Press, 1994). Other examples include Mary Louise Roberts, *Civilization Without Sexes: Reconstructing Gender in Postwar France, 1917–1927* (Chicago: University of Chicago Press, 1994), and Daniel J. Sherman, *The Construction of Memory in Interwar France* (Chicago: University of Chicago Press, 2000). For a recent rumination on the cultural history of World War I as informed by postmodern theory, see Sherman, "Culture War?" *Radical History Review* 70 (1998): 149–55.

7. Northrop Frye, *Anatomy of Criticism: Four Essays* (Princeton: Princeton University Press, 1957), 207.

8. J. M. Barrie, *Peter Pan* (1911; reprint, New York: Signet, 1987), 101.

9. "1914," in Tim Cross, ed., *The Lost Voices of World War I: An International Anthology of Writers, Poets and Playwrights* (Iowa City: University of Iowa Press, 1989), 55.

10. Eric Leed, *No Man's Land: Combat and Identity in World War I* (Cambridge: Cambridge University Press, 1979), ch. 2.

11. See Modris Eksteins, *Rites of Spring: The Great War and the Birth of the Modern Age* (New York: Houghton Mifflin, 1989), ch. 1.

12. See Cross, *Lost Voices,* 80.

13. See Chapter 4.

14. See John Keegan, *The Face of Battle: A Study of Agincourt, Waterloo, and the Somme* (1976; reprint, New York: Penguin, 1978), 238.

15. See Smith, *Between Mutiny and Obedience,* 233.

16. A. J. P. Taylor, *The First World War: An Illustrated History* (London: Hamish Hamilton, 1963), 123.

17. Joseph Roth, *The Radetzky March,* trans. Eva Tucker and Geoffrey Dunlop (Woodstock, N.Y.: Overlook, 1983 [originally published in German in 1932]).

18. Elaine Showalter, *The Female Malady: Women, Madness, and English Culture, 1830–1980* (New York: Penguin, 1985), ch. 7. Showalter draws heavily on Leed, *No Man's Land,* ch. 5.

19. Showalter, *Female Malady,* 172.

20. See Leed, *No Man's Land,* 173–76.

21. In July 1917, Sassoon wrote a lengthy denunciation of the war to his commanding officer which ended up being read in Parliament and published in the *Times.* Through the massive intervention of his friend and fellow war writer Robert Graves, Sassoon was not court-martialed but sent to a mental hospital for officers at Craiglockhart in Scotland.

22. Showalter, *Female Malady,* 187.

23. The edition used here is *All Quiet on the Western Front,* trans. A. W. Green (New York: Ballantine, 1991).

24. See Michel Foucault, *Discipline and Punish: The Birth of the Prison,* trans. Alan Sheridan (New York: Vintage, 1979 [originally published in French in 1975]).

25. See ibid., part 3, ch. 1.

26. Remarque, *All Quiet,* 295.

27. See Marcus Paul Bullock, *The Violent Eye: Ernst Jünger's Visions and Revisions on the European Right* (Detroit: Wright State University Press, 1992), 22.

28. Quoted in Leed, *No Man's Land,* 153.

29. See Bruce M. Gudmundsson, *Stormtroop Tactics: Innovation in the German Army, 1914–1918* (New York: Praeger, 1989).

30. Quoted in Leed, *No Man's Land,* 158–59.

31. Winter and Baggett, *Great War,* 399.

32. Ibid., 409.

33. See Lyotard, *Postmodern Condition,* ch. 10.

34. Carolyn Walker Bynum, "In Praise of Fragments: History in the Comic Mode," in *Fragmentation and Redemption: Essays on Gender and the Human Body in Medieval Religion* (New York: Zone, 1991), 11–26; and Lynn Hunt, "Introduction: History, Culture, and Text," in *The New Cultural History* (Berkeley: University of California Press, 1989), 1–22.

35. For example, in *Fragmentation and Redemption* Bynum applies the comic mode to medieval Christian theologies of bodily mutilation and putrefaction.

36. Bynum, "In Praise of Fragments," 24.

37. The edition used here is *The Good Soldier Svejk,* trans. Cecil Parrott (London: Penguin, 1973).

38. Ibid., part 1, ch. 7.

39. On the Annales paradigm and its limitations, see Hunt, "Introduction." This section also expands on some of the arguments made in *Between Mutiny and Obedience,* ch. 10.

40. See particularly Jean-Jacques Becker, *1914: Comment les Français sont entrés dans la guerre* (Paris: Presse de la Fondation National des Sciences Politiques, 1977).

41. Guy Pedroncini, *Les Mutineries de 1917* (Paris: Presses Universitaires de France, 1967). I turn to my differences with Pedroncini below.

42. J. G. Fuller, *Troop Morale and Popular Culture in the British and Dominion Armies* (Oxford: Clarendon, 1990).

43. Tony Ashworth, *Trench Warfare, 1914–1918: The Live and Let Live System* (New York: Holmes & Meier, 1980).

44. In the end, it should be noted, Ashworth and the soldiers he describes succumb to the tragic narrative. He concluded that the command structure

found effective ways to ratchet up levels of violence in the front lines, mostly through increasing the density of weaponry and through raids. The objective was to provide incidents that would provoke a vicious circle of violence by inculcating a desire for revenge. He posits an essentially nonaggressive self of the soldier that in the end was defeated by the technologies of military power.

45. See Smith, *Between Mutiny and Obedience,* especially ch. 5.

46. Stéphane Audoin-Rouzeau and Annette Becker, "Violence et consentement: La 'culture de guerre' du premier conflit mondiale," in Jean-Pierre Rioux and Jean-François Sirinelli, eds., *Pour un Histoire culturelle* (Paris: Seuil, 1997), 252. All translations are my own unless otherwise noted.

47. See, for example, Jean-Jacques Becker, Jay M. Winter, Gerd Krumeich, Annette Becker, and Stéphane Audoin-Rouzeau, eds., *Guerres et Cultures, 1914–1918* (Paris: Armand Colin, 1994); and John Horne, ed., *State, Society, and Mobilization in Europe During the First World War* (Cambridge: Cambridge University Press, 1997).

48. Stéphane Audoin-Rouzeau, *Men at War, 1914–1918: National Sentiment and Trench Journalism in France During the First World War,* trans. Helen McPhail (Providence: Berg, 1992 [originally published in French in 1986]).

49. *Le Crapouillot,* February 1917, quoted in ibid., 87.

50. Annette Becker, *La Guerre et la foi: De la mort à la mémoire* (Paris: Armand Colin, 1994), 15.

51. J. Bellouard, *Le Chemin de croix de ceux qui sont restés* (1916), quoted in ibid., 32.

52. See Chapter 1.

53. For a recent reconsideration, see Jean-Jacques Becker, *1917: Année impossible* (Brussels: Editions Complexe, 1997).

54. Arno Mayer, *Political Origins of the New Diplomacy, 1917–1918* (New Haven: Yale University Press, 1959).

55. See Gloden Dallas and Douglas Gill, *The Unknown Army: Mutinies in The British Army in World War I* (London: Verso, 1985); and Desmond Morton, " 'Kicking and Complaining': Demobilization Riots in the Canadian Expeditionary Force, 1918–1919," *Canadian Historical Review* 41 (1980): 334–60.

56. This meant that a crisis was reached when enough casualties were incurred for soldiers to conclude that they were statistically unlikely to survive the war. See Keegan, "Army Downs Tools."

57. István Deák, *Beyond Nationalism: A Social and Political History of the Habsburg Officer Corps, 1848–1918* (New York: Oxford University Press, 1990), 198.

58. See Colin Gordon, "Government Rationality: An Introduction," and Michel Foucault, "Governmentality," in Graham Burchell, Colin Gordon, and Peter Miller, eds., *The Foucault Effect: Studies in Governmentality* (Chicago: University of Chicago Press, 1991), 1–51, 87–104.

59. See Pedroncini, *Les Mutineries de 1917.*

60. This section draws from Smith, *Between Mutiny and Obedience,* ch. 8, and two articles published after this book appeared. Both considered the French army as a whole. See "The French High Command and the Mutinies of the Spring of 1917," in *Facing Armageddon, 1914–1918: The War Experienced,* Peter Liddle and Hugh Cecil, eds. (London: Leo Cooper/Pen and Sword, 1996), 79–92; and "Remobilizing the Citizen-Soldier through the French Army Mutinies of 1917," in Horne, *State, Society, and Mobilization,* 144–59.

61. The term "soldiers" refers to those who were the object of command authority in the field, principally common soldiers, noncommissioned officers, and junior officers.

62. Quoted in Smith, *Between Mutiny and Obedience,* 188.

63. Quoted in ibid., 192.

64. Quoted in ibid., 194.

65. Quoted in ibid., 195.

66. This analysis relies on Elise Kimmeling Wirthschafter, *From Serf to Russian Soldier* (Princeton: Princeton University Press, 1990); and John Bushnell, *Mutiny amid Repression: Russian Soldiers in the Revolution of 1905–1906* (Bloomington: Indiana University Press, 1990).

67. Allan K. Wildman, *The End of the Russian Imperial Army: The Old Army and the Soldiers' Revolt (March–April 1917)* (Princeton: Princeton University Press, 1980), 95. My analysis relies on this volume and its sequel: *The End of the Russian Imperial Army: The Road to Soviet Power and Peace* (Princeton: Princeton University Press, 1987).

68. Of course, the French mutinies actually occurred some months later.

69. Mark von Hagen, *Soldiers in the Proletarian Dictatorship: The Red Army and the Soviet Socialist State, 1917–1930* (Ithaca: Cornell University Press, 1990).

70. See Chapter 10.

71. I have intentionally avoided the term "deconstructed." Deconstruction is a precise technique of textual analysis and the term is best used in that context.

CHAPTER 6

Mobilizing Economies for War

GERALD FELDMAN

In undertaking the task of discussing the economic mobilization of the great belligerents during the First World War, I could not help but remember that this was the subject of the first undergraduate seminar I taught at Berkeley in 1963. I had just finished my dissertation, which was to be published as *Army, Industry, and Labor in Germany, 1914–1918* three years later.[1] I emerged from my work, a genuine *Fachidiot* (that is, a specialist to the point of idiocy) who had forgotten most of what he had studied and who huddled insecurely in the scholarly trench that he had inhabited for the previous few years. The undergraduate seminar was an opportunity to capitalize on what I knew to excess and to move about more freely on the terrain with which I was familiar. I taught a seminar on the comparative domestic history of the First World War. Nevertheless, I do not want to treat my participation in this volume as yet another nostalgic journey. Instead, I see it as an opportunity to take stock of more than three decades' historical research and new perspectives— and, I hasten to add, of research and perspectives inevitably influenced by the momentous events of the recent past.

Let me begin by illustrating this point with one of the books I assigned my students (and myself) in 1963, Michael T. Florinsky's

End of the Russian Empire.[2] The 1931 book was the summary volume of the twelve-volume Russian Series of the Social and Economic History of the World War, published by the Carnegie Endowment for International Peace. This great project on the war, which had comparable series for the various combatant nations, remains one of the major and persistently underexploited sources on the war and its consequences. Florinsky's volume, which "endeavored to explain why and how the monarchy came to its doom and was replaced by a Communist dictatorship," was reprinted in 1961 in a paperback edition because, as Florinsky noted in his preface, "the place of the Soviet Union in world affairs being what it is, the subject of this book is perhaps even more timely today than it was when the volume was written."[3] When one reads Florinsky's description of Russia's mobilization and his conclusion, then perhaps yet a new edition would be timely:

> The source of the catastrophe which overcame the Empire may, undoubtedly, be traced far back in the history of the Russian people. As long as the country was not asked to make the supreme and heroic effort imposed upon it by the war, it managed to trail, and not without a certain degree of success, behind the other European countries along the road of economic development and progress. The Great War put the whole framework of the Empire to a severe test. The obsoleteness and the imperfections of its political, social, and economic structure could no longer be concealed and ignored. Following the example of England, France and Germany, who, reacting from the blows they were receiving, made superhuman efforts to meet the emergency, Russia, or rather her educated classes, tried to organize their country for the war; but their attempts were sporadic, uncoordinated, and almost pathetic in their helplessness.[4]

Russia's mobilization under the Communists for the Second World War and the Cold War were, of course, more impressive efforts, but the demise of the Soviet Union and the present condition of its successor states certainly suggest that Russia's socioeconomic problems and political structures have remained inadequate to the demand of her international requirements and aspirations and that there are powerful lines of continuity from tsarist Russia to the present.

As Florinsky's conclusion makes clear, however, the Russian Empire was a participant in rather than an outsider to processes of mobilization that profoundly tested the great European powers and eventually the United States. Whatever the variations among the combatant nations—I spell out below the more important of these—they all responded in analogous ways to the demands of war. The outcome of these responses, at both the national and international levels, produced profound transformations in every significant aspect of economic and social life. While it is difficult to spin out so massive a counterfactual as that of what would have happened had the First World War not occurred, it is certainly safe to say that the economic and financial growth of the United States, the globalization of international trade, changes in the relative balance and significance of industrial sectors, the expansion of welfare legislation, and collective bargaining would have gone forward in any case. The war made a difference to the way these processes took place and defined the conditions under which they occurred.

As I have argued elsewhere in a specific reference to Germany that can be generalized, the First World War was the great transformer through which the currents of history emerged with newly determined strengths and directions.[5] By this I do not mean, however, that the results were any more positive than what emerged from the transformers of Baron Frankenstein. For a very long time there was a strong tendency on the part of postwar critics, historians, and other academic analysts to see in the organization of the wartime economy and in its social tendencies the promise of a future economic order based on planning, rational organization, and the collaboration of social groups and the state, and to see the failures of the interwar period as social and economic consequences of the peace and efforts to restore the prewar order. Such criticisms mirrored the shattered hopes and expectations of such wartime planners and organizers as Walther Rathenau, Albert Thomas, and Etienne Clémentel, as well as the fantasies of socialist theorists like Rudolf Hilferding.

In my view, the time has come to shed such illusions and to recognize that the consequences of the peace were the consequences of the war, and that the same conditions that made it impossible to go back to the prewar period also made it impossible to go forward to the much happier reconstruction after the Second World War and to the promise of a reconstruction based on market capitalism and international cooperation that *may* be possible in Central and Eastern Europe now that the "real existing" Socialist systems have collapsed and the Cold War has ended. That is, economic mobilization in the First World War was not the potential prelude to an aborted new economic and social order but rather a massive disturbance and distortion of the promise held forth by the evolution of the international capitalist system prior to 1914.

Let us begin by recalling that economic mobilization was the nightmare that prewar soldiers and statesmen—leaving aside a few fanatics—refused to face. They were well aware of the profound dangers of a long war, and this was one of the roots of the short war illusion, as well as the belief of people like Norman Angell that modern industrial capitalism and major wars were incompatible.[6] Interestingly, it seems to have been Count von Schlieffen, the author of the famous plan that bears his name, who was most explicit in rejecting the possibility of long wars under modern conditions. He argued in 1909 that "such wars are impossible in an age when the existence of the nation depends on the uninterrupted continuation of commerce and industry. . . . A strategy of exhaustion cannot be conducted where the sustenance of millions requires the expenditure of billions."[7] There have been some recent arguments that

Schlieffen's successor, the younger Moltke, anticipated a long war and urged greater economic preparedness. With some prescience, Moltke removed the Netherlands from the neutral countries to be invaded so that Germany could receive some supplies from Dutch ports.[8] There is no evidence, however, that he or anybody else in a decision-making capacity in any of the future warring states demanded mobilization of the civilian economy.

Indeed, there was a studied effort to avoid facing the implications of a great international conflict, and it is no accident that the sphere in which significant preparatory measures did take place was the least transparent, the realm in which governmental authorities could most convincingly fool the public because they first had to fool themselves; namely, the realm of money and finances. As Barry Eichengreen has shown in his splendid book *Golden Fetters*,[9] the operation of the gold standard before 1914 was never as automatic, rule-driven, and London-controlled as some of its admirers had thought, and it is difficult to imagine that its functions would not have been modified and transformed over time. Nevertheless, the habits and practices of international cooperation in the monetary sphere insured its perpetuation so long as those who were cooperating did not decide to start killing one another instead. Furthermore, the prewar international monetary system was the linchpin holding together practices in international trade and domestic finance that, taken as an entirety, promoted commerce and required governments to live more or less within their means. The gold standard, in short, promoted a world of "trading states" as opposed to a world of states engaged in political and military rivalry.[10]

Unhappily, the atavistic tendencies in the international order proved stronger than the progressive ones. Even before the war, nations were upsetting their domestic finances in the armaments race, undermining their capacities for economic development and trade as well as violating the so-called rules of the game by hoarding gold and making preparations to suspend convertibility, artificially maintain exchange rates, and violate contracts and other financial obligations in the event of war.[11] One of the curiosities of the financial mobilization for war was that it almost invariably involved measures of what can only be called financial demobilization as well. The Russians provided a particularly stunning illustration of such financial demobilization by introducing prohibition even though the liquor monopoly was the government's chief source of revenue. The only liquidity that this reduced, of course, was that of the state treasury, which was compelled to produce masses of currency that, like the moonshine now concocted in millions of homes, resulted in diminishing satisfaction the more it was consumed.[12] If one leaves aside this peculiar dependence on liquor, however, Russia's financial methods were not all that much different from those of the continental powers that relied largely on domestic war loans rather than taxes to cover the increasing expenditure of war. Russia, like France, did have access to loans from its wealthier allies, first Britain and then the United States, but the bulk of the costs were covered by war bond issues and the printing press. Austria-Hungary, too, was able to borrow from Germany to some extent, but Germany was unable to borrow from anyone and became the most notorious case of a major country that chose to finance the war by domestic war loans rather than taxation.[13]

The war bond drives in Germany and elsewhere constitute an important and insufficiently examined aspect of domestic mobilization for the war, especially from the vantage point of propaganda. But again I emphasize the peculiar limits of the financial mobilization and the profound implications of the financial costs of the war. Both the Germans and the French were notoriously unwilling to tax their citizens, and they effectively promised to cover the costs of the war by winning it and making the enemy pay without ever explaining how indemnities or reparations were to be paid if, as both the allies and the Central Powers planned to do by 1917, one were at the same time fighting an economic war after the war with one's former enemies. The British were perhaps most successful in financing their war costs with taxation, and, as Theodore Balderston has correctly argued, the British, unlike the Germans, had a banking community used to holding government debt and willing to do so.[14] This did not mean, however, that the propertied classes in Britain or anywhere else were willing to accept a continuation of those wartime taxes on profits and income. Financial mobilization, such as it was, took place in an environment of a national emergency that was expected to end with the war, but also in an environment where fiscal discipline had been lost, where businessmen anticipated high expenses in converting back to peacetime production and in restoring their trading positions—a matter that is taken altogether too lightly by socially minded historians—and where the lower classes had developed expectations that took very little account of the need to restore the value of currencies or to reconstruct the national and international economies. As Barry Eichengreen has put the problem:

> The war upset understandings regarding the burden of taxes and the distribution of income. Following the armistice, the wealthy demanded that new income taxes be eliminated and that preexisting ones be rolled back to prewar levels; representatives of labor, in contrast, demanded capital levies to eliminate the windfall profits and capital gains reaped by the owners and operators of war-related industries. Any attempt to restore the prewar fiscal system was complicated by permanent new demands on the government finances; a land fit for heroes required the provision of war pensions, medical care, unemployment benefits, and housing subsidies. Additional revenues had to be found. The question was whether they should be raised along prewar lines or through the retention of wartime expedients. This was the single most contentious issue postwar governments would face.[15]

It would have to be done, however, in the context of a revolution in international financial relations caused by interallied debts and compounded by reparations, depreciated currencies and inflation, the rise to creditor status of the United States, a nation in no way experienced in acting as an international creditor and as a lender of last resort with a poor idea of what international economic cooperation entailed. Schlieffen and Norman Angell may have been wrong in thinking that advanced industrial societies were incapable of fighting long wars, but they were right in thinking that they could not really afford them. With this in mind, let me turn from the financial mobilization that, as I have tried to show, was combined with a demobilization of the traditional financial and fiscal virtues of the prewar gold standard system, to the mobilizations of the so-called real economy.

There are two aspects of the mobilization of the real economy that are interconnected but that nevertheless are usefully analyzed separately. One of these is the mobilization of the industrial economy for war production. The other is the problem of provisioning and of welfare in wartime—that is, of meeting the basic necessities of life and grappling with maintaining the living standards for the civilian population. For a variety of reasons, the least of which being that Germany is the country of my greatest expertise, I think it helpful to view Germany as ideal-typical of the problems in both areas. As a blockaded nation and the most advanced industrial state in Europe, Germany experienced provisioning difficulties and the need for raw materials control very early in the war and developed organizational structures that became a model for other warring nations. At the same time, Germany exhibited conflicts over provisioning controls that were to have analogues elsewhere. Similarly, the issues and processes involved in Germany's relatively slow transition to "total mobilization" received more explicit articulation than their counterparts elsewhere. In part this was because Germany was a highly organized society with a well-developed civilian and military bureaucracy, strong employer and business organizations, large trade unions, and significant corporatist traditions. At the same time, imperial Germany was an odd mix of liberalism and authoritarianism, a constitutional state with growing tendencies toward parliamentarism, as well as a powerful opposition to political and social liberalization. It had a tradition of self-administration by economic interest groups that rested on a combination of liberal economic principles and expectations of state support and encouragement of key economic actors. It possessed a system of social welfare that combined government intervention with organized participation from below. Germany was a nation that far more than any other in Europe had made the most of the prewar international economic order, and its prosperity was most vulnerable to its upset. At the same time, however, it was the nation whose military and foreign policy had done most to destabilize international relations. Economic mobilization threatened all of the delicate balances on which the Second Empire and its achievements rested, and it is thus not surprising that many of the issues involved in economic mobilization were so openly expressed in the German case.

The resistance of the civilian and military bureaucracy to economic and social mobilization for war in Germany, therefore, is not to be understood as a sign of retardation, but rather as an instinctive system-preserving response to the dangers such mobilization presented. Initiatives, therefore, necessarily came from outside the bureaucracy. The most famous of these was the proposal of Walter Rathenau and Wichard Von Moellendorff for the creation of the Raw Materials Section of the Prussian War Ministry, in which industrial self-government would be employed to procure and distribute scarce raw materials in accordance with priorities defined by the military authorities.[16] This organizational model was to be widely emulated by other combatant nations, including the United States, and Rathenau and Moellendorff saw it as a prototype for the reorganization of the economy in peacetime. It is important to recognize, however, that the vast majority of German businessmen showed little enthusiasm for such ideas. They swallowed them because of wartime necessities but sharply opposed their perpetuation with increasing vehemence throughout the war. The proponents of war socialism à la Rathenau and Moellendorff were seldom found in the business community but rather among young technocrats, scientists, and some Socialists who grasped at the opportunity to give their ideals some content for a change.

It was to be two years, however, before the technocrats were to have another go at organizing the war economy. The Prussian War Ministry, which was responsible for the economic mobilization, pursued an extremely conservative course despite the growing demand for war production and the need to exempt skilled workers and reclaim workers from the front. Indeed, liberal Britain was to take the lead in the organizational effort by creating the Munitions Ministry in 1915. Appearances, however, can deceive. The German army was a conscript army, and although the War Ministry conscripted too many workers who were needed on the home front because the war was expected to be short, it was a mistake that the ministry could correct. In Britain the workers marched off voluntarily, and it was only after conscription was introduced in 1916 that one could move toward a coordinated manpower policy. What the Prussian War Ministry did seek to do, and what ultimately proved impossible, was to control the financial, economic, and social consequences of the unexpectedly long war for as long as possible. Instead of a military-industrial complex, therefore, there was military-industrial tension, the War Ministry seeking to prevent an excessive number of exemptions from military service and returns from the front, to reduce strains on the economy and contain costs by moderating demands and limiting profits, and to maintain morale by preventing the employers from exploiting their workers and encouraging mediation and arbitration through joint worker-employer committees and use of trade union personnel and good offices to reduce conflict and control turnover. This moderate policy had the support of Germany's civilian leaders, who were well aware of the sociopolitical dangers of what was to become known as total war.[17]

The great battles of matériel on the Somme in the summer of 1916, and the appointment of the radical militarist Erich Ludendorff and his fanatical adviser Major (later Lieutenant Colonel) Max Bauer to the supreme command, ended this moderation. These events introduced the full-scale economic mobilization influenced and organized by industrialists eager to make full use of plant facilities and hungry for manpower; military bullies wanting to do away with what they saw as bureaucratic *Schlamperei;* and technocratic dreamers, like Moellendorff, who thought that the crisis could be used to realize their programs for economic rationalization and the creation of a new economic order based on industrial self-government and state tutelage. The results were, first, a munitions scheme (the Hindenburg Program) whose guiding principle was excess and which threw the economy into chaos by creating coal shortages and transportation bottlenecks and vastly increasing the inflation; second, a reorganization of the management of the war economy through the creation of the War Office, which was led by well-meaning and able people but in the end worsened the bureaucratic problems; and, finally, the Auxiliary Service Law, which was intended to mobilize the population for the war effort and to control labor turnover but which actually was used by special interest groups to protect war profiteering and wage increases, promoting rather than discouraging turnover. Indeed, the Auxiliary Service Law has often been regarded as the magna carta of organized labor in Germany, which was surely not the intention of the Supreme Command or the industrialists. Interestingly enough, women were excluded from the law despite the wishes of the Supreme Command because the civilian authorities argued, quite correctly, that those capable of being employed were already employed and that they had shifted into the war industries.

The reasons for the failure of the Supreme Command and of industrialists to have their way, and for labor's success, are fairly obvious. In the absence of a totalitarian dictatorship it is impossible to undertake a mobilization of the civilian population without providing compensation in the form of special privileges, increased rights, and promises for the future. This was especially the case in Germany during World War I, when Socialist support of the war effort could not go without recognition and when the blockade created food and clothing shortages that heightened the dissatisfaction as well as the claims and demands of the labor force. The management and mismanagement of these provisioning problems had profound social consequences. The entire system of production, price, and distribution regulations built up during the first two years of the war and collectively known as the *Zwangswirtschaft*, or controlled economy, was designed to favor the urban working classes over the farmers and retailers. The latter groups bore the brunt of what was described as "consumer socialism," a system of endless regulations, confiscations, judicial proceedings, fines, and even imprisonment. Since the government had always claimed to support the so-called *Mittelstand* of farmers, retailers, and craftsmen, their sudden decline and fall was all the more galling.

Yet the system did not really work—first, because the food shortage was an absolute one, and second, because excess regulation and insufficient price incentives promoted what we have since learned they always promote: black marketeering and inflation. The result was a genuine criminalization of German society, as well as the nurturing of deep resentments between city and country, between workers and farmers, between middle class and workers, and between middle class and upper class. By late 1917 economic regulation and mobilization had called forth a gigantic revulsion in large segments of German society. Industrialists, merchants, craftsmen, and farmers were united in common hostility toward wartime controls and actually organized public meetings and demonstrations against their projected perpetuation in peacetime. At the same time, the breakdown of the provisioning system had a disillusioning effect on the working class as well, and promoted a loss of faith in the bureaucracy. These problems, along with war weariness, were responsible for the wave of strikes in 1917–18. If the German people held out, it likely was because they were misinformed about the military situation and continued to believe in the possibility of military victory.

At the same time, general disgust with the bureaucracy and a loss of confidence in the authorities paved the way for an inflation-greased alliance between the forces of organized industry and labor at the end of the war.

So much for the German "model." How does it compare with that of the other warring nations? The question of provisioning is the one most easily dealt with, and it is probably the most important in determining the relative success or failure of economic mobilization. The management of the Austrian food supply was analogous to the German system in both its organization and results. While theoretically the Austro-Hungarian monarchy should have been better provisioned than its ally, the Hungarians refused to supply their partner, and enemy occupation of other grain areas, conscription, and the requisition of horses and fodder severely reduced production and supply. Austria's increasing uselessness as an ally and its regime's interest in a separate peace certainly have much to do with this situation.[18] Failures of organization and mounting tensions between city and country also affected the Russian food supply and general provisioning situation, but the context was a somewhat different one. As in Germany and Austria, the Russians sought to concentrate the economic management of the war effort by setting up special councils in the summer of 1915 for national defense, transport, fuel, and food supply. There does appear to have been enough food in production, and the peasants initially prospered from the war insofar as the massive conscription of peasants permitted them to survive it. In contrast to the Central Powers, it was the army that suffered deprivation, and the problems of provisioning were above all a reflection of Russian industrial backwardness, an inadequate transportation system, an absence of sufficient manufactured goods to supply the rural population, and a peasantry increasingly unwilling to accept paper money for its produce and prepared to retreat into sullen self-sufficiency and resentment toward other social classes.[19]

This sketchy survey of the provisioning problems of Central and Eastern Europe only highlights the great advantages enjoyed by the allies. The most extreme example of this, as Jay Winter has shown us, was Great Britain, which enjoyed access to food supplies from abroad and which used price and wage incentives to increase production at home. It is remarkable that rationing was not introduced until 1918. If the supply of food diminished and the composition of diets changed and—as difficult as this is to imagine in the case of English food—became less tasty, there does seem to have been a high coordination between labor mobilization and provisioning in Britain. The recruitment of previously lower paid workers into the war industries to replace the skilled workers who had gone off to war, and the willingness of the government to let wages keep up with inflation, meant a general increase in living standards. Inflation in Germany raised the incomes of the lower paid groups but lowered the living standards of everyone, but this seems not to have been the case in Britain. Provisioning was indeed the great failure of the German war economy when compared to the British economy, and while I am not certain I would go as far as Winter does in suggesting that "the outcome of the war may well have been reversed" if the Germans had enjoyed such success, I would certainly agree that there was "much greater deprivation, stress, and despair as well as deteriorating standards of health among a German population which paid the price British civilians never had to pay for their country's war effort."[20] France, too, was greatly advantaged when compared to Germany, thanks to its agricultural base and access to imports. Once again rationing did not even begin until 1917, and it was not generalized until 1918, when price incentives were given to the farmers, who apparently did quite well out of the war. While the "war profiteering" of the farmers produced resentment in both Britain and France, especially when there were brief shortages or when one had to queue up, the hostility between city and country that existed in Central and Eastern Europe was an experience that the Western allies were spared.[21]

What all this suggests is that access to food and to a reasonably liberal system of provisioning was a powerful advantage enjoyed by the Western allies and probably was more decisive than was economic mobilization of the more dirigiste kind. Nevertheless, the production of weapons and munitions was no incidental matter, and one must also ask how typical was the German model among the warring states.

Successful pursuance of the war effort seemed to depend in part on the organization and collaboration, voluntary or imposed, of the forces of industry and labor. It was a measure of Russia's backwardness but also of its prewar movement toward greater economic modernity that liberal-minded industrialists took the initiative to establish war industries committees in the summer of 1915 and even sought to enlist the collaboration and participation of labor. In May 1916 labor representatives were actually elected to twenty regional and ninety-eight district committees, despite the ferocious opposition of the Bolsheviks. Unhappily, the negative collaboration of the Bolsheviks and the reactionary regime that took power later in 1916 proved more powerful than the nascent positive collaboration between industry and labor; the labor representatives were arrested at the beginning of 1917, and, if the tsarina had her way, the businessmen on the war industries committees would have been arrested also.[22]

Italy is a particularly interesting example of parallels despite the profound developmental differences among the countries involved. Italy was a late-developing nation, and its mobilization, while rapid once the country entered the war, was strongly influenced by foreign models, above all the British War Ministry. In its practice, however, the Italian model was closest to Austria in its extraordinary repressiveness. On the one hand, the Italian Socialists opposed the war effort, so that it was impossible to speak of a political truce in the Italian case. On the other hand, the employers were eager to keep labor under strict control. As a result, the MI, or industrial mobilization agency set up at the beginning of the war, was based on the militarization of the industrial economy. Effectively, the Italian workers were treated as forced labor, denied the right to strike, and subjected to military discipline. As in Germany and Austria, the administration of the industrial mobilization was in the hands of the military, in this case, General Alfredo Dallolio. But in contrast with the Prussian War Ministry prior to the Hindenburg Program and the War Office afterward, the MI, like its Austrian counterparts, took a fundamentally anti-labor stance in its early days. The arbitration system over which it presided excluded labor representatives. By late 1916, however, Dallolio, like his counterparts in Germany (including General Wilhelm Groener), came to the conclusion that industrial peace could not be maintained by repression. Much to the aggravation of the industrialists and the General Staff, he began to mandate the improvement of working conditions as well as to encourage wage increases to meet inflationary conditions by urging the employers "to concede of your own free will, before you are forced to."[23] Increasingly, representatives of trade unions were used to control the inflationary situation and the discontent, especially after the disaster at Caporetto. The military sought to make a sharp distinction between "economic" and "political" strikes, but in a very real sense it was an artificial one, because the fundamental aim of strikes was to force the government to impose concessions on the employers. In the end both labor and industry looked to the state to protect their interests and claims rather than trying to seek an escape from state controls through collaboration with one another. What the Italian historian Giovanni Procacci has termed "corporative social fragmentation"[24] was an outcome of the war economy. It was very different from the corporatist collaboration that grew out of the war economy in Germany and that characterized the wartime economies of England, to a greater degree, and of France, to a lesser degree.

In contrast to Germany, Austria, Italy, and Russia, the wartime economic mobilizations of England, France, and the United States were in the hands of civilian authorities, and all three countries benefited at the crucial period of the war from the leadership of heads of state who enjoyed popular mandates and had democratic credentials. When the going got rough, harsh measures, especially against labor, had democratic legitimacy and were always softened by wage concessions to labor and the involvement—and, therefore, the implication—of the trade unions in the war effort. The concessions to labor were especially important in England, where trade union rights were well established and where work-rule violations through the dilution of the labor force required compensation and promises to a higher degree than in France, where the unions were weaker. In the last analysis, however, economic mobilization under democratic auspices was more productive of illusions about the future than of real change in the social order. Albert Thomas's policies, as Gerd Hardach has convincingly argued, left industrialist profits intact, while his rhetoric about the future of war socialism and his programs for future economic controls only increased industry's desire to return to prewar conditions. The British situation was more ambiguous, since Lloyd George never abandoned his reformist past and since some businessmen, like Sir Alfred Mond, were interested in collaborationism. Nevertheless, the urge to return to prewar conditions remained strong among British industrialists, and the condition of the pound and the power of the city weighed on the entire British establishment. Here, as elsewhere, the growing concern with demobilization in 1917–18 was increasingly characterized by a thirst for decontrol rather than for a permanent installation of state-run corporatism or even societal corporatism based on voluntary collaboration of interest groups. From this perspective, American "exceptionalism" in the realm of economic mobilization—that is, its reliance on ad hoc, informal, temporary, and limited agencies and instrumentalities—may be less exceptional than it seems. It reflected the advantages of distance, rich resources, and limited involvement, the luxury of a nation that could enter the war late and abandon responsibility for its consequences early.[25]

In the end, therefore, what now seems most interesting about the mobilization for war between 1914 and 1918 are not its modalities but rather its consequences and trajectories.[26] Thus considered, much of the romance is gone. The financial mobilization, such as it was, destroyed prewar arrangements and left behind inflation and destabilization, which at once paved the way for the depression and for its mismanagement. The controlled economy in Eastern and Central Europe deepened urban-rural tensions, alienated farmers and the lower middle class, discredited the state, nurtured black marketeering, became identified with Socialism, lived on in various forms in the practices of the Socialist-command economies that have recently collapsed, and continue to live on in the pollution and criminality they have left behind. The future of the controlled economy, in short, is to be found in the *Mangelwirtschaft,* the economy of consumer shortage from which various European nations have suffered in this century. The legacy of the wartime mobilization was important in influencing the economic mobilizations of the Second World War, but this was not what war socialism enthusiasts were dreaming about. Rathenau's and Moellendorff's ideas seem to have influenced Lenin as Soviet Russia moved toward the NEP, but this is not much of a recommendation, any more than is the fact that Albert Speer was influenced by them as well. Mussolini brought back Dallolio in 1923 when he established his Board of Civilian Mobilization, and the Fascist Labour Charter of 1926 was inspired by wartime compulsory arbitration and Mussolini's approval of the experience. The more voluntary corporatist arrangements entered into after the First World War were often undertaken in rejection of the experiences of the war economy, and they all failed anyway. In short, I see little continuity or positive influence from the wartime mobilizations, and I seriously question even their positive potential. I would conclude, therefore, that it was not the experience of the First World War economic mobilizations but rather the experience of the Great Depression that inspired the social and economic reforms and international cooperation of the post-1945 period.

NOTES

1. Gerald D. Feldman, *Army, Industry and Labor in Germany, 1914–1918* (Princeton, 1966; reprinted, New York: Berg, 1992).

2. Michael T. Florinsky, *The End of the Russian Empire* (1931; 2nd ed., New York: Collier, 1961).

3. Ibid., vi.

4. Ibid., 246–47.

5. Gerald D. Feldman, *The Great Disorder: Economics, Politics, and Society in the German Inflation, 1914–1924* (Oxford, 1993), 25.

6. Norman Angell, *The Great Illusion* (London, 1910).

7. Reichsarchiv, *Der Weltkrieg 1914–1918. Kriegsrüstung und Kriegswirtschaft* (Berlin, 1930), 328.

8. The argument that key members of the German General Staff were conscious that the war would be a long one has been made by Stig Förster. See the newspaper reports, "Mit Hurra und vollem Bewußtsein in die Katastrophe: Der Erste Weltkrieg und das Kriegsbild des deutschen Generalstabs," *Frankfurter Rundschau*, September 8, 1994. I do not find that the evidence presented really refutes the idea of a "short war illusion."

9. Barry Eichengreen, *Golden Fetters: The Gold Standard and the Great Depression, 1919–1939* (Oxford, 1991).

10. Richard Rosecrance, *The Rise of the Trading State: Commerce and Conquest in the Modern World* (New York, 1985).

11. Eichengreen, *Golden Fetters*, 67–74.

12. Florinsky, *End of the Russian Empire*, 41–47.

13. For a brief introduction to war finance in the various countries, see Gerd Hardach, *The First World War, 1914–1918* (Berkeley, 1977), ch. 6. For a detailed account of the German system, see Feldman, *Great Disorder*, ch. 1.

14. Theo Balderston, "War Finance and Inflation in Britain and Germany, 1914–1918," *Economic History Review* 41 (1989): 222–44.

15. Eichengreen, *Golden Fetters*, 77–78.

16. Feldman, *Army*, 46–55.

17. Ibid., chs. 2–4 for this discussion, and Feldman, *Great Disorder*, ch. 2.

18. Hardach, *First World War*, 112–23. On the Austro-Hungarian war economy, see Robert J. Wegs, *Die österreichische Kriegswirtschaft 1914–1918* (Vienna, 1979).

19. Florinsky, *End of the Russian Empire*, 35–37, 117–18.

20. J. M. Winter, *The Great War and the British People* (London, 1985), 245.

21. Jean-Jacques Becker, *The Great War and the French People* (New York, 1985), especially 217–31.

22. Florinsky, *End of the Russian Empire*, 127–33.

23. Giovanni Procacci, "State Coercion and Worker Solidarity in Italy (1915–1918): The Moral and Political Content of Social Unrest," and Luigi Tomassini, "Industrial Mobilization and State Intervention in Italy in the First World War: Effects on Labor Unrest," Leopold Haimson and Giulio Sapelli, eds., *Strikes, Social Conflict and the First World War: An International Perspective* (Milan, 1992), 145–77, 179–211, quote on p. 157.

24. Ibid., 177.

25. On Britain, see Keith Middlemas, *Politics in Industrial Society: The Experience of the British System Since 1911* (London, 1979), chs. 3–5, and Noel Whiteside, "Concession, Coercion or Cooperation? State Policy and Industrial Unrest in Britain, 1916–1920," in Haimson and Sapelli, *Strikes, Social Conflict and the First World War*, 107–21. On France, see especially Gerd Hardach, "Industrial Mobilization in 1914–1918: Production, Planning and Ideology," and

Alain Hennebicque, "Albert Thomas and the War Industries," in Patrick Fridenson, ed., *The French Home Front, 1914–1918* (Providence, 1992), 57–132. On the United States, see David M. Kennedy, "American Political Culture in a Time of Crisis: Mobilization in World War I," in Hans Jürgen Schröder, ed., *Confrontation and Cooperation: Germany and the United States in the Era of World War I, 1900–1924* [Germany and the United States of America, Krefeld Historical Symposia, vol. 2] (Providence, 1993), 213–28.

26. For a fuller development of these arguments for the German case, see Gerald D. Feldman, "Der deutsche organisierte Kapitalismus während der Kriegs- und Inflationsjahre 1914–1923," in *Vom Weltkrieg zur Weltwirtschaftskrise. Studien zur deutschen Wirtschchafts- und Sozial-geschichte 1914–1932* [Kritische Studien zur Geschichtswissenschaft, vol. 60] (Göttingen, 1984), 36–54, and "War Economy and Controlled Economy: The Discrediting of 'Socialism' in Germany During the First World War," in Schröder, *Confrontation and Cooperation*, 229–52. For a comparative discussion, see Gerald D. Feldman, "Die Demobilmachung und die Sozialordnung der Zwischenkriegszeit in Europa," *Geschichte und Gesellschaft* 9, no. 2 (1983): 156–77.

CHAPTER 7

Labor and Labor Movements in World War I

JOHN HORNE

World War I occupies a place apart in the history of labor. Site of the defining revolution of the twentieth century, source of the great socialist schism, it has generated charged historiographies in the competing traditions of the left. Many of the issues that feature in those histories remain central—such as the collapse of the Second International, socialist "pacifism," industrial protest, the two Russian revolutions in 1917, and revolutionary potential elsewhere. Yet it is only recently, thanks to a generation of detailed and less partisan studies of these and other questions, that it has become possible to reintegrate labor into the history of the war. Even so, many studies remain more concerned with labor than with the war, and few are comparative or transnational in scope. The challenge remains to rethink this history in terms of the war. In this chapter I suggest, in light of this newer scholarship, how three key features of World War I affected labor (understood as the working classes as well as organized labor and socialism), and how labor's responses in turn shaped the war. They are the outbreak of war; the industrial war; and national mobilization for what became a prolonged war of attrition. Space limits the discussion to the principal European countries.

The Trauma of 1914

Conventionally, August 1914 has been seen as a moment of labor disarray. Chauvinist crowds demonstrating on the boulevards of European cities signaled the triumph of nation over class. The failure of the Second International to avert the war, along with socialist support for (and sometimes participation in) governments of national unity, symbolized the bankruptcy of prewar internationalism and even the "treason" of socialist leaderships. There are good reasons to stress the significance of working class and socialist responses to the outbreak of war, but a closer look lessens the emphasis on rupture and suggests longer-term, structural explanations.

Working-class involvement in the national solidarity generated by the outbreak of war is explained by (among other things) the still limited support for labor and socialist organizations before 1914. Even in Germany, where the Social Democratic Party (SPD) had become the largest party and a truly massive force with over a million members and a third of the popular vote, many workers had other political and trade union allegiances. This was truer still of countries, such as France and Britain, with powerful nonsocialist political traditions appealing to artisans and industrial workers and, in the French case, a much weaker trade unionism. In a different way, the illegality of most labor and socialist organizations in an authoritarian late-industrializer like Russia also reduced opposition to the war.[1] Yet the evidence that workers participated in a frenzy of chauvinism is thin. In both the French and German cases, detailed research points to a public mood of resignation or even resolve, rather than enthusiasm.[2] In Russia, weaker impulses of national cohesion limited the potential for popular mobilization.[3] Cheering crowds certainly gathered, but they were less representative, and less working class, than they once seemed.

Nineteen-fourteen as a moment, therefore, points to the relative integration of the working classes into the nation without, for all that, dissolving the distinctive labor cultures and organizations that had become a feature of many European societies. But assessing just how indicative it was of longer-term trends is complex. One school of thought has argued for the growing "nationalization" of European working classes. Influenced by earlier studies of organized labor, especially of the paradoxical integration of the SPD into Wilhelmine Germany, they hold that a series of developments (from national capital accumulation to primary education, suffrage and social welfare) combined to shape the self-definition and institutional articulation of working-class identities within national parameters before 1914. Where these processes were most developed, in the more "advanced" countries of Central and Western Europe, the national adhesion of the working class was greatest.[4]

Such a view has the merit of stressing the shaping force of the political context and the growing sense of national "community" within which labor evolved in this period.[5] Yet other historians have noted that precisely these societies were also marked by new forms of working-class organization and militancy in the early twentieth century, as well as by a surge of industrial radicalism in the half decade before the war. This last was the case in Germany and Britain (less so in France) as much as in Italy and Russia. Even here, it has been argued, national and political forms of mediation significantly helped control and defuse labor radicalism in those societies with a more "nationalized" working class (Britain and Germany), whereas in Russia and Italy the outcome was unmediated, overtly political conflict and state repression.[6] Still, the point stands that even in the most developed industrial societies the tendency to political incorporation faced powerful contrary processes of class conflict and labor militancy. The latter were driven by a variety of economic and social developments. These included price rises, changing industrial organization as the workshop gave way to the factory with its restructured skilled and semi-skilled workforce (especially in engineering), and growing industrial cities and suburbs that reinforced class identity and solidarity.[7]

The process of "nationalization" might therefore be thought of as one that was certainly operative before the war, but along a spectrum from relatively mature and integrated national polities (Britain, France, Germany) to extremely fragile states and nations, such as those (in different ways) of Italy, Russia, and Austria-Hungary. It was also under strain from potentially fragmentary forms of class tension. Peaking in 1914 with the mobilization for war, nationalization channeled a complex process of working-class formation that, in other circumstances, stood to undermine it by reinforcing class antagonisms.

Explanations of the "collapse" of the Second International parallel this analysis. The contradiction between national allegiance and socialist internationalism that proved fatal in 1914 was built into the Second International from the outset. Unlike its predecessor, the new body founded in 1889 was a federation of virtually autonomous national parties, each of which reflected the national circumstances of its own development. This is not to deny the profoundly internationalist culture of the Second International, shaped above all by the Marxism of the SPD and its chief philosopher-theorist, Karl Kautsky, nor its belief in socialist unity. The International aspired to social transformation (symbolized by the ideal of "revolution") through a vision of proletarian dominance forged by inexorable historical forces. Reducing the cataclysms of Marxist class theory to abstractions, it was infused with an optimistic rationalism that turned socialism into the most advanced expression of "civilization."

With rising international tension from 1905, this vocation of moral custodianship made the prevention of war—seen as a product of the capitalist order that socialism was destined to replace—a high priority of the International. Yet the incorporation of the socialist parties into very different national political cultures and systems provoked bitter disagreements over the means to be used. This was partly because the parties made varying assessments of what they stood to lose through the different tactics proposed. The SPD, for example, shied away from any commitment to an automatic general strike against war that might risk its suppression and jeopardize the considerable gains already made. But it was also because the logic of national incorporation meant that not all wars conformed to class criteria, as debates over the new theories of "imperialism" indicated. An older logic of justifiable wars of national defense, or even national liberation, in order to safeguard the genesis and growth of progressive movements lay just beneath the surface. Occasionally it emerged explicitly, as in *The New Army,* the 1910 book by the French socialist Jean Jaurès, which sought to reconcile international proletarian action to prevent capitalist and colonial wars with the right of the working class to national self-defense, a right rooted in the French republican tradition.

Behind the facade of socialist unity, therefore, the Second International was riven by the politics of national difference. Although this has long been evident in the congresses of the International, the depth of the divisions in its bureaucracy, especially between French and German socialists, has only emerged more recently.[8] The divisions were even more apparent in the emergence of the parallel International Federation of Trade Unions, in which the dominant Germans, with their rigid separation of industrial and political questions, systematically blocked the attempt by the French General Confederation of Labor (CGT) to use industrial tactics inspired by revolutionary syndicalism against the threat of war.[9]

No less significantly, a younger, more radical generation of leaders (Lenin, Trotsky, Liebknecht, Rosa Luxemburg) contested the culture and bureaucracy of the Second International. They drew on the new forms of labor militancy noted above for an activist reinterpretation of the revolutionary potential of the period. This is seen most clearly in Trotsky's theorizing of the soviets and Luxemburg's advocacy of the revolutionary mass strike, both following the 1905 Russian revolution. But the tension also perhaps reflected in socialist circles something of the wider intellectual revolt against bourgeois rationalism and optimism that marked fin-de-siècle culture. For the humanism and inevitable gradualism that characterized the socialist culture of the Second International, and the elaborate diplomacy that was the price of socialist unity, could both be seen as a parody of the liberal bourgeois world. No socialist intellectuals involved in the International went as far as Georges Sorel in theorizing labor as the mythic source of violence that would destroy bourgeois culture.[10] The continual reframing of Marx preserved the notion of a history ruled by scientific laws. But the shift of emphasis by younger radicals to active intervention and to the power of popular militancy suggests a reworking of socialism as an intellectual project that reflected the contemporary fascination with violence and action.[11] Above all, it altered the relationship between war and revolution, with war increasingly seen as inevitable and, in the case of Lenin and Luxemburg, as one path to revolution.[12]

The circumstances of the July 1914 crisis magnified the disarray of international socialism. The fact that the conflict was triggered not by an imperialist convulsion (which is how the 1911 Moroccan crisis had been credibly portrayed) but by nationalist antagonisms in an arena, the Balkans, where the International claimed to have localized an earlier war, in December 1912, meant that it failed to fit the prevailing anticipation of how a European war might occur. The presentation of the crisis on all sides as one of national defense, and even survival, fatally undermined whatever socialist will remained to resist national governments.[13] But even had the crisis been different, the deeper tensions in the International (as in national socialist movements) made a fundamentally different outcome unlikely. The process of national incorporation and the inchoate reconfiguration of revolutionary (and other) options had fatally qualified the International's capacity for action in advance.

Yet if such an analysis downplays the importance of August 1914 as the cause, rather than the occasion, of the rupture of labor internationalism, the significance of the moment for socialism as an ideological system remains. The shock was immense, especially for those immersed in the dominant political culture of the Second International. The assassination of Jaurès by a deranged nationalist on the eve of French mobilization heightened the disarray. The unitary model of international socialism fractured, along with the dominant linguistic tropes of revolution and anti-militarism and an entire representational system for portraying labor and the working class. But full disintegration was an extended cultural process, lasting throughout the war and beyond.

The Industrial War and Labor

In 1914 labor and socialist leaders shared the "short war illusion" of most Europeans. The significance of the conflict seemed to lie in its imminent resolution by purely military means. Gradually there emerged contrary indications that the war would be long, and that its dynamism would stem from its own internal processes as much as from its outcome. Most obviously the trench deadlock meant that mass armies would stay in the field for the foreseeable future. But the accompanying shell shortages that afflicted every major combatant power from fall 1914 to spring 1915 also showed that war was now an industrial contest, with victory belonging to the side that could most effectively deliver its economic resources to the battlefield. There was a tension between these two realities. Mobilization for the "short war" had been dominated by a military paradigm, that of maximizing the men under military command for rapid victory with minimum civil interference. Realization that the outcome would be determined by economic capacity as much as by military manpower reversed the paradigm. It meant reorganizing the mobilization process on the basis of the division and specialization of labor, with some recognition of the civilian specificity of the domestic effort. The main economic actors could not simply be incorporated into the military paradigm. Labor acquired a powerful market position (having been initially sidelined by the disruption of the military mobilization), and the worker became as crucial as the soldier for victory.[14] Against expectations, the war reasserted, even redefined, industrial labor. This process was doubly critical, for military effectiveness and for the preservation of national cohesion. The crucial question is how it affected the balance of tendencies toward the integration or alienation of labor, within and between different countries, and in particular whether it generated a countermobilization against the war.[15]

Structurally, the war reinforced some of the principal sources of prewar labor conflict and militancy. By vastly expanding metalworking (the core of war production), it gave enlarged prominence to the longer-term struggle over the restructuring of production while intensifying it through wartime labor shortages. Prewar skilled workers were clawed back from the front and assigned to armaments factories, often far from their homes. But the only way of reconciling competing military and industrial claims on crucial adult males was by diversifying the labor supply, with recourse above all to women and, to a lesser degree, youths and (in France) immigrants. Peasants, men and women, were also important in Italy and Russia. The employment of such semi-skilled labor was accompanied by the "dilution" of skilled work, with craft workers often promoted but with their expertise incorporated into more integrated and mechanized systems of production controlled by management. The "rationalization" of labor propagated by the American industrial engineer F. W.

Taylor and his European acolytes was applied in various forms (including piece-rates and bonuses) to munitions production.[16]

The threat to the place of skill in the armaments factories spurred craft workers to new heights of militancy. This entailed a certain friction with the semi-skilled workers, especially in Britain, where engineering craft workers defended a heritage of protective customs that employers, in a still fragmented industry, had found it hard to reduce. Even there, however, skilled workers sought to make common cause with the semi-skilled. Such collaboration was especially relevant where the metallurgical firms were bigger and the sector more highly integrated, as in Germany, and where (as in many countries) craft workers were prepared to accept the logic of industrial rationalization but on their own terms. In a manner familiar from the prewar period, skilled and semi-skilled workers cooperated, the former transmitting the traditions of labor organization and resistance to the latter, in an effort to win collective control over conditions, discipline, and the restructured labor process in the war factories. Factory and regional-level leaderships, cutting across established trade union structures, emerged in most major centers of war production, resulting in distinctive shop stewards or workers' delegate movements from Glasgow to Petrograd and from Turin and Paris to Berlin. These cross-grade alliances of workers in the armaments factories were at the hub of wartime labor protest.[17] Wartime shifts in industrial geography, which reinforced the role of large (and capital) cities, underlined labor militancy. Concentrations of war workers turned neighborhood, district and suburb, as well as factory, into sources of solidarity and sites of collective action.[18]

Structural changes in industrial labor were not confined to arms production. While export industries languished, other sectors such as food, clothing, and leather retained their importance, thanks to military contracts or by virtue of their place in the war economy (as with mining and railways). Although the skill composition and internal hierarchies of these industries were not remodeled in the same way as in the metal trades, a tight labor market gave workers a new capacity for industrial action and unionization. Wartime strikes were not the preserve of armaments workers and cities, also affecting more traditional sectors and settings. Textile workers (many of them women), for example, provided more strikers than any other industry in Italy and France, and they helped turn Moscow into a major center for strikes in 1917.[19] The position of women workers itself illustrates the key changes in the wartime labor force. Contrary to a conventional view, the war did not always transform the number of women wage-earners in absolute or relative terms, since women had long worked in industry, nor is it clear whether many women entered wage work because of the war. But women switched from traditionally feminized areas (textiles, domestic service) to male-dominated sectors like engineering, and where they remained in traditional sectors they acquired a new militancy.[20]

In some ways the war had an even more disruptive impact on living standards than on the structure of the working class. Inevitably the assignment of a high proportion of national income to destructive ends placed domestic consumption under strain. Calculating real wages, let alone total (and family) incomes, is technically fraught, and a myriad of qualifications makes generalization difficult. Nonetheless, it can be suggested first that real working-class incomes generally declined but did so least in the war industries; second, that workers did not see their living standards (though lower to start with) fall as much as some other groups less well connected to the war economy; and, third, that the evolution of working-class living standards differed significantly from country to country.

From early in the war, inflation eroded wages. The universal failure to impose centralized state direction on the war economy made this inevitable. But the process was fueled by the reluctance of employers to grant wage increases for what were seen as temporary price rises (or, less charitably, by their reluctance to reduce profits), as well as by the initial decline in industrial conflict—resulting from legal constraints, weakened trade unions, and (not least) labor patriotism. In the second half of the war wages increased and in many cases narrowed the inflationary gap. Nonetheless, average real wages declined throughout the war—by 20 percent in France, for example, and, in Germany, by 23 percent for male war workers and 44 percent for men in other industries.[21] More refined analysis based on family incomes or personal trajectories (e.g., women transferring into munitions work) would doubtless reveal that some groups increased their real wages. But this was against the trend. Yet industrial workers (especially war workers) were better off in relative (and possibly even absolute) terms than were those in the middle and lower-middle classes who faced wartime inflation on fixed or falling incomes from investments, state incomes, or declining businesses.[22]

Living standards were also determined by the absolute availability of vital necessities, however, and it is here that major differences emerge between the belligerent states. True, some shortages were common to all countries. This was so with housing. Rapid urban expansion at a time when construction was virtually impossible (there was some experimentation with temporary buildings) created a crisis in working-class accommodation even if, in absolute terms, it was grimmer in Petrograd than Paris. But the availability of other crucial items, such as food and fuel, was determined (given inevitable national shortages) by access to the international economy. In this respect, as Avner Offer has demonstrated, agricultural resources shaped the outcome of the war.[23] Owing to the allied blockade, for which conquests in Eastern Europe never compensated, Germany experienced shortages from early 1915 that had become acute by the last two years of the war. Improved real wages in 1917–18 meant little in the face of empty shelves and the black market. Life, especially for working-class mothers, was exhausting and disruptive—and the position was even worse in Austria.[24]

In Britain and France, by contrast, access to the world economy—plus governments that were responsive to the needs of the civilian population and effective at meeting them—meant that living standards suffered much less. Comparison of civilian mortality rates tells the story. Whereas these rose significantly in Germany during the last two years of the war, reflecting malnutrition though not outright famine, they were relatively stable in France and slightly improved for the most vulnerable members of the British working class, indicating the leveling effect of national rationing.[25] Outright shortages in Italy in 1917 provoked violent protests before a government galvanized by the defeat of Caporetto claimed access to the inter-allied monopoly on international food supplies. Such a solution was irrelevant to Russia, however, a major prewar grain exporter. By 1916 the country's transport system and internal market had collapsed, resulting in food shortages and popular protest unmatched elsewhere.[26]

The war, then, intensified certain longer-term sources of labor militancy and industrial conflict in a climate of acute pressure on working-class living standards, and at a time when mechanisms of national integration were strained by the length and human cost of the conflict. An extremely tight labor market ensured that labor and working-class grievances would find expression in strikes, and there was a surge of industrial and related protest virtually everywhere in 1917–18, which continued into 1920. In many countries it constituted a strike wave of unprecedented magnitude, though the peaks typically came after the war itself.[27] The strikes were driven by a variety of economic motives—most notably anti-inflationary wage demands and issues of "control" in the war industries—and drew in many categories and sectors with little history of industrial militancy, including white-collar and professional workers.[28] The question of their political potential, however, brings out both deeper and longer-term differences between the various belligerent powers, and also the political constraints on the industrial sphere.

The local and regional shop stewards' movements that emerged in the war industries provided fertile ground for the development of a radical labor culture in which the prewar traditions of mobilized skilled workers and the rebelliousness of wartime adolescents combined with radical socialist or revolutionary syndicalist ideas. It was here that the strongest support was found for the politicization of strikes in wider protest against the war, or even in favor of revolution. Given considerable working-class war-weariness, even in countries like Britain and France, in 1917–18 these movements of more politicized labor militancy struck a sympathetic chord with broader currents of popular opinion, a connection amplified by other forms of protest.

The latter have received less attention than have strikes, but it is clear that inflation and above all scarcity forced workers to think and act as consumers as well as producers. Several historians have argued that the war witnessed a resurgence of older languages of consumer entitlements (the traditional "moral economy" of the poor), providing a crucial source of protest.[29] Concern with food and other necessities permeated strikes in Britain and France. The parliamentary enquiry into the British strikes of May 1917 found food prices to be the most widespread cause of unrest. Denunciation of "hoarders," "speculators," and "profiteers" was rife and led to labor demands for controls and rationing—which in France were couched in the revived language of Jacobinism. But it was the countries with more sharply declining living standards and absolute shortages that experienced the most serious consumer revolts. The German strikes of April 1917 were in part a food protest triggered by a reduced bread ration, while an attempt at worker control of food supplies ran through the three strike movements that convulsed Austria in May

1917 and January and June 1918.[30] The most serious Italian upheaval, in Turin in August 1917, was a mixture of strike, food riot, and insurrection unleashed by a bread shortage. Much of the upheaval in Russia around the February revolution reflected older forms of consumer revolt as much as strike action.[31]

These movements of protest that, starting from work-place and consumer grievances, spread to denunciations of the war and demands for peace, represented one of the most serious challenges to national cohesion faced by the wartime state—along with mass military disobedience and movements of national secession. The German strike movements of April 1917 and January 1918, those in Austria already referred to, the French strikes of May 1918, the Milan strike of May 1917 and the Turin insurrection of August, and—in Russia—February 1917 and the July days (when the popular movement turned against the Provisional Government) might all be seen as falling into this category. Yet closer scrutiny suggests that, for all the elements in common, there are major distinctions between the national cases. These are partly a question of real differences between the various war economies and in the decline of living standards. Britain and France never experienced the scale of consumer protest that marked Italy and Russia, or even Austria and Germany. Just as important, it was a matter of the deeper processes of social integration and of the "maturity" of the working class.

For in the most advanced industrial societies, wartime strikes and industrial protest occurred in the context both of developed prewar habits of industrial bargaining and of states prepared to intervene in labor affairs to an unprecedented degree in order to maximize war output and manage social conflict. War conferred sweeping repressive powers on the state by virtue of exceptional legislation and of the military mobilization of many adult males. But what stands out is the *relative* economy with which such powers were used and the extent to which labor was part of the corporatist approach common in the industrial effort. The danger from militarizing labor, in short, was considerable and usually avoided.[32]

The British experience was perhaps exceptional because the absence of military conscription until 1916 made it imperative from the outset to find an alternative mechanism to military mobilization for directing the labor flow and restructuring the production of munitions. This was provided by the Munitions of War Act of July 1915, which was the foundation of British wartime industrial relations and gave Lloyd George, as minister of munitions, considerable control over the mobility, "dilution" and material conditions of labor in the armaments industries. But it also provided for labor participation in its administration, imposed some constraints on employers (including excess profits taxation), and rested on the prior agreement of the trade union movement. It paved the way for the spread of tripartite institutions that by the last phase of the war regulated substantial areas of industrial relations and conferred wide recognition on trade unions.[33]

In France and Germany the state directly controlled mobilized males. But the disadvantages of keeping such workers under a military regime, as well as the increasing recruitment of nonmilitarized labor, in reality limited the use of military authority as an instrument of industrial regulation. In both countries mobilized workers were allowed to join trade unions and earn civilian wages. The French minister of Armaments, Albert Thomas (a socialist), consulted trade unions over the industrial mobilization from the start and set up a participatory system of wage-regulation, including factory level worker delegates, when he banned strikes by nonmobilized war workers in January 1917—a system maintained by Clemenceau in the last year of the war.[34] The sanction of being returned to the front was powerful but used sparingly—following a disastrous confrontation with mobilized militants in the Loire, in December 1917. The Prussian Ministry of War, which presided over German industrial mobilization in 1914–16, also consulted trade unions in the teeth of employer opposition and, in June 1916, the highly restrictive Imperial Associations Law was replaced by more favorable trade union legislation.[35] As in Britain, both states preferred to use trade unions as partners in settling the strikes of 1917–18.

True, the Hindenburg Program, which aimed to galvanize munitions output and militarize the labor force, including women, was nothing less than an attempt to institute a command economy by authoritarian heavy industrialists, allied with the third Supreme Command against the War Ministry. This had no parallel in Britain or France. But more significant was the failure not only of its illusory production targets but also of the Patriotic Auxiliary Labor Law of December 1916. Far from militarizing labor, this conceded major gains to the trade unions, including factory committees and participatory wage regulation similar to those introduced in Britain and France.[36]

All this suggests that in Britain, France, and Germany the wartime state displayed real (if circumscribed) autonomy in relation to the economic mobilization, and a readiness to collaborate with organized labor both to anticipate conflict and to settle even theoretically illegal strikes, often to labor's advantage. This helps explain the wage increases noted in all three countries in the last two years of the war. Radical local labor leaderships were inevitably a part of this complex process, and they remained beset by the tension between the possibility of politicizing industrial action and the logic of securing the tangible gains that were the strikes' immediate goals. Often the more pragmatic side won out. This is not to deny the political thrust of much industrial radicalism that in the German case, anticipated the workers' council movement, which suddenly bloomed in the November revolution at the end of the war. Even here, however, the moderate and constitutional orientation adopted by most in the early council movement, and the fact that as the wartime state col-

lapsed labor and business leaders arrived at their own institutionalized conflict regulation (the Stinnes-Legien accord of November
1918), indicate the political limits to industrial radicalism during the
war.[37] In a victorious Britain and France, with the state intact, the
political (let alone revolutionary) appeal of industrial action was
even more restricted.[38]

The real contrast is with Russia and Italy—that is, with precisely
those countries where the prewar working class was the least "nationalized," where industrial conflict was the least mediated (and most
politicized), and where the state enjoyed the weakest popular legitimacy. In Italy the state and industrialists began with a highly coercive
industrial mobilization, partly because the conservative elites had entered the war in 1915 to reverse the reformism of Giolitti's liberal regime. It was headed by a military figure, General Dallolio, and many
male workers remained full soldiers. Even here, domestic unrest and
military setback necessitated a more mediatory approach from 1917,
including regional committees with labor representation, which frequently benefited workers—though industrial discipline remained
extremely harsh.[39] But in a highly polarized society, politicized strikes
became part of a broader coalition of popular hostility to both
the war and the regime—though one that bred an equally powerful reaction, ultimately feeding into fascism. In Russia, however,
the entire industrial mobilization conducted by the War Industries
Committees remained a parallel, voluntary affair seen as dangerously
corrosive of autocratic state power by the tsarist bureaucracy. When
an attempt was made to regulate labor questions in 1915 by incorporating worker representation (the "workers groups"), the government remained profoundly skeptical—perhaps with reason, since by
the end of 1916 the "workers groups," like the War Industries Committees themselves, had joined the opposition that led to the February Revolution.[40] In a more one-sided social polarization against the
state than in Italy, industrial protest (while retaining an instrumental,

economic logic down to the October revolution) also contributed directly to a revolutionary dynamic. Despite the political symbolism of the Russian revolution for labor elsewhere, the social impact of the war on Russian labor was the exception, not the rule.[41]

The War and Socialist Politics: Reform, Peace, and Revolution

Ultimately, the war conferred a certain primacy on politics and culture. For the mobilization process, though expressed most directly in the military and industrial efforts, derived more fundamentally still from the authority and legitimacy of the state and from the cultural representations (ideas, values, images) that were enrolled behind the conflict.[42] Economic issues impinged on the political and cultural spheres, but the latter encompassed much more, including the perceived goals of a "total" war and the sacrifices involved in fighting it. The crucial relationship of labor with the war, therefore, occurred at this level of power and representation. And although labor was by no means co-terminous with socialism (labor having other political expressions, socialism having supporters in other social groups), socialism claimed to speak for labor, which made it the latter's most significant political expression when working-class support for the war was so vital.

There is no lack of accounts of wartime socialism explaining its divisions and realignments in terms of the broader evolution of socialist organizations and ideas.[43] What matters here are the integral processes and key events of the war, which shaped this evolution. On the one hand, the parameters of the process were set by the fracturing of the unitary model and socialist culture of the Second International in 1914. On the other, they were determined by the relationship of national mobilization with central features of the war, including not only the industrial war but also the strain placed on the legitimacy of both state and nation by the costly military stalemate, and the diplomatic outcome of the fighting. The war's relationship with socialism also depended on the latter's diverse functions—political movement, intellectual project, state power, or broader cultural force. Seen thus, it might be suggested that the war confronted socialists in three basic guises—reform, peace, and revolution.

Reform emerged as a corollary of socialist support for the war. National mobilization did not mean the suspension of socialist politics in 1914 but rather their rapid readjustment to the war through a process of "self-mobilization." The terms on which this occurred varied with different national experiences of the outbreak of war and with contrasting labor and socialist traditions. French socialists and British Labour leaders combined distinct views of August 1914 (legitimate defense against German invasion in the one case, violation of Belgian neutrality and international law in the other) with a common conviction that Prussian militarism directly threatened labor and the working class. The link between socialism and wars of national defense or liberation was revived, reemphasizing the Jacobin template of much French socialism. As Paris momentarily faced a siege in September 1914, the capital's labor movement rediscovered the language of 1870 and revolutionary patriotism.[44] Likewise, German Social Democrats accepted their government's carefully contrived illusion of a war for national survival against a reactionary Russia that they had long considered a major threat to their own achievements.[45] Defending socialism (or its prospects) through the nation was even a strong enough ideal to rally part of the exiled leaderships of Russian revolutionary socialism. By a specific "choice of 1914," therefore, socialists accepted the nation's claim on labor but also asserted the converse—that the war gave socialists a claim on the nation.

The translation of this claim into a fully fledged reform program was complex and varied. Initially, the sense of national crisis precluded overt political bargaining. SPD leaders hoped that the fully democratized Germany for which they considered the party to be fighting would simply follow from support for the war. The veteran French socialist Jules Guesde and his followers justified socialist participation in government on the grounds of national defense, not class collaboration, a blend of Jacobinism and Marxism that seemed to preclude major reform. Other socialist and labor leaders, however, argued from early on that the war's social impact on workers required immediate reforms, including institutional consultation with organized labor. The rhetoric of solidarity and equal sacrifice generated by national mobilization, along with a host of grievances, resulted in a distinctive wartime social morality that was characterized by competing claims of obligation, entitlement, and social justice—and of which the "moral economy" of popular consumption already referred to was but one element. This social morality was by no means the prerogative of labor and the working class. As noted, other groups suffered greater relative material decline, and there were other issues than material ones. By reference to the ultimate sacrifice of death on the front, for example, war workers were often portrayed by peasant and lower-middle-class soldiers and families as privileged "shirkers," *embusqués*, or *imboscati*.[46] Nonetheless, the language of sacrifice and recompense was used by labor and socialist leaders to demand both immediate and more fundamental reforms. The British Labour Party, for example, qualified its reluctant acceptance of military conscription in 1916 with a compensating demand for the "conscription of riches," or capital, in which wartime social justice combined with socialist principles.[47]

The lessons of the economic mobilization reinforced this tendency. If labor and socialist leaders were critical of the inequalities and inefficiencies of this process, they were nonetheless impressed by the economic intervention of the wartime state and the potential of its corporatist orientation. Convinced that the same impulse could

be channeled into planned demobilization and sweeping social reform, they began to project the postwar period as one of fundamental "reconstruction" or "economic reorganization," in which the
working class would play a key role in a profoundly modified capitalism—whose ultimate replacement by some form of democratically
controlled and collectivized economy seemed a distinct possibility.
Located in labor grievances and the social morality of wartime, this
vision was far more than an intellectual project, though intellectuals
played a key role in defining it.[48] In different forms, but typically
turning on the nationalization of specific industries and the introduction of comprehensive social welfare, it redefined the program of
the British Labour Party (committing it to socialism), reoriented
the majority of the CGT away from revolutionary syndicalism, and
strongly affected both the SPD and Austrian socialism—in all cases
with significant popular support.

In effect, the process of national mobilization, by redefining the
relationship of labor with the nation, fostered a distinctive variant of
reformist socialism.[49] This was no defensive rationalization of the
collapse of socialist internationalism in 1914 but the expression in
transformed wartime circumstances of the "nationalizing" tendencies long apparent in different variants of socialism, nationally as
well as in the Second International itself. Significantly, the attempt in
1919–20 to revive the International on its old, unitary base turned
on an alliance of British Labour and the German majority Social
Democrats, just as the reformist CGT played a comparable role in
the International Federation of Trade Unions. In both cases nationalization and social reform within the framework of liberal democratic politics—the watchwords of war reformism—defined the new
orientation.[50]

Reformist socialism was deprived of immediate effect not only by
the bitter opposition of reoriented variants of revolutionary socialism but also by the broader postwar context. In victorious Britain

and France a confident state presided over a resurgent conservative politics that refused to apply the politics of wartime mobilization to peace. Unlike in 1945, there was no shift in the balance of domestic power allowing the implementation of left-wing reform programs. In Central Europe conditions appeared more propitious for just such change. But the crisis of state and regime that accompanied military defeat in fact meant that German and Austrian Social Democracy had to grapple with the prior task of state reconstruction and the legitimization of a new democratic regime, under the menace of both radical social revolution and violent counter-revolution, plus the threat of allied occupation. For various reasons (which have been intensively debated, especially in the German case) the limited attempts to plan and implement economic reform in both countries, notably through the nationalization of industry, achieved few results, the principal gains of the immediate postwar period lying in social reform.[51] Nonetheless, by unambiguously linking the ideal of economic expropriation and social reform to parliamentary democracy and by stimulating a flurry of plans and programs for nationalization and a decentralized socialist economy, the war and its immediate aftermath permanently redefined reformist socialism in Central and Western Europe down to 1945 and beyond.[52]

The war confronted socialism in a radically different way through the question of peace. By 1915, minority voices in most European socialist parties and many trade union movements had begun to question socialist commitment to the national efforts and to seek an end to the fighting. Aided by the action of neutral socialists (both moderate Dutch and Scandinavians and more radical Swiss and Italians), a number of meetings were held, notably in the Swiss villages of Zimmerwald and Kienthal, in September 1915 and April 1916. The hope that socialists might stop the war was fanned by Woodrow Wilson's attempted peace mediation and by the anti-war feeling in Russia following the February revolution. It culminated in the project of an international conference in Stockholm, in 1917.

In many respects this development also drew on prewar themes within European socialism. Whereas national mobilization portrayed the war as the defense of "civilization" and "culture" against the barbarism of the enemy, critical socialists perceived war itself to be the real barbarism. There was nothing especially socialist in this. It was the basis of much liberal opposition to the war, including that of Romain Rolland in his September 1914 pamphlet *Above the Battlefield*, which resonated strongly in minority socialist circles.[53] But it was also, as we have seen, a value embedded in the prewar culture of the Second International. It was logical in reasserting it to see the revival of the International as the means of giving it force—even if the permanent bureau, mired in the hostility between opposed majority socialists, refused to take the lead in doing so.

The language of the Zimmerwald and Kienthal resolutions remained that of conventional prewar Marxism. The war was seen as the product of capitalism and imperialism; an internationally coordinated movement maximizing labor and socialist opposition was the way to end it. But peace, not revolution, was the goal. Although the two terms coexisted in the same semantic frame there was a potential conflict of emphasis and underlying interpretation illustrated clearly by the clash between Lenin and Kautsky. The latter, in a tussle between the moral and "scientific" impulses of his Marxism, after the 1911 Moroccan crisis, had decided that imperialism (as the most advanced, internationalist stage of capitalism) did not necessarily entail war. Socialists might therefore with some confidence resist war as a distinct project from bringing about socialism. It was a distinction that chimed with the growing gradualism of Kautsky's revolutionary prognosis, and it was shared by Jaurès and much of French socialism. Lenin, however, once the conflict broke out, considered that imperialism made war inevitable and that war was the likely path to revolution—understandably, from a Russian perspective. He bitterly attacked Kautsky and sought to subordinate peace to revolution through his policy of "revolutionary defeatism." Although Lenin may have believed it possible to create a unitary, revolutionary International longer than is usually supposed, he considered the old International dead in 1914 and later moved toward a policy of splitting the hard-line revolutionaries from the rest, including moderate pacifists.[54]

It was, however, the reverse emphasis on peace rather than revolution that prevailed in the socialist and trade union opposition to the war, both at Zimmerwald and down to Stockholm. The language of this socialist pacifism has not been systematically studied. But it might be suggested that the moral aversion to war already clearly present in the prewar International now became its dominant motif. The leaders of the emergent minority in Germany (Bernstein, Kautsky, and Haase) described the war as combining the "cruelty of barbaric ages" with the "most sophisticated tools of civilization" in their statement of June 1915, *The Demand of the Hour,* and the same terms were used elsewhere.[55] The Zimmerwald resolution prefaced its formulaic explanation that "the war which has provoked this chaos is the product of imperialism" with a description of the chaos itself: "Millions of corpses cover the battlefields. Millions of men will remain mutilated for the rest of their days. Europe has become a gigantic slaughter-house for men. All the civilization created by the labor of previous generations is destined to be destroyed. Savage barbarism is today triumphing over everything that heretofore constituted the pride of humanity."[56] It is not clear how much this language of moral protest reflected (or emanated from) the experience of the soldiers or war-weary civilians, and how much it sprang from the disturbed sensitivities of socialist intellectuals.[57] Nor have the variations of its nuances between countries been established. But it was important (if for nothing else) as the attempt by socialists, whose anti-militarism hampered strictly military analysis, to grasp and respond to the radical novelty of industrial war and a scale of destruction that strained the terms of conventional class analysis.

Further proof of the importance of socialist pacifism comes from its protean nature by 1917, as evidenced by the preparation for the Stockholm conference. Pro-national defense socialists were rarely apologists for war, but their commitment to the logic of ultimate victory made it hard for them to condemn the particular horror of the warfare of attrition. Extreme revolutionaries (such as the Zimmerwaldian left) saw the war as symptomatic of the crisis rather than as the crisis itself. It was therefore a broad coalition of pacifists, widely divergent on other criteria (such as reform and revolution), that provided a socialist formulation of the popular currents of war weariness that appeared in many countries in 1917. The formation of the German Social Democratic opposition into an independent party in April 1917, the Independent German Social Democratic Party (USPD)—extending from the revisionist, Bernstein, to the extreme left Spartacists—epitomized the political realignment forced by the question of peace.[58] But the same dynamic was at work elsewhere. It drew in both revolutionaries (hoping to use peace to win converts) and also pro-national defense majorities who, even if they remained skeptical over a negotiated peace, insisted (reflecting the deepening human misery of the war) that their own national aims should be nonexpansionist and help abolish future war.[59]

By the same token, the failure of Stockholm demonstrates how illusory was any socialist consensus on peace in 1917. Even had the French and British governments not forbidden their respective delegations to attend, the impossibility of socialist agreement on the terms of a compromise settlement doomed the conference in advance. The logic of conflicting national war aims remained too powerful. The SPD was trying to distance itself from the radical expansionism of the military dictatorship but still believed in a justifiable war of national defense. The British and French majorities remained convinced of German aggression in 1914 and in part wished to use Stockholm to confront the SPD with its complicity in this, thereby helping keep Russia, and especially the Petrograd soviet, in the war.[60] When the conference failed to take place, the Zimmerwaldian left (predominantly Bolsheviks and Spartacists) met at Stockholm to bury the attempted revival of the International and unequivocally to harness the peace movement to revolution. Between moral revulsion against the "catastrophe" of the war (that is, the military slaughter) and agreement on how to end it (that is, its political significance) lay a gulf in which the Stockholm project foundered. It was the same gulf that, outside Russia (and perhaps Italy), prevented movements of industrial and popular protest with their anti-war overtones (including the French mutinies) from turning into outright rejection of the national defense. As the French minority socialist leader Jean Longuet commented during the German spring offensive in 1918: "Before such a danger . . . for the liberty of the world, there is no socialist, nor internationalist, who would express any other thought . . . than that of resistance . . . in the face of the Germanic onslaught."[61]

Yet for the same reason, peace remained the defining issue for Central and Western European socialists during the last year of the war. If the hope had gone of short-circuiting the bloody conflict by socialist consensus and diplomacy, it became more important than ever to ensure that the war's true meaning and outcome should be that it never occurred again, and this in turn meant directing the moral thrust of pacifism and national defense alike into the project of a new world order, independently of any socialist revolution. The key ideas of liberal internationalism—universal disarmament and a Society of Nations—had already surfaced in the International before the war. But they now acquired a totemic status, uniting the broad center ground both programmatically and through the outpouring of socialist (and popular) support for Wilson and Wilsonism. Faced with the war's ineluctable progression, only an eschatological belief in permanent world peace seemed capable of redeeming its horror.[62]

Revolution (outside Russia) may seem curiously muted in this realignment of socialist horizons during the war. In fact, the opposite was the case, but revolution was even more complex and polyvalent than peace, with considerable variations according to socialist tradition and national situation. Moreover, the response to the Russian experience was one whose defining impact on European socialism observed a different chronology in different countries, and generally occurred as much in the two postwar years (down to the second and decisive congress of the Communist International in August 1920) as during the war itself. From the viewpoint of the war, what emerges sharply is the distinction between the two Russian revolutions of February and October 1917.

Since the Russian revolution was born of war it is not surprising that the issue of peace should have been central to its own unfolding and international impact. In fact, the dominant revolutionary model available to contemporaries, the French revolution, had engendered war rather than emanating from it, and the belief that the February revolution would create a democratic national mobilization on the Jacobin model was initially a powerful one in allied (and especially French) opinion. This included a number of pro-war socialists who were sent by their governments to Russia to encourage precisely this outcome.[63] In an opposed but parallel interpretation the extreme right of the SPD took the February revolution as evidence of the effectiveness of the German military effort in the east. The Provisional Government under Kerensky (a right-wing socialist) did indeed attempt to implement the Jacobin model, resulting in the failed offensive of the summer of 1917 and the final disintegration of the imperial army.[64] But from the outset the opposed policy of a general negotiated peace resonated throughout the popular revolutionary movement (without necessarily implying abandonment of the national defense). It was advocated notably by the Petrograd soviet, without whose impetus the brief socialist convergence on the project of Stockholm would not have occurred.

It was this call to peace that electrified European socialists and explains much of the influence of the February revolution. Revolution, in other words, embodied the hopes for peace that accompanied the crises of morale afflicting virtually every belligerent nation in 1917. The identification of the message with the soviets and other forms of revolutionary representation conveyed a sense of controlling fate that contrasted with the feeling of powerlessness induced by the military stalemate and wartime social conditions. "Take your destiny into your own hands," a revolutionary pamphlet celebrating the Russian revolution declared to Leipzig workers during the strike of April 1917.[65] Elsewhere, too, the example of the soviets encouraged radical industrial militants to see their local power as a means of pressing for peace. In France, where the political culture of labor drew on a broader revolutionary tradition, the Russian revolution strengthened the tendency for economic and political protest (including the demand for peace) to be expressed in revolutionary language and imagery, as Jean-Louis Robert has shown in his detailed study of Paris workers.[66] Even in Britain, where the political culture of labor was anything but revolutionary, the prestige of Russian events gave a fillip to the yearning for peace, including the extraordinary meeting of socialist opposition groups held in Leeds in June 1917, which called for the establishment of Councils of Workers and Soldiers.[67]

October 1917, however, by subordinating peace to revolution in the dramatic form of the Brest-Litovsk treaty the following March, reduced the revolution's appeal for socialist movements still caught up in the war. This was particularly so with Russia's allies. French and British socialists in general judged the Bolsheviks harshly for unilaterally withdrawing from the war and allowing the Germans to launch their offensive in the west, in the spring of 1918.[68] In Germany, Kautsky went much further in 1918, opening a major polemic with Lenin by condemning the Bolshevik "dictatorship" as a vehicle of socialist revolution.[69] Only on the extreme left did the priority of revolution over peace begin to realign socialism and syndicalism in support of the Bolshevik revolution. This was the case, among others, with the Spartacists in Germany, with left-wing syndicalists and socialists in France, and with the major elements of Italian socialism. Turin socialists (including Gramsci) hailed Lenin well before the October revolution.[70] Helped by the scarcity of news, the revolution remained an idealized image onto which each group (including anarchists and syndicalists) projected its own fantasy.[71]

In the longer term, Bolshevism transformed the meaning of revolution as an ideological and imaginary category for European socialism. This involved more than creating a new type of International, based on splitting, not uniting, national movements and on subordinating the latter to Bolshevik revolutionary politics. War, and the memory of war, were central to the process. Communists derived their immediate revolutionary credentials from the claim that they had been consistent in their absolute rejection of the war, and their founding mythology included a demonized history of the war and the "treason" of the "social chauvinists." Postwar communism used the moral discourse of pacifism widely but it did so to underline its monopoly on revolutionary legitimacy—until the Popular Front era in the 1930s changed its attitudes to war.

Reformist socialists, by contrast, found Bolshevik violence and authoritarianism deeply offensive and considered it part of the more brutal world the war had created. Their own gradualist path to postwar socialism explicitly sought to avoid the chaos of such a revolution. With the tension between national defense and pacifism now resolved, peace—that is, the creation of a democratic world order to eliminate conflict—became central, both as a program and as an ideal, in what amounted to a reformulation of the humanist values of pre-1914 socialism. It was also a process that helped reconcile reformists with some of the noncommunist currents of revolutionary socialism which flourished for several years after the war.[72] In opposed ways, the unprecedented death and destruction of the war continued to redefine the division of socialism that the war itself had occasioned.

Conclusion

Closer integration of the history of labor with that of the war runs some risks. Most obvious is that of exaggerating the role of the war at the expense of longer-term processes that determined the evolution of labor. As in other domains, war did not exist apart from more permanent structures and more durable processes. Historians have rightly warned that much that was caused by the war may well have happened anyway, and this is especially so outside the immediate sphere of the military conflict.[73] The acceptance by labor and socialist opinion of the outbreak of war in 1914, it is clear, can be understood only in relation to deeper processes of labor integration into nation states and national communities. Equally, the patterns of labor protest during the war have many connections with prewar industrial militancy and class conflict. Reformists and revolutionaries of various kinds did not wait for the war to engage in bitter conflict.

Yet in the nonmilitary as in the military sphere, the war consisted of distinctive processes, experiences, and consequences that stemmed from the requirements of a mass industrial conflict that locked on the battlefield into a murderous trial of endurance. These constitute the originality of the war, and it is important to see them in something of their totality. As far as labor is concerned, it is less a question of determining whether the war integrated labor and the working class into the nation or alienated them from it, than of seeing that it did both simultaneously, and in very particular ways. Workers were called on as soldiers and citizens as well as producers. Labor participated in the political and cultural process of national mobilization as well as in the industrial mobilization. In the French strikes of May 1918, for example, the two came into conflict as a protest against aspects of the industrial effort acquired an anti-war edge—only to find itself isolated by a national remobilization (including much of the working class) against renewed invasion.

The outcome of the opposed forces to which the war subjected labor depended on underlying patterns of the "nationalization" of labor but also on circumstances deriving from the war itself. What stands out, for all the shared features of labor's wartime experience, is the resulting difference between national cases. In Britain and France, nation-states with a high level of popular legitimacy (reflected in the political cultures of labor and socialism) and developed mechanisms for resolving industrial conflict, combined with a less serious wartime degradation of material conditions than elsewhere to limit working-class disaffection and socialist mobilization against the war. The reverse was true (though in very different ways) in Russia and Italy. In the pivotal German case the density of social arrangements capable of mediating industrial conflict (for all the serious decline in living standards) contrasted with the crisis of the state that the war initiated and defeat confirmed. Together they marked the distinctive parameters of a German "revolution" in which labor and socialism, though vital, were only one of many actors.

These are perhaps the most familiar kind of conclusions about the reciprocal relationship of World War I and labor. A newer, cultural reading of the war has yet to be applied to the theme of labor in a systematic way. But it is already clear that a focus on experience and representation has much to offer (as in the parallel case of gender). The scope and limitations of labor protest, for example, cannot be understood in isolation from the wider social morality of wartime that aligned and opposed different groups in often novel ways. Even more than the material structure the representational worlds of political movements and social groups (as Jean-Louis Robert has shown for Parisian workers) were deeply affected by the war. Currents of popular eschatology generated by the length and suffering of the conflict created a sometimes messianic fervor for ideas of transformation and redemption (Wilsonism, revolution) that shaped the cultural environment of labor. Key elements of representational systems changed their meaning, as the evolving significance of reform, peace, and revolution demonstrates in the case of socialism. Above all, the war itself proved an experience that strained existing socialist ideas and values beyond the limit, dissolving the political culture of the Second International. In ways that remain fully to be established, the unassimilable memory of World War I remained inseparable from the history of labor and socialism during the interwar period and beyond.[74]

NOTES

1. For an overview of pre-1914 developments, see D. Geary, ed., *Labour and Socialist Movements in Europe Before 1914* (Oxford: Berg, 1989).

2. For France, see J.-J. Becker, *1914: Comment les français sont entrés dans la guerre* (Paris: Editions de la Fondation Nationale des Sciences Politiques, 1977), and J.-J. Becker and A. Kriegel, *1914: La Guerre et le mouvement ouvrier français* (Paris: Colin, 1964). On Germany, see G. Krumeich, "L'Entrée en guerre en Allemagne," in J.-J. Becker and S. Audoin-Rouzeau, eds., *Les Sociétés européennes et la guerre de 1914–1918* (Paris: Centre d'Histoire de la France Contem-

poraine, University of Paris X-Nanterre, 1990), 65–74; J. T. Verhey, "The 'Spirit of 1914': The Myth of Enthusiasm and the Rhetoric of Unity in World War One Germany" (Ph.D. thesis, University of California at Berkeley, 1991); and W. Kruse, *Krieg und Nationale Integration* (Essen: Klartext Verlag, 1993).

3. No detailed study of this subject appears to exist in English, but see D. C. B. Lieven, *Russia and the Origins of the First World War* (London: Macmillan, 1984).

4. See in particular M. van der Linden, "The National Integration of European Working Classes, 1871–1914," in *International Review of Social History* 33, no. 3 (1988): 285–311, and R. Gallissot, "La Patrie des prolétaires," *Le Mouvement Social* 147 (1989): 11–25. The debt to the work of D. Groh on the SPD is explicit (D. Groh, *Negative Integration und revolutionärer Attentismus: Die deutsche Sozialdemokratie am Vorabend des ersten Weltkrieges* [Frankfurt: Ullstein Buch, 1974]). But there are also similarities with the integrationist study of the working classes as a whole by P. N. Stearns, *Lives of Labour* (London: Croom Helm, 1975).

5. For an overview, see E. J. Hobsbawm, *Nations and Nationalism Since 1780: Programme, Myth, Reality* (Cambridge: Cambridge University Press, 1990), ch. 4.

6. L. Haimson and G. Sapelli, eds., *Strikes, Social Conflict, and the First World War: An International Perspective* (Milan: Fondazione Giangiacomo Feltrinelli, 1992), especially 13–21. The violent and polarized nature of Red Week in Italy in June 1914 was due in part to the deliberate rejection by Salandra's conservative government of the conciliatory policies toward labor adopted by Giolitti in his previous decade of political predominance.

7. For a synopsis of these tendencies, see J. E. Cronin and C. Sirianni, eds., *Work, Community, and Power: The Experience of Labor in Europe and America, 1900–1925* (Philadelphia: Temple University Press, 1983), and especially J. E. Cronin, "Rethinking the Legacy of Labor, 1890–1925," 3–19, and "Labor Insurgency and Class Formation: Comparative Perspectives on the Crisis of 1917–1920 in Europe," 20–48.

8. Notably by the pioneering work of Georges Haupt and those who worked with him on the archives of the Second International. See especially G. Haupt, *Socialism and the Great War: The Collapse of the Second International* (Oxford: Clarendon, 1972); G. Haupt, "Guerre ou révolution?: L'Internationale et l'union sacrée en août 1914," in G. Haupt, ed., *L'Historien et le mouvement social* (Paris: Maspero, 1980), 199–235; J. Howorth, "French Workers and German Workers: The Impossibility of Internationalism, 1900–1914," *European History Quarterly* 15 no. 1 (1985): 71–97; and R. Gallissot, R. Paris, and C. Weil, "La Désunion des prolétaires," *Le Mouvement social* 147, special issue, 1989.

9. S. Milner, *The Dilemmas of Internationalism: French Syndicalism and the International Labour Movement, 1900–1914* (Oxford: Berg, 1990).

10. G. Sorel, *Reflections on Violence* (1906; English trans., London: George Allen and Unwin, 1916).

11. This argument has not yet been developed systematically and comparatively. At the very least it suggests that the cultural history of socialist intellectuals and of socialism as an intellectual project during the decade 1910–20 is ripe for exploration. Such an approach has been initiated by C. Prochasson, *Les Intellectuels, le socialisme et la guerre 1900–1938* (Paris: Seuil, 1993), and F. Furet, *Le Passé d'une illusion: Essai sur l'idée communiste au XXe siècle* (Paris: Robert Laffont/Calmann-Lévy, 1995), especially chs. 2–5. For important hints on the influence of fin-de-siècle culture on left oppositionist leaders (who were almost all educated in the crucial decade of the 1890s), see I. Deutscher, *Trotsky*, vol. 1: *The Prophet Armed* (Oxford: Oxford University Press, 1954), and P. Nettl, *Rosa Luxemburg* (Oxford: Clarendon, 1969), 19–20.

12. For example, in the famous Lenin-Luxemburg amendment to the resolution of the 1907 Stuttgart congress of the International on war, which envisaged using the "violent economic and political crisis" occasioned by war to bring about revolution (Nettl, *Rosa Luxemburg*, 268–71).

13. Haupt, *Socialism and the Great War*; A. Kriegel, "La IIe Internationale (1889–1914)," in J. Droz, ed., *Histoire générale du socialisme*, vol. 2: *De 1875 à 1918* (Paris: Presses Universitaires de France, 1974), 555–83.

14. For the disruption caused by the outbreak of war and the suspension of normal economic activity, see J. Lawrence, M. Dean, and J.-L. Robert, "The Outbreak of War and the Urban Economy: Paris, Berlin, and London in 1914," *Economic History Review* 45, no. 3 (1992): 564–93.

15. For good overall discussions of key national cases, see J. Kocka, *Facing Total War: German Society, 1914–1918* (1973; English trans., Leamington Spa: Berg, 1984), ch. 2; B. Waites, *A Class Society at War: England, 1914–18* (Leamington Spa: Berg, 1987), ch. 4; and P. Fridenson, "The Impact of the War on French Workers," in R. Wall and J. Winter, eds., *The Upheaval of War: Family, Work, and Welfare in Europe, 1914–1918* (Cambridge: Cambridge University Press, 1988), 235–48. There are no thoroughgoing syntheses on a comparative or transnational basis of the monograph literature on labor (as opposed to trade unionism and socialism) during the war.

16. J.-L. Robert, "Ouvriers et mouvement ouvrier parisiens pendant la grande guerre et l'immédiat après-guerre" (Doctorat d'Etat thesis, University of Paris-I, 1989), part 1; for divergent views on the restructuring of the working class and leveling of the skill differential in Britain, see Waites, *Class Society at War*, 130–48, who broadly supports the case, and A. Reid, "The Impact of the First World War on British Workers," in Wall and Winter, *Upheaval of War*, 221–33, who is more skeptical.

17. P. Spriano, *Storia di Torino operaia e socialista* (Milan: Einaudi, 1958), ch. 16; D. Mandel, *The Petrograd Workers and the Fall of the Old Regime* (Lon-

don: Macmillan, 1983), 46; J. Hinton, *The First Shop Stewards' Movement* (London: Allen and Unwin, 1973); D. Geary, "Revolutionary Berlin," in C. Wrigley, ed., *Challenges of Labour: Central and Western Europe, 1917–1920* (London: Routledge, 1993), 24–50; J.-L. Robert, *Les Ouvriers, la patrie et la révolution: Paris, 1914–1919* (Besançon: Annales Littéraires de l'Université de Besançon no. 592, Série, Historiques no. 11, 1995).

18. J.-L. Robert and J. M. Winter, *Capital Cities at War: Paris, London, and Berlin, 1914–1919* (Cambridge: Cambridge University Press, 1997).

19. D. Koenker, *Moscow Workers and the 1917 Revolution* (Princeton: Princeton University Press, 1981), 21–22; L. Tomassini, "Industrial Mobilization and the Labour Market in Italy During the First World War," *Social History* 16, no. 1 (1991): 59–87 (75).

20. U. Daniel, *The War from Within: German Women in the First World War* (1989; English trans., Washington D.C.: Berg, 1996), and U. Daniel, "Women's Work in Industry and Family: Germany, 1914–1918," in Wall and Winter, *Upheaval of War*, ch. 10; J.-L. Robert, "Women and Work in France During the First World War," ibid., ch. 9; D. Thom, "Women and Work in Britain," ibid., ch. 11; A. Woollacott, *On Her Their Lives Depend: Women Munitions Workers in the Great War* (Berkeley: University of California Press, 1994), ch. 1; F. Thébaud, *La Femme au temps de la guerre de 1914* (Paris: Stock, 1986).

21. Fridenson, "Impact of the War on French Workers," 239; Kocka, *Facing Total War*, 23–24.

22. Kocka, *Facing Total War*, ch. 3; Waites, *Class Society at War*, ch. 3; Robert and Winter, *Capital Cities at War*.

23. A. Offer, *The First World War: An Agrarian Interpretation* (Oxford: Clarendon, 1989).

24. R. Sieder, "Behind the Lines: Working Class and Family Life in Wartime Vienna," and A. Triebel, "Variations in Patterns of Consumption in Germany in the Period of the First World War," both in Wall and Winter, *Upheaval of War*, 109–38 and 159–95, respectively.

25. J. M. Winter, "Some Paradoxes of the First World War," in Wall and Winter, *Upheaval of War*, 9–42. For a comparison of state provisioning policy and the differences in national experience, see J. Horne, ed., "Nouvelles pistes d'histoire urbaine, 1914–18," special dossier in *Guerres mondiales et conflits contemporains*, 183, 1996, with essays by T. Bonzon on Paris, B. Davis on Berlin, J. Manning on London, and L. Tomassini on Italy.

26. M.-C. Dentoni, *Annona e consenso in Italia, 1914–1919* (Milan: Franco Angeli, 1995); P. B. Struve, *Food Supply in Russia During the World War* (New Haven: Yale University Press, 1930), 407–29.

27. A major advance in the comparative study of these waves of industrial protest has been made by the publication of the proceedings of three linked conferences, drawing together the work of scholars from a number of countries,

viz. L. Haimson and C. Tilly, eds., *Strikes, Wars, and Revolutions in an International Perspective: Strike Waves in the Late Nineteenth and Early Twentieth Centuries* (Cambridge: Cambridge University Press, 1989); Haimson and Sapelli, *Strikes and Social Conflict and the First World War;* and Wrigley, *Challenges of Labour.*

28. J. Wishnia, *The Proletarianizing of the Fonctionnnaires: Civil Service Workers and the Labor Movement Under the Third Republic* (Baton Rouge: Louisiana State University Press, 1990), on France; Kocka, *Facing Total War,* 91–102, on Germany; Waites, *Class Society at War,* 240–64, on Britain.

29. See B. Waites, "The Government of the Home Front and the 'Moral Economy' of the Working Class," in P. H. Liddle, ed., *Home Fires and Foreign Fields: British Social and Military Experience in the First World War* (London: Brassey's Defence, 1985), 175–93; G. Procacci, "State Coercion and Worker Solidarity in Italy (1915–1918): The Moral and Political Content of Social Unrest," in Haimson and Sapelli, *Strikes, Social Conflict, and the First World War,* 145–77, and G. Procacci, "Gli Effetti della grande guerra sulla psicologia della popolazione civile," *Storia e problemi contemporanei* 10 (1992): 77–91; Horne, "Etat, société et économie morale: L'approvisionnement des civils pendant la guerre de 1914–18."

30. H. Hautmann, "Vienna: A City in the Years of Radical Change, 1917–20" in Wrigley, *Challenges of Labour,* 87–104.

31. The argument that rather than being specifically labor or socialist there was a popular movement of protest in tsarist Russia, in which rural and preindustrial traditions and consciousness played a key role, has been persuasively made for the prewar period by C. Read, "Labour and Socialism in Tsarist Russia," in Geary, *Labour and Socialist Movements in Europe,* 137–81 (especially 169–71). See also B. Engel, "Not by Bread Alone: Subsistence Riots in Russia During World War 1," *Journal of Modern History* 69 no. 4 (1997): 696–721.

32. For a comparative view, see Chapter 6. Also relevant are G. Hardach, *The First World War, 1914–1918* (1973; English trans., London: Allen Lane, 1977), ch. 4, and on corporatism, the classic study by C. S. Maier, *Recasting Bourgeois Europe: Stabilization in France, Germany, and Italy in the Decade After World War I* (Princeton: Princeton University Press, 1975). On Britain, see C. Wrigley, "The Ministry of Munitions: An Innovatory Department," in K. Burk, ed., *War and the State: The Transformation of British Government, 1914–1919* (London: Allen & Unwin, 1982), 32–56; R. J. Q. Adams, *Arms and the Wizard: Lloyd George and the Ministry of Munitions* (London: Cassell, 1978); K. Middlemas, *Politics in Industrial Society: The Experience of the British System Since 1911* (London: André Deutsch, 1979); and J. Turner, "The Politics of 'Organized Business' in the First World War," in J. Turner, ed., *Businessmen and Politics: Studies of Business Activity in British Politics, 1900–1945* (London: Heinemann, 1984), 33–49. On France, see R. F. Kuisel, *Capitalism and the State in Modern France: Renovation*

and *Economic Management in the Twentieth Century* (Cambridge: Cambridge University Press, 1981); J. F. Godfrey, *Capitalism at War: Industrial Policy and Bureaucracy in France, 1914–1918* (Leamington Spa: Berg, 1987); and P. Fridenson, ed., *The French Home Front, 1914–1918* (Providence: Berg, 1992), especially 1–13, 89–132. For Germany, see G. Feldman, *Army, Industry, and Labor in Germany, 1914–1918* (1966; new ed., Providence: Berg, 1992).

33. C. Wrigley, *David Lloyd George and the British Labour Movement* (Brighton: Harvester, 1976); C. Wrigley, *A History of British Industrial Relations*, vol. 2: *1914–1939* (Brighton: Harvester, 1987); Reid, "The Impact of the First World War on British Workers"; and G. R. Rubin, *War, Law and Labour: The Munitions Act, State Regulation, and the Unions, 1915–1921* (Oxford: Clarendon, 1987), for a detailed study of how the machinery of wartime industrial relations often worked to labor's advantage.

34. Horne, *Labour at War*, ch. 5.

35. Fridenson, "Impact of the First World War on French Workers"; Horne, *Labour at War*, 63–83, 176–96; Feldman, *Army, Industry, and Labor in Germany*, 120–23; J. A. Moses, *Trade Unionism in Germany from Bismarck to Hitler, 1869–1918* (London: George Prior, 1982), vol. 1, chs. 10, 11.

36. Feldman, *Army, Industry, and Labor in Germany*, chs. 1–4; Kocka, *Facing Total War*, 46.

37. Feldman, *Army, Industry, and Labor in Germany*, 525–27.

38. Robert, *Les Ouvriers*, 291–406; K. Amdur, *Syndicalist Legacy: Trade Unions and Politics in Two French Cities in the Era of World War I* (Urbana: University of Illinois Press, 1986).

39. Tomassini, "Industrial Mobilization and the Labour Market in Italy"; G. Procacci, "La Legislazione repressiva e la sua applicazione," in G. Procacci, ed., *Stato e classe operaia in Italia durante la prima guerra mondiale* (Milan: Franco Angeli, 1983), 41–59 (especially 57).

40. L. H. Siegelbaum, *The Politics of Industrial Mobilization in Russia, 1914–17: A Study of the War Industries Committees* (London: Macmillan, 1983).

41. W. G. Rosenberg and D. P. Koenker, "Strikes and Protest in Revolutionary Russia: Worker Activism in Petrograd and Moscow Between February and October 1917," in Haimson and Sapelli, *Strikes, Social Conflict, and the First World War*, 453–77.

42. For the process of national mobilization, see J. Horne, ed., *State, Society, and Mobilization in Europe During the First World War* (Cambridge: Cambridge University Press, 1997).

43. For good syntheses, see M. Rebérioux, "Le Socialisme et la première guerre mondiale (1914–1918)," in Droz, *Histoire générale du socialisme*, vol. 2: *De 1875 à 1918*, 585–641; A. S. Lindemann, *A History of European Socialism* (New Haven: Yale University Press, 1983), chs. 5, 6; and D. Kirby, *War, Peace, and Revolution: International Socialism at the Crossroads, 1914–1918* (London: Gower, 1986).

44. On the "self-mobilization" of French and British labor, see J. Horne, *Labour at War: France and Britain, 1914–1918* (Oxford: Clarendon, 1991), ch. 2. On the internationalist traditions of British labor, see D. J. Newton, *British Labour, European Socialism, and the Struggle for Peace, 1889–1914* (Oxford: Oxford University Press, 1985). For the Paris labor and socialist movement in the fall of 1914, see J.-L. Robert, "Mobilizing Labor and Socialist Militants in Paris During the Great War," in Horne, *State, Society and Mobilization*, ch. 5.

45. F. Fischer, *Germany's Aims in the First World War* (1961; English trans., London: Chatto & Windus, 1967), chs. 2, 3; C. Schorske, *German Social Democracy, 1905–1917: The Development of the Great Schism* (Cambridge: Harvard University Press, 1955); S. Miller, *Burgfrieden und Klassenkampf: Die deutsche Sozialdemokratie im Ersten Weltkrieg* (Düsseldorf: Droste, 1974); S. Miller and H. Potthoff, *A History of German Social Democracy from 1848 to the Present* (Leamington Spa: Berg, 1986), ch. 5.

46. The question of wartime social morality has only begun to be explored, with little yet attempted on a comparative basis. See, however, Procacci, "Gli Effetti della grande guerra sulla psicologia della popolazione civile," 77–91, and J. Horne, "Social Identity in War: France, 1914–1918," in T. G. Fraser and K. Jeffery, *Men, Women and War* (Dublin: Lilliput, 1993), 119–35.

47. Horne, *Labour at War*, ch. 6.

48. For France, see Prochasson, *Les Intellectuels, le socialisme et la guerre*, 122–29, and for Britain, J. M. Winter, *Socialism and the Challenge of War: Ideas and Politics in Britain, 1912–18* (London: Routledge and Kegan Paul, 1974).

49. For a generic study of this phenomenon, based on a comparison of the French and British cases, see Horne, *Labour at War*, especially ch. 7. For the importance of nationalization, see J. Horne, "L'idée de nationalisation dans les mouvements ouvriers européens jusqu' à la deuxième guerre mondiale," *Le Mouvement social*, 134 (1986): 9–36. On the British case, see also D. Tanner, *Political Change and the Labour Party, 1900–1918* (Cambridge: Cambridge University Press, 1990). On Germany, see Schorske, *German Social Democracy*, and Miller and Potthoff, *History of German Social Democracy*, ch. 5.

50. For the international dimension of labor reformism, see A. Van der Slice, *International Labour, Diplomacy and Peace, 1914–1919* (Oxford: Oxford University Press, 1941), and Horne, *Labour at War*, ch. 8.

51. On the German case, see G. Ritter and S. Miller, *Die Deutsche Revolution, 1918–1919* (Frankfurt/Main: Fischer Bücherei, 1968), 140–41, Maier, *Recasting Bourgeois Europe*; G. Eley, "The SPD in War and Revolution, 1914–1919," in R. Fletcher, ed., *Bernstein to Brandt: A Short History of German Social Democracy* (London: Edward Arnold, 1987), 64–89, and E. Kolb, *Vom Kaiserreich zur Weimarer Republik* (Cologne: Kiepenheuer und Witsch, 1972); id., *The Weimar Republic* (1984; English trans., London: Unwin Hyman, 1988), 3–22. On Austria, see O. Bauer's remarkable personal account of the immediate postwar period,

Die Oesterreichische Revolution (1923), translated as *The Austrian Revolution* (London: Leonard Parsons, 1925).

52. Horne, "L'Idée de nationalisation dans les mouvements ouvriers européens."

53. R. Rolland, *Above the Battlefield* (1914; English trans., London: Macmillan, 1914).

54. Extraordinarily, there is no thorough study of Lenin's wartime revolutionary politics nor a biography comparable in stature to that of Trotsky by Isaac Deutscher. On Lenin and Kautsky and the debate on imperialism, see M. Donald, *Marxism and Revolution: Karl Kautsky and the Russian Marxists, 1900–1924* (New Haven: Yale University Press, 1993), 188–220.

55. S. Miller, "Bernstein's Political Position, 1914–1920," in Fletcher, *Bernstein to Brandt*, 98.

56. Conférence socialiste internationale. Zimmerwald (Suisse): September 5–8, 1915 (Paris [1915]), 22, reproduced in A. and C. Sowerwine, *Le Mouvement ouvrier français contre la guerre, 1914–1918* (Paris: Editions d'Histoire Sociale, 1985), vol. 5: *Le Comité pour la reprise des relations internationales*.

57. For the relationship with its readership of the important pacifist paper *La Vague*, edited by the French "Kienthal" socialist deputy Pierre Brizon in 1918, see T. Bonzon and J.-L. Robert, *Nous crions grâce: 154 lettres de pacifistes, juin–novembre 1916* (Paris: Editions ouvrières, 1989).

58. D. Morgan, *The Socialist Left and the German Revolution: A History of the German Independent Social Democratic Party, 1917–1922* (Ithaca: Cornell University Press, 1975).

59. For France, the standard studies remain A. Kriegel, *Aux Origines du communisme français* (Paris: Mouton, 1964), 2 vols., especially vol. 1., and R. Wohl, *French Communism in the Making, 1914–1924* (Stanford: Stanford University Press, 1964). For Britain, see W. Kendall, *The Revolutionary Movement in Britain: The Origins of British Communism* (London: Weidenfeld and Nicolson, 1969), 174–76.

60. Kirby, *War, Peace and Revolution*, 155–56.

61. J.-J. Becker, "Jean Longuet et l'union sacrée (1914–1918)," in G. Candar, ed., *Jean Longuet, la conscience et l'action* (Paris: Revue Politique et Parlementaire, 1988), 43–54 (52).

62. The key works on the diplomatic context and Wilsonism remain A. J. Mayer, *Political Origins of the New Diplomacy, 1917–1918* (New Haven: Yale University Press, 1959), and ibid., *Politics and Diplomacy of Peacemaking: Containment and Counter-Revolution at Versailles, 1918–1919* (London: Weidenfeld and Nicolson, 1968).

63. The British Labour leader Arthur Henderson and the French socialist armaments minister Albert Thomas went as plenipotentiaries to the Provisional Government. Other socialists visited the Petrograd soviet (Cachin and Moutet

for the French Socialist Party). On French attitudes to the February revolution, see I. Sinanoglou, "Frenchmen: Their Revolutionary Heritage and the Russian Revolution," *International History Review* 2, no. 4 (1980): 566–84, and F. Furet, *Le Passé d'une illusion*, ch. 3.

64. S. Fitzpatrick, *The Russian Revolution*, 2nd ed. (Oxford: Oxford University Press, 1994), ch. 2; and (on the army), A. Wildman, *The End of the Russian Imperial Army*, vol. 1: *The Old Army and the Soldiers' Revolt (March–April 1917)*, and vol. 2: *The Road to Soviet Power and Peace* (Princeton: Princeton University Press, 1980, 1987).

65. P. Broué, "La Révolution russe et le mouvement ouvrier allemand" in M. Ferro et al., *La Révolution d'octobre et le mouvement ouvrier européen* (Paris: Etudes et Documentation Internationales, 1968), 51–74 (58).

66. Robert, *Les Ouvriers*, 145–50. For the importance of the language of revolution, including the example of the soviets, in expressing what were substantively much more restricted demands during the French mutinies in May–June 1917, see G. Pedroncini, *Les Mutineries de 1917* (Paris: Presses Universitaires de France, 1967), 309–13.

67. S. R. Graubard, *British Labour and the Russian Revolution, 1917–1924* (Cambridge: Harvard University Press, 1956).

68. Graubard, *British Labour and the Russian Revolution*, 44–63; R. Page Arnot, *The Impact of the Russian Revolution in Britain* (London: Lawrence and Wishart, 1967), 117–20; A. Kriegel, "L'Opinion publique française et la révolution russe," in Fay et al., *La Révolution d'octobre et le mouvement ouvrier européen*, 75–104; Robert, *Les Ouvriers*, 217–20.

69. K. Kautsky, *The Dictatorship of the Proletariat* (1918; English trans., London: National Labour Press, 1919); Donald, *Marxism and Revolution*, 221–46.

70. For the Italian case, see J. Cammet, *Antonio Gramsci and the Origins of Italian Communism* (Stanford: Stanford University Press, 1967), 35–62, and G. Arfé, *Storia del socialiso italiano, 1892–1926* (Turin: Einaudi, 1965), 239–49.

71. This tendency is perfectly illustrated by the enthusiasm of key French revolutionary syndicalists for the Bolshevik revolution and their subsequent rejection of communism. See the writings of Pierre Monatte in C. Chambelland, ed., *La Lutte syndicale* (Paris: Maspero, 1976), and J. Jennings, *Syndicalism in France: A Study of Ideas* (London: Macmillan, 1990), 175–78.

72. These alternative currents of revolutionary socialism are studied in A. S. Lindemann, *The "Red Years": European Socialism versus Bolshevism, 1919–1921* (Berkeley: University of California Press, 1974). For an intellectual history of the particular susceptibility of French left-wing intellectuals to the communist appropriation of the key term "revolution," see Furet, *Le Passé d'une illusion*, ch. 3, and C. Prochasson and A. Rasmussen, *Au Nom de la patrie: Les intellectuels et la première guerre mondiale (1910–1919)* (Paris: Editions la découverte, 1996), ch. 6.

73. For recent discussions of labor from this perspective, see C. L. Bertrand, ed., *Situations révolutionnaires en Europe, 1917–1922: Allemagne, Italie, Autriche-Hongrie* (Montreal: Centre Interuniversitaire d'études européennes, 1977); D. Geary, *European Labour Protest 1848–1939* (London: Croom Helm, 1981), ch. 4; Haimson and Sapelli, *Strikes, Social Conflict, and the First World War,* especially 13–21; and Wrigley, *Challenges of Labour,* ch. 1.

74. For one attempt, focusing on key leaders, see D. S. White, *Lost Comrades: Socialists of the Front Generation, 1918–1945* (Cambridge: Harvard University Press, 1992).

Part

III

_____

The

Shadow

of

War

CHAPTER 8

The War, Imperialism, and Decolonization

A. S. KANYA-FORSTNER

The First World War, Lenin wrote in 1920, had indeed been "imperi-alistic (that is, an annexationist, predatory, plunderous war) on the part of both sides; it was a war for the division of the world, for the partition and repartition of colonies, 'spheres of influence' of fi-nance capital, etc."[1] This may have been pitching it a little high; but Lenin's claim was not totally unfounded. No power, not even Ger-many, went to war in 1914 specifically for the purpose of expanding its colonial empire.[2] By then the principal objectives of German *Weltpolitik* were continental: the creation of a German-dominated economic union in Central Europe and the extension of German influence into the Balkans and the Middle East.[3] But the construc-tion of a territorially unified empire out of her possessions in East, West, and South-West Africa was still one of the goals of German world policy, and *Mittelafrika* could be created only by taking ter-ritory from Portugal, Belgium, and France. Such ambitions had prompted the German demand for the whole of the French Congo and part of Gabon during the Moroccan crisis of 1911. Although the Franco-German Agreement of November 1911 failed to give Ger-many everything she wanted, the Cameroons did gain access to the

Congo-Ubangi river system and hence a short common frontier with the Belgian Congo.[4] The agreement with France was soon followed by intermittent talks with Britain over the future of central Africa, including a possible partition of the Portuguese and Belgian colonies.[5] Chancellor Bethmann Hollweg's last-minute bid to secure British neutrality on July 29, 1914, also made it clear that *Mittelafrika* was still on the German agenda. In his conversation with the British ambassador, Bethmann Hollweg promised that a victorious Germany would make no territorial demands on France in Europe, but he pointedly refused to extend this guarantee to the French colonial empire.[6] The chancellor's notorious September Programme, drafted when victory on the Western Front still appeared imminent, did not elaborate on the "question of colonial acquisitions, where the first aim is the creation of a continuous Central African colonial empire."[7] The German colonial minister, however, was willing to be much more explicit. Portugal, although still neutral, would have to cede Angola and the northern half of Mozambique; Belgium would have to give up the Congo; France would have to surrender Equatorial Africa as far north as Lake Chad, Dahomey, and the northern part of the Niger Bend, along with Timbuktu. And if Britain were to be defeated as well, she would have to part with Nigeria![8] This was colonial repartitioning with a vengeance.

Britain and France did not have similar designs on the German colonial empire, but the outbreak of war gave them opportunities that they were quick to seize. Two days after its declaration of war the British government decided to attack the German colonies "[in order] to harm Germany as much as possible everywhere we can."[9] German Togoland was invaded on August 7, more than a week before the British Expeditionary Force landed in France, and German resistance was quickly overcome. British and French forces, the latter accompanied by some Belgian troops, also invaded the Cameroons, although fighting there continued until February 1916. All the other German territories in Africa and the Pacific were occupied one by one, and it was clear from the start that they would not be returned. The possibilities for global repartition grew larger still when the Ottoman Empire entered the war on the side of the Central Powers at the end of October 1914. British and French overseas war aims were soon expanded to include the Arab Middle East, and both powers recognized their Russian ally's age-old claims to Constantinople and the Straits of the Dardanelles.[10]

During the course of the war British objectives overseas were defined by a succession of Cabinet committees: the Committee on Asiatic Turkey (March 1915); the Territorial Changes Committee (August 1916); the Territorial Desiderata Committee (March 1917); and the Eastern Committee (March 1918). Despite the shifting fortunes of war, the partition of the German and Turkish empires remained high on the list of British priorities. Nor was the imperial emphasis in British war aims altogether surprising. After the palace coup that brought Lloyd George to power in December 1916, the War Cabinet included the two grand old men of British imperialism—Lord Milner, the former high commissioner for South Africa, and Lord Curzon, the former viceroy of India—to say nothing of the prime minister himself. Lloyd George made no secret of his imperial ambitions, not even to the Americans. As he told Colonel House in November 1917, British objectives included "the African colonies [of Germany] both east and west; an independent Arabia under the suzerainty of Great Britain, Palestine to be given to the Zionists under British or, if desired by us, under American control; an independent Armenia and the internationalization of the Straits."[11] Lloyd George's list was not even complete; he could have added South-West Africa and the German colonies in the Pacific, all of them reserved for the Dominions, as well as Mesopotamia.

By contrast, the imperialists responsible for shaping French colonial war aims were to be found outside rather than inside the government. When dealing with colonial issues the government's policy was to proceed "not on the basis of any general programme but exclusively on the basis of prevailing circumstances, taking account only of immediate concrete interests."[12] For most of the war, consideration of colonial war aims thus remained the more or less exclusive concern of the leaders of the French colonialist movement and their allies among officials in the Ministries of Colonies and Foreign Affairs. Only in February 1918 did the government finally establish an official commission, the Commission d'étude des questions coloniales posées par la guerre, to draft a comprehensive set of colonial war aims for a possible future peace conference, and this commission too was little more than a colonialist pressure group. Its secretary-general and most of its *rapporteurs* were prominent colonialists, as were its two vice-presidents and most influential members: Eugène Etienne, the undisputed leader of the French "colonial party," and Gaston Doumergue, a former minister of colonies and the leading colonialist politician in the senate.[13] Not surprisingly, therefore, French claims to enemy territory were scarcely less ambitious than those of their British allies. In the Middle East the goal was to establish a French sphere of influence over *la Syrie intégrale:* all of Syria, from the Taurus mountains to Sinai and from the Mediterranean to the desert, including Palestine.[14] In North Africa, the French wanted their Moroccan protectorate freed from the restrictions imposed, as a result of German pressure, by the Algeciras Act. And as their share of the German colonial empire they wanted all of the Cameroons and as much of Togoland as they could get.

Nor were British and French ambitions limited to enemy possessions. As part of their colonial planning both sides developed a bewildering array of proposals for taking territory from each other, as well as from other allies and neutrals. The prizes for the French in North Africa were the international city of Tangier and the Spanish zone of Morocco. In West Africa the goal was to create a "unified empire" by acquiring the British, Portuguese, and Spanish enclaves, as well as the independent state of Liberia. Among the "enclaves" included in the most extravagant of these plans were the Gold Coast and Nigeria.[15] British designs on the French colonial empire were somewhat more modest, concentrating for the most part on Djibuti and French interests in Ethiopia. But various British discussion papers at one time or another suggested the acquisition of Tahiti, the French share of New Hebrides Condominium, French possessions in India, Dahomey, St. Pierre and Miquelon, and the Newfoundland Fisheries, not to mention parts of the Belgian Congo and Portuguese Africa.[16]

Britain and France were not the only powers to dream of colonial aggrandizement. The Belgians hoped to secure Cabinda and the south bank of the Congo from the Portuguese through an ingenious three-cornered exchange, giving Britain the territory that their troops had occupied in the northwest corner of German East Africa, in return for which the British would compensate the Portuguese in the southern part of German East Africa or possibly in South-West Africa.[17] Greediest of all were the Italians, who had been drawn into the war by Anglo-French promises of territory in Europe, the Middle East and Africa. The Italian Colonial Ministry's "maximum programme," drawn up in November 1916, laid claim to British Somaliland, Jubaland with Kismayu, French Somalia with Djibuti and the Djibuti–Addis Ababa railroad, an exclusive sphere of influence in Ethiopia, and the extension of Libya south to Lake Chad.[18]

All this was heady stuff, but the realities of global repartition proved rather less exciting. The disposition of the German colonies was determined largely by the manner of their conquest. The first to fall was Togo. By the end of August it had been occupied by troops from the Gold Coast and Dahomey and provisionally partitioned, with the French obtaining a larger slice of territory but the British gaining control of the capital, Lomé, and the colony's railway lines.

In the Cameroons, the territories ceded by France to Germany in 1911 were simply reincorporated into French Equatorial Africa. The rest of the German colony was initially administered as an Anglo-French condominium and then partitioned between the two allied powers in February 1916. When the partition talks began, François Georges-Picot claimed nine-tenths of the Cameroons for France and was more than a little surprised to have his demands immediately accepted. What Picot did not know was that his British counterparts had instructions to give him anything he asked for, "provided that we got a quid pro quo in the fact that they [the French] made no claims to East Africa."[19] Picot drew the partition line on a small-scale map "in a casual way with with a blue pencil," without regard for ethnic boundaries or the interests of the local populations who, needless to say, were not consulted during this bizarre exercise.[20] German South-West Africa was occupied by British South African troops. Most of German East Africa also fell to the British; but its conquest proved much more difficult than anticipated and eventually required some assistance from the Belgians, who occupied the provinces of Ruanda and Urundi in the northwest. In the Far East, Kiaochow on the Shantung peninsula and the German Pacific islands north of the Equator were taken by the Japanese, Samoa by New Zealand, and the remaining Pacific islands as well as New Guinea by Australia.[21]

The most important of the wartime partitions was that of the Arab Middle East. Here the notorious Sykes-Picot Agreement of 1916 allotted France direct control over Cilicia and Lebanon, along with a sphere of influence in Syria as far east as the Persian border. The British received direct control over Haifa and Acre on the Mediterranean coast and over southern Mesopotamia, together with a sphere of influence that included what later became Transjordan. The two spheres of influence were in turn to form an independent Arab state in which Britain and France were to have exclusive rights to provide economic assistance and advisers in their respective spheres. In this roundabout way the British government hoped to reconcile its commitments to France and its own imperial ambitions with the pledge it had earlier given Sharif Husain of Mecca "to recognize and support the independence of the Arabs" outside the areas of direct European control. Palestine (which may or may not have been included in the undertaking to Husain) was to be placed under an international administration, with the details to be decided after consultation with Russia, Italy, and the representatives of Husain. Neither side, however, considered this part of the agreement definitive. Picot soon obtained a secret assurance of Russian support in any future negotiations to bring Palestine within the French sphere. Sykes, for his part, soon began to consider the possibility of using the Zionist movement as a way to bring Palestine under a British protectorate.[22]

As it turned out, nothing ever came of the more grandiose plans for global repartition inspired by the war. Anglo-French territorial exchanges proved impracticable because neither side had anything to trade. Dreams of a French Nigeria or Gold Coast could never be realized without massive concessions elsewhere in the world, which virtually nobody was prepared to contemplate.[23] The prolonged dispute over the future of Tangier, which lasted into the mid-1920s, merely served to embitter Anglo-French relations. In the end the city retained its international status.[24] More modest proposals also came to naught. The French, for their part, were determined not to surrender any essential part of their empire, which for the Commission d'étude included not merely Djibuti but St. Pierre and Miquelon and the Newfoundland Fisheries as well.[25] The British found the notion of abandoning parts of their empire equally difficult to swallow. Any proposal to cede territory in Africa, the parliamentary undersecretary at the Foreign Office complained in December 1918, was bound to be met by objections that "there is an aeroplane station, or a submarine base, or that it is the oldest colony, or it will offend some New Zealand politician if we do it, or something of that kind."[26] Although suggestions for a deal involving the Gambia continued to be floated from time to time, none of them ever made it to the bargaining table.[27]

Repartitions of the sort envisaged by the imperial powers seemed even more farfetched in the new international climate created by the Russian revolutions of 1917 and America's involvement in the war. President Wilson's appeal for a statement of belligerent war aims in December 1916 and his call for "peace without victory" a month later had already given notice that secret plans for the "division of the world" would face an uncertain future. The Anglo-French reply to Wilson's appeal contained no reference to the German colonies. As Louis Mallet of the Foreign Office noted, "It would be very awkward to tell Dear Mr. Wilson of our intentions for fear he would never understand our arguments."[28] The American declaration of war on Germany in April 1917, sandwiched between the abdication of the tsar and the mutinies in the French army on the Western Front, made Wilson even more of a force to be reckoned with, for it soon became obvious that the American contribution to winning the war would be decisive. Nor did the president wait long to make his own intentions clear. On January 8, 1918, he issued his famous Fourteen Points, one of which called for colonial settlements to be based on the principle that "the interests of the populations concerned must have equal weight with the equitable claims of the government whose title is to be determined." In his Four Principles a few weeks later he went further still, insisting that territorial settlements must be concluded "in the interests and for the benefit of the population concerned, and not as part of any mere adjustment or compromise of claims against rival states."[29] By then the Provisional Government had already renounced Russia's territorial ambitions, and at the end of 1917 the victorious Bolsheviks had formally denounced the secret treaties partitioning the Ottoman Empire, which they then proceeded to publish.[30]

The significance of this changing climate was not lost on allied leaders, whose chief preoccupation after America's entry into the war was to give their imperialist objectives at least the appearance of conforming to Wilsonian principles of self-determination. In June 1917 the French government disclaimed "any thought of conquest or the subjection of foreign populations." At the same time, Lloyd George declared "the wishes, the desires and the interests" of the indigenous population to be the "dominant factor" in determining the future of the German colonies, and a few months later he reaffirmed his commitment to the "general principle of self-determination."[31] Henceforth, claims to a share of the German colonies would have to be based not on the right of conquest or on strategic requirements but on the interests of the indigenous inhabitants. "Whether one likes it or not," Albert Duchêne of the French Colonial Ministry noted in January 1918, "the African question will not be settled at the end of the war simply according to the imperialist ambitions of the Great Powers. [The peace-makers] will also take account, if not of the rights then at least of the interests and perhaps even the wishes of the native populations."[32]

The Soviet publication of the Sykes-Picot Agreement also made it impossible to reconcile Anglo-French ambitions in the Middle East with the new Wilsonian principles. By March 1918, Sykes himself was convinced that the agreement was "dead and gone and the sooner scrapped the better." "It is no use thinking in terms of the past," he warned his French colleague. "President Wilson's voice is now the important one, and ideas that do not fit in with his speeches won't have much influence on the Peace Conference. Any question of annexation or direct control as a post-war form of settlement I think is now fairly disposed of."[33] The French were obliged to agree with Sykes' sentiments, if not with his conclusions, and the principle of self-determination was duly embodied in the Anglo-French declaration of November 7, 1918, to the peoples of the Ottoman Empire.[34]

French officials were especially worried by the threat of misplaced American idealism. According to Gaston Doumergue of the Commission d'étude, America now represented the chief obstacle to the achievement of French imperial objectives: "She is the key to everything." In deference to American scruples, the partition of the German colonies would have to be based on the principle that "[they] will be given to countries which have colonies next to them and which seem most capable of guiding them along the path of civilization. . . . Thus for Togo and the Cameroons we shall be in a very favourable position."[35] The work of the Peace Conference would also have to be limited to the disposition of the German colonies. Other imperial issues, including Anglo-French colonial exchanges, which could so easily appear "contrary to the general sense of the peace," would have to be insulated from American interference and settled through bilateral negotiations.[36] Meanwhile in London, the French ambassador tried to convince the British Foreign Secretary of the need to settle all outstanding issues before the Peace Conference began, "so that when the President [Wilson] came over, he would find himself face to face with a united opposition and an accomplished fact." To reinforce his argument Paul Cambon even raised the specter of a future war that would pit Britain and France against the combined might of the United States and Germany! But the British would have none of this. A. J. Balfour dismissed Cambon's "new apocalyptic revelations" as "little short of insanity."[37] Curzon for his part warned the Eastern Committee on December 2, three weeks after the Armistice, that "the great power from whom we have most to fear in future is France." Jan Smuts came to the same conclusion: "France may be our great problem, and therefore we should make friends with America. That is the line of policy for us to pursue."[38]

French imperialists had to contend with an even more serious obstacle: their own prime minister. Although the passionate anti-colonialism of his earlier years had mellowed with the passage of time, Georges Clemenceau was still, by his own admission, "the least colonialist of all Frenchmen,"[39] and when the war ended in November 1918, he alone determined French foreign policy. Clemenceau's overriding objective was to ensure complete French security against any possible threat of renewed German aggression in Europe, which in concrete terms meant the return of Alsace-Lorraine and French control over the left bank of the Rhine. In pursuit of this objective he therefore proposed "to make concessions to Wilson and the British on any question which doesn't involve our frontier, so that we can then become intransigent."[40] Clemenceau's strategy had two immediate consequences for the achievement of French imperial ambitions. In December 1918, even before the Peace Conference convened, he disregarded the advice of his Foreign Ministry and agreed to Lloyd George's request for the transfer of Mosul and Palestine to the British sphere of influence in the Middle East.[41] In January 1919, when the future of the German colonies came up for discussion at the conference, he listened to his minister of colonies, Henri Simon, make an eloquent case for annexing the German colonies outright, and then accepted the principle of trusteeship that came to be embodied in the League of Nations Mandate system.

In the event, the American challenge to European imperial designs proved to be less of a threat than many had feared. The Americans, it is true, were eager to consult the peoples of the Middle East about their future—as indeed were the British. Husain's son Faisal, who now governed most of Syria with British assistance, was invited to the Peace Conference as the representative of the Arabs and was able to put the case for Syrian independence to the Supreme Council. The Zionisis too were allowed to put their case for Palestine. In order to keep the balance, the French arranged for their clients in the

Comité Central Syrien and a delegation from Mount Lebanon to address the Council as well.[42] Afterward, at Wilson's suggestion, an allied commission of enquiry was sent to ascertain the wishes of the population directly. But the British and French quickly decided not to take part, and the conclusions of the all-American enquiry were ignored by everyone, including the Americans.[43] At British insistence the White Dominions and India were also represented at the Peace Conference, ostensibly on the grounds of their contributions to the war effort.[44] The French did not demand similar representation for their empire. On their own initiative, Algerian, Tunisian, and Vietnamese nationalists submitted lists of demands based on Wilsonian principles. But all of them were ignored, and when the future Ho Chi Minh tried to call on Wilson he was promptly shown the door. Nobody at the Peace Conference, least of all the Americans, took the notion of extending self-government to Germany's African colonies seriously. According to G. L. Beer, Wilson's chief colonial expert, "the negro race has hitherto shown no capacity for progressive development except under the tutelage of other peoples." Beer even suggested that such incapacity might be biologically determined, pointing out that many scientists accepted "as an established physiological fact that the cranial sutures of the Negro close at an early age," so preventing "organic intellectual progress thereafter."[45] The only expression of African opinion at the conference came through the Pan-African Congress, which was organized in Paris with the unofficial support of the French government, in the face of American attempts to block it.[46]

In any case the colonial powers would have had little to fear from such an airing of nationalist aspirations; at this stage most nationalists sought reforms rather than independence. The Jeunes Algériens of Emir Khaled called for the nomination of an Algerian delegate to the Peace Conference, representation for Algerian Muslims in the French Parliament, and access to French citizenship without the loss of Muslim personal status.[47] The Pan-African Congress did not demand self-government for Africans; it merely requested "the right to participate in government as fast as their development permits."[48] Even Ho Chi Minh's demands stopped short of independence, calling instead for representation in the French Parliament, a guarantee of basic freedoms, equal rights, an amnesty for political prisoners, an end to forced labor, and the abolition of the salt tax.[49]

The German colonies were eventually designated as mandates of the League of Nations, with sovereignty over them residing formally in the League and the mandatory powers answerable to the League for their administration. But Simon was not far off the mark when he told Beer, soon after the mandatory principle had been accepted, that there was "no difference between a colony and . . . [a] mandated area."[50] The Pacific colonies and South-West Africa were classified as "C" Mandates, to be administered "under the laws of the Mandatory as integral portions of its territory," subject only to a ban on the slave, arms, and liquor trades, as well as on the construction of military bases.[51] The choice of mandatories—Japan, Australia, New Zealand, and South Africa—merely confirmed their status as the occupying powers. The tropical African colonies were classified as "B" Mandates and assigned to Britain, Belgium, and France, more or less along the wartime partition lines, although the partition of Togo was modified so as to give the French Lomé and the railway lines. The mandatory powers in tropical Africa were prohibited from imposing protectionist customs duties, but this was the only additional restraint on their freedom of action. After prolonged negotiations with the British and the Americans, the French even secured the right to raise troops and use them for metropolitan defense in the event of another European war—which was all that really mattered to Clemenceau.[52]

The disposition of the Ottoman Empire's Arab provinces proved much more difficult and contentious. The distinction between spheres of influence and direct control embodied in the Sykes-Picot Agreement inevitably disappeared. Instead, the Arab territories were classified as "A" Mandates, whose "existence as independent nations can be provisionally recognised subject to the rendering of administrative advice and assistance by a Mandatory until such time as they are able to stand alone." The future of Syria in particular became the subject of a protracted and acrimonious Anglo-French dispute; on one occasion Clemenceau, then aged 78, was supposed to have offered Lloyd George the choice of pistols or swords.[53] In the end, however, the broad lines of the Sykes-Picot partition, as modified by the Clemenceau–Lloyd George accord of December 1918, were confirmed. At the San Remo Conference in April 1920, the mandates for Syria and Lebanon were assigned to France; those for Palestine (including Transjordan) and Iraq went to Britain.[54]

The peace settlements overseas were thus shaped less by the new principle of self-determination than by the much older dictum "To the Victors go the Spoils." Having lost the war, Germany lost all her prewar influence overseas, not merely her African and Pacific colonies and concessions but also the economic advantages that she had enjoyed in Morocco under the terms of the Algeciras Act. Even the venerable Berlin Act of 1885 was revised to deprive Germany of her rights as one of the signatories. With the loss of her Arab territories the Ottoman Empire effectively ceased to exist and eventually became the Turkish Republic. For a time after 1920, even parts of Anatolia and Constantinople itself were occupied by the allies. The allies, of course, no longer included Russia, which had signed a separate peace with Germany in March 1918 and thereby placed itself among the vanquished.[55] Indeed, the Treaty of Brest-Litovsk amputated vast tracts of the prewar Russian empire from the infant Soviet state—from Finland and the Baltic littoral in the north to the Caucasus in the south, along with Poland and the Ukraine.[56] Although some of these territories were eventually reincorporated into the Soviet Union, others, such as Finland, were lost forever.

As was to be expected, the lesser powers among the victorious allies received the smallest shares of the spoils. "Gallant Little Belgium" never did acquire the south bank of the Congo. She did obtain a portion of German East Africa, but her mandate over Ruanda and Urundi actually comprised less territory than her troops had occupied during the war. The Portuguese, who entered the war late and took virtually no part in the conquest of the German colonies, received practically nothing: a scrap of territory in the southeast corner of German East Africa known as the Kionga Triangle.[57] Italy did not participate in the war outside Europe either, and her pickings were correspondingly slim. Despite wartime promises, Italy eventually received nothing from the partition of the Ottoman Empire and had to settle for whatever her allies were willing to give up in North Africa: Jubaland and minor changes to the Libyan frontiers.[58]

As was also to be expected, the chief beneficiaries of the peace settlements overseas were Great Britain (together with the Dominions) and France, which emerged from the war with their empires not merely intact but considerably enlarged. The British empire grew by about one million square miles in Africa and the Pacific. The French also managed to add about a quarter of million square miles, and three million people, to their African holdings. These imperial extensions, of course, came in the form of mandates rather than outright acquisitions of territory. But the terms of the mandates were so loose and the powers of the League so limited that the distinction was largely academic. The war and the influence of the United States on the peace settlement also forced the colonial powers to change their imperial rhetoric and to justify their empires in terms of the benefits conferred upon their subject peoples. But the postwar emphasis on the ideals of trusteeship, self-determination, and eventual self-government was less radical than it appeared. Such concepts had long been included in the canon of British imperialism, and trusteeship if not self-government formed part of the French *mission civilisatrice* as well as Belgian *moralisation*. Moreover, these were general principles, not necessarily guides to policy. There was as yet no serious thought of dismantling empires and granting colonies independence in the near or, in the case of Africa, even in the foreseeable future. The rise of Labour and pressure for domestic reform in Britain may have diluted popular support for imperialism there, but it produced no broadly based demand for imperial devolution.[59] In France, the imperial contribution to the war effort made the Empire, perhaps for first time in its history, widely if not deeply popular.[60]

Nevertheless, historians have some grounds for choosing the First World War as the conventional starting point for their surveys of decolonization, even if its short-term effects were largely indirect and its full impact would not be felt for several years.[61] Of most immediate significance was the role of the various colonial empires in the war itself; indeed, the French colonial empire's newfound popularity after 1919 was itself a function of its massive contribution to the war effort. In all, the Empire mobilized some 600,000 soldiers for active service, most of them from Algeria and French West Africa. It also sent more than 200,000 civilian workers to France, the majority from Indochina and the Maghreb. Imperial troops distinguished themselves on the Western Front, where a Moroccan regiment became the most decorated unit in the French army. The *tirailleurs sénégalais* also fought at Gallipoli and in the Balkans, as well as in various African campaigns. After the war they helped to garrison Syria and formed part of the French occupation force in the Rhineland, where outraged German protests over their (vastly exaggerated) depredations made them even more popular in French eyes.[62] The imperial contribution to the British war effort was much more impressive still. Well over a million troops from the White Dominions took part in the fighting, and many of their exploits—whether of the Canadians on the Western Front or of the Australians at Gallipoli—became the stuff of legend. India alone raised almost 1.5 million men, more than a million of whom (including noncombatants) served overseas, along with 250,000 British troops previously garrisoned in the Viceroyalty. Indian contingents fought, albeit briefly, on the Western Front, as well as in the Balkans, in East Africa and above all in the Middle East, where they made up half the total British force. India's financial contribution—almost £1.5 billion by 1920—was equally important. Most of the money was raised through war loans, but it included an outright gift of £100 million in 1917.[63] In addition to men and money, the empires also supplied food and raw materials. A persistent shortage of shipping prevented the French colonies from sending as much food as metropolitan planners had anticipated. The bulk of Indochina's rice exports, for example, remained in the Far East. But imports from Canada, Australia, and India, along with the U.S., were vital for keeping Britain fed during the war, just as food shortages may have played a role in Germany's collapse.[64]

The demands of the war were bound to intensify the impact of colonial rule on its subjects. More intensive production, recruitment drives, the requisition of supplies and labor, price rises in food and other essential commodities, all these new burdens brought home the full reality of colonial subjection—in many regions of sub-Saharan Africa, for the first time. These increased exactions were in turn accompanied by a weakening of the European presence on the ground as local administrators, traders, and colonists volunteered or were called up. The extension of the war to the Ottoman Empire in November 1914 posed additional problems for the British and the French, raising serious fears about the continued loyalty of their Muslim subjects in India and North Africa.

Wartime pressures created a potentially dangerous situation in both the British and the French colonies. Most parts of the French empire were shaken by disturbances, though imperial control was never seriously threatened anywhere. The first large-scale recruiting drive in West Africa provoked a major rebellion in the Niger Bend at the end of 1915.[65] There was widespread unrest in southeastern Algeria at the end of 1916[66]; revolts in southern Madagascar and Niger in 1916–17, the latter organized by the Sanusiyya, which had already driven the Italians out of Fezzan[67]; and scattered insurrections in Indochina throughout the course of the war. The British had to cope with similar challenges in many of their African possessions, although the level of unrest never reached the same proportions. Indeed, the most famous wartime rebellion against British rule—the Chilembwe rising in Nyasaland—was also the least serious.[68] The most notable exception to this pattern of unrest was India, where the outbreak of war prompted a massive demonstration of loyalty to the Raj, not least by Indian nationalists hoping for a rapid advance to self-government once the war had been won. This wave of imperial enthusiasm soon dissipated as prospects for an early victory receded. In 1916 the "Extremist" leader Bal Gangadhar Tilak and Annie Besant of the Indian National Congress organized their Home Rule Leagues to agitate for self-government, and at the end of the year Tilak forged an alliance between Congress and the Muslim League. But the Extremists were now much less extreme than they had been a decade before, and their agitation posed no real threat to British control.[69]

The war and its challenges were bound to affect imperial policies. As their coercive powers weakened, colonial rulers were forced to rely more on persuasion and to offer their subjects some reward for their continued loyalty. These considerations produced a number of wartime reforms, along with promises of much more to come. In December 1914, Algerian volunteers and their fathers, as well as migrant workers who spent more than a year in France, were exempted from the *indigénat,* the system of summary native justice imposed on most French colonial subjects. The extension of compulsory military service to the inhabitants of the "Four Communes" of Senegal in 1915–16 was accompanied by a confirmation of their rights as French citizens, regardless of their Muslim personal status.[70] In January 1918, Blaise Diagne, the first Black African elected to the French Parliament, was sent to organize the last great recruiting drive in West Africa and to announce new reforms: tax exemptions for volunteers, some relaxation of the *indigénat,* and access to French citizenship for decorated war veterans. At the same time, the government announced its intention to create a special category of citizenship, compatible with Muslim personal status, for Algerian war veterans.[71] These were, at best, modest reforms of limited scope. But the British seemed willing to take much bolder steps in order to ensure the loyalty of their Indian subjects. In August 1917 the secretary of state for India officially announced the government's commitment to "the increasing association of Indians in every branch of the administration, and the gradual development of self-governing institutions with a view to the progressive realization of responsible government in India as an integral part of the Empire."[72]

The end of the war brought new challenges with it as well. The principal British war aim overseas had been the traditional one of Indian security and control over the routes to her most important Asian possession. By 1919 the British position in India seemed as fully insured as anyone could have wished. British predominance on the East African coast was now solidly established with the acquisition of the Tanganyika mandate. Control over Egypt and the Suez Canal had been consolidated in December 1914 with the proclamation of a British protectorate; it was soon to be reinsured by the Palestine mandate. With Palestine, Transjordan, and Iraq added to her existing spheres of influence in Persia and Afghanistan, Britain also dominated a virtually uninterrupted swathe of territory stretching all the way from South Africa to India, while Australia and New Zealand, at the other end of the "East of Suez Arc," expanded the orbit of subimperial control with their mandates over the German colonies in the Pacific. And to make Indian assurance doubly sure, British troops were garrisoned in the Caucasus and Transcaspia. But all this amounted to a caricature of imperial overreach, and almost immediately British predominance in Asia threatened to crumble under the weight of her Indian insurance policies. The deportation of the nationalist leader Saad Zaghlul from Egypt in March 1919 provoked massive protests that quickly turned violent. By the summer British troops were fighting in Afghanistan, and by the end of the year British attempts to consolidate their primacy in Persia were also coming unstuck. In May 1920, Mustafa Kemal began to organize Turkish resistance against the allies in Anatolia, and in July a rebellion broke out in Iraq. By February 1921, with the signature of treaties between the Soviet Union, Persia, Afghanistan, and Turkey, the Russian bogeyman had reappeared on the northwest frontier of India. For a time India itself threatened to go up in flames. The Punjab riots and the Amritsar massacre in April 1919 swung even moderate nationalists against the British. In 1920, Gandhi launched his campaign of noncooperation, which India's Muslims, spurred on by the allied occupation of Constantinople and the harsh peace terms imposed on Turkey, quickly joined. Asian unrest was bad enough. Worse still, it coincided with an imperial crisis much closer to home in Ireland, and with labor unrest in Britain itself. Given the losses suffered during four years of war and the massive pressure for rapid demobilization afterward, it was obvious that the British world system could not be managed according to the old rules any longer.[73]

French imperial overreach was not quite so dramatic. But French losses in the war—almost 1.5 million dead and twice that number seriously wounded—were by far the heaviest of the Western allies, and the security of their eastern frontier against the possible threat of a resurgent Germany was bound to be the chief French postwar concern. Nevertheless, France too had to face her share of crises in her newly enlarged global empire, many of them of her own making. To strengthen their hold over their Middle Eastern mandates, the French created Greater Lebanon by adding the predominantly Muslim regions of Tripoli, Tyre, Sidon, and the Beqaa Valley to the traditional heartland of their Maronite Catholic clients in Mount Lebanon. The consequences of that decision were to haunt the Middle East for more than half a century.[74] By the beginning of 1920, Turkish resistance in Cilicia had turned into a full-scale war. Faced like the British with pressures for rapid demobilization, the French were unable to send reinforcements and were quickly pushed back. Fighting with the Turkish nationalists continued for more than a year until the French were forced to make peace, more or less on Ataturk's terms, in June 1921.[75] In Syria itself, the French installed themselves by force, driving Faisal out of Damascus in July 1920. They then carved up their mandate along ethnic and religious lines, creating a separate state for the Druzes in the south and another for the Alawis around Latakia on the Mediterranean coast. Even Aleppo and Damascus were initially placed under separate administrations.[76] But the arrangement satisfied nobody and did not bring an end to unrest. In 1925 a rebellion broke out among the Druzes and quickly spread to the rest of the mandate. Homs and Aleppo were attacked, and Syrian insurgents seized parts of Damascus.[77] In North Africa the French became involved in a costly war against Abd el Krim of the Rif, whom they had helped to arm when the latter was fighting the Spaniards. Abd el Krim was eventually overwhelmed by a combined Franco-Spanish assault, but not before the French government had been obliged to send 100,000 troops to Morocco, with Marshal Pétain, the hero of Verdun, to command them.[78] There were crises as well in Indochina, where the French had to deal with a series of rural insurrections after 1925, along with a mutiny by part of the garrison at Yen Bai on the Red River in February 1930.[79]

The British empire was able to weather its crises with some fancy footwork and its fair share of luck.[80] Southern Russia was soon deemed expendable, and British troops were withdrawn in the summer of 1920. Troops were also withdrawn from Persia at the end of the year, and in December 1921 Britain conceded the Irish Free State. The Egyptian protectorate was abrogated in March 1922, but Britain retained control over the defense of Egypt and the administration of the Sudan. The rebellion in Mesopotamia was duly suppressed, and in June 1921 the British made Faisal, whom the French had recently driven out of Syria, king of Iraq. Calm eventually returned to India as well. At the end of the war, the British did try to make good on some of their wartime undertakings, and in 1919 the Government of India Act introduced a degree of responsible government at the provincial level. But the provincial governors retained control over finance and law and order, and wartime security measures also remained in force. More fortuitously, when Gandhi's noncooperation movement turned violent at the end of 1921, the Mahatma—true to his principles—called it off, and the British promptly imprisoned him.[81]

In dealing with their imperial problems, the French were rather heavier handed. The Jonnart Law of February 1919 did give the vote in local elections to more than 400,000 Algerian Muslims and increased the number of Muslim seats on municipal councils. But Muslims could vote only for their own representatives, who were still heavily outnumbered by the European settlers. Despite wartime promises, access to French citizenship remained conditional upon the renunciation of one's Muslim personal status. Only some 300 Algerians applied for citizenship under the new law between 1919 and 1923, and only 200 of those applications were approved.[82] Although some marginal improvements in local representation and other limited reforms were also introduced in sub-Saharan Africa and Indochina, the record there was scarcely any brighter.[83] When colonial opposition became violent, the French usually responded with overwhelming force. To suppress the 1925 insurrection in Damascus, the military command did not hesitate to shell the city, killing several hundred people in the process. Vietnamese insurgents were dealt with just as ruthlessly. There were 700 summary executions in 1930 alone, and by 1932 more than 10,000 nationalists had been imprisoned. Gandhi's civil disobedience may have earned him two years in an Indian jail. Had he been a French colonial subject, as Ho Chi Minh remarked, "he would long since have entered heaven."[84]

The moral impact of the war appeared to pose no real threat to the survival of empire either. The significance of Wilsonian idealism was certainly not lost on the emerging elites of the colonial world; but the proceedings of the Peace Conference allayed imperial concerns on that score. The Russian Revolution represented a potentially much more serious danger. At its Second Congress in July 1920, Lenin committed the Communist International to the support of "revolutionary liberation movements" in the colonial world, and the Comintern reaffirmed this commitment at its fourth congress two years later.[85] But colonial liberation was not one of the Comintern's principal goals and was always seen as dependent on the victory of socialism in the advanced capitalist world. In the Comintern's first manifesto, Trotsky declared the "emancipation of the colonies" to be possible "only in conjunction with the emancipation of the metropolitan working class," a position that Lenin fully endorsed.[86] The Bolshevik victory in Russia undoubtedly had an impact on anticolonialist movements, particularly in India, Indonesia, and Indochina. But it was disillusion over the failure to introduce promised reforms as much as Communist agitation that drove colonial nationalists to adopt revolutionary strategies.

The First World War and its aftermath may thus have done little in the short term to shake the foundations of the European empires.

But some Europeans at least were beginning to feel them tremble. In March 1919, Sir Harry Johnston, the former British proconsul in East and Central Africa, warned the Royal African Society that the war had brought the "beginning of revolt against the white man's supremacy."[87] In November 1920, France's most celebrated imperial proconsul, Hubert Lyautey, warned that "the time has come for a radical change of course in native policy and Muslim participation in public affairs. . . . Concepts of the rights of peoples to self-government and revolutionary change have spread across the earth. For this a price will have to be paid."[88] Gloomier still was Albert Sarraut, the former governor-general of Indochina and the Third Republic's longest-serving minister of colonies. "In the minds of other races," he wrote in 1931, "the war has dealt a terrible blow to the moral standing of a civilization which Europeans claimed to be superior, yet in whose name they spent more than four years savagely killing each other. Europe's prestige, particularly in Asia, has been gravely compromised. It has long been a commonplace to contrast European greatness with Asian decadence. That contrast now seems reversed. The renaissance of Asia confronts the decline of the West."[89] Scarcely a decade later, as the Japanese overran the southeast Asian empires of Britain, France, and the Netherlands alike, Sarraut's fears became reality.

NOTES

1. V. I. Lenin, *Imperialism: The Highest Stage of Capitalism*, preface to the French and German editions (Moscow, n.d.), 9. The preface was first published in *The Communist International*, no. 18 (October 1921).

2. Why the powers did go to war has been the subject of endless debate ever since the war itself broke out in August 1914. The question is touched on by many of the contributions to this collection.

3. On German objectives before the war, the best known work is F. Fischer, *Krieg der Illusionen* (Düsseldorf, 1969), also translated as *War of Illusions* (London, New York, 1975).

4. The convoluted Franco-German negotiations over the Congo can be followed most conveniently in J. C. Allain, *Agadir 1911* (Paris, 1976), 398–418.

5. On the Anglo-German discussions, see J. Willequet, "Anglo-German Rivalry in Belgian and Portuguese Africa?" in P. Gifford and W. R. Louis, eds., *Britain and Germany in Africa: Imperial Rivalry and Colonial Rule* (New Haven, 1967), 245–73; P. H. S. Hatton, "Harcourt and Solf: The Search for an Anglo-German Understanding Through Africa, 1912–1914," *European Studies Review* 1, no. 2 (1971): 123–45.

6. Goschen to Grey, July 29, 1914, *Collected Diplomatic Documents Relating to the Outbreak of the European War* (London, 1915), no. 85.

7. F. Fischer, *Germany's Aims in the First World War* (London, 1967), 104. However, for a more critical assessment of the September Programme and its significance, see W. C. Thompson, "The September Program: Reflections on the Evidence," *Central European History* 11, no. 4 (1978): 348–54.

8. Fischer, *Germany's Aims*, 102–3.

9. G. R. Clerk (Chief Clerk, War Department), August 10, 1914, cited in P. J. Yearwood, "Great Britain and the Repartition of Africa, 1914–1919," *Journal of Imperial and Commonwealth History* 18, no. 3 (1990): 319.

10. The standard accounts are W. R. Louis, *Great Britain and Germany's Lost Colonies, 1914–1919* (Oxford, 1967); and J. Nevakivi, *Britain, France, and the Arab Middle East, 1914–1920* (London, 1969). See too C. M. Andrew and A. S. Kanya-Forstner, *France Overseas: The Great War and the Climax of French Imperial Expansion* (London, 1981).

11. C. Seymour, ed., *The Intimate Papers of Colonel House* (Boston, 1928), 3: 235.

12. Albert Duchêne, "Rapport sur les accords interalliés conclus pendant la guerre pour les colonies," February 20, 1918, Archives du ministère de Affaires étrangères [AE] A Paix 186.

13. On the role of the French colonial party in the formulation of colonial war aims, see C. M. Andrew and A. S. Kanya-Forstner, "The French Colonial Party and French Colonial War Aims, 1914–1918," *Historical Journal* 17, no. 1 (1974): 79–106; Andrew and Kanya-Forstner, "France and the Repartition of Africa, 1914–1922," *Dalhousie Review* 57, no. 3 (1977): 475–93. The secretary-general of the Commission d'étude was Etienne Fournol, a leading member of the "Syrian party." The *rapporteurs* included Auguste Terrier, secretary-general of the Comité de l'Afrique française; Camille Fidel, secretary-general of the Société des Etudes coloniales et maritimes; Henri Lorin, a future vice-president of the Groupe colonial de la Chambre; Philippe Millet of *Le Temps,* "very much in the inner circle of French colonial politics"; Robert de Caix, the most influential of the younger French colonialists; and Albert Duchêne, head of the colonial ministry's African department, whom the *Bulletin du Comité de l'Afrique française* described as "l'un des meilleurs et des plus anciens ouvriers de l'expansion africaine."

14. See C. M. Andrew and A. S. Kanya-Forstner, "La France à la recherche de la Syrie intégrale, 1914–1920," *Relations internationales*, no. 19 (Fall 1979): 263–78.

15. Andrew and Kanya-Forstner, "France and the Repartition of Africa," 478–79. Terrier suggested an exchange of Sierra Leone and the Gold Coast for French India and the French share of the New Hebrides Condominium. The proposal to acquire Nigeria came from the governor-general of French West Africa, Marie-François Clozel. Clozel did not specify what he would offer the British in return.

16. See especially Yearwood, "Great Britain and the Repartition of Africa," 316–41. In 1915, for example, the colonial secretary, Lewis Harcourt, had suggested the acquisition of Djibuti and the French share of the New Hebrides Condominium in exchange for all of Togoland and a larger French share of the Cameroons, or alternatively the acquisition of all of Togoland and Dahomey in exchange for almost all of the Cameroons and the British share of the New Hebrides Condominium. Harcourt, "The Spoils," March 25, 1915, cited in Louis, *Germany's Lost Colonies*, 59–60.

17. The proposal (which came to nothing) is discussed in B. Digre, *Imperialism's New Clothes: The Repartition of Tropical Africa, 1914–1919* (New York, 1990), 105–18, 150–56. See too Louis, *Germany's Lost Colonies*, 73–74, 150–52.

18. On Italian colonial ambitions, see R. L. Hess, "Italy and Africa: Italian Colonial Ambitions in the First World War," *Journal of African History* 4, no. 1 (1963): 105–26.

19. Bonar Law, War Committee minutes, February 22, 1916, Public Record Office, Cabinet Office Papers [CAB] 42/9.

20. On the details of the partition, see P. Yearwood, " 'In a Casual Way with a Blue Pencil': British Policy and the Partition of Kamerun, 1914–1919," *Canadian Journal of African Studies*, 27, no. 2 (1993): 218–44.

21. The most convenient account of these campaigns is Louis, *Germany's Lost Colonies*, chs. 2–3.

22. There is a vast literature on the Sykes-Picot Agreement and its subsequent history. Nevakivi, *Arab Middle East*, provides a useful and accurate account. The fullest account based on the French documentary record is Andrew and Kanya-Forstner, *France Overseas*. The British undertaking to Sharif Husain of October 24, 1915, was the price paid for Husain's agreement to raise an Arab revolt against the Turks, the revolt that was to make Lawrence of Arabia famous. Whether or not the undertaking included Palestine has been the subject of fierce and often acrimonious debate ever since. The fullest account is Elie Kedourie, *In the Anglo-Arab Labyrinth: The McMahon-Husayn Correspondence and Its Interpretation, 1914–1939* (Cambridge, 1976); but for a very different view see A. L. Tibawi, *Anglo-Arab Relations and the Question of Palestine, 1914–1921* (London, 1977). See too the exchange between Isiah Friedman and A. J. Toynbee, "The McMahon-Hussein Correspondence and the Question of Palestine" and "The

McMahon-Hussein Correspondence: Comments and a Reply," *Journal of Contemporary History* 5, nos. 2, 4 (1970): 83–122, 185–201. On Britain's relations with the Zionists, see inter alia L. Stein, *The Balfour Declaration* (London, 1961); I. Friedman, *The Question of Palestine, 1914–1918* (London, 1973); M. Vereté, "The Balfour Declaration and Its Makers," *Middle Eastern Studies* 6, no. 1 (1970): 48–76.

23. Henri Simon, the minister of colonies, did not rule out the possibility of acquiring the two British colonies in return for adequate compensation, but he did not specify what compensation he had in mind. In return for Nigeria, the head of the Quai d'Orsay's African department, de Peretti della Rocca, was prepared to make major concessions in the Middle East, but this view was not shared by his senior colleagues in the Ministry. Simon to Minister of Foreign Affairs [M. A. E.], December 17, 1918, no. 304, Archives nationales, Section Outre-Mer [ANSOM] Affaires Politiques [AP] 1044; Note de la sous-direction d'Afrique, n.d. [December 1, 1918], AE Afrique 116; "Observations a/s de la note de la sous-direction d'Afrique, January 16, 1919, AE Tardieu MSS 55.

24. On the Anglo-French negotiations over Tangier, see Andrew and Kanya-Forstner, *France Overseas*, especially 173–74, 185, 192–93, 214, 223–26, 233–35.

25. Doumergue to Simon, November 13, 1918; n.d. [March 11, 1919], ANSOM AP 96.

26. Eastern Committee minutes (Robert Cecil), December 9, 1918, CAB 27/24.

27. Governor-General, French West Africa to Minister of Colonies [M. C.], December 5, 1928; Chargé d'Affaires, London to M. A. E., January 16, 1929, encl. in M. A. E. to M. C., January 30, 1929, ANSOM AP 517/15.

28. Mallet to Drummond, December 23, 1916, cited in J. S. Galbraith, "British War Aims in World War I: A Commentary on 'Statesmanship,' " *Journal of Imperial and Commonwealth History* 13, no. 1 (1984): 30. On the more general question of the British response to Wilson's various peace initiatives, see S. J. Kernek, *Distractions of Peace During War: The Lloyd George Government's Reactions to Woodrow Wilson, December 1916–November 1918*, Transactions of the American Philosophical Society, NS 65, part 2 (Philadelphia, 1975).

29. H. W. V. Temperley, *A History of the Peace Conference of Paris* (London, 1920–24), 1: 193, 195.

30. On these developments, see Rex Wade, *The Russian Search for Peace: February–October 1917* (Stanford, 1969); C. J. Smith, Jr., *The Russian Struggle for Power, 1914–1917: A Study of Russian Foreign Policy During the First World War* (New York, 1956).

31. *Journal Officiel, Débats parlementaires, Chambre*, June 5, 1917; "Address of Prime Minister Lloyd George at Glasgow on Peace Terms," June 29, 1917, cited in Digre, *Imperialism's New Clothes*, 97; Temperley, *Peace Conference*, 1: 227.

32. Duchêne, Rapport no. 8, January 11, 1918, ANSOM AP 1044.

33. Sykes to Wingate, March 3, 1918; Sykes to Picot, March 3, 1918, PRO Foreign Office Papers [FO] 800/221 Sykes MSS.

34. The text of the declaration is reproduced in Nevakivi, *Arab Middle East*, 264. In it, the two powers committed themselves to the "complete and definite emancipation of the peoples so long oppressed by the Turks and the establishment of national governments and administrations deriving their authority from the initiative and free choice of the indigenous populations."

35. Minutes of the Commission d'étude, June 24, July 1, November 4, 1918, ANSOM AP 97.

36. Doumergue to M. C. November 13, 1918, ANSOM AP 96; M. C. to M. A. E., December 5, 1918, ANSOM AP 1044.

37. Balfour to Lloyd George, November 29, 1918, House of Lords Record Office, Lloyd George MSS F3/3/45.

38. Eastern Committee minutes, December 2, 1918, CAB 27/24.

39. Minutes of the Council of Four, May 21, 1919, in P. Mantoux, *Les délibérations du Conseil des Quatre, 24 mars–28 juin 1919* (Paris, 1955), 2: 139.

40. R. Poincaré, *Au service de la France* (Paris, 1928–74), xi, 112 (diary entry for February 2, 1919).

41. What Clemenceau obtained in return for these concessions remains unclear. According to Lloyd George, the agreement was unconditional and simply reflected Clemenceau's recognition of Britain's preponderant role in the conquest of the Middle East. But this claim was hotly disputed by Clemenceau himself and seems quite implausible on the face of it. André Tardieu, one of Clemenceau's closest associates, later claimed that the prime minister received an assurance of British support for French claims on the Rhine. According to a note in the Quai d'Orsay archives, however, the assurances of British support covered French claims in the Middle East: "L'accord loyal et entier proposé par M. Lloyd George et accepté par M. Clemenceau comprend deux termes: une concession sur Mossoul, que nous faisons largement; et, en contrepartie, un appui sans restrictions des délégués anglais à la conférence pour les revendications françaises sur la Syrie et la Cilicie." D. Lloyd George, *The Truth About the Peace Treaties* (London, 1932), 2: 1038; Lloyd George to Clemenceau, October 19, 1919; Clemenceau to Lloyd George, November 9, 1919, *Documents on British Foreign Policy* 4, nos. 334, 357; A. Tardieu, "Mossoul et ses pétroles," *L'Illustration*, June 19, 1920; Note a/s d'une entente franco-anglaise sur la question de la Syrie, February 10, 1919, AE A 1096/6.

42. Minutes of the Supreme Council, February 6, 13, 15, 27, 1919, *Papers Relating to the Foreign Relations of the United States; Paris Peace Conference* 3: 889–94, 1024–38; 4: 2–5, 161–70.

43. The fullest account of this episode is H. N. Howard, *An American Inquiry in the Middle East: The King-Crane Commission* (Beirut, 1963). After a tour of the region in the summer of 1919, the commission reported that the majority of the population wanted a unified Syria, including Palestine and Lebanon, under an American mandate. The second choice of the people was a British mandate; a French mandate was unacceptable. The findings of the com-

mission, however, had no effect whatsoever on how the Middle Eastern mandates were apportioned, and the American government did not even communicate the report to its allies.

44. Canada, Australia, South Africa, and India (including the Native States) were each allotted two delegates; New Zealand was allotted one. In addition, their chief delegates formed a panel from which one was always selected to sit as a member of the British Empire delegation. On the Dominions at the Peace Conference, see M. Hankey, *The Supreme Control at the Paris Peace Conference 1919* (London, 1963), chs. 3–4. The special interests of Australia and New Zealand are discussed in R. C. Snelling, "Peacemaking 1919: Australia, New Zealand, and the British Empire Delegation at Versailles," *Journal of Imperial and Commonwealth History* 5, no. 1 (1975–76): 15–28.

45. G. L. Beer, *African Questions at the Paris Peace Conference* (New York, 1923), 179.

46. "The Pan-African Congress: A Report," *Crisis* 17, no. 1 (May 1919). On the attitudes of the French and British governments, see the correspondence in AE Afrique 27.

47. On Emir Khaled, see C.-R. Ageron, "L'émir Khâled, petit-fils d'Abd el-Kader, fut-il le premier nationaliste algérien?" in *Politiques coloniales au Maghreb* (Paris, 1973), 248–88. Khaled was the grandson of Abd el-Kader, the Algerian nationalist hero who led the resistance against the French invasion during the 1830s and 1840s. French citizenship made one subject to French laws; an Algerian Muslim who took French citizenship, therefore, could not have more than one wife.

48. "The Pan-African Congress: A Report," *Crisis* 17, no. 1 (May 1919).

49. See W. J. Duiker, *The Rise of Nationalism in Vietnam, 1900–1941* (Ithaca, 1976), 196.

50. Cited in W. R. Louis, "The United States and the African Peace Settlement of 1919: The Pilgrimage of George Louis Beer," *Journal of African History* 4, no. 3 (1953): 421.

51. Covenant of the League of Nations, Art. 22.

52. On the assignment of these mandates, see Louis, *Germany's African Colonies*, ch. 4; C. M. Andrew and A. S. Kanya-Forstner, "France and the Disposition of Germany's African Colonies, 1914–1922," in *Etudes africaines offertes à Henri Brunschwig* (Paris, 1982), 209–23.

53. The story may not have been entirely apocryphal. In his younger days Clemenceau had been a fearsome, and much feared, duelist.

54. On the assignment of the Middle Eastern mandates, see Nevakivi, *Arab Middle East*, chs. 7–12; Andrew and Kanya-Forstner, *France Overseas*, chs. 8–9.

55. The reasons for the Russian defeat are discussed in Chapter 2. Some of Fuller's conclusions sharply contradict those of the best-known work in English on Russia's military performance: Norman Stone, *The Eastern Front, 1914–1917* (London, 1975).

56. The classic study of the Treaty of Brest-Litovsk is J. W. Wheeler-Bennett, *Brest-Litovsk: The Forgotten Peace, March 1918* (London, 1938). See too R. K. Debo, *Revolution and Survival: The Foreign Policy of Soviet Russia, 1917–18* (Toronto, 1979), ch. 7.

57. Digre, *Imperialism's New Clothes*, 186–96.

58. Hess, "Italy and Africa," 119–26.

59. The Labour Party's "Memorandum on War Aims," published in December 1917, called for "the full and frank abandonment by all the belligerents of any dreams of an African Empire [and] the transfer of the present Colonies of the European Powers in Tropical Africa . . . to the proposed Super-National Authority or League of Nations." But the proposal was quickly abandoned as "too advanced and too adventurous" (Sidney Webb). See Louis, *Germany's Lost Colonies,* 86–92. See too S. N. Gupta, *Imperialism and the British Labour Movement, 1914–1964* (London, 1975), ch. 2.

60. For the impact of the war on French perceptions of their colonial empire, see C. M. Andrew and A. S. Kanya-Forstner, "France, Africa, and the First World War," *Journal of African History* 19, no. 1 (1978): 11–23.

61. E.g., R. von Albertini, *Decolonization: The Administration and Future of the Colonies, 1919–1960* (New York, 1971). The author of one recent survey, however, has felt it necessary to note that "the end of the First World War may appear as a somewhat premature point at which to begin an outline history of European decolonization." R. F. Holland, *European Decolonization, 1918–1981: An Introductory Survey* (London, 1985), 1.

62. On Algeria, see C.-R. Ageron, *Les Algériens musulmans et la France* (Paris, 1968), 2: 1140–89; G. Meynier, *L'Algérie révélée: La guerre de 1914–18 et le premier quart du XXe* siècle (Geneva, 1981). The definitive study of West Africa's contribution to the war effort is M. Michel, *L'appel à l'Afrique: Contributions et réactions à l'effort de guerre en AOF, 1914–1919* (Paris, 1982). On the African troops in the Rhineland, see K. L. Nelson, "The 'Black Horror' on the Rhine: Race as a Factor in Post–World War I Diplomacy," *Journal of Modern History* 42, no. 4 (1970): 606–27; S. Marks, "Black Watch on the Rhine: A Study in Propaganda, Prejudice, and Prurience," *European Studies Review* 13, no. 3 (1983): 297–334.

63. On the Indian contribution, see especially J. M. Brown, "War and the Colonial Relationship: Britain, India and the War of 1914–1918"; and S. D. Pradhan, "Indian Army and the First World War," in D. C. Ellinwood and S. D. Pradhan, eds., *India and World War I* (Manohar, 1978). See too K. Jeffrey, " 'An English Barrack in the Oriental Seas'? India in the Aftermath of the First World War," *Modern Asian Studies* 15, no. 3 (1981): 374.

64. Andrew and Kanya-Forstner, *France Overseas*, 141–42. For the importance of food supplies as a factor in determining the outcome of the war, see A. Offer, *The First World War: An Agrarian Interpretation* (Oxford, 1989).

65. See Michel, *L'appel à l'Afrique*, ch. 5.

66. See Ageron, *Les Algériens musulmans*, 2: 1150–57.

67. On the revolts in Niger, see A. Salifou, *Kaoussan ou la révolte sénoussiste* (Niamey, 1973); J.-L. Dufour, "La révolte touareg et le siège d'Agadès (13 décembre 1916–3 mars 1917)," *Relations internationales*, no. 3 (1975): 55–77; F. Fuglestad, "Les révoltes des Touareg du Niger (1916–17)," *Cahiers d'Etudes africaines* 13, no. 1 (1973): 83–120.

68. The standard account is G. Shepperson and T. Price, *Independent African: John Chilembwe and the Origins, Setting, and Significance of the Nyasaland Native Rising of 1915* (Edinburgh, 1958).

69. On the Home Rule Leagues, see H. F. Owen, "Towards Nation-Wide Agitation and Organisation: The Home Rule Leagues, 1915–1918," in D. A. Low, ed., *Soundings in Modern South Asian History* (Berkeley, 1968), 159–95.

70. Ageron, *Les Algériens musulmans*, 2: 1141. On the Four Communes, see M. Michel, "Citoyenneté et service militaire dans les quatre Communes du Sénégal au cours de la Première Guerre mondiale," in *Perspectives nouvelles sur le passé de l'Afrique noire et de Madagascar: Mélanges offertes à Hubert Deschamps* (Paris, 1976), 299–314.

71. On Diagne's mission, see M. Michel, "La genèse du recrutement de 1918 en Afrique noire française," *Revue française d'Histoire d'Outre-Mer* 58, no. 4 (1971): 433–50. On the Algerian reforms, see Ageron, *Les Algériens musulmans*, 2: 1203–4.

72. On the background and significance of the Montagu Declaration, see Brown, "War and the Colonial Relationship."

73. The argument outlined above has been stated most trenchantly in J. A. Gallagher, "Nationalisms and the Crisis of Empire, 1919–1922," *Modern Asian Studies* 15, no. 3 (1981): 355–68; and J. A. Gallagher, *The Decline, Revival, and Fall of the British Empire* (Cambridge, 1982), especially 86–99.

74. On the creation of Greater Lebanon, see L. Lohéac, "Le Liban à la Conférence de la Paix," maîtrise d'histoire, Paris-Nanterre, 1972; L. Lohéac, *Daoud Ammoun et la création de l'Etat libanais* (Paris, 1978).

75. On Franco-Turkish relations, see Andrew and Kanya-Forstner, *France Overseas*, ch. 9; S. R. Sonyel, *Turkish Diplomacy, 1918–1923: Mustafa Kemal and the Turkish National Movement* (London, 1975).

76. Aleppo and Damascus, along with Latakia and Alexandretta, were united in 1922; but Latakia was removed from the federation in 1925. Latakia and the Jebel Druze were incorporated into the Syrian Republic in 1936, only to be split off once more in 1939. Alexandretta was ceded to Turkey in 1938–39.

77. On the revolt, see J. L. Miller, "The Syrian Revolt of 1925," *International Journal of Middle East Studies* 8, no. 4 (1977): 545–63.

78. For a popular but scholarly account, see D. S. Woolman, *Rebels in the Rif: Abd el Krim and the Rif Rebellion* (Stanford, 1968).

79. Duiker, *Nationalism in Vietnam*, ch. 8.

80. The analysis below is based largely on J. Darwin, "Imperialism in Decline? Tendencies in British Imperial Policy Between the Wars," *Historical Jour-*

nal 23, no. 3 (1980): 657–79; and K. Jeffrey, "Sir Henry Wilson and the Defence of the British Empire, 1918–22," *Journal of Imperial and Commonwealth History* 5, no. 3 (1977): 270–93. The general approach has been labeled the " 'fancy footwork' school of imperial history" by some of its critics. See B. R. Tomlinson, "The Contraction of England: National Decline and the Loss of Empire," *Journal of Imperial and Commonwealth History* 11, no. 1 (1982): 58–72.

81. Gandhi called off his campaign in January 1922. Shortly afterward he was sentenced to six years' imprisonment for sedition but was released in 1924.

82. Ageron, *Les Algériens musulmans*, 2: 1211–24.

83. For a brief summary, see Andrew and Kanya-Forstner, *France Overseas*, 243–44.

84. Cited in A. P. Thornton, *Imperialism in the Twentieth Century* (Minneapolis, 1977), 136.

85. "Theses on the National and Colonial Question adopted by the Second Comintern Congress," July 28, 1920; Executive Committee of the Communist International, "Manifesto on the Nationalist Movement in French North Africa," May 1922; "Theses on the Eastern Question adopted by the Fourth Comintern Congress," November 1922; "Theses of the Fourth Comintern Congress on the Negro Question," November 30, 1922, in J. Degras, ed., *The Communist International, 1919–1943* (London, 1971 [1956]), 1: 138–44, 351–52, 382–93, 398–401.

86. "Manifesto of the Communist International to the Proletariat of the Entire World," March 6, 1919, ibid., 43; "Theses on the National and Colonial Question," July 28, 1920, ibid., 141: "The entire policy of the Communist International on the national and colonial question must be based primarily on bringing together the proletariat and working classes of all nations and countries for the common revolutionary struggle for the overthrow of the landowners and bourgeoisie. For only such united action will ensure victory over capitalism, without which it is impossible to abolish national oppression and inequality of rights." In 1928 the Finnish communist O. Kuusinen, who drafted the "Theses on the Revolutionary Movement in Colonial and Semi-Colonial Countries," admitted that "colonial work as a whole" was one of the weakest aspects of the Comintern's activity. Ibid., 2: 526.

87. Cited in R. Rathbone, "World War I and Africa: Introduction," *Journal of African History* 19, no. 1 (1978): 4–5.

88. H. Lyautey, "Coup de barre," November 18, 1920, cited in H. Grimal, *Decolonization: The British, French, Dutch and Belgian Empires, 1919–1963* (London, 1978), 100.

89. A. Sarraut, *Grandeur et servitude coloniales* (Paris, 1931), 19. Sarraut was minister of colonies from January 1920 to March 1924, and again from June 1932 to September 1933.

CHAPTER 9

The War, the Peace, and the International State System

ZARA STEINER

The peace treaties of 1919 have a bad press.[1] From the time of the peace conference contemporaries and historians have been harsh in their criticisms of the peacemakers. John Maynard Keynes' *Economic Consequences of the Peace,* it could be argued, had far greater influence on interwar European opinion than his theories had on economic practice. When compared to the Vienna settlement of 1815, the devices contrived for maintaining peace after 1918 have been condemned by all schools of theorists, idealists, realists or neorealists, by anti-theoreticians like the late Sir Harry Hinsley and by historian-practitioners like George Kennan and Henry Kissinger. Since the dismantling of the Berlin Wall and the collapse of the Soviet Union a reevaluation of these settlements may prove more profitable as one looks back at the fragmented European continent of an earlier postwar decade.

It is my general argument that the Great War and the peace settlements, taken together, had a profound impact on the international state system. These changes are better understood when viewed with long-range glasses. In terms of interstate relations, the 1920s represented a break in diplomatic practice and procedures. The decade had a character of its own, different from the one that preceded and the one that followed it. The 1920s was a period of experimentation conducted against a background of political, economic, and social dislocation. There was an expansion of the diplomatic map, both geographically and in the area of multilateral negotiation. New states entered the global system, and a range of problems—economic, financial, social, and cultural—was placed on the international agenda. There was even an international committee on intellectual cooperation created to promote conversations between the brightest and the best. New agents appeared on the international stage with competencies far removed from those associated with the "old diplomacy." Both at home and abroad, foreign ministries faced unusual forms of competition in their conduct of foreign affairs. Summit and conference diplomacy, from which foreign ministers were often excluded, multiplied in number and in importance. New forms of international agreement emerged, bilateral and multilateral: nonaggression pacts of the Soviet variety, arms limitation treaties, the Locarno guarantees, the Kellogg-Briand Pact, an international "peace kiss" renouncing war, and, of course, the Convenant of the League of Nations. Some of these innovations had their roots in pre-1914 practice or in novel forms of wartime cooperation. Others were the direct product of the experiences of "total war" and the new problems created by a conflict of such length and destructiveness. Some of the new practices, particularly with respect to multilateral negotiation, were abandoned under the impact of the depression and the rise of Hitler and were not to be revived. Many, however, resurfaced, albeit in altered forms after 1945.

Historians, unlike political scientists, are uncomfortable with the idea of breaks in continuity. The year 1919 could not and did not represent an entirely new chapter in the history of diplomacy. The expanded concept of internationalism dates to the prewar period when the effects of an enlarged electorate in many states and the transportation-communication revolutions were already producing changes in diplomatic practice. There were clear signs, too, of the challenge posed by the extra-European states to the supremacy of the continental powers, though this challenge was still to be translated into political terms. The war was responsible, however, for key shifts in the pattern of international relations. It acted as a catalyst for the altered international positions of the United States and Japan and for the creation of new states. It changed, temporarily at least, the power hierarchy of the European states. Less dramatically than the war of 1939–45, it affected the relationship between the European imperial powers and their non-European dependents, despite the continued importance of traditional racial assumptions. The extent and ferocity of the war forced the governing elites both to face the problems created by the conflict and to consider wartime techniques that might be used to solve them. Reform movements within and outside elected governments in both the victorious and defeated states pressed for the reconsideration of the premises on which the "old diplomacy" rested and demanded an overhaul of the diplomatic machinery of the prewar order.

The peacemakers could not start afresh. They were realists and pragmatists responding to concrete situations in a highly volatile international environment. As most of the postwar statesmen came to political maturity before 1914, there was a natural inclination, with some notable exceptions, to look backward, at past practices and at their own experiences, either during the war or in those prewar years that were rapidly transformed into a much-regretted "golden age" of peace. It was not without significance that the British preparations for the peace conference included a study of the Congress of Vienna. Not unexpectedly, the international system that resulted from the peace was a compound of old and new as the statesmen grappled with immediate and longer term problems. Recent commentators on this postwar international order have called attention to its schizophrenic nature. "At the one level, the powers participated in an elaborate myth." Ian Clarke writes in *The Hierarchy of States*, "At the more profound level, the powers were very consciously aware of the underlying reality of the situation. The most fitting account of the interwar period is, then, that during the 1920s the myth and the reality managed to coexist with each other whereas in the 1930s the myth was destroyed and only the reality remained."[2] If one understands the degree to which the old regime had been destroyed or was discredited by the Great War and looks at the actual working of the reconstituted system, the splintered behavior of the statesmen becomes at least understandable and the gap between myth and reality appears less sharp.

It was not possible to reconstruct the old system because so much of it had vanished by 1919. The mechanisms that had kept the peace of Europe, whether based on the concert of Europe and the balance of power or on alliances and ententes, had failed. The statesmen gathered at Paris were witnesses to the terrible price of failure. At the systemic level, four empires—three European and the Ottoman—had disappeared and their ruling dynasties toppled. The Habsburg Empire was wiped off the face of the map; the German, Russian and Ottoman empires reappeared, carrying some of the baggage of their predecessors but with new boundaries, new governments, and new goals. Both within these old empires and outside, the positions of monarchies were shaken and the cause of republicanism promoted. The key political problems facing the peacemakers arose from these massive transformations.

The problem of the German state was the central issue at debate in Paris. Germany was defeated but not destroyed. Despite military defeat and the fall of the imperial government, the outcome of the war left her future in any reconstituted system undecided. The victors could not agree on the terms of the treaty to be imposed nor on the question of its enforcement. David Stevenson has convincingly argued that it was mainly geopolitical considerations that kept the allied coalition together, and that once Germany was beaten there was little to hold the victors together. The lack of consensus of what to do with Germany was critical in the subsequent undermining of the Treaty of Versailles, for the compromises that were reached at Paris did not create a common will to enforce them. These compromises deprived Germany of territory, her former military power, and, temporarily at least, some of the sources of her economic strength, but she was left intact and capable of again becoming the dominant power of Europe. The Treaty of Versailles was a truce, "an Armistice for twenty years," and represented, as did the war itself, an indecisive ending to the struggle for power in Europe. The Germans signed what they viewed as a "diktat," refusing to accept the reality of a situation that their political and military leaders had acknowledged.

The three key figures at the peace conference started from similar premises but followed different scenarios. Clemenceau, Lloyd George, and Woodrow Wilson each held Germany responsible for the war and insisted on punishment. Wilson proved, in the end, to be perhaps even more vindictive than his colleagues. The three statesmen assumed that Germany would recover and seek to return to great power status. The French and British thought in traditional balance-of-power terms. Clemenceau hoped to use the German defeat to construct a peace structure that would delay her reemergence. He wanted to provide France with the opportunity to make up some of those differences in strength that the war had so tragically confirmed and to slow and restrain Germany's industrial and commercial growth. The "Tiger" knew that Germany, regardless of defeat, remained more populous and stronger than France. With dismemberment ruled out, he sought through the territorial, financial, economic, and military clauses of the treaty to weaken Germany and strengthen France. Yet already at the peace conference Clemenceau acknowledged that France could secure her future goals only if backed by the British and Americans. Though French security demands shaped the treaty, Clemenceau was forced to compromise in order to secure the abortive Anglo-American guarantee and the possibility of their future cooperation. Every subsequent French premier, including Poincaré, considered France too weak to secure her future against Germany alone.

Lloyd George also thought about a renewed balance of power. He hoped that the Germans would learn from their defeat and accept their reduced position as the price of bringing on the war. A vengeful Germany would disrupt the peace, but a chastened nation could be encouraged to return to the European concert. The treaty settlements could then be revised in the Germans' favor. Such revision would check French hegemonic ambitions, promote European prosperity (with reservations about an export drive at British expense), and provide a barrier against the spread of Bolshevism. Like others in his cabinet, Lloyd George looked to the creation of a new European equilibrium that would allow Britain to carry out its main objectives, which were imperial and colonial. Having secured Britain's war aims—that is, the destruction of Germany's fleet and the distribution of its colonies—the Welsh wizard saw himself as the future broker between Paris and Berlin, with Britain as the balancer of Europe. The prime minister did not question whether his country had actually played this part in the past or if it had the strength to play it in the future. It is not at all clear that the prime minister understood the price Britain had paid for its victory in the war.

Woodrow Wilson offered a different and more radical scenario. The German defeat and its seeming dependence on American involvement in the war appeared to place the president in a pivotal position as the peace conference opened. In fact, he was unable to force his two partners to accept his views and had to compromise his goals in order to preserve a measure of unity. Wilson was not interested in reestablishing a European equilibrium. In his view, all the

European states were tainted in one way or another. The American president looked to the construction of a new international system that would replace the discredited balance-of-power structure. He would sacrifice much in terms of his principles to secure the establishment of the League of Nations. While he abandoned earlier ideas of immediate German participation, he intended that a democratic Germany would join the League and that the new organization would correct the imperfections of the Versailles Treaty. He hoped, like Lloyd George, that the new Germany would reenter the liberal world trading system and become the economic dynamo of the new Europe. The reparations settlement and the harsh (in Wilson's judgment) economic clauses of the treaty could be revised once the defeated enemy had reformed itself and joined the new world organization. The peace treaty was not the one he wanted, but it was the most he could get. He defended it in the hope that it would be subject to revision.

The subsequent withdrawal of the United States from the peace settlement exacerbated the differences between the British and French over the interpretation of the treaty terms. It seems hard to believe, in the atmosphere of 1919, that any peace devised by the victors would have seemed "just" to the Germans. Nevertheless, while one might question whether this was a "Carthaginian peace," it can be argued that the treaty was "too severe where it should have been lenient" and vice versa. It could have been made to work only "by using force to compel German compliance or by securing German cooperation." The French and British, if they had agreed, might have done either. Instead, their disagreements left the Germans not only unwilling to accept the Versailles settlement but in a position to secure its revision and ultimately overthrow it. Revision when it came after 1925 was too slow and piecemeal to quell German nationalism or to strengthen the domestic appeal of the Weimar Republic sufficiently to weather the future economic storm. Nor did it result in the kind of cooperation between London and Paris that might have strengthened the admittedly fragile stabilization.

Instead of five Great Powers in Europe as in the prewar period, there were only two or possibly three (Italy was considered the least of the Great Powers) responsible for the establishment of a new equilibrium in Europe until in 1925 Germany rejoined the concert of Europe. The reduction in the number of European major players made the balance unstable, particularly as each acted independently of each other. The conflicting aims of status quo and revisionist powers and the "haves" and "have-nots" made any semblance of stability short-lived. The war and the peace settlements, moreover, created new medium- and small-sized states. There would be no similar expansion of the state system until the 1950s, and in Europe, the 1990s. The "Balkanization of Europe" was the direct result of the collapse of the Habsburg Empire and the fall of tsarist Russia. An interplay between war, civil strife, and social and economic upheaval, compressed in some instances to a period of a few months, produced support for aspiring leaders. Representatives of the major nationalities were already pressing for recognition of their claims before the peacemakers assembled at Paris. President Wilson's espousal of the principle of self-determination and the ideas of the "New Europe" group in London were of considerable importance in their triumph. So, too, were French hopes, articulated earlier in Paris than in London or Washington, to create a series of independent states as a barrier to German expansion. It must be remembered, however, that there were divided counsels in the victor capitals, and until 1918 uncertainties remained whether the Habsburg Empire should be reformed or destroyed. Wilson's Fourteen Points implied the continued existence of Austria-Hungary, and the armistice still assumed the empire's unity despite the commitments already made to Serbia, the future Czechoslovakia, and Poland. In fact, nothing, barring the use of military force, that the peacemakers could have done would have reconstituted the old Habsburg state. For the most part, they were faced with a fait accompli.

Poland was re-created from the vanished Austro-Hungarian, German, and Russian empires. Czech and Slovak refugees secured allied recognition for their new nation even before it was accepted by their co-nationals at home. Serbia became the base for a Serbo-Croat-Slovene state only officially designated as Yugoslavia in 1929. Along the former Russian borders, Finland, Estonia, Latvia, Lithuania, Georgia, Azerbaijan, and Armenia came into existence, the last three enjoying only short periods of independence. Existing states extended their territories. Italy and Romania tried with some success to capitalize on wartime promises and the anarchical situation in adjacent lands. The Italians got less than they thought they deserved; the Romanians more than doubled their prewar population and territory. The Greeks occupied much of Anatolia, giving substance to the vision of the "great idea." They were unfortunately encouraged in their ambitions (mainly by the British) to make further gains at the expense of the defeated Turks. The emergence and victory of Nationalist Turkey checked the Greek advance and allowed Mustapha Kemal to win a revised peace treaty at Lausanne in 1923. The Treaty of Lausanne proved the most enduring of the peace settlements, and the new Turkey became a force for stability and peace in the Near East.

Even as the territorial committees of the peace conference met to draw the boundaries of the new successor states, wars were raging on most of their frontiers. There was no status quo, and in the east little prospect of an immediate settlement. Because in most instances the Council of Four was otherwise engaged, the boundaries settled by the experts, with the exception of Poland, were accepted by the "big three." The experts had to take into account not only the complex nationalities map of East-Central Europe but also wartime promises and the divergent aims of the victor powers both before and after

1917. As far as possible, apart from Germany, an attempt was made to uphold the principles of self-determination. Where modified, consideration was taken of geography, past history, economic, and strategic factors. The peacemakers were unduly optimistic about the prospects for democracy and toleration. With the exception of Czechoslovakia, authoritarian governments emerged in all the new states. The creation of national states (which halved the number of people living under "alien" governments) inevitably produced dissatisfied national minorities. To their credit, the peacemakers did not consider annihilation, as a later generation was to do. There were expulsions, half a million Turks and 1.2 million Greeks were "repatriated," and, either by agreement or with some degree of compulsion, 770,000 German speakers had left the "lost territories" for the Reich by 1925.[3] Minority treaties were concluded between the allied powers and the successor states containing protection clauses guaranteeing the rights of minority nationalities, including the Jews. The League was required to hear grievances and to censure if necessary but was not empowered to take any further concrete action. These safeguards did not prevent governments of the dominant nationalities from imposing their rule, even by force, on their own minorities. The problem of the German-speaking populations left outside the pre-1914 boundaries of the Reich would provide Nazi Germany with a "legitimate" reason for the early stages of its expansionism.

In the Baltic the defeat first of Russia and then of Germany set the stage for independence. The peacemakers intervened in Latvia, where a German brigade under General von der Goltz first fought Bolsheviks and then groups of Latvians. Polish forces assisted the Lithuanians against the Bolsheviks, seizing Riga at the same time. The British gave military and naval assistance to both the Latvians and Estonians in their struggle against the Bolsheviks. The issue in the Baltic was resolved only when the Red Army beat the White Russian Baltic Army and all foreign forces left the region. In 1920 the

Soviet Union recognized the independence of the three Baltic states and Finland. There was a confused situation in the Transcaucasian region involving Reds, Whites, the British (who soon pulled out their forces), and the Nationalist Turks. Agreements concluded between the Bolsheviks and Nationalist Turks paved the way for a settlement. Azerbaijan, the part of Armenia lying in the former Russian Empire, and finally Georgia, whose independence was formally recognized by the Bolsheviks in 1920, were reabsorbed as republics into the Soviet Union. No independent Armenia was created from the former Ottoman Armenian lands that remained part of Turkey. The Polish-Russian frontier was not settled until the Treaty of Riga (1921), which brought the Polish-Soviet war to an end. Large Byelorussian and Ukrainian areas remained in Poland, but most of the Ukraine was left to the USSR. This new border remained in place until 1939.

None of the statesmen in Paris knew how to handle the problem of the Soviet Union still engulfed in civil war, lacking recognition and absent from the peace proceedings. During 1919 allied and American troops were withdrawn from Russia, but there was no agreement in the delegations about what should be done about the revolutionary government. The principals tended to neglect or postpone decisions, and their juniors had to deal with immediate problems without direction from above. The impact of the Bolshevik threat on the peacemakers and on the peace treaties is still debated, but Lenin's worldview directly challenged both the balance of power assumptions of the British and French and the liberal internationalism of the American president. The Bolsheviks were pledged to the total abolition of the international system. Lenin assumed that the revolution would spread and the capitalist states would be attacked from within. There would be no need for foreign ministers, foreign ministries, or foreign policies. In a much-quoted statement, Trotsky, the first people's commissar for foreign affairs, said he would "issue a few revolutionary proclamations to the peoples and then close up the shop." The young revolutionary government quickly learned how to use the tactics of "open diplomacy" to publicize its cause. The failure of the revolutionary movements in Europe would force the Soviet government to reenter the capitalist arena despite its declared and continued abhorrence of the rules. It proved to be the only way to safeguard the revolution in Russia and to maintain the new regime.

It was not only the old state system that was in disarray. The global financial structure had collapsed, and the global economy was disrupted and distorted by the war. The so-called self-regulating gold standard no longer existed. The length and character of the war meant that the quest for peace and stability could not be divorced from the revival of trade and credit. In contrast to Wilson's revolutionary ideas about the future world order, his economic and financial preconceptions were highly traditional. The Americans wanted to return to the laissez-faire system of the prewar period and to the "open door" principles they had long professed. Unexpectedly, financial and commercial issues came to the forefront of international politics, first in Paris and then in the post-peace period. The creditor position of the United States and its enhanced economic and commercial strength ruled out any return to the prewar situation, whatever may have been the hopes of the Bank of England, the Treasury, and the City of London. The United States, through official and private actions, would take a crucial part in the reconstitution of the global trading and financial system. Even where not directly involved, American financial strength influenced the outcome of European conflicts. Reparations emerged as the battleground for establishing the new European equilibrium. It was not reparations as such that was the issue, for many historians today argue that Germany could have afforded the total sum set in 1921 had her government agreed to pay. It was the international conflicts of interest resulting from the quarrels over reparations that put in question the enforcement of the peace. The ensuing struggle between France and Germany over payment "emerged as the chief bone of contention in the Franco-German struggle for political and economic dominance in Europe. It marked, in short, the continuation of war by other means."[4] With the Americans not officially represented on the Reparations Commission but with the only source of funds that could break the deadlock, it was a war whose outcome they would help to determine.

How was the new international regime created, and what were its enduring features? By regime or system I am referring to the norms, rules, and practices inherited or devised by statesmen to regulate the behavior of their states and citizens in the pursuit of their international goals. These may grow up over a long period of time; they can be altered suddenly or gradually, but they require some form of recognition by the participating states. As the war spread, the geographic base of the international order broadened. The participation of Japan and the United States in the peacemaking process, as well as the crowds of non-European petitioners present in Paris, pointed to possible alterations in the Eurocentric character of the prewar system. In political terms this geographic expansion proved less revolutionary than some feared. The Japanese enjoyed their new status as one of the Great Powers. The peace conference was the first international conference at which the country was officially represented. Her representatives, however, maintained a relatively low profile in Paris and accepted their exclusion from the Council of Four except when Japan's special interests were involved. The Japanese failed in their attempt to secure a racial equality clause in the Covenant, but their claim to Shantung, bitterly contested by President Wilson, was recognized on May 4, a day, incidentally, of key importance for the Chinese nationalist movement. During the next ten years Japan accepted and worked within a European-dominated global system and, for the most part, adopted the course set by the

European powers. The Japanese were good Geneva citizens, serving in the League Secretariat and participating in international meetings. There was a strong pro-League movement in Japan. Nonetheless, the Japanese continued to play a restricted global role. Their accommodation to a European-directed system had much to do with the withdrawal of the United States from the League and the creation of separate security arrangements for the Pacific. While the Far East was included in the global order, it also stood apart. There remained, too, a cultural gulf between the Western powers and Japan, accentuated by a legacy of unspoken racial assumptions hardly changed by the war, which accentuated the separation between West and East.

In security terms the American impact on the postwar order was also less dramatic than anticipated in 1918. Neither the British nor the French had any doubts about the crucial importance of the American intervention in the war or about the need to tap her resources for postwar reconstruction. Indeed, one of the main reasons why the allied powers accepted an armistice concluded between President Wilson and the Germans was the fear that if the war continued, it would be an American and not a European peace. Both Lloyd George and Clemenceau courted Wilson in full recognition of the formidable power of the country he represented. It became clear at the peace conference, however, that Wilson was unable to impose his views and that, with the League of Nations secured, he could be forced to give way when pressed on other issues. America's financial and economic strength was not used to secure political goals. Wilson left his mark on the peace settlements but did not shape them. Those who expected the most from the president became his most disillusioned critics. The subsequent Senate rejection of the Versailles treaty and the electorate's unwillingness to join any global security system left that system mainly in European hands. The potential hegemony of the 1920s did not fully emerge.

It was not that the Republican administrations lacked a political agenda for Europe (including the cutting of land armaments) but successive presidents believed that the European nations had to solve their own problems before the United States would consider any form of involvement. The widespread disillusionment with Europe and European practices in the postwar period went far beyond Capitol Hill. French and British efforts to bring the Americans into some form of security system repeatedly failed. The American absence had a negative effect on the restoration of the European equilibrium, for it left the burden of sustaining the balance and enforcing the rules to France and Britain. The former proved incapable of assuming it, as the Ruhr occupation proved. The latter proved unwilling to try, given its military weakness and worldwide interests. The costs of the recent continental involvement seemed excessively high. Even when the two governments agreed to a policy of peaceful treaty revision in the West, the British refused to underwrite the eastern settlements, leaving the most volatile areas of the continent without a guarantor.

The League owed its existence to Wilson's single-minded efforts, though its form reflected earlier British thinking rather than the president's more nebulous ideas. The Wilsonian concept was revolutionary in its theoretical formulation. It was the first attempt to give a legal shape to the way the international order was organized. In Wilson's view it was to be something more than an enlarged Concert of Europe though something less than a super-state. The sovereign states were to recognize that peace was indivisible and that an attack on one was an attack on all to be met by common action. In conception, if not in reality, it aimed at universality and open diplomacy. The very terms of the Covenant illustrated the difficulties implicit in translating the ideals of "collective security" (the term became common only in the early 1930s) into a workable system. Even in the compromised form in which the League of Nations emerged, it proved unacceptable to either the French or the British, who were left with the task of making the new system operative. It was, from the start, a victors' League, but with one of the key victors missing. Already in the 1920s the new institution operated as an adjunct to the traditional system and not as a substitute for balance-of-power politics, as Wilson had intended. Even if the Americans had joined the League they would have rejected the Wilsonian vision of its role and reinforced the minimalist British interpretation of its functions. Other regional systems supplemented or, as some have argued, weakened the League's claim to a global security role.

While rejecting Wilson's ideas of liberal internationalism, neither Clemenceau nor Lloyd George were willing to publicly disavow his principles. As a consequence, from its inception the idea of the League was divorced from its practices. During the 1920s, governments, responsive to domestic opinion, encouraged the illusion of an alternative system of preserving the peace while using the methods of the past to settle interstate disputes. The Council of the League developed techniques for handling disputes that succeeded in some cases but not in others. There was no upward curve of progress. The representatives of the small powers found an important international platform, and some, Beneš of Czechoslovakia and Beck of Luxembourg, were strong advocates of the Geneva system; but their influence was limited and often exercised through traditional diplomatic channels. After 1925, though the Locarno statesmen regularly attended Council meetings, all the major questions, including the Council agenda, were settled in private exchanges in their Geneva hotel rooms. The representatives of the other member states bitterly complained about the Locarno tea parties. Protests against this revival of the "old diplomacy" fell on deaf ears. At the same time, the British, French, and German leaders identified themselves and their countries with the maintenance of the League of Nations in its security role. If there was a "myth" of collective security, the statesmen helped to encourage and sustain it.

There were moments when genuine efforts were made to strengthen the League's peacekeeping machinery. The French made numerous, if unsuccessful, attempts to extend the coercive powers of the League in their efforts to maintain the treaty status quo. Seeking security above all, they hoped the League might provide what neither the Americans nor the British would offer. For a brief moment, during the Ethiopian crisis, the only case where sanctions were actually invoked, the Baldwin cabinet hoped that the League might succeed in brokering a settlement that Mussolini would accept. The national and international interest in a compromise solution temporarily coincided. After this failure, no further attempt was made to use the League's coercive powers. No British statesman was prepared to put the Geneva system into operation during the Rhineland operation. The Soviet Union tried, with minimal success, to revive the League's security functions in the hope of reducing the risks of its isolation. When Churchill called for an active League of Nations in 1938, he hoped to attract all-party support for military alliances to encircle Germany. After 1936, British and French leaders abandoned the "myth" of collective security. Its abandonment did not promote the cause of peace. *Realpolitik,* in the sense of appeasement or alliances, had little effect on Hitler and did not prevent the resort to war.

The American contribution to the stabilization of the world's financial and trading structure, though of considerable importance, was hardly a coherent or integrated reconstruction program. There is a continuing debate about the extent to which the United States accepted its responsibilities as a creditor nation to stabilize the global system. There was no possibility, given the climate of opinion in the United States in 1918–19, that any government could consider war debt cancellation or transfer the cost of reparations to the American taxpayer. Nor would any Washington government shoulder the financial burden of European reconstruction, as happened after the Second World War. The Americans did make a contribution to

European recovery, but it was limited in terms of intention and scope and was divorced from specific foreign policy goals. Administration policies were frequently shaped by diverse and even opposing domestic interests as filtered through Congress. The war debt and trade agreements had to take into account the electorate's belief that countries should pay their legitimate debts and that the domestic economy had to be protected when under competitive threat. Republican administrations, even when working with private interest groups in the international arena, placed renewed emphasis on the concepts of individualism and voluntary action that had characterized the country's wartime mobilization.

Because the Americans were not dependent on external trade for prosperity, even the politicians who recognized the the need to foster European recovery moved with caution. Much of the burden of assisting the Europeans could be left to private initiative and funding. American and European interests on the official level did not necessarily coincide. From the American administration's point of view, the terms offered for the settlement of war debts were generous, or at least as generous as Congress would accept. The situation looked very different from London or Paris, where it was thought that the United States should take on the burden of financing the war. The new trade treaties, based on the unconditional most-favored-nation principle, gave special protection to American producers despite the professed official attachment to open markets and nondiscrimination.[5] It has been argued that it was not American tariff policy which accounted for the country's trade surplus but the greater efficiency and competitiveness of its economy. On a comparative scale, American practices were probably no more discriminatory than those of other trading nations. Nonetheless, the disparity between what was said at international conferences and what was done in Washington could not have been more marked. The United States did not assume Britain's place as the world's largest importer of goods even though she was challenging the latter's lead in the export of capital. The introduction of a "liberal world trading system" remained a blueprint for an ideal future.

Republican administrations did encourage the goals of currency stabilization and the settlement of the reparations question. They would not, however, actively participate in their achievement. Washington would wait until the Europeans settled the political problems thought to be the fundamental causes of the current financial chaos. Once the Germans and French composed their differences over reparations and the European debtors settled their accounts with the Americans, the way would be open for the experts to devise the solutions needed to put Germany and Europe back on the road to prosperity. When after the Ruhr occupation the opportunity arose for a solution of the reparations question through American participation, private individuals, in contact with government officials, worked out the details of the Dawes agreements. The J. P. Morgan partners, again backed by American officials, played a key role in brokering the subsequent arrangements. However responsible and responsive the partners may have been to the broader national interest, Morgan's "primary responsibility," to quote Stephen Schuker, "lay in ensuring the safety of bonds syndicated by the firm."[6] Their financial concerns had political consequences. The Dawes Plan and the London agreements, as Schuker has shown in his innovative study *The End of French Predominance in Europe,* strengthened the power position of Germany at the expense of France. Though the American government backed the new settlement, it neither intervened directly in the working of the Dawes regime nor did it exercise any control over the amounts or direction of private investment in Germany. The difficulties in the situation became clearer as Germany became more dependent on the flow of American funds for its prosperity. The interests of the American taxpayer in the payment of war debts diverged from the interests of Wall Street and its clients, whose main interest was in the continued prosperity of Germany. There was a connection between war debts and reparations, not in terms of any circular flow, but in the way the French and British, mainly for political reasons, linked the two questions. Ultimately, Germany received as much in the way of loans as they paid in reparations. It has been argued that since the Americans received only negligible direct reparations and little in the way of war-debt repayment, "the major burden of the capital transfer to Germany fell in one way or another on the American investor and taxpayer."[7]

Insofar as American and British financial stabilization policies (and the latter depended heavily on American cooperation) were successful and a form of restored gold standard put in place, its management rested on the voluntary cooperation of central bankers. American views on the necessary conditions for stabilization enlisted the support of the British Treasury and Bank of England. Both shared an official aversion to using loans and investments to achieve political goals. The Ango-American financial community was highly critical of French "financial imperialism." Whether the line between the two spheres of action was as sharp as they claimed is dubious, but the divorce between the two placed limits on what could be achieved in the way of effective stabilization. Though some of the weaknesses of the mid-decade equilibrium lay beyond the range of American influence, the American policy of financial stabilization without political involvement was bound to add to the fragility of the European settlement.

Whether in the political or in the financial and commercial spheres, America's participation in world affairs was erratic and unpredictable. Presidents were highly sensitive to shifts in the political winds, which were difficult for Europeans to understand. After 1925, when stabilization policies began to bear fruit and signs of economic recovery engendered some measure of optimism, European attitudes toward the United States began to change. Continuing attempts were made to bring Washington into some form of European security arrangements, but British and French politicians came to accept the American absence from the League (particularly after the more extreme policies of nonassociation were abandoned) and to assess more realistically the possibilities of American participation in continental political affairs. Stresemann, who viewed the American contribution to Germany's recovery as essential to its restoration to great power status, looked toward a European political solution. Briand accepted the British terms for a readjustment of the European balance in the hope of securing London's support should the appeasement of Germany fail. Austen Chamberlain took pride in the fact that the Locarno treaties were a European arrangement in which the Americans took no part. "With America withdrawn," the British foreign secretary wrote in 1925, "or taking part only where her interests are directly concerned in the collection of money, Great Britain is the lone possible influence for peace and stabilization. Without our help things will go from bad to worse." The Imperial Conference was told that Locarno was "in large measure a British achievement and was recognized as such by the other parties. As a result British friendship is cultivated, British counsel asked, British aid sought and as in the days of Castlereagh Great Britain stands forth again as the moderator and peacemaker of the new Europe created by the Great War."[8] Such an exaggerated view of British influence may have been necessary to impress the imperial statesmen, but it also reflected a return of confidence in Britain's balancing role. Some years later, in 1932, the British prime minister, Stanley Baldwin, summed up the prevailing mood in Whitehall when he complained that "you will get nothing from Americans but words, big words but only words."[9]

The limited American participation in European affairs seemed less damaging to the stability of Europe after 1925 than in 1919. The allied powers had never wanted the Americans to be the supreme arbiters in their political concerns. In the later 1920s they did not expect or want them to be an arbiter at all. Even as European entrepreneurs copied American industrial models or, in some cases, invited American direct investment, resentment of its economic predominance grew. While neither the Germans nor the British would countenance an anti-American common market, there is little doubt that the roots of the abortive Briand Plan were fed by French concern over the American "invasion" of European markets. By the end of the decade, the anti-American current was gathering force, above all, in France, but in other European states as well.

If the new world order reflected the ambiguities of America's new international position, it also had to contend with the challenge posed by the USSR. The Soviet impact was less damaging than the peacemakers feared. In particular, the fear of a Bolshevik tidal wave in Europe began to subside before the peacemakers left Paris. With the suppression of the Spartacists in January and the Bavarian Soviet Republic in April 1919, the German temperature chart began to dip despite the attempts of the new Berlin government to keep fears of the threat alive. In August 1919 the Hungarian Soviet Republic under Bela Kun fell when Romanian military forces entered Budapest. A communist uprising in Switzerland was ruthlessly crushed. The new if uneasy Soviet Turkish entente created in 1919–20 spelled the end of the independence of the Transcaucasian republics, but Ataturk's Turkey was virulently anti-Bolshevik at home, and Turkish diplomacy at the Lausanne Conference of 1922 confirmed the tactical nature of Ankara's pro-Soviet policies. Even the Russo-Polish war did not bring the French, not to speak of the British, to the Polish barricades, and the final Polish success owed relatively little to allied support. Without any major effort on the part of the imperialist-capitalist victors, the Bolshevik tide in Europe receded.

It left its mark. The revolutionary moment in Europe was not forgotten. As Communist parties appeared in a majority of European states, the Bolshevik threat seemed ominously present. The failed Communist actions in Germany in 1923 when the unity of the state seemed in question was a powerful reminder of the dangers posed by revolutionary parties. Some governments outlawed the Communists while others, as in Britain, viewed the party's activities as potentially seditious and dangerous to the stability of the state. No Western government accepted the Soviet claim that the Comintern was an independent organization for which the Moscow government was not responsible. At the international level, it was the potential threat from Russia that had to be considered. France's eastern alliance system was intended not only to check the Germans but to create a cordon sanitaire in the East. The Rapallo treaty, concluded by the two pariah nations of Europe during the Genoa conference, nourished Anglo-French fears of a German-Russian partnership. Nonetheless, recent research suggests that the importance of the treaty in terms of either British or French policy can be exaggerated. Attention in both capitals was focused on Berlin rather than on Moscow. In 1925, Briand and Chamberlain were to see the Locarno treaties as a way of detaching Germany from the Soviet Union and in Chamberlain's words, "saving the soul" of the German nation. When asked to prepare a memorandum on Britain's policy in Europe, Harold Nicolson, a Foreign Office official, left Russia out not because she was unimportant, for she was the "most menacing of all our uncertainties," but because "the Russian problem is for the moment Asiatic rather than European." The Soviet Union was only a "storm cloud upon the Eastern horizon of Europe—impending, imponderable, but, for the present, detached."[10] British disinterest in Eastern Europe in 1925 was stronger than the prospect of the future storm. Bolshevik activities in China and at home created more anxiety than Soviet policy in Europe. The temporary break in British relations with the Soviet Union had little to do with European affairs, though Stalin worked up a war-scare atmosphere in Moscow in anticipation of an Anglo-Polish attack on Russia. With the Locarno agreements in place, Briand looked to the inclusion of the Soviet Union in an Eastern Locarno that would underwrite his Eastern allies against German revisionism. It was not an idea with which the Poles had any sympathy. For Pilsudski, Russia was always the more dangerous enemy.

Throughout the postwar decade, foreign attitudes toward the Soviet Union were composed of a strange amalgam of political, commercial, and ideological concerns. This had begun at the peace conference; witness the difference of views between Lloyd George, Lord Curzon, and Winston Churchill. In none of the European capitals, Rome included, was there a single or consistent view on relations with Moscow. The inconsistencies in foreign attitudes were paralleled and in some instances caused by the shifts in Soviet policy. With world revolution ruled out for the immediate present, Lenin concentrated on securing trade and investment from the West. The Soviets worked hard to secure such agreements, yet as was made clear at Genoa, Lenin would not compromise on the essentials of the Soviet revolutionary position at home in order to achieve them. Stalin, preparing to use Russia's own resources to accelerate industrialization, was willing to negotiate with the capitalist powers without ever believing that peaceful coexistence was possible. The possibility of clashes between the ideals of world revolution and "socialism in one country" faded as the Comintern and local Communist parties became instruments for the exclusive promotion of the interests of the Soviet Union.

Whereas Germany was brought back into the European concert after 1925, the Soviet Union remained outside. Even when the Russians reentered the diplomatic stage and Litvinov became a familiar figure in Geneva during the disarmament talks, the activities of the Comintern, the Communist parties and Soviet agents abroad reenforced the conviction of many Western diplomats that Russia stood outside the borders of the global order. Notwithstanding the trade agreements of the period and the recognition of the Soviet Union by a growing number of European states, Stalin's government remained an object of intense suspicion. Writing of his official tour of Russia in 1925, the first to be made by a member of the British diplomatic service, Owen O'Malley recalled, "It was with an indescribable sense of relief that I left Russian and entered Persian territory, and although I can give no rational explanation of this sentiment, I record it as the outstanding recollection of my journey."[11] These feelings of being in an alien and oppressive land, remote from civilization (in 1942 O'Malley was to speak of his relief in crossing into "civilised Manchukuo"), were intensified by the massive anti-foreign campaign unleashed in Russia with the introduction of the first Five Year Plan. The very existence of the Soviet state introduced a new ideological element into the international order. There was no parallel with prewar tsarist Russia, nor with Mussolini's Fascism, which many diplomats admired, nor even, as became clear, with Hitler's National Socialism.

"It [the European center] retained enough power to be able to plunge the world into disorder in the future," Klaus Hildebrand writes, "not least because the USA and . . . the USSR, who both postulated a new world cut to their own ideological pattern, for the time being behaved in a reserved and abstinent manner as far as international politics was concerned. Soviet Russia . . . was forced to cut back in the field of power politics for a considerable length of time. The USA, bitterly disappointed by the old world, began her political and military retreat into 'fortress America.'"[12] Both the creation of the new international order and its maintenance lay, for the most part, in European hands. Though the war had produced changes on the peripheries that complicated European security dilemmas, the focus of world politics remained in Europe.

Changes in domestic politics also had their effects on the way foreign affairs were conducted. Diplomacy was in a state of transition, though the new guideposts were not yet in place. The leaders of all the victorious powers were elected representatives responsible to their electorates. All had to consider the political context in which they operated. In the defeated states, too, representative governments emerged. The triumph of self-determination was linked, at least temporarily, with the creation of democratic and parliamentary regimes. Second, the massive mobilization of men and resources during the war created social and economic dislocations that persisted into the postwar period. Even where social revolutions were contained, some response to the conditions that produced these upheavals was required. Finally, because the war had produced an expansion in the power and authority of governments, there was the expectation that they would deal with problems previously ignored. Even where, as in Britain, there was a strong demand for the quick dismantling of wartime controls, there remained, above all in working-class circles, new assumptions about what the state should do. In Germany, somewhat exceptionally, wartime experiences bred a strong anti-liberal reaction, fostering a distrust of the noninterventionist state that left private interest groups free to set their own terms in the marketplace.

In the postwar period the traditional lines between domestic and foreign policy became increasingly blurred. The peace was made in a highly charged political atmosphere. Lloyd George and Woodrow Wilson responded to the Germanophobe atmosphere in their respective countries. The anti-colonialist Clemenceau had to take notice of the imperialist wave in French political circles. Orlando and Sonnino knew what the political price would be if they failed to respond to the mounting nationalist pressure over Fiumi. Wilson, encouraged by the massive acclaim with which he was received, tried to go over the heads of the Italian representatives directly to the Italian people only to find that he had misjudged the popular mood.

Orlando fell in June, a victim to the Fiumi agitation. "Vox populi, vox diaboli," Clemenceau was to complain, but even the most conservative statesmen could not ignore the changed atmosphere in which diplomacy had to be conducted. Public opinion, however ignorant, volatile, or misled, became a more important pawn on the diplomatic chess board than in the period before 1914. The disarmament talks of the later 1920s continued despite the belief in British and French governing circles that they were dangerous as well as futile because neither government would face the public consequences of their abandonment. Foreign ministries recognized the importance of public opinion, whether at home or abroad, by creating or expanding special departments for press relations and propaganda purposes. The "populist perspective" in foreign affairs was an indirect consequence of "total war."

The need to satisfy electorates, parties, or special interest groups meant that most interstate financial and commercial negotiations had a Janus-like quality. The battles over reparations, for instance, were not only the key to the balance-of-power struggle on the continent but a critical element in the relations between governments and their electorates. Harold James in *The German Identity* suggests that in the absence of any other common interest on which to build a national consensus, "reparations were the relatively cheap price for keeping Weimar democracy alive."[13] Foreign policy issues were part of domestic agendas; solutions to internal problems were sought in the international sphere. This was not new but occurred on a much expanded scale.

The war itself added to the international agenda and provided the stimulus for multilateral action. Some issues, such as communications and transport, were already subjects of international agreement before 1914. These agreements required massive revision in view of the changed European situation. Other problems, such as the exchange of populations or the question of refugees, stateless persons, or national minorities were the result of the war, the revolutions, or the peace settlements. This expanded diplomatic arena, a foretaste of what was to happen after 1945, was not anticipated by the peacemakers. Woodrow Wilson distrusted the functional approach to peacekeeping, and Article 23 was far from central to his concerns. Yet the continuing development of efforts and institutions to deal with social, economic, and humanitarian concerns stood in marked contrast to the collapse of the League's security functions in the 1930s.

Quite apart from the conferences called to discuss financial and commercial affairs, the League secretariat was asked to take on responsibilities arising out of the peace treaties. Whether with regard to the mandate system or to the treatment of national minorities, a small group of Secretariat officials, without any powers of coercion, was laying the basis for a broadened concept of internationalism. The whole idea of an international civil service was new. A few individuals, Fridjof Nansen, for one, gave institutional shape to humanitarian impulses. Despite the constant struggle for funds and recognition and the reluctance of states to countenance what was often seen as attacks on their sovereignty, these activities set new standards of concern and accountability. The idea of national representatives appearing before a Mandates Commission whose rebukes increased in number and severity before the end of the decade represented a modest step forward in this respect. Dismissed as a "fig leaf" for colonialism, the mandate system was, after all, the world's first experiment in the international control of dependent territories. Without challenging the basis of imperial rule it had some effect on the "official mind." What could be done for refugees or for the stateless even in the pre-Hitler period was restricted in scope, but each attempt set a precedent for a broadened conception of shared responsibility that somehow survived the darkness that enveloped Europe.

One consequence of this expansion in the subject matter of diplomacy was the increased use of nondiplomatic specialists and experts in international affairs. At the highest level there was the postwar growth of ministerial diplomacy at the expense of foreign secretaries and their professional advisers. Presidents and prime ministers, then as now, called in private individuals to give advice and assist in deliberations. Domestic departments, increasingly involved in foreign affairs, appointed specialist attaches to serve abroad. In a multitude of professional fields it became common practice for experts, both official and private, to confer with one another and to make recommendations for action. Foreign ministries, partly by choice, found themselves excluded from such meetings, though many of the decisions reached had important political consequences.

The professional diplomats had already suffered a diminution in prestige and reputation during the war despite taking on a whole range of nontraditional responsibilities (blockade, propaganda, intelligence). In the early 1920s, a major effort was made to reequip the foreign ministries so as to strengthen their competence in such fields as commerce, finance, cultural services, news, propaganda, and intelligence. The creation of the League of Nations itself led to important innovations, particularly in those smaller states forced to reconsider their neutral positions and isolationist traditions. Resident delegations were established in Geneva, and some dozen states established special offices for League affairs at home. The reforming spirit soon died; the public demands that had forced the services to expand their sources of recruitment and reorganize their departments lost their force. Financial stringency and the natural conservatism of the diplomatic profession led to cutbacks and retreat. Confidence in traditional diplomacy revived at the time of the Locarno negotiations when political relations and security questions took center stage and foreign secretaries and their staffs enjoyed a temporary revival of power. It proved to be a false dawn.

The depression and ascendancy of Hitler produced a retreat from internationalism and multinational diplomacy. The Second World War War destroyed both the diffused nature of the 1919 international power structure and the Eurocentric character of the global state system. Apart from Alexis de Tocqueville and a handful of clairvoyant observers, few predicted a world dominated by the United States and the Soviet Union. Whatever their real or potential power, neither country had reshaped the interwar order as Wilson and Lenin each intended. European domination of the non-European world also vanished during and after the Second World War. As A. S. Kanya-Forstner has argued, neither the Great War nor its aftermath undermined the foundations of Europe's empires. It was not at all clear in the interwar period that Britain and France were already at the apex of their imperial power. Where there were difficulties in maintaining imperial rule accommodations were made, but without threatening the continuation of the imperial system. It can be argued that the British Empire appeared more stable in the 1930s than in 1919. It was the Second World War that radically speeded up the deceit process.

Some features of the 1919 settlements proved more enduring than later critics have suggested. "The map of Europe today," Christopher Seton-Watson wrote in early 1989, "is not all that different from the map drawn in 1919." The main differences, apart from the divisions of Germany, lay in the westward expansion of the Soviet Union and Poland. Even this frontier was close to that of the "Curzon line" adopted by the Paris Peace Conference and rejected by the Poles. The Ukrainians, divided among four different nations in 1919, were placed under Soviet rule in 1945. The three Baltic states were again part of Russia but preserved their national frontiers. "There have been only three minor frontier changes in Europe: the adjustment of the Italian-Yugoslav frontier in Yugoslavia's favor; the return to Bulgaria of the Southern Dobrudja by Romania; . . . and the award to Greece of the Dodecanese which Italy had seized from the Turks in 1912," Seton-Watson wrote. "It is ironic that the frontier which Italy requested at the 1946 Paris Peace Conference was exactly that proposed by Wilson in 1919 but rejected by the Italians."[14] Some scores were settled; the Czechs expelled their German and Hungarian minorities. In the case of the Hungarian minority in Romania and the Albanian minority in Yugoslavia, old grievances continued unabated.

Since Seton-Watson wrote this essay, the European map has been dramatically redrawn. The present breakup of empires and states, however, only underlines the "persistence of nationalist aspirations." Ethnic particularism and the continuing sense of national identity has proved far stronger (and not only in the former Soviet empire and in ex-Yugoslavia) than the leaders of the victorious powers of the Second World War could have imagined. Whether these feelings were just beneath the surface during the Nazi and Communist periods or were actually diminishing only to be revived when political vacuums were created is a still a much-debated question. There are similarities between the ethnic conflicts of the 1990s and those of the 1920s. The hopes of the 1919 peacemakers that the "new states" would become democratic, illusory in the short term, may, in some measure and in some states, now be fulfilled. More utopian were the dreams that the dominant nationalities would learn to respect the rights of their minorities. If the statesmen of 1919 realistically assessed the strength of nationalist feeling in Europe (if blind to the full implications of self-determination for the future of Germany), they failed to grasp the degree to which the principles of self-determination might undermine European rule elsewhere. There were elements of self-doubt among the imperial rulers and traditional racial conceptions came under attack, particularly in the Far East, yet the old order did not collapse and the second European war opened with much of it intact.

The post-1919 generation's reading of the causes of the Great War convinced many that there had to be a change in the international order if future catastrophes were to be avoided. The League of Nations embodied some of their hopes. It was, it is now argued, a misconceived attempt to find a substitute for the power considerations on which all international state systems are built. The real indictment of the postwar leaders, in my view, lay not in their acceptance of the Covenant but in their perpetration of Wilsonian myths that did not correspond with the reality of the League structure. If the Geneva system had been viewed as an addition to, rather than as a substitute for, the traditional ways of preserving the peace, it might have had a less harmful effect on the conduct of international affairs. The League represented a "sub-system" operating within the wider international order, affecting as well as reflecting its international environment. It offered an enlarged framework for multilateral diplomacy. It developed new mechanisms and techniques for handling disputes and for dealing with problems requiring cooperative action. These might have evolved without the League, but the Geneva structure gave them shape and promoted the minimal consensus that enabled them to function.

Participation in the League's activities affected the way that statesmen viewed and conducted foreign affairs. Geneva became a center of world politics. Some warmed to the "Geneva spirit"; others found it repellent. The Geneva "talking shop" served a purpose, and the "small change" of diplomacy was handled with some measure of success. But the League could not fulfill its central security purpose nor handle the problem of multilateral disarmament. The assumption that disarmament would eradicate militarism and that multinational disarmament would promote peace proved as dangerous as the doctrine of "self-determination." The League's campaign for disarmament, which absorbed more time and energy than any other issue, was not only unsuccessful but highly damaging to its reputation. The new institution had a place in the international system, but it was not the place that the liberal internationalists reacting to the devastating experience of the war demanded. It was unfortunate that it was their vision of the League that replaced its reality in the minds of so many of its supporters.

*   *   *

It was a tribute to the endurance of this much-battered concept that in 1944 a new attempt was made to create a global security system. Again, a world war had highlighted the price paid for living in an anarchical world. The United Nations was built on the institutional framework of the League of Nations. Despite its altered and more realistic structure, it too failed in its fundamental purpose. The peace, where it was kept, appeared to depend on a balance of military power too destructive to challenge. Despite its failure to fulfill the hopes of its American creator, the United Nations remains very much part of the international landscape; few actually want to see it vanish. On the contrary, since the breakup of the bi-polar world, there has been a continuous search for ways to strengthen the U.N.'s peacekeeping functions. As long as sovereign states are the units of power in the international state system, there can be no collective security system. This has not, and should not, stop the search for forms of collective action that might make life in the international order more bearable and humane. If the illusions of the Wilsonians have been shattered, their echoes remain.

The United Nations inherited the humanitarian, social, and economic functions of the League of Nations. The Bruce Report, published on August 22, 1939, the date of the Nazi-Soviet pact, called attention to the need to expand the nonpolitical aspects of the League's work, an attempt to provide the institution with a continuing raison d'etre. The Bruce Report pointed to the creation of the United Nation's Economic and Social Council and provided the model for an integrated approach to economic and social problems. Today the

United Nations is but one multilateral agency operating in these fields of activity. Many of its agencies have become semi-independent if not independent organizations. The present range of multinational activity and the growth of governmental and nongovernmental transnational institutions dwarfs the meager efforts of the interwar period. Nonetheless, these latter attempts to develop nonpolitical areas of cooperation represented an important stage in the recognition of the needs of an increasingly interdependent world.

The international order that emerged from the Great War looked very different from the alliance structures of the prewar period. How different was a subject of fierce debate in the 1920s as it became clear that neither a new balance of power nor a Wilsonian system of collective security had emerged. Somewhat optimistically, in 1929, the reparation powers assembled at the Hague for "The Conference on the Final Liquidation of the War." No new system was actually put in place in 1919; what developed was an amalgam of old and new in a highly uneasy relationship with each other. Wars hasten changes in the international system. The changes that followed the Great War were more revolutionary than those of 1815. The peace settlements were also far less successful than those of 1815 in maintaining the stability of Europe. David Stevenson may be correct when he claims that the peace fell apart so quickly because the peacemakers "lacked the foresight or the willingness to maintain concerted action in order to promote lasting stability." The explanation for failure, however, must take into account the transformations of the prewar period that had already undermined the Concert of Europe and produced the increasingly antagonistic relations between the states and the willingness of statesmen to resort to war. One must understand why, for instance, so many in London, and not just the "scaremongers," assumed that Germany harbored Napoleonic ambitions, a central question that remains on the historical agenda. It must also take into account what had happened during the war itself that made reconstruction so difficult at every level. This is not just a question of war aims nor of political or even economic change. It must include the extent of the killings and maiming, the attitudes toward war that the conflict engendered, and the dreams and nightmares that war provoked. Historians must assess the changes that the war itself made to the assumptions at the base of the international system. The peacemakers were aware of these changes but found no unanimity on which were to be accepted and which rejected. Reference must be made to the ambiguities of the power relations of the states both within and outside continental Europe and the difficulties of re-creating structures of international discourse when so many of the shared assumptions that had held Europe together were questioned, threatened, or demolished during the course of the war. The postwar decade was transitional; the transformations begun before the 1914–18 war and speeded up as a consequence of its extent and length were far from complete. The European truce lasted only twenty years, and for that the peacemakers must take some share of the blame. Europe was left in a fragmented state, and its victorious leaders could not agree on how to rearrange its parts to give the separate states the best chance to preserve their independence and promote their prosperity. Yet it must be said, even without subscribing to the "great man" theory of history, that it was Hitler who destroyed the peace of Europe and who had the clearest vision of how it could be reconstructed. There were aspects of the peace settlement that held out the promise of a new international state system based on the recognition of a changing world. Some reemerged in the post-1945 period. This is not to ignore the new situation created by the Second World War. It is to suggest that some of the ideas that emerged from the peace conference and the institutions and methods evolved during the 1920s have had an important afterlife in our own day. I would plead only that the dismissal of the decade as a sterile period in the evolution of the international state system requires reconsideration.

NOTES

1. This lecture and article were composed before the publication of Manfred F. Boemeke, Gerald D. Feldman, and Elisabeth Glaser, eds., *The Treaty of Versailles: A Reassessment After Seventy-Five Years* (Cambridge, 1998), which is now the most detailed collection of essays on its subject.

2. Ian Clarke, *The Hierarchy of States* (Cambridge, 1989), 157.

3. Niall Ferguson, *The Pity of War* (London, 1998), 441.

4. Stephen A. Schuker, "Origins of American Stabilization Policy in Europe," in Hans-Jürgen Schröder, ed., *Confrontation and Cooperation: Germany and the United States in the Era of World War I, 1900–1924* (Providence, 1993), 398. See also Schuker, *The End of French Predominance in Europe* (Chapel Hill, N.C., 1976).

5. See Elisabeth Glaser-Scmidt, "German and American Concepts to Restore a Liberal World Trading System After World War 1," in Schröder, *Confrontation and Cooperation*, 353–357.

6. Schuker, "Origins of American Stabilization Policy in Europe," 402.

7. S. Schuker, "American Reparations to Germany, 1919–1933," in Gerald D. Feldman, ed., *Die Nachwirkungen der Inflation auf die deutsche Geschichte, 1924–1933* (Munich: R. Oldenbourg, 1985), 371.

8. Cab 32/47, 11109/1/18 Memorandum Respecting the Policy of Locarno Presented to the Imperial Conference 1926.

9. K. Middlemas and J. Barnes, *Baldwin: A Biography,* (London, 1969), 729.

10. Memorandum by Harold Nicolson, 20/2/25, DBFP, 1st ser., vol. 27, doc. 205.

11. Owen O'Malley papers, in private possession of author, dated 1925.

12. K. Hildebrand, "The Transformation of the International System, from the Berlin Congress (1878) to the Paris Peace Treaty (1919–1920)," in R. Ahmen, A. M. Birke, and M. Howard, eds., *The Quest for Stability: Problems of West European Security, 1918–1957* (Oxford, 1993), 32–33.

13. H. James, *A German Identity, 1770–1990* (London, 1989), 134.

14. Christopher Seton-Watson, "1919 and the Persistence of Nationalist Aspirations," *Review of International Studies* (1989), 15, 316.

CHAPTER 10

Of Men and Myths
The Use and Abuse of
History and the Great War

HOLGER H. HERWIG

> The poor condition of the logical analysis of history is shown by the fact
> that neither historians, nor methodologists of history, but rather repre-
> sentatives of very unrelated disciplines have conducted the authoritative
> investigations into this important question.
>
> —MAX WEBER

Weber's comment regarding the "poor condition of the logical analysis of history" refocused my thoughts on my article "Clio Deceived," wherein I posed the question of whether a perverse law
operated whereby those events that are most important were hardest
to understand because they attracted the greatest attention from
mythmakers and charlatans.[1] It also brought to mind John F. Kennedy's commencement address at Yale University on June 11, 1962,
wherein he warned that the "great enemy of truth" all too often was
the "myth—persistent, persuasive and unrealistic."

I use the term "myth" not in Joseph Campbell's sense, whereby
myths are designed to teach us how to search for meaning, to seek
the essence of being alive, and to feel the spiritual potentialities of
life.[2] Rather, I use the term in its classic Greek sense, in which the

myth, for all its inconsistencies and absurdities, when accepted as truth, represents the learning and wisdom of a society. It is often a strange composite of primitive historical science and religion. Ancient Greeks and modern Europeans both resorted to mythmaking to serve existing social structures. Thus, as Euripedes used the tale of Theseus to restore a faltering Athenian democracy, Germans after 1918 used the myths of "war-guilt" and "stab-in-the-back" to restore a lost imperial order. But universal acceptance of myths as accepted truth is not in most cases the ultimate result. To make this point I have selected five instances for analysis of what I consider to have been "historical pollution" and "mythmaking."

Finally, I decided to concentrate on the mythmaking, and the misdeeds, of Germany and Austria for several reasons. First, these are the two states that I have studied for the past thirty years, and thus they are the ones with which I am most familiar. Second, while all major participants in the Great War early on presented "color books" containing carefully selected diplomatic documents, and while all states offered up their own versions of mythologized battle experience, the relative degree and virulence of mendacity manifested by mythmakers in Berlin and Vienna stands in marked contrast to the more benign efforts of Paris and London to fudge the historical record. Thus, for counterpoint I have included the story of the French "bayonet trench" at Verdun. Third, mythmakers, especially in Germany but also in Austria, had more immediate reason to reforge their histories than did the allies. Their efforts were part and parcel of a national campaign of "patriotic self-censorship" designed to counter the allies' charges in the Treaty of Versailles of sole war guilt and the attendant issue of reparations. At stake were lands "lost" to Belgium, Czechoslovakia, Denmark, France, and Poland; and colonies surrendered first and foremost to Great Britain. Finally, I selected especially the German case to highlight the role—ranging from pollution of the historical record to official denial to publish, from falsification of documents to government barring of lecture trips—that Clio's muses played in denying nonconformist scholars access to the public debate. For it was nothing short of a tragedy, in Hermann Hesse's words of 1930, that "90 or 100 prominent men" conspired "to deceive the [German] people on this vital question of national interest."[3]

War Guilt and War Denial: July 1914

German war guilt was laid down in the Treaty of Versailles in June 1919. Under Article 231, Germany accepted "responsibility . . . for causing all the loss and damage . . . of the war" since the conflict had been brought about solely "by the aggression of Germany and her allies." Article 232 stated that Germany "will make compensation for all damage done" to allied populations and property, including the "complete restoration" of major areas of combat.[4] These charges set off a tortuous and at times devious historical investigation that has intrigued scholars to this day. Character assassinations, denials of career and research opportunities, and falsification and destruction of evidence are its hallmarks. For the Great War, as Modris Eksteins has put it in this volume, was a "war about the gist of history."

As early as August 3, 1914, the day before the "war of Austrian succession" officially began, Berlin published its account of the origins of the war in the *Deutsches Weissbuch*.[5] The Foreign Office's color book was the product of a hasty sifting of its archives; half of the thirty documents were blatant forgeries. Nevertheless, it was the starting point of the war guilt debate. Thereafter, Legation Secretary Bernhard Wilhelm von Bülow, political archivist at the Wilhelmstrasse, undertook a careful "ordering" of the documentary record concerning July 1914. The sensational publication of materials pertaining to the outbreak of the war by the Socialists Kurt Eisner and Karl Kautsky only hastened Bülow's reordering of the files, which he completed in May 1919 by way of a special card index of seven thousand documents. Bülow divided his documents into two major groups: "defense" and "offense."[6]

By 1920 the Wilhelmstrasse had created a special War Guilt Section, whose job was threefold: to "order" and "cleanse" the Foreign Office's records with regard to the origins of the war; to produce a massive documentary publication for the period 1871 to 1914 to show Germany's peaceful policies; and to subsidize scholars, both at home and abroad, who were willing to tout the official German line for July 1914.

The first task was perhaps the easiest. Researchers in the Foreign Office Archives in Bonn today will not find a single document pertaining either to German deliberations or to Austro-German discussions at Potsdam on July 5–6, where Reich leaders issued Vienna the famous "blank check." Nor will they discover Berlin's reaction to Vienna's ultimatum to Serbia; nor any notes of German discussions with the representatives of foreign powers during the month of July; nor any record of the Kaiser's talks with military or diplomatic leaders that July; nor any trace of telephone calls, telegraphs, or verbal communications.[7] The Wilhelmstrasse quietly gave all potentially incriminating materials back to such people as Chancellor Theobald von Bethmann Hollweg and Foreign Secretary Gottlieb von Jagow as "private" papers. Most of this material disappeared in the 1920s and 1930s with the help of willing "patriotic censors."

The second task was also completed successfully. Between 1922 and 1927 the Foreign Office, through a committee of private scholars, published the forty-volume series *Die Grosse Politik der Europäischen Kabinette 1871–1914*, which, in the words of one historian, "established an early dependence of all students of prewar diplomacy on German records."[8] Few non-German scholars appreciated that this seemingly complete publication was badly flawed: poten-

tially incriminating documents were omitted or shortened or severely edited; a few were prejudicially falsified.

Perhaps most interesting, the Wilhelmstrasse used a number of
prominent American historians to put its case before the scholarly
community. The Harvard historian Sidney B. Fay's sympathetic
two-volume *The Origins of the World War* was translated into German and French and distributed by the Foreign Office at taxpayers'
expense, and its author was wined and dined by Berlin.[9] Similarly,
Harry E. Barnes of Smith College was singled out for support as his
writings upheld the German position.[10] Barnes' works were translated into German and French, distributed for free, and Barnes
toured Berlin as a government guest no fewer than three times in
1926 alone. By contrast, Bernadotte Schmitt's critical *The Coming of
the War, 1914* was never translated into German, and Berlin in 1928
rejected a suggestion by its consul at Chicago that Schmitt tour
Germany.[11] The Wilhelmstrasse declined to have what it termed this
"incorrigible" historian spread his message within the Reich.[12]

Other incorrigible historians fared no better. To research the
legal questions surrounding the origins of the war, the Reichstag's
First Committee of Enquiry had turned to the eminent Freiburg
jurist Hermann Kantorowicz. The latter finished his work in 1923,
completed minor textual revisions two years later, and sent cor-
rected galleys to press in 1927. The book appeared in 1967—as a private manuscript.[13] What had delayed publication for four decades?

Kantorowicz concluded after his careful study of extant documents that responsibility for the war lay largely with the Central Powers: with Austria-Hungary for the way it had exploited the Sarajevo
murder to launch a war with Serbia, regardless of its ramifications;
and with Germany for supporting Vienna to the hilt and for rejecting
all subsequent peace feelers from Britain and Russia. Jew, Democrat, Republican, and anglophile, Kantorowicz experienced the full

wrath of officialdom. In 1927, Foreign Minister Gustav Stresemann vetoed Kantorowicz's appointment to a chair at Kiel University. Next, Stresemann denied Kantorowicz private publication of his findings. Then the Finance Office withdrew the 40,000 to 50,000 RM promised to Kantorowicz as a subsidy for the official publication. Final degradation came in 1933 when Kantorowicz was one of the first German professors fired from academia by the Nazis, his writings burned publicly for being anti-German.[14]

Nor was Kantorowicz's case an isolated one. In 1932 Germany's conservative historians denied the young radical scholar Eckart Kehr the Rockefeller Fellowship that Charles A. Beard had helped him secure for study in the United States. As recently as 1964, West German Foreign Minister Gerhard Schröder, acting on the advice of senior conservative historians, rescinded Goethe Institute travel funds awarded to Fritz Fischer for a planned lecture tour in the United States—a tour that the doyen of German historians, Gerhard Ritter, compared to a "national tragedy."[15]

Last but not least, this official censorship was paralleled by an equally effective and insidious unofficial campaign to keep memoirs and diaries from coming to light. The argument of postmodernists notwithstanding, historical scholarship, at its best, comes down to the use of evidence; at its worst, to the abuse of evidence. We may disagree about the interpretation and weighting of documents, the motivation of major actors, the precise timing of critical decisions, and the mindset of statesmen and soldiers at precise points in their careers; but we should never agree to falsify or pollute the historical record, much less to destroy it.

In Germany the critical papers of leading figures were systematically "cleansed" (destroyed) by self-appointed "patriotic censors." A few examples will make the point. In 1919, General Helmuth von Moltke's widow, Eliza, sought to publish the general's papers dealing with the outbreak of the war. She was cautioned against this by a former Prussian general, a Prussian diplomat, and "certain [other] persons," with the result that the memoirs that appeared in 1922 were virtually devoid of information on the July crisis. Moreover, Moltke's papers were so neatly cleansed by the general's eldest son, Wilhelm, that, in the words of the historian John Röhl, "they contain not a single document worth reading from the pre-War period."[16]

Much the same apparently applies to the papers of Field Marshal Paul von Hindenburg, which are still held by his grandson, Hubertus, and which were cleansed in the 1960s by the nationalist historian Walther Hubatsch. Hindenburg's published memoirs for the years 1911 to 1934 were, in fact, written by Colonel Hermann Mertz von Quirnheim of the Potsdam Reichsarchiv.[17] General Erich Ludendorff's papers likewise are still held by his son-in-law, Franz Karg von Bebenburg, who has stated that they no longer contain any materials relevant to the Great War.[18] One can only guess at the "patriotic censor" in this instance.

Even when important collections were not destroyed—despite the wishes of their authors—controversy surrounds their handling and originality. A case in point is the papers of Kurt Riezler, Bethmann Hollweg's senior adviser in July 1914. As late as the 1950s the conservative historian Hans Rothfels, a fugitive from Nazi Germany, advised Riezler against publication for fear that it would reopen the debate concerning the origins of the Great War. After Riezler's death in 1965, his brother destroyed a substantial part of the papers. When Riezler's sister, Mary White, eventually consented to their publication, the job was handed to an archconservative historian, Karl Dietrich Erdmann, who carefully "ordered" the papers once more—and then had them locked up for eight years in the Federal Archive at Koblenz. In the process, the critical notes for the period from July 7 through August 14, 1914, were edited and reedited so many times that their authenticity has been questioned.[19] Historical evidence has been so profusely and purposefully polluted by patriotic censors from the 1920s to the 1960s that we have every right to question the legitimacy of segments of the German historical profession.

Mobilization 1914:
The Great Austro-Hungarian "Conspiracy"

Franz Conrad von Hötzendorf, the Austro-Hungarian chief of the General Staff in 1914, has enjoyed widespread veneration in both the professional and popular press. Austrian writers—ranging from such military historians as Rudolf Kiszling, Edmund Glaise von Horstenau, and August von Urbánski to publicists such as Karl Friedrich Nowak and Oskar Regele—have championed Conrad as their country's greatest military leader since Prince Eugene of Savoy. Cyril Falls, an English military historian, has claimed that Conrad was the "best strategist at the outset, probably of the war."[20] A French scholar, Marc Ferro, deemed Conrad the "best strategist among the Central Powers."[21] Conrad certainly agreed with such verdicts in his five-volume memoirs, stating that the 1914 mobilization against Serbia and Russia "proceeded smoothly,"[22] and blaming failures in the field either on the uncooperative German ally or on incompetent subordinates. Papers that might have shown Conrad at fault were "ordered" by Viennese military archivists and historians.[23]

With regard to the mobilization of July–August 1914, the prevailing view of the past seventy years has been that Conrad was caught on the horns of a geographic-strategic dilemma—whether to concentrate first against Russia or Serbia—and that he handled it about as well as could be expected. In fact, Conrad "solved" the mobilization dilemma by sending the bulk of his army south against Serbia to deal it a quick, mortal blow, banking on the anticipated snail's pace of Russian mobilization to buy time for the expected clash in southern Poland. But when Russia mobilized much faster than planners in Vienna had believed (or hoped?) possible, Conrad turned for succor to Major Emil Ratzenhofer and Colonel Johann Straub of the Railroad Bureaus in the General Staff and the War Ministry. Thus, on Ratzenhofer's advice, Habsburg forces continued their travels to Serbia, disembarked, reembarked, and finally headed for Galicia. In Winston Churchill's inimitable words, they left General Oskar Potiorek in Serbia before they could "win him a victory," and they returned to Conrad "in time to participate in his defeat."[24] Almost all writers from 1914 to Norman Stone's *The Eastern Front* in 1975 have stressed that Conrad's situation was hopeless and that he did the best that could have been expected.

In truth, Conrad failed to adhere to the sound plan that he had developed before 1914: to send the greater part of his forces (A-Staffel) to Galicia, to hurl a smaller body of two armies (Minimalgruppe Balkan) against Serbia, and to maintain twelve divisions (B-Staffel) as a strategic reserve, to be deployed in the decisive theater at the decisive moment. Instead of holding back his strategic reserve and watching Russian and Serbian mobilization unfold, Conrad, for political and psychological reasons, immediately dispatched B-Staffel to Serbia, where it was to deploy by August 10. "Dog Serbia," in Conrad's view, had to be crushed at all costs; nothing less than the survival of the Empire depended on this. No amount of warnings about the speed of the Russian buildup in Galicia—from Conrad's former military attaché to Russia, the Foreign Ministry at the Ballhausplatz, the German military, or Kaiser Wilhelm II—could deter Conrad from his Serbian obsession.

Ratzenhofer and Straub before the war had planned mobilization for war against Russia (War Case R) and Serbia (War Case B) separately and independently of each other, and they had failed to prepare a mutual War Case R+B. Thus there existed in Vienna in 1914 no contingency plans for deployment against Serbia, followed by redeployment against Russia—the most likely scenario in any war. Caught off-guard by the quick Russian mobilization and without a plan to deal with it, Ratzenhofer and Straub adamantly insisted that Conrad continue deployment against Serbia. Any change in plans, they argued, would throw all existing preparations into "chaos." Even when it became clear that Russian troops were deploying in southern Poland by August 6, Conrad ordered B-Staffel to continue to Serbia to undertake a military "demonstration" along the Save-Danube line.

Conrad's bungled mobilization resulted in 230,000 men being killed and wounded in the Balkans, and 250,000 being killed and wounded (as well as 100,000 taken prisoner) in Galicia. At the height of the Battle of Lemberg between August 28 and 30, B-Staffel (now reconstituted as the Second Army) still lacked its IV and VII Corps, which were secure in trains en route from Serbia to Poland. But the world never learned the truth about the Austro-Hungarian mobilization, which Conrad hid even from the German ally. Instead, Conrad sought to cover his ineptitude by launching vitriolic denunciations of Berlin for its alleged failure to send major forces to the Eastern Front immediately after the outbreak of war.

What quickly became the "official" picture of a heroic Conrad beset by unsolvable strategic dilemmas was cast in stone after 1918 as former officers rallied around Conrad and the *k.u.k.* Army. Nothing less than their survival was at stake: the Law of Exclusion of December 19, 1918, denied officers with the rank of major or higher rights in the new republic.[25] Public criticism of Conrad became anathema for these officers, as it would tarnish the glory of the venerable Imperial and Royal Army. And since they enjoyed a monopoly on access to military archives thanks to the archivists Glaise von Horstenau and Kiszling, these official apologists dominated the writing of Habsburg military history on the Great War.

Specifically, Major Ratzenhofer, the architect of the mobilization debacle of August 1914, wrote the story of the Habsburg *Aufmarsch* in the first volume of the official history, *Österreich-Ungarns Letzter*

Krieg, 1914–1918. Published in 1929, Ratzenhofer's apologia was so marred by factual errors that the volume had to be recalled. When rewritten and rereleased in 1931, it turned out that Ratzenhofer yet again had penned the vital section on mobilization! Seventeen members of the erstwhile *k.u.k.* Army wrote the official history—the only case in which an official history of the Great War was written exclusively by former officers.[26] Moreover, two of Conrad's hagiographers, Kiszling and Glaise von Horstenau, controlled the preparation of all the volumes of *Österreich-Ungarns Letzter Krieg*, down to the last one, published in 1938. Thus they reinforced the "Conrad legend" and suppressed evidence that might have cast Conrad in an unfavorable light.

In the interwar years these onetime Habsburg officers dedicated themselves to spreading the mobilization myth. Ratzenhofer served as editor of the most prominent Austrian military history journal, *Militärwissenschaftliche Mitteilungen*, wherein he maintained strict orthodoxy regarding the "official" view of the 1914 mobilization. Kiszling, after consulting with the German Reichsarchiv, produced a series of books on the Dual Monarchy's major battles and campaigns in Russia between 1914 and 1918; here also Kiszling used his powerful position to whitewash Conrad's 1914 mobilization. More: by publishing numerous articles in the *Berliner Monatshefte*, Kiszling spread his view of Conrad and mobilization to a larger German readership. Kiszling never deviated from his apologia in the countless articles, chapters, and books that he wrote between 1922 and 1984.[27] As chief administrator of the Vienna War Archive from 1939 to 1945, Kiszling held a position of power from which he controlled the research and writing of Austrian military history; as well, he staffed the archive with loyal supporters. We will never know how many potentially incriminating documents Kiszling and his minions cleansed or ordered.

Still, the real story of Austro-Hungarian mobilization could not be suppressed forever. In 1993 the world finally received a detailed research book on Habsburg mobilization that debunked the Ratzenhofer-Straub-Kiszling-Glaise von Horstenau "official" mythology. In Jack Tunstall's words, Conrad's mobilization blunder was a classic case of "cognitive dissonance": a blind faith in a quick victory over Serbia in time to meet the Russian threat in Poland with full force, one that was contrary to all available evidence.[28] This academic "conspiracy" served neither the Austrian Republic nor historical investigation.

Tannenberg: Reality and Myth

East Prussia in 1914 was a most unlikely place for making myths and heroes. A maze of irregular hills covered with brush and trees, a low terrain that alternated between barren stretches of sandy soil and bogs and lakes, Germany's easternmost province had been designated a holding area under the Schlieffen plan. Six infantry divisions and one cavalry were to stem the onslaught of the Russian "steamroller"—two armies consisting of nineteen infantry and seven cavalry divisions supported by rifle and artillery brigades. After a series of inconclusive clashes in and around Gumbinnen, General von Moltke cashiered the commander of his Eighth Army, General Max von Prittwitz und Gaffron—the first time in modern German military history that an army commander was relieved of command in this manner. Although few could have suspected it, Moltke therewith set the stage for the most renowned military partnership in German history.

At 4 A.M. on August 23, 1914, a special military train pulled into the station at Hanover. On board was a brilliant but eccentric staff officer, General Erich Ludendorff, who had recently received the coveted Pour le mérite (Germany's most prestigious military decoration) for storming the Belgian belt fortresses at Liège. On the platform, dressed in Prussian blue, stood the stout and imperturbable General Paul von Hindenburg. Kaiser Wilhelm II was pleased with neither choice: he regarded Hindenburg not just as simple but as simpleminded, and Ludendorff as a technician and careerist lacking in social graces. As the train rolled eastward, Ludendorff briefed Hindenburg on the situation in East Prussia. "Before long," Hindenburg later wrote, "we were at one in our view of the situation."[29] The two generals quickly agreed that it was of paramount military, political, and psychological importance to keep the Eighth Army east of the Vistula River, and not to execute a retreat into West Prussia. Then both soldiers went to bed.

Unbeknown to Hindenburg and Ludendorff, Prittwitz's First General Staff Officer, Lieutenant-Colonel Max Hoffmann, had already given orders for German forces to halt their retreat in the north before General P. K. Rennenkampf's First Army, and to concentrate against General A. V. Samsonov's Second Army in the south. Upon arriving at Eighth Army headquarters on August 24, Hindenburg and Ludendorff approved Hoffmann's dispositions. Although outnumbered 485,000 to 173,000 in East Prussia, the triumvirate at Marienburg quickly agreed that their only chance lay in a bold gamble: to concentrate first against Samsonov below the Masurian Lakes and then to force-march all available troops north against the phlegmatic Rennenkampf.

And therewith the first Tannenberg legend came into being. Hoffmann, writing his memoirs after the event and bitter at having been bypassed for senior command, told a fascinating account of a blood feud that he had witnessed as a military observer during the Russo-Japanese War. At the railway station in Mukden, Captain Hoffmann had seen how two Russian officers, A. V. Samsonov and P. K. Rennenkampf, had blamed each other for the Russian debacle, had hurled epithets at each other, had rolled on the ground in front of their troops, and had vowed never to aid one another, come what may.[30] In August 1914, remembering the incident, Hoffmann claimed that he devised the plans for Eighth Army to concentrate against each of the two Russian commanders, secure in the knowledge that neither Samsonov nor Rennenkampf would come to the aid of the other. Thus was the campaign in East Prussia won on the dusty plains of Mukden.

The incident vividly expressed what every Western observer believed of the prewar Imperial Russian Army: that it was structurally inefficient and staffed with incompetent court favorites. Surely it was not inconceivable that Tsar Nicholas II and his stable of sycophants at military headquarters were quite willing to entrust a campaign that depended on close cooperation for its success to two commanders who hated each other. The legend was born—and it persists to the present day.[31]

But the incident never occurred. Rennenkampf was, in fact, in the hospital being treated for a battlefield wound at the time of the alleged scuffle with Samsonov. He would have required the services of several litter-bearers to have reached the railway station.[32] And while Hoffmann had indeed been in the Far East in 1905, he had been attached not to the Russian but rather to the Japanese army as a military attaché.

This notwithstanding, Hindenburg/Ludendorff accepted Hoffmann's plan to concentrate first against Samsonov below the Masurian Lakes, which divided East Prussia into northern and southern theaters of operations; a single cavalry division stood between Rennenkampf and the Vistula. There was no talk that day of a new Cannae, only of a chance to strike the Russian Second Army in the flanks. At dawn on August 27, I Corps unleashed a hurricane bombardment against Samsonov's left wing, which fled the battlefield, thereby exposing Second Army's center. On August 28, after a failed attack by Samsonov's center, the Germans charged both flanks of the Second Army. A rout ensued. Only 2,000 Russian soldiers escaped the deadly German ring; 50,000 died or were wounded, and 92,000 surrendered. Samsonov committed suicide at Pivnitz, near Willenberg.[33]

The second Tannenberg legend was about to unfold. At 5:30 P.M. on August 28, Ludendorff began to draft his report of the battle with the words "Frögenau—leave the exact time open." Thus Ludendorff accurately gave the village of Frögenau as the site of the battle. Hoffmann quickly realized that this would not do, and persuaded Ludendorff to "transfer" the victory to another nearby village, Tannenberg. There, on July 15, 1410, as every German schoolboy knew, a Polish-Lithuanian force had dealt the Teutonic Knights a crushing defeat, ending Germanic eastward expansion. Ludendorff readily concurred with Hoffmann, and thus the legend of the Teutonic Knights helped establish the legend of the Battle of Tannenberg.

The official German history of the war, *Der Weltkrieg 1914 bis 1918*, in the mid-1920s embellished Tannenberg with revelations about a Russian reign of terror in August and September 1914. Entire villages—Domnau, Abschwangen, Ortelsburg, Bartenstein, among others—had been burned to the ground. Women and girls had been systematically raped. About 100,000 draft-eligible men had been hauled eastward as "hostages." Bridges and rail centers, factories and communications facilities had been destroyed. Overall, the Reichsarchiv's military historians set German losses due to Russian pillage and plunder at 1,620 civilians, 17,000 buildings, 135,000 horses, 200,000 pigs, and 250,000 cows.[34] In the absence of accurate Russian records it is impossible to verify or debunk the German claims. But there is no question that the Russian "reign of terror" in East Prussia in 1914 was remembered well by another invading German army in 1941.

The reality of Tannenberg quickly became the myth of Tannenberg. Hindenburg, awarded the Pour le mérite for the battle, became the Great War's first hero. His picture adorned newspapers and walls throughout Germany. Barbers copied his now famous mutton-chops. War loans were sold by allowing subscribers to drive nails into his wooden statue in Berlin. The Imperial Navy christened a battle-cruiser in his honor. Silesia renamed the industrial town of Zabrze for the "savior of the fatherland." The official history of the war touted Tannenberg as the "greatest battle of encirclement in world history" after Leipzig (1813), Metz, and Sedan (1870). Even Cannae paled in comparison.[35]

Every legend needs its commemorative shrine. German veterans' associations after the war raised funds for a fitting monument. The architects Johannes and Walter Krüger, taking Stonehenge as their model, designed a great stone memorial by blending "myth and acoustics." Eight large towers were linked by a massive wall; each served a specific function, such as chapel, battle-flag hall, youth hostel, and the like. Mass graves attested to the titanic "clash of empires" that had taken place at Tannenberg in 1914. The "sacred space" inside the towers and wall formed a circle large enough to hold 10,000 people. Nordic imagery thus gave reality to the Tannenberg legend.[36] Schoolchildren undertook pilgrimages to the shrine. In 1935, Adolf Hitler buried Hindenburg in the Tannenberg memorial with full military honors. In 1945, German engineers destroyed the monument rather than have it fall into Russian (later Polish) hands.

Verdun 1916: Obfuscation by Myths and Numbers

Verdun. The word still conjures up images of almost incomprehensible carnage. Legends concerning "heaps of dead" and "streams of blood" dominate virtually all accounts. Cyril Falls termed Verdun "assuredly one of the most hellish of conflicts . . . still one of the most famous of the war."[37] Basil Liddell Hart informed his readers that "no battle of the whole war was more heroic or more dramatic in its course."[38] A. J. P. Taylor acerbically asserted that "Verdun was the most senseless episode in a war not distinguished for sense anywhere."[39] Marc Ferro assured us that it "gripped the imagination" and that its veterans "were lauded" in every land.[40] The list of German combatants includes the legendary air aces Manfred Baron von Richthofen and Oswald Boelcke, the future tank master Heinz Guderian, the novelist Arnold Zweig, and two eventual leaders of the Nazi party, Rudolf Hess and Ernst Röhm.

It seems almost perverse to apply the terms "myths" and "legends" to a bloody encounter that quickly became a symbol of the monotonous mass murder of the First World War. I do not for a moment intend to belittle the hell of the Meuse "meat grinder" of 1916. Both sides hurled 10 million artillery shells, or about 1.35 million tons of steel, at each other between February and December. The German Fifth Army alone in a single day expended 17.5 railway wagons of shells. Hill 304 in three months became Hill 297 as seven meters of earth were blasted off its crown. Phosgene, a novel asphyxiating gas, was first used at Verdun. Flame-throwers gave a special "face"—not to mention smell—to the battle in the subterranean caverns of Forts Vaux and Douaumont.[41] Steel helmets changed the very appearance of what Ernst Jünger called the new "workers of war."

The battlefield was a hellish nightmare of sounds and sights. In what Mary R. Habeck calls the "view from below" (Chapter 4), the men of 1914–18 quickly learned what a double-edged sword the new technology of war had become. Soldiers caught in the barbed wire or hit by shrapnel lay screaming for hours in no-man's-land before overworked medics could reach them. Many bled to death. Horses suffered in the mud and the sleet and snow of early 1916, easy prey for both artillery and snipers. Many combatants retained images of horses with belly wounds still kicking their legs in deep shell holes five and six days after being shot. The lunar craters, which a French aviator compared to the "humid skin of a monstrous toad," turned gray and brown as men and beasts filled them. The fields soon reeked of decaying human flesh. Rats ate well and often. Lime chloride was dumped between the stacked bodies of the dead to aid decomposition. Even the soil was unclean: cultivated and fertilized for centuries by the excreta of animals, it was laden with pathogenic bacteria that led to horrendous rates of infection and amputation through deadly gas gangrene. Wound mortality ran as high as 40 percent.

No, the myths and legends of Verdun pertain to what was made of the battle both then and later, by combatants as well as by journalists and scholars. For there can be no denying that "Verdun" took on a meaning of its own, quite beyond what took place there in 1916. Germany's Great Captains of the Second World War, for example, never lost sight of Verdun's mythical significance. In July 1944, when the German military commander in France, General Carl-Heinrich von Stülpnagel, was implicated in the attempted assassination of Hitler, he returned to his old post at Verdun, where he had served as captain in 1916, and tried to commit suicide. As late as 1966, Charles De Gaulle, also a captain at Verdun, could still not bring himself to invite either Germans or Americans to the fiftieth anniversary commemorations at this national shrine for fear of polluting its sacred soil with a foreign presence.[42] It remained for French President François Mitterrand and German Chancellor Helmut Kohl to break the taboo two decades later.

Almost immediately Verdun became enshrouded in myths. The French dubbed it a "sacred city." Field Marshal von Hindenburg spoke of it as a "beacon light of German valor."[43] The *mentalité* that is Verdun was consecrated in the Treaty of Versailles, signed in June 1919 in the Hall of Mirrors at Louis XIV's shrine of conspicuous self-veneration at the same table at which Otto von Bismarck had proclaimed the German Empire in January 1871. It stipulated that French graves were to be individual and sited in villages and towns, whereas German graves were to be massed and placed in remote areas; that crosses on French graves were to be white (for purity), while German crosses were to be black (for shame).[44]

Casualty figures for Verdun likewise became legendary. When I toured the battlefield with my children on the cold, bleak, and dreary July 4, 1992, the guide solemnly informed us that one million men had died (!) there in the spring, summer, and fall of 1916. When we visited the ossuary, pointedly inscribed "pour la France," we were assured that behind its glass panes alone rested the bones of 250,000 *poilus*. Nor can historians agree on the butcher's bill: Ferro claims 350,000 French casualties; Taylor 315,000 French losses; Alistair Horne 350,000 men per side; and James L. Stokesbury would have us believe that 89,000 French *poilus* and 82,000 German *Landser* died on Dead Man Hill alone.[45] In truth, the German Fifth Army, which fought the Battle of Verdun, reported 81,668 men either killed or missing at Verdun between February and September 1916.[46]

The mythology of Verdun sufficed to give coin to the most outrageous actions. In 1916, in the best tradition of *opéra-bouffe*, the Prussian Army awarded the Pour le mérite to Lieutenant Cordt von Brandis, commander of 8 Company of the 24th Brandenburg Regiment—not for storming Fort Douaumont, in which he had only a tertiary role, but for telephoning the news of its fall to staff headquarters.[47] The truth concerning the storming of Fort Douaumont is shrouded by layers and layers of claims and counterclaims, memoirs and memoir "corrections," to the point that it is almost impossible to sort fact from fiction. According to one account, the fort was entered first by a Sergeant Kunze and ten men of the Pioneers. More likely that honor fell to Reserve Lieutenant Eugen Radtke of 6 Company, followed by Captain Hans Joachim Haupt, commander of 7 Company. Brandis merely followed their tracks through the snow into the world's greatest bastion, which had fallen to the Germans without a shot being fired. As Haupt secured the fort against a possible French attempt to retake it, he instructed Brandis to pass news of the fort's capture to Battalion Headquarters; from there, Brandis received permission to put Regimental Headquarters in the picture as well.

News of this incredible *coup de main* immediately landed on the desk of the Prussian crown prince, commander-in-chief of the Fifth Army. Prince Wilhelm seized the moment: Brandis and Haupt, both regular officers, were awarded the Pour le mérite; Radtke and the enigmatic Kunze, one a reserve officer and the other a noncommissioned officer, received nothing. Brandis' noble ancestry undoubtedly advanced his cause with the crown prince. Schoolchildren received a day off and church bells pealed to celebrate Douaumont's fall. After the war a Prussian village was renamed in Brandis' honor. Mythmaking and class bias had combined in the person of Cordt von Brandis, who took full advantage of the opportunity to embellish his claim to sole credit for the storming of Douaumont—"He who conquers the bride also gets to lead her home"[48]—both then and after the war.

As a counterpoint to the deliberate German and Austrian efforts at mythmaking, the French managed to stumble onto another myth: *la tranchée des baïonettes*. Visitors to the battlefield today are led to a squat gray concrete bunker, barely six feet high and replete with twisted and rusted bayonets sticking out of the ground, allegedly still clutched by French soldiers from 3 Company of the 137th Infantry Regiment from the Vendée, who had defended the sacred ground to their last breath. Cameras click. Videocams roll. Visitors stand in awe. But, as the French journalist Jean Norton Cru first exposed in 1930 and as the German radio journalist German Werth reiterated in 1979, the tranchée was the creation of an eccentric American millionaire, a "benefactor" who decided to create a macabre shrine for effect.[49] The truth is that two companies, French 21st Division, had surrendered to a Bavarian unit and dropped their rifles on this spot on June 12, 1916. Did some of the French soldiers die on the spot, still clutching their bayonet-tipped rifles? Had some (surely not all) been buried alive by the German artillery bombardment of June 10–11? Had the Germans found the dead French soldiers; hastily shoveled dirt over them; and used their rifles in the absence of crosses? Or had it been a combination of all of these possibilities? The French chaplain of the ossuary willingly informs knowledgeable visitors that he finds it harder each year to replace the rusted bayonets! The power of the myth remains supreme: the saga of the tranchée, replete with its contradictory and fragmentary evidence, is kept alive in France through children's comic strips.

Even the distribution of medals for valor on the field of battle escalated beyond comprehension during and after Verdun. Germany awarded no fewer than 5.9 million Iron Crosses between 1914 and 1924. Staff officers at Verdun routinely joked that one could escape this decoration only by committing suicide.[50] Morale and the "poor bloody infantry," to use Leonard Smith's analogy (Chapter 5), were fused in part by this lavish outpouring ("algebraic variable") of national souvenirs.

German military writers in the interwar period struggled to create a final myth: that Verdun had not been a military defeat but rather the apex of a kind of modern technological warfare that rendered meaningless traditional concepts of victory and defeat. And the mythology of Verdun continued well into the Second World War. In November 1942, Adolf Hitler, a veteran of the Western Front, assured the Nazi Old Guard at Munich on the anniversary of the "beer-hall putsch" of 1923 that Stalingrad, then raging at its climactic height, would never become a "second Verdun."[51] The remnants of the German Sixth Army, 93,000 men, surrendered to the Soviets two months later.

Dolchstoss: The Granddaddy of Myths

On November 18, 1919, Field Marshal von Hindenburg strolled to the Reichstag in Berlin, ostensibly to "testify" on the technical issue of the timing of unrestricted submarine warfare in 1916–17. Instead, Hindenburg, ably stage-managed by the Conservative Party leader Karl Helfferich and his former quartermaster-general Ludendorff, turned his "testimony" into a triumphant farce. Escorted by an honor guard, the "wooden titan" took his place in a witness box adorned with chrysanthemums tied with ribbons of the imperial colors of black, white, and red. Resolutely ignoring the Committee of Enquiry's specific questions on the timing of the U-boat campaign, Hindenburg instead read a prepared statement. Under oath he swore that neither the Kaiser, his government, nor the general staff had wanted war in 1914; and that, as verified by no less an authority than a "British general," the German Army "was stabbed in the back" by the home front in 1918.[52] A stunned committee was barely able to cross-examine the "witness."

While the term "stabbed in the back" had been in circulation among soldiers and statesmen well before the end of the Great War, Hindenburg's "testimony" gave official birth to the *Dolchstosslegende*. From that point on, the alleged "November criminals"—Jews, Marxists, and pacifists—were equated in the public's mind with defeat and revolution. A year later Hindenburg repeated the charge of domestic treason in his memoirs—written, as stated earlier, by Colonel Mertz von Quirnheim—with reference to the ancient Germanic Nibelungen saga. "Like Siegfried, stricken down by the treacherous spear of savage Hagen, our weary front collapsed."[53] Five years before Hitler set down on paper his notion of the "big lie," Hindenburg had already demonstrated its effectiveness.[54]

And yet Hindenburg could hardly have been further from the truth, as he well knew. For the German army was badly beaten by

August 1918. In four years of bitter warfare, the Reich had enormous casualties—1.8 million men killed, 4.2 million wounded (including 1.1 million invalids), and 618,000 prisoners of war. The process of demoralization and decimation within its ranks had escalated, especially in the summer of 1918. According to General Hermann von Kuhl, the German Army had lost about one million men during Operation Michael in March to July; concurrently, U.S. Army forces in France increased by one million men. Moreover, 420,000 more Germans were killed and wounded and 340,000 were missing and taken prisoner between mid-July and the Armistice of November 11, 1918.

Anglo-Saxon scholars often overlook that German battalions, divisions, and corps were mere skeletons by 1918. One corps within the Second Army, for example, was down to 2,683 combatants and 2,000 reserves—against a normal strength of about 40,000 men. More than one-third of the divisions in army groups Crown Prince Rupprecht of Bavaria and Crown Prince Wilhelm of Germany were down to 600 men—as compared to full strength of about 15,000. Many units experienced 20 percent loss of personnel whenever front- and rear-echelon troops were exchanged. Desertions had reached epidemic proportions: the official history placed their number as high as 1 million in the late months of the war.[55] In truth, the German Army had been decisively beaten at the latest by July 19, when General Ferdinand Foch counterattacked at Château Thierry—and not stabbed in the back by the equally suffering and demoralized home front.

But this military defeat had not been reported to the German people under cover of military censorship, which helps account for the success of the stab-in-the-back legend. One minute German troops stood victorious on the soil of France and Belgium, Russia, and Romania; the next minute they allegedly collapsed and sued for peace at any price. How could this be? The Dolchstosslegende provided a powerful and convenient explanation, one that was widely and readily accepted, especially by the German middle classes, denied political direction and threatened with social and economic chaos by the collapse of the Hohenzollern Monarchy and the outbreak of revolutions throughout Germany.

"Proof" was piled on top of "proof." General Hans von Seeckt, the future "father" of the Reichswehr, had ruminated as early as the political crisis of July 1917 on Chancellor von Bethmann Hollweg's alleged "weakness" in directing the war effort. "Why do we bother going on fighting?" Seeckt mused. "The home front has stabbed us in the back and therewith the war is lost."[56] General Ludendorff, about to flee Germany (and thus responsibility for the military defeat) on September 29, 1918, maliciously instructed the Supreme Command to turn power over "to those circles which primarily have brought us to this state of affairs. . . . Let them now stew in their own juice."[57] The German official history incorporated the Dolchstosslegende into its final volume.[58]

At the lower end of the scale of officer ranks, Lieutenant Martin Niemöller, commander of *U-67* at Pola in the Adriatic Sea, also allowed his thoughts to turn to the search for those responsible for the sudden collapse after Operation Michael. Surely, Niemöller wondered, those at home must have had a hand in the inexplicable and sudden demise?[59] On November 18, 1919, Field Marshal von Hindenburg merely gave his stamp of approval (and legitimacy) to such thoughts.

Hindenburg knew well that German Jews, for example, had served in large numbers in the front lines during the Great War. In October 1916, shortly after his appointment as chief of the General Staff, the Prussian army had undertaken a "Jew count" (*Judenzählung*) in its ranks to find out whether charges from the radical Right that Jews refused to serve were true. The final tabulations, published only after the war, were revealing. About 100,000 Jews, or 17.3 percent of the German Jewish population, had served in the armed forces; of these, 84,000 had been in the front lines, where one in seven had died or been lost. Just over 35 percent of those Jews who served had been decorated, and 23 percent had been promoted.[60] The figures compared favorably to those for German non-Jews.

Yet, to make quite certain that no one misunderstood who had wielded the proverbial knife, Heinrich Class, head of the Pan-German League, on October 19, 1918, suggested that his followers single out the Jews as a convenient "lightning rod for all that is unjust" in the German collapse. Citing Heinrich von Kleist's shrill outcry of 1809 against Napoleon's rape of Prussia, Class concluded with reference to the Jews: "Beat them to death; the court of world history will not ask for your motives."[61] Is it too far off the mark to suggest that the "twisted road to Auschwitz" began with the Dolch-stosslegende? After the period of what Zara Steiner in her essay calls the "truce" of the Peace of Paris of 1919, a new generation willingly allowed Germany's rulers to remove the "criminals of 1918" from the body politic.

Conclusion

The Spanish-born American philosopher George Santayana once perspicaciously observed, "Myths are not believed in, they are conceived and understood." I have tried on the basis of five case studies to document the power of myths. It remains to draw conclusions from this saga of deliberate mythmaking and charlatanry. Are the myths merely the ruminations, however intriguing, of a pedantic German historian? Or are there deeper and more universal "lessons" to be learned?

For the professional historian, some conclusions are apparent. The scholar who goes to Bonn seeking to find the proverbial smoking gun concerning the July 1914 crisis in the files of the Foreign Office will be sadly disappointed. These were "cleansed" of potentially damaging documents at the latest by 1920. Similarly, the researcher who goes to the Federal Military Archive at Freiburg and works through the Moltke papers will also be denied a single document that sheds light on the origins of the war. And even should someone have the proper credentials to gain access to the private papers of Hindenburg and Ludendorff, I suspect that they will discover that these, too, have been well ordered by patriotic censors.

The situation in Vienna is somewhat the same. Historians can trace the information traffic on Foreign Minister Leopold von Berchtold's desk at the Ballhausplatz month by month, right up to June 27, 1914. Then a gap appears. The paper trail resumes only on July 5—that is, after the decision for war had been taken and the "blank check" received from Berlin.[62] Recent scholarship suggests that Berchtold's papers were cleansed long before Hugo Hantsch's 1963 biography.[63] Across town at the War Archive, students will find that the records of the Intelligence (Evidenz) Bureau of the Habsburg Army likewise underwent cleansing. Its files contain three copies of the telegram of June 28, 1914, from General Potiorek in Sarajevo informing Vienna of the assassination of Archduke Franz Ferdinand; the next entry is a request for war supplies from the Eastern Front one year later.[64]

But sheer perseverance and doggedness can partially compensate for this lack of first-source materials. Numerous historians, beginning with Fritz Fischer and his host of students, have mined regional archives at Dresden, Munich, and Stuttgart for information shared by Berlin with the former royal legations of Saxony, Bavaria, and Württemberg. As a result, the picture largely has been filled in, much as a mosaic is pieced together chip by chip and stone by stone.

The process is neverending. Let me offer but one example. In October 1993 I undertook a research trip to the Bavarian archives. Knowing that under Article 11 of the German Constitution the Federal Council needed Bavaria's votes to gain the required two-thirds majority vote for war—and thus had to keep Munich in the picture—

I combed the files of the Bavarian legation in Berlin. Indeed, Munich was kept in the loop. On July 9, 1914, Undersecretary of State Arthur Zimmermann informed the Bavarians that Berlin saw the moment as "very propitious" for Vienna to launch a "campaign of revenge" against Serbia, believing that the war could be localized in the Balkans. Nine days later Berlin instructed Munich that it fully backed Vienna's decision "to use the favorable hour" to settle accounts in the Balkans, "even given the danger of further entanglements." The latter reference was cleared up by the Wilhelmstrasse with the comment that it would back Austria-Hungary even at the risk of "war with Russia." And to confuse European capitals, Berlin informed Munich that it was sending Kaiser Wilhelm II on his annual Norwegian sailing trip, and Generals Helmuth von Moltke and Erich von Falkenhayn on their yearly vacations.[65] One could hardly find a more direct recitation of the scenario of July 1914—one designed strictly in confidence for King Ludwig III of Bavaria.

At a more general level, such ongoing research helps not only explode the myths put forth by the mythmakers and charlatans from the 1920s to the 1960s, but also the recent fascination with computer-assisted simulations. In a word, the "1914 analogy" used by political scientists such as Ole Holsti—and alluded to by Michael Howard in this volume—simply does not stand up to closer scrutiny. It all comes down to the GIGO factor: garbage in, garbage out. As long as computers are programmed to accept that in July 1914, in the words of Henry Kissinger, "nation after nation slid into a war whose causes they did not understand but from which they could not extricate themselves,"[66] we will never get beyond a superficial understanding of the origins of the Great War. A quick perusal of American history textbooks, for example, shows that most American students read only that the Great War was caused by the existence of two rival alliances.[67]

Finally, and most important, disinformation, pollution of historical scholarship, and patriotic self-censorship go well beyond the history of any country or the origins of any war. They raise basic questions about the role of the historian in society, about scholarly integrity and public morality. They illustrate the universal problem of establishing the critical record of events sufficiently vital to the national interest to become the objects of partisan propaganda. They cause us to query whether a nation is well served when its intellectual establishment conspires to distort the historical record, and to obstruct honest investigation into national catastrophes, on which past, present, and future vital national interests can be reassessed.

Despite this dismal tale of campaigns of delay, obfuscation, preemptive historiography, and mass campaigns of disinformation, I close on an optimistic note: while in the short run myths may serve immediate political and psychological goals, in the long run they serve neither the nation nor the truth—and are doomed to failure.

NOTES

1. Holger H. Herwig, "Clio Deceived: Patriotic Self-Censorship in Germany After the Great War," *International Security* 12 (Fall 1987): 7. The themes first expressed there I followed up in *The First World War: Germany and Austria-Hungary, 1914–1918* (London, 1997).

2. Joseph Campbell, *The Power of Myth* (New York, 1988). See also William H. McNeill, "Mythistory or Truth, History and Historians," in *Mythistory and Other Essays* (Chicago, 1985), 3–22.

3. Cited in Eckart Klessmann, "Als politischer Zeitkritiker neu entdeckt: Hermann Hesse," in *Die Zeit: Zeitmagazin* 15 (April 14, 1972), 10.

4. Lawrence Martin, ed., *The Treaties of Peace, 1919–1923* (New York, 1924), 1: 123.

5. The story of the German "patriotic censors" has been told by Ulrich Heinemann, *Die verdrängte Niederlage: Politische Öffentlichkeit und Kriegsschuldfrage in der Weimarer Republik* (Göttingen, 1983); Wolfgang Jäger, *Historische Forschung und politische Kultur in Deutschland. Die Debatte 1914–1980 über den Ausbruch des Ersten Weltkrieges* (Göttingen, 1984); Erich J. C. Hahn, "The German Foreign Ministry and the Question of War Guilt in 1918–1919," in Carole

Fink, Isabel V. Hull, and MacGregor Knox, eds., *German Nationalism and the European Response, 1890–1945* (Norman, Okla., 1985), 43–70; and Herman J. Wittgens, "War Guilt Propaganda Conducted by the German Foreign Ministry During the 1920s," Canadian Historical Association, *Historical Papers* (1980). The German *White Book* was paralleled by the Austro-Hungarian *Red Book*, the British *Blue Book*, the French *Yellow Book*, and the Russian *Orange Book*.

    6. Herwig, "Clio Deceived," 12.

    7. Imanuel Geiss, ed., *Julikrise und Kriegsausbruch 1914* (Hanover, 1963), 1: 33–34.

    8. Wittgens, "War Guilt Propaganda," 231.

    9. Sidney B. Fay, *The Origins of the World War* (New York, 1928), 2 vols.

    10. Harry E. Barnes, *The Genesis of the World War: An Introduction to the Problem of War Guilt* (New York, 1927), and *In Quest of Truth and Justice: DeBunking the War Guilt Myth* (New York, 1927).

    11. Bernadotte E. Schmitt, *The Coming of the War, 1914* (New York, 1930), 2 vols.

    12. Wittgens, "War Guilt Propaganda," 238–39, 240–45.

    13. Hermann Kantorowicz, *Gutachten zur Kriegsschuldfrage 1914*, ed. Imanuel Geiss (Frankfurt, 1967).

    14. Herwig, "Clio Deceived," 34–36.

    15. Ibid., 36.

    16. John Röhl, ed., *1914: Delusion or Design? The Testimony of Two German Diplomats* (London, 1973), 37–38. See also Helmuth von Moltke, *Erinnerungen. Briefe. Dokumente 1877–1916. Ein Bild vom Kriegsausbruch, erster Kriegsführung und Persönlichkeit des ersten militärischen Führers des Krieges*, ed. Eliza von Moltke (Stuttgart, 1922). The few papers that survived were collected by Moltke's younger son, Adam.

    17. Even Walther Hubatsch, *Hindenburg und der Staat. Aus den Papieren des Generalfeldmarschalls und Reichspräsidenten von 1878 bis 1934* (Göttingen, 1966), 53, concedes this point. The Hindenburg Papers at the Federal Military Archive at Freiburg contain only notes by Hindenburg on Mertz von Quirnheim's edition of his "memoirs."

    18. Egmont Zechlin, "Ludendorff im Jahre 1915. Unveröffentlichte Briefe," *Historische Zeitschrift* 211 (1970): 318.

    19. Karl Dietrich Erdmann, ed., *Kurt Riezler: Tagebücher, Aufsätze, Dokumente* (Göttingen, 1972). The recent discovery of Erdmann's letters from the 1930s has destroyed his claims to have remained aloof from the Nazis. For the controversy over the originality of the papers, see Bernd Sösemann, "Die Tagebücher Kurt Riezlers: Untersuchungen zu ihrer Echtheit und Edition," *Historische Zeitschrift* 236 (1983): 327–69; Erdmann replied in "Zur Echtheit der Tagebücher Kurt Riezlers: Eine Antikritik," ibid., 371–402. See also Bernd F. Schulte, *Die Verfälschung der Riezler Tagebücher. Ein Beitrag zur Wissenschaftsgeschichte der 50iger und 60iger Jahre* (Frankfurt, 1985), 9, 146.

20. Cyril Falls, *The Great War* (New York, 1959), 36.

21. Marc Ferro, *The Great War, 1914–1918* (London, 1973), 70.

22. Franz Baron Conrad von Hötzendorf, *Aus meiner Dienstzeit, 1906–1918* (Vienna, 1923), vol. 4, 304.

23. See Rudolf Jerábek, "Die österreichische Weltkriegsforschung," in Wolfgang Michalka, ed., *Der Erste Weltkrieg: Wirkung, Wahrnehmung, Analyse* (Munich, 1994), 954–56.

24. Winston S. Churchill, *The Unknown War: The Eastern Front* (New York, 1931), 132.

25. Graydon A. Tunstall, Jr., *Planning for War Against Russia and Serbia: Austro-Hungarian and German Military Strategies, 1871–1914* (New York, 1993), 189.

26. Peter Broucek, "Militärgeschichte in Österreich von 1918 bis 1938/45," *Vorträge zur Militärgeschichte*, vol. 4: *Militärgeschichte in Deutschland und Österreich vom 18. Jahrhundert bis in die Gegenwart* (Bonn, 1985), 97.

27. Ibid., 98.

28. Tunstall, *Planning for War*, 222.

29. Paul von Hindenburg, *Out of My Life* (London, 1933), 61.

30. Max Hoffmann, *War Diaries and Other Papers*, vol. 2: *War of Lost Opportunities* (London, 1929), 41–51.

31. Holger H. Herwig and Neil M. Heyman, eds., *Biographical Dictionary of World War I* (Westport, 1982), 188.

32. Dennis E. Showalter, *Tannenberg: Clash of Empires* (Hamden, Conn., 1991), 134.

33. Reichsarchiv, *Der Weltkrieg 1914 bis 1918*, vol. 2: *Die Befreiung Ostpreussens* (Berlin, 1925), 230.

34. Ibid., 325–30.

35. Ibid., 242–43.

36. Showalter, *Tannenberg*, 348.

37. Falls, *Great War*, 186.

38. B. H. Liddell Hart, *The Real War, 1914–1918* (Boston, 1930), 215.

39. A. J. P. Taylor, *The First World War: An Illustrated History* (London, 1963), 94.

40. Ferro, *Great War*, 75.

41. See Herwig, *First World War*, 183 ff.

42. German Werth, *Verdun. Die Schlacht und der Mythos* (Bergisch Gladbach, 1979), 11, 399.

43. Paul von Hindenburg, *Aus meinem Leben* (Leipzig, 1920), 140.

44. See Articles 225 and 226 of the Treaty: Martin, *Treaties of Peace*, 1: 119–20; also Werth, *Verdun*, 396.

45. James L. Stokesbury, *A Short History of World War I* (New York, 1981), 145.

46. Hermann Wendt, *Verdun 1916. Die Angriffe Falkenhayns im Maasgebiet mit Richtung auf Verdun als strategisches Problem* (Berlin, 1941), 243.

47. Werth, *Verdun*, 117. The most recent study is by Alain Denizot, *Douaumont; 1914–1918: Vérité et légende* (Paris, 1998), 39ff.

48. Cited in Werth, *Verdun*, 117. See also Eugen Radtke, *Douaumont: Wie es eigentlich war* (Berlin, 1934).

49. See Jean Norton Cru, *Du Témoignage* (Paris, 1967), 76; in English, *War Books: A Study in Historical Criticism* (San Diego, 1976), 31–32.

50. Josef Stürgkh, *Im Deutschen Grossen Hauptquartier* (Leipzig, 1921), 110.

51. Max Domarus, *Hitler. Reden und Proklamationen, 1932–1945* (Munich, 1965), vol. 4, 1933.

52. *Stenographische Berichte über die öffentlichen Verhandlungen des 15. Untersuchungsausschusses der Verfassunggebenden Nationalversammlung nebst Beilagen* (Berlin, 1920), vol. 2, 701. See also Joachim Petzold, *Die Dolchstosslegende. Eine Geschichtsfälschung im Dienst des deutschen Imperialismus und Militarismus* (East Berlin, 1963), 45–46; and John G. Williamson, *Karl Helfferich, 1872–1924: Economist, Financier, Politician* (Princeton, 1971), 309–11. The British general alluded to was either Frederick Maurice or Neill Malcolm.

53. Hindenburg, *Aus meinem Leben*, 403.

54. Adolf Hitler, *Mein Kampf* (Munich, 1939), 182–83.

55. Figures calculated by Wilhelm Deist, "Der militärische Zusammenbruch des Kaiserreichs. Zur Realität der 'Dolchstosslegende,'" in Ursula Büttner, ed., *Das Unrechtsregime. Internationale Forschung über den Nationalsozialismus* (Hamburg, 1986), 1: 112–18. On the transfer of German units from Russia to France, see Tim Travers, "Reply to John Husey: The Movement of German Divisions to the Western Front, Winter 1917–1918," *War in History* 5 (1998): 367–70.

56. Cited in Wilhelm Deist, ed., *Militär und Innenpolitik im Weltkrieg, 1914–1918* (Düsseldorf, 1970), 2: 796 fn. 35. Letter of July 16, 1917.

57. Cited in Albrecht von Thaer, *Generalstabsdienst an der Front und in der O. H. L. Aus Briefen und Tagebuchaufzeichnungen, 1915–1919*, ed. Siegfried A. Kaehler (Göttingen, 1958), 235.

58. Reichsarchiv, *Der Weltkrieg 1914 bis 1918*, vol. 14: *Die Kriegführung an der Westfront im Jahre 1918* (Berlin, 1944), 763, 768.

59. Notes of an interview with Niemöller on July 22, 1970 at Wiesbaden.

60. Werner T. Angress, "Das deutsche Militär und die Juden im Ersten Weltkrieg," *Militärgeschichtliche Mitteilungen* 19 (1976): 136–37.

61. Cited in Werner Jochmann, "Die Ausbreitung des Antisemitismus," in Werner E. Mosse, ed., *Deutsches Judentum in Krieg und Revolution, 1916–1923* (Tübingen, 1971), 440–41. Kleist's comments are in *Germania an Ihre Kinder* (published 1813).

62. Haus-, Hof- und Staatsarchiv, Vienna, I PA Cabinet des Ministers. Protokoll 1913–1915, Nr. 592.

63. Jerábek, "Die österreichische Weltkriegsforschung," 961.

64. Österreichisches Staatsarchiv-Kriegsarchiv, Conrad Archiv, B Flügeladjutant, vol. 3; and ibid., Büro Generalstab 91.

65. Bayerisches Hauptstaatsarchiv, Munich, MA 3076, Militär-Bevollmächtigter Berlin. Reports of July 9 and 18, 1914.

66. Cited in Marc Trachtenberg, *History and Strategy* (Princeton, 1991), 99; original in *New York Times,* March 11, 1976. Kissinger repeated the same fluff in chs. 7 and 8 in *Diplomacy* (New York, 1994). See Ole R. Holsti, "The 1914 Case," *American Political Science Review* 59 (1965): 365–78, and *Crisis, Escalation, War* (Montreal, 1972).

67. For example, Robert A. Divine et. al., eds., *America, Past and Present* (Glenview, Ill., 1987), 698; Arthur S. Link et. al., eds., *The American People: A History,* vol. 2: *Since 1865* (Arlington Heights, Ill., 1981), 654; and George Brown Tindall, *America: A Narrative History* (New York, 1988), 985.

CHAPTER 11

The Cultural Legacy of the Great War

MODRIS EKSTEINS

While serving in the front line of battle in 1916, Colin Ross, Scottish in name though German in nationality, reflected, "A poet will come who will write the history of this world war, after a few decades, perhaps after a few centuries." He of course had the existing literary canon in mind: Homer on the Trojan war, Tolstoy on Napoleon's invasion of Russia, and perhaps Zola on the French debacle of 1870. Without saying so outright, Ross was suggesting that, despite the contributions of historians, only the poet-artist would in the end be able to cut through the shibboleths of the war experience to capture a higher meaning. And if ever there was an event that cried out for sublime interpretation, it was the horrific war in which Ross found himself in 1916.[1]

Ross was evoking a grand Western tradition, going back to at least Aristotle, that venerated the artist as a seer, a man of grace who could perceive and express truths that remained hidden from mere mortals. Ultimately these truths could be captured only through superior intuitive and imaginative effort, not through normal observation and analysis. For facts to become memorable an element of fiction was essential. The historian, as empirical observer and interpreter, was of little assistance when humanity was confronted by the ineffable. In May 1918 the cultural historian and critic Egon Friedell mused that if some historian were to prove one day, with the help of a monstrous technical apparatus—huge footnotes, endless bibliography—that Troy had never existed, Homer would still have truth on his side forever.[2]

That historian whom both Ross and Friedell debunked was of course central to the European social and intellectual experience of the previous century. In that century of extraordinary European expansion—"Expansion is everything," said Cecil Rhodes—in industry and territory, in bridges and ships, the historian had become the secular theologian, the learned scholar, who gave intellectual order and validity to this imperial thrust emanating from Europe. For Thomas Carlyle and most of the historians of the nineteenth century, history had moral value. It was, Carlyle said, "not only the fittest study but the only study, . . . 'the universal Divine Scripture.' "[3] Leopold von Ranke, too, took up the religious analogy and spoke, on occasion, of historians as priests.

Progress, gain, achievement, growth—these were the key urges of the nineteenth-century European bourgeoisie; the Macauleys, Guizots, and Rankes were, in turn, driven by similar notions. These were historians who reaffirmed the faith of the European middle classes in themselves; these were historians whose raison d'être was control, understanding, and success.[4] Of his professional forebears, the British historian Herbert Butterfield wrote in 1931: "It is astonishing to what an extent the historian has been Protestant, progressive, and whig, and the very model of the 19th century gentleman."[5] G. W. Prothero even appropriated Charles Darwin's achievement for the historians: "What is the theory of evolution itself," he asked in 1894, ". . . but the achievement of historical method."[6] By 1914 the History Honours School at Oxford finally had more students than the school of *Literae Humaniores* or classical studies.[7] The nineteenth century had indeed been the *saeculum historicum,* the century of history.

When war broke out in August 1914 university establishments in all belligerent countries joined in the public enthusiasm. Lecture halls emptied. Of Oxford and Cambridge, Gilbert Murray said, "There are perhaps no institutions in England whose response to the requirements of the war has been more swift, or whose sacrifice more intense and enduring, than the two ancient universities."[8] Historians were at the forefront of the patriotic affirmation. It was their task to explain the crisis and to reassure their compatriots of the righteousness of the national cause. The Oxford history faculty was in print with a statement *Why We Are at War* within weeks of the outbreak.[9] Of the forty-three holders of chairs in history at German universities who voiced an opinion, as many as thirty-five would aver publicly that Germany had joined the war only because it had been attacked.[10]

As, in the course of 1915 and then particularly 1916, the war bogged down into stalemate and attrition, and as it turned, in the process, into a trial not only of military strength but of moral fortitude, and, indeed, of civilizations, historians on all sides were called upon to justify the cause of their respective nations. Of all academic disciplines and intellectual pursuits, history was involved in the war most intensely. This was, after all, a war about the gist of history. Ortega y Gasset recognized this early on. "History," he wrote, "is trembling to its very roots . . . because a new reality is about to be born."[11]

As, in the course of the war, the gulf between promise and reality widened, as all systems and structures, practical and intellectual, began to be questioned, history too—as the key to knowledge and self-understanding—came to be doubted by some. In the nineteenth century history was, for most of its practitioners, synonymous with optimism and progress. After the Great War, however, Oswald Spengler declared, while predicting the end of Western civilization, that "optimism is cowardice." "The need for optimism," he said, "is basically a sentimental and decadent frame of mind."[12] While Gottfried Benn spoke of the "dissolution of history," Walter Benjamin put forward his theory of historical discontinuity.[13] He likened history to "flashes of memory" at moments of danger and conjured up a phantasmagoric vision of the angel of history: the angel is facing the past but, caught in a violent storm, is unable to close its wings; it is, as a result, driven backward into the future. Benjamin's "theses on the philosophy of history" were loaded with images and metaphors of violence: storms, explosions, revolutions, debris. The historian, he said, must be "man enough to blast open the continuum of history."[14] Ranke's notion of history—to portray the past "as it actually was"— Benjamin called "the most powerful narcotic of the nineteenth century."[15] By 1930, Egon Friedell said flatly, "History does not exist."[16] And Siegfried Kracauer chimed in: "Reality is a construction."[17]

Such cultural pessimism was, one might be tempted to conclude, a largely German phenomenon, the product of defeat and disillusionment. But there were many interesting non-German variants. For the French poet and veteran Drieu la Rochelle, history was "dream": "Men turn life into a dream, and this dream they have called history."[18] After some time in the trenches, Ford Madox Ford became a pessimist about history. "If, before the war, one had any function it was that of historian," he wrote. All intellectual issues were approached from a historical point of view. "But now, it seems to me, we have no method of approach to any of these problems."[19] Tietjens, the central character of Ford's tetralogy *Parade's End*, loses his memory in the trenches.

In their splendid sendup of British history, *1066 and All That*, first published in 1930, those two wonderful ironists Sellar and Yeatman pointed out, in a different vein but with a similar intent—the intent to blast open the continuum of history: "History is not what you thought. It is what you can remember. All other history defeats itself." Despite the comic mode, is the idea not the same as Benjamin's depiction of history as flashes of memory? At the end of their 62-chapter, 123-page romp through history, Sellar and Yeatman concluded, some sixty years before Francis Fukuyama, that with the Great War history had come to a "." And they in fact entitled their final section "Up to the End of History."[20]

What Friedell, Benn, Ford, Sellar, and Yeatman meant of course was that history as arbiter, history as purposeful meaning, history as teleology had not survived the war. Instead of being a goddess, Herbert Butterfield suggested in 1931, history was "an old reprobate, whose tricks and juggleries are things to be guarded against."[21] Paul Valéry spoke in similar terms in the same year—"History is the most dangerous product that the chemistry of the intellect has invented."[22] Aware that *histoire* tended to be a synonym for *patrie*, a French syndicalist leader stated bluntly, "In order to secure a definitive peace, stop teaching history."[23] More recently Michel Serres would say that history is the last ideology, the most tenacious of them all.[24]

If Ranke had urged the historian to conceal himself and to allow his sources to speak, Lucien Febvre, a founder of the Annales group, now asserted: "There is no History. There are only historians." It is not the past that conjures up the historian, he went on to point out, it is the historian who gives birth to history. Like the doctor who studies cadavers not to learn about cadavers but to learn about life, the historian, too, should be driven by relevance.[25] Begun in 1929, "the *Annales* project," that enormously influential reorientation of historiography from a study of momentous events to a concern with long-term economic and social determinants, was fueled by the need for innovation.

In the gargantuan crisis of authority that has been the twentieth century, the discipline of history, emanating in its modern form from the age of enlightenment and European imperialism, has suffered a rude fate.[26] If professional historians have been slow to respond to the crisis, public awareness and taste have not.[27] In its frenzied preoccupation with newness and change, our century has been intensely antihistorical. At the heart of the self-doubt of Western civilization in this century has been this crisis of history.

The Great War of 1914–18 was in part a product of this crisis—doubts about the validity of history and reason had, as we shall see, considerable momentum before 1914—but in the dimensions and passions of the conflict, and in its nihilistic energy, the war magnified the doubt immeasurably. The promoters of reason, law, empire, and history won the war militarily; but I suggest that they lost it spiritually. In the end the loser conquered. *Vincebamur a victa Graecia*—conquered Greece our conqueror—said Cicero of the relationship between Greece and Rome in antiquity. *Vincebamur a victa Germania*—conquered Germany our conqueror—Cicero might well say of the outcome of the two world wars and of this century as a whole.[28]

Although there were many pressures and sources for change in the fin-de-siècle world a hundred years ago, no single country was more involved in that change than Germany. It was of course a new state, established only in 1871. Its population and economy had grown enormously since then. It threatened soon to double France in population size. As for industrial benchmarks, in the production of steel, that key building material for the new age, it surpassed, by 1914, the combined output of Britain, France, and Russia. In even newer industries—chemicals and dyestuffs, electricals, optics, and machine tools—it was a world leader. Germany's labor movement was the largest and best organized in the world, and it was looked to for leadership by socialists around the globe. Its youth and women's movements were, in comparative terms, large and influential, as were those movements encouraging alternative lifestyles, involving for instance diet or sexuality. Magnus Hirschfeld, who headed a movement to decriminalize homosexuality, pointed out that while admittedly there was much to be done in Germany, an affair like the Oscar Wilde scandal in Britain could never have occurred there. German military strength was of course renowned, and at the turn of the century Germany began building a navy with the intention of challenging Britain's sea power, which had been so instrumental in the *pax Britannica* of the nineteenth-century world. To Britain its navy was not just an instrument of imperial power and security. It was a symbol of geographical reality, of moral authority, and of history. Any challenge to that navy was a challenge to the very essence of Britishness.

Planck, Einstein, Bosch, Haber, Röntgen, Diesel. . . . In science and technology, as these names suggest, the German contribution was stunning. In architecture and design, from Peter Behrens and Hans Poelzig to the Werkbund, the German achievement was equally impressive, so much so that non-German critics of the modern style as a whole associated it with Germany. Of the relatively stark lines of the newly constructed Théâtre des Champs-Elysées in Paris, Alphonse Gosset, an architect, remarked in 1913: "That the Germans . . . should accept this sort of reclusion is perhaps understandable, but Parisians, avid of bright lights and elegance, no!"[29] Similar charges and countercharges held for modern art as well. The opponents of cubism and of the more general move away from representational art blamed the new experimentalism on German influence and German brutality. After all, the main art dealer in Paris for the cubist painters was the German Daniel-Heinrich Kahnweiler, and he had a habit of whistling Wagnerian themes while showing off the Picassos and Braques in his gallery in the rue Vignon.[30] Homosexuality, too, was looked on in many quarters as a German vice, a counterpart to the excessive German emphasis on military training. Friedrich Gundolf and Friedrich Wolters, who were members of the circle around the poet Stefan George, were not at all offended by such categorization. "We have always believed," they insisted in 1912, "that something essentially formative for German culture as a whole is to be found in these relations." Their vision was of a culture committed to "heroized love."[31]

Change, self-assertion, rebellion, and innovation were the essence of both the German reality and the German image in the early years of this century. And it is no wonder that German-speaking historians and philosophers were also at the forefront of the assault on the idea of scientific inquiry in history. In the second half of the century Jacob Burckhardt and Friedrich Nietzsche built on Arthur Schopenhauer's earlier doubts about objectivity. "Clio, the muse of history," Schopenhauer had said, "is as permeated with lies as a street-whore with syphilis."[32] Historical accounts, said Burckhardt (in the same vein though in the milder language), were "mere reflections of ourselves." "If anything lasting is to be created," he wrote in 1870, "it can only be through an overwhelmingly powerful effort of real poetry." And what was the role of history? "Obviously: to amuse people as intensively as possible," he stated.[33] Nietzsche agreed: only if historians ceased to make unwarranted connections and to preach could history have any genuine meaning.

This assault on empiricism and objectivity was popularized by the likes of Julius Langbehn and that eccentric Englishman who became a German, Houston Stewart Chamberlain. Any pretense to objectivity among historians, said Chamberlain, was "academic barbarism" (*wissenschaftliche Bildungsbarbarei*); history should be poetry; history should be art.[34] Kaiser Wilhelm II read Chamberlain avidly, as did Adolf Hitler.

In fact Germany's intellectual influence in the world at the beginning of the twentieth century was astounding. "As a rule," wrote the British historian Sir John Seeley, "good books are in German."[35] Institutions of higher learning throughout the world patterned their structure and organization on the model of the German university. In 1875, 83 percent of the professors in Russia had received their first degrees in Germany.[36] In 1895 one-half of the historians in the United States had received some part of their training in Germany.[37] If its military and political leadership claimed that Germany was, by 1907, "encircled" by forces in a hostile alliance system intent on suffocating it culturally as well as militarily, Germany's intellectual influence abroad belied such claims entirely. The place in the sun that the Kaiser desired for Germany politically was in fact occupied by that country, to international acclaim, intellectually. "There have been, among the nations, some *parvenus* of power and wealth," wrote the Italian journalist and historian Guglielmo Ferrero of Germany's position in the world in 1914; "but one had not hitherto seen the *parvenu* of civilization: a people become, in a few dozen years, capable of teaching to every one, even to its former masters. Our age has witnessed this extraordinary phenomenon."[38]

The armed conflict that began in early August 1914 was a response to specific political and military considerations. But in the broadest sense the war grew out of the "German problem": how was one to deal with Germany and the effervescence and turbulence it symbolized? The outbreak of war was interpreted by Germans as a *Befreiungskrieg,* a war of liberation—a war to liberate potential, instinct, and spirit, a war to break away from outworn notions of history. In a café in Aachen in August 1914 a German scientist told the American journalist Irvin Cobb: "We Germans are the most industrious, the most earnest, the best educated race on this side of the ocean." In referring to "this side of the ocean" he was obviously being diplomatic. He continued: "Russia stands for reaction; England for selfishness and perfidy; France for decadence. Germany stands for progress. . . . After this war—if we Germans win it—there will never be another universal war."[39] For the French and the British the war represented a struggle to preserve tradition, law, and empire, to preserve a world with boundaries, regulations, and definitions, against the technically brilliant but morally anarchic thrust of "the modern," represented by Germany. Germany, it was said, was a country without a sense of limits, without natural frontiers, either geographical or spiritual.

The inability to bring the war to a quick and decisive conclusion led to the acceleration of tendencies associated with the modern. As the war dragged on, as casualties mounted, as the all-consuming effort continued, authority at all levels was undermined, including, on the grandest level of all, the authority of Western civilization as hitherto conceived. That civilization, Ezra Pound snarled, was an old bitch gone in the tooth. In the wake of that war, which mobilized some sixty million men, killed off about one in six, and mutilated about one in three, nothing could look or sound the same as before. Prewar harmonies, though reproduced ad nauseam, rang hollow. The connections were gone. Meaning, like a huge artillery shell, had exploded into endless fragments. Nonsense, dada now kept insisting, was far more rational than sense. History was, in short, absurd. And so, like a latter-day Nero, the survivor, often missing a limb or two, jiggled his yo-yo—quite appropriately the great toy of the limbless twenties—while the ruins smoldered.

What had kept that Great War going was of course the very values for which it supposedly was being fought, notions of duty, honor, sacrifice, and commitment. As authority was ravaged, those values too were ravaged. In the end, for many, only personal experience counted, beyond meaning, beyond interpretation. The soldier became the equivalent of the avant-garde artist. They were both outsiders. Colin Ross's memoir of his front experience was entitled *Wir draußen*—"we out there." Both the soldier and the artist were at the front, in fact on the frontier of possibility and respectability. Theirs was, Apollinaire pointed out, a battle of the frontiers. The task of both soldier and artist was to venture into no-man's-land, to cross this murderous strip and to achieve victory on the other side. "Things go beyond mere strength here," wrote one young German soldier from the front. "Here the impossible is made possible."[40] R. H. Tawney, the economic historian, said as much in different words: he likened the front-line soldier of the Great War to a "mischievous ape tearing up the image of God."[41] In this process the war democratized the instincts of the avant-garde.

For many who experienced the war but especially for that generation that came to maturity during it or immediately after, the war did not end in November 1918. Ernst von Salomon, sixteen years old in November 1918, joined a Hamburg Freikorps unit and went off to the Eastern Baltic to continue the battle. But a battle for what? To protect the Baltic Germans, descendants of the Teutonic Knights, against the Bolsheviks? Against indigenous nationalists, especially Latvians and Estonians? The purpose was always murky. It was the act of rebellion and the experience that were all-important. Here, again on the frontier, in a geographical and psychological sense, "we were cut off from the world of bourgeois norms," wrote Salomon. "The bonds were broken and we were free." The adventure was the essence. The absurdity of the situation, when analyzed in conventional terms, was captured by Salomon's superior, in an address to his troops: "We are German soldiers who theoretically are not German soldiers, and we are defending a German town which theoretically is not a German town. And out there are the Letts and the Estonians and the English and the Bolsheviks—and by the way, I like the Bolsheviks the best of all that crew—and further south are the Poles and the Czechs, and then—well, you know it all as well as I do. . . . Have you got a cigarette for me, youngster?"[42]

"And by the way, I like the Bolsheviks the best of all." So said the Freikorps officer. Freikorps and Bolsheviks, a fraternity united by fantasies of violence as well as the fact that neither side ever took prisoners—this was the fraternity of the aggrieved and the disenchanted, to be sure; but it was also the fraternity of the vital nihilist, for whom struggle had become the most important value. For Ernst Jünger, too, the most popular modern German writer next to Thomas Mann, Prussianism and Bolshevism were kindred spirits.

"Une armée de bandits!" the French military attaché in Riga called the Freikorps crowd.[43] Bandits? Criminals? Maybe, but bandits have had a strange way of becoming heroes in the twentieth century. Again the definitions and boundaries blur. The point is that Hitler, the Nazi, and Stalin, the Bolshevik, had a cultural context for the pact they were to sign in 1939. Stalin said of that pact that it was signed in blood.

"Words . . . slip, slide, perish / Decay with imprecision, will not stay in place," wrote T. S. Eliot in "Burnt Norton."[44] If words do not stay in place, how can frontiers, ideologies, treaties, constitutions, or for that matter history? "The situation of our time," said W. H. Auden in his "New Year Letter" of 1940, "surrounds us like a baffling crime."[45]

People like Marinetti, d'Annunzio, Salomon, and especially Ernst Jünger, would aestheticize this experience of violent eruption. The event, the sensational moment, and the surprise were all superior to morality, purpose, and history as process.[46]

Naturally, few soldiers or civilians could articulate the "deconstruction" of language and power that took place in the course of the war, and "disenchantment" as a cultural and social phenomenon was principally a postwar manifestation, but the war experience sowed the seeds of doubt that then came to bloom later. "Il fait beau, allons au cimetière," wrote Emmanuel Berl between the wars.[47]

The war produced a profound moodswing in the modern temper.[48] Whereas the experimentation of the prewar avant-garde was fueled by a good measure of anger, frustration, and sarcasm, there was nonetheless an overriding optimism and titanism in the new religion of art. The war, along with its political and economic aftershocks, changed all that. Despair and hope, resentment and decency traded places. After the war H. M. Tomlinson saw everywhere the "spectres of a shadowland which now will never pass."[49] The parapet, the wire, and the mud were permanently fixed, he said, in our imagination. "Which is to say," Paul Fussell added some years ago in his remarkable book *The Great War and Modern Memory,* "that anxiety without end, without purpose, without reward, and without meaning is woven into the fabric of contemporary life."[50] The state of emergency had become the permanent condition. In this contrary atmosphere, the anti-hero became the hero, the victim became the leader. Franz Kafka became, as Frederick Karl has put it, "representative man,"[51] and we all became Joseph K., the main protagonist in Kafka's *The Trial,* a man who does not understand why he has been arrested but who feels guilty nonetheless. Charlie Chaplin, the little vagabond, led us down endless highways and byways. And Adolf Hitler—who, as his valet reported, was wont to stand, like the wicked fairy-tale queen, in front of a mirror and to ask whether he looked like a *Führer*—Adolf Hitler became the *Führer.*[52] In 1930, Carroll Carstairs ended his book *A Generation Missing* with the words: "It's a weary world and the raspberry jam sent me from Paris is all finished now."[53]

In the space of a few years a Victorian world of respectability, predictability, and heroes had been replaced by a culture of experience, surprise, and victims. Victims had become agents; the outsider had become the insider. The forces that ante bellum Germany had represented and unleashed—the energy and moral thrust of the newcomer, and the resentment of the outsider—had become the dominant voices. Neither Lenin nor Mussolini, let alone Stalin or Hitler, would have stood a chance of political success without the backdrop of the Great War. The *Sonnenkinder* of the 1920s, people like W. H. Auden, Christopher Isherwood, and Stephen Spender, were far more interested in Germany than in France. They went off not like their fathers to Paris but, much to the chagrin of their mothers, to Berlin and Hamburg, took working-class lovers, and reveled in what Lionel Trilling later called the "adversary culture." Looking back on his interwar youth Richard Cobb remembered that "at school, and in books written for boys, one was so constantly reminded that we had won the war that my school friends and I found our curiosity excited by those who had lost it. Losing seemed much more original and stimulating than winning."[54]

The great moral issues of our century—which in turn have provoked the most exciting cultural endeavor—have been posed by the losers, or perhaps by guilt-ridden victors. Losing has, paradoxically, meant winning. *Vincebamur a victa Germania.*

In 1916, in the middle of the Great War, Ernst Troeltsch published an essay in the main German historical journal, the *Historische Zeitschrift,* in which he admitted that any concept of the unity of human history was impossible to maintain. Instead of a single history there was a variety of histories. And then he came to a striking conclusion: these various histories would not necessarily understand each other.[55] Martin Heidegger, whose shadow now looms so large over our own age, argued along similar lines in the 1920s. There is no history, there are only histories. Our approach to history in our postcolonial, postmodernist, and, some might say, posthistorical age has, it seems to me, validated this analysis. In the process, history has become a statement not of hope and confidence, as it was for the most part in a previous century, but at best of humility and respect.[56] Despite all the disasters that have befallen our century, I propose that that development has been all to the good.

NOTES

1. Colin Ross, *Wir draussen: Zwei Jahre Kriegserleben an vier Fronten* (Berlin: Ullstein, 1916), 11. Ross, who served on four fronts during the war, became a prolific travel writer after the war. One of his books was a "journey inward": *Der*

Wille der Welt: Eine Reise zu sich selbst (Leipzig: Brockhaus, 1932). There, on page 31, this peripatetic journalist wrote, not surprisingly: "The will of the world is change."

2. Egon Friedell, *Abschaffung des Genies: Essays bis 1918*, ed. Herbert Illig, 2nd ed. (Vienna: Löcker Verlag, 1984), 260.

3. Thomas Carlyle, "On History Again," *Critical and Miscellaneous Essays*, 7 vols. (London: Chapman and Hall, 1890), 4: 212–13, 220. Also G. P. Gooch, *History and Historians in the Nineteenth Century*, 2nd ed. (New York: Longmans, Green, 1913), 324.

4. Friedrich Meinecke, "Drei Generationen deutscher Gelehrtenpolitik," *Historische Zeitschrift* 125 (1922): 248–83, esp. 249. More recently: Utz Haltern, "Geschichte und Bürgertum: Droysen—Sybel—Treitschke," *Historische Zeitschrift* 259 (1994): 59–107.

5. Herbert Butterfield, *The Whig Interpretation of History* (London: G. Bell and Sons, 1931), 3–4.

6. G. W. Prothero in *The National Review*, December 1894, 461, quoted in Lord Acton, *The Study of History* (London: Macmillan, 1895), 131. "History," Carlyle had said in 1830, "lies at the root of all science." "On History," *Critical and Miscellaneous Essays*, 2: 253.

7. Stuart Wallace, *War and the Image of Germany: British Academics, 1914–1918* (Edinburgh: John Donald, 1988), 59.

8. Gilbert Murray, in an essay entitled "Oxford and the War," in *Faith, War, and Policy: Addresses and Essays on the European War* (Boston: Houghton Mifflin, 1917), 212.

9. Ernest Barker et al., *Why We Are At War: Great Britain's Case* (Oxford: Clarendon, 1914). See also the chapter "Historians and the War," in Wallace, *War and the Image of Germany*, 58–73.

10. Otto Hintze, Friedrich Meinecke, Hermann Oncken, and Hermann Schumacher, eds., *Deutschland und der Weltkrieg* (Leipzig: Teubner, 1915). Klaus Schwabe, "Zur politischen Haltung der deutschen Professoren im Ersten Weltkrieg," *Historische Zeitschrift* 193 (1961): 601–34. See also his *Wissenschaft und Kriegsmoral: Die deutschen Hochschullehrer und die politischen Grundfragen des Ersten Weltkrieges* (Göttingen: 1969), esp. 23. Wolfgang Jäger, *Historische Forschung und politische Kultur in Deutschland: Die Debatte 1914–1980 über den Ausbruch des Ersten Weltkrieges* (Göttingen: Vandenhoeck & Ruprecht, 1984), 14–43. Herbert Flaig, "The Historian as Pedagogue of the Nation," *History* 59, no. 195 (February 1974): 18–32.

11. Cited by Robert Wohl, *The Generation of 1914* (Cambridge: Harvard University Press, 1979), 217.

12. Oswald Spengler, *Man and Technics: A Contribution to a Philosophy of Life*, trans. C. F. Atkinson (New York: Knopf, 1932). Also, Spengler to Paul Reusch, September 28, 1931, *Spengler Letters, 1913–1936*, ed. and trans. Arthur Helps (London: Allen & Unwin, 1966), 260–61.

13. Gottfried Benn, "Expressionismus," *Sämtliche Werke,* ed. Gerhard Schuster, Band IV/Prosa 2 (Stuttgart: Klett-Cotta, 1989), 79, 82.

14. Walter Benjamin, "Theses on the Philosophy of History," in *Illuminations,* ed. Hannah Arendt, trans. Harry Zohn (New York: Schocken, 1969), 255–62. On the theses, see Gerhard Kaiser, *Benjamin, Adorno: Zwei Studien* (Frankfurt a.M.: Athenäum Verlag, 1974), 1–77.

15. H. D. Kittsteiner, "Walter Benjamins Historismus," in Norbert Bolz and Bernd Witte, eds., *Passagen: Walter Benjamins Urgeschichte des neunzehnten Jahrhunderts* (Munich: Wilhelm Fink Verlag, 1984), 163–97, esp. 171. On Benjamin's view of the present as a perpetual state of emergency, see Richard Wolin, *Labyrinths: Explorations in the Critical History of Ideas* (Amherst: University of Massachusetts Press, 1995), 55–82.

16. In the epilogue to his *Cultural History of the Modern Age,* 3 vols., trans. C. F. Atkinson (New York: Knopf, 1954), 3: 467.

17. "A hundred reports from a factory do not add up to the reality of that factory, but remain forever a hundred views from a factory. Reality is a construction." Siegfried Kracauer, *Die Angestellten: Aus dem neuesten Deutschland* (1929; reprint, Frankfurt a.M.: Suhrkamp, 1971), 16.

18. Pierre Drieu la Rochelle, *Interrogation: Poèmes* (Paris: Editions de la Nouvelle Revue Française, 1917), 32.

19. In James Longenbach, *Modernist Poetics of History: Pound, Eliot, and the Sense of the Past* (Princeton: Princeton University Press, 1987), 9.

20. Walter C. Sellar and Robert J. Yeatman, *1066 and All That* (London: Methuen, 1930), v, 111–15. By 1955 the volume had been reprinted thirty-eight times. It is, in mood and tone if only indirectly in subject, a war book, inspired by and a counterpart to Robert Graves's *Goodbye to All That.*

21. Butterfield, *Whig Interpretation,* 132.

22. Paul Valéry, *History and Politics,* trans. Denise Folliot and Jackson Matthews (New York: Pantheon, 1962), 114.

23. In Ann-Louise Shapiro, "Fixing History: Narratives of World War I in France," *History and Theory,* Theme issue 36 (1997): 117.

24. Michel Serres, "L'univers et le lieu," in *L'Arc* 72 (Aix-en-Provence, n.d.), 65.

25. Lucien Febvre, in his introduction to Charles Morazé, *Trois essais sur histoire et culture* (Paris: Armand Colin, 1948), vii–viii.

26. "Authority has vanished from the modern world," wrote Hannah Arendt in her essay "What Is Authority?" *Between Past and Future* (New York: Viking, 1968), 91.

27. In his presidential address to the American Historical Association in 1969, C. Vann Woodward said, "Whatever contemporary paintings they hung on their walls or modern literature they kept on their shelves, little of the spirit that informs these arts seemed to enter into the monographs the historians wrote." In his *The Future of the Past* (New York: Oxford University Press, 1989), 17.

28. Among the most interesting contributions of late to the debate about Germany and modernism are those of Peter Fritzsche: *A Nation of Fliers: German Aviation and the Popular Imagination* (Cambridge, Mass.: Harvard University Press, 1992); "Machine Dreams: Airmindedness and the Reinvention of Germany," *American Historical Review* 98 (1993): 685–709; "Landscape of Danger, Landscape of Design: Crisis and Modernism in Weimar Germany," in Thomas W. Kniesche and Stephen Brockmann, eds., *Dancing on the Volcano: Essays on the Culture of the Weimar Republic* (Columbia, S.C.: Camden House, 1994), 29–46; "Nazi Modern," *Modernism/Modernity* 3, no. 1 (1996): 1–21.

29. In Pierre Lavedan, *French Architecture* (Harmondsworth: Penguin, 1956), 227.

30. Corona Hepp, *Avantgarde—Moderne Kunst, Kulturkritik und Reformbewegungen nach der Jahrhundertwende* (Munich: Deutscher Taschenbuch Verlag, 1987); Klaus-Jürgen Sembach et al., *1910: Halbzeit der Moderne* (Stuttgart: Hatje, 1992); Kenneth E. Silver, *Esprit de Corps: The Art of the Parisian Avant-Garde and the First World War, 1914–1925* (Princeton: Princeton University Press, 1989), 6–9; Pierre Assouline, *An Artful Life: A Biography of D. H. Kahnweiler, 1884–1979*, trans. Charles Ruas (New York: Grove Weidenfeld, 1990), 52.

31. James D. Steakley, *The Homosexual Emancipation Movement in Germany* (New York: Arno Press, 1975), 49; Lillian Faderman, ed., *Lesbian-Feminism in Turn-of-the-Century Germany* (Weatherby Lake, Mo.: Naiad, 1980); George L. Mosse, "Nationalism and Respectability: Normal and Abnormal Sexuality in the Nineteenth Century," *Journal of Contemporary History* 17, no. 2 (1982): 221–46; and Samuel Hynes, *A War Imagined: The First World War and English Culture* (London: Bodley Head, 1990), 223–24.

32. Arthur Schopenhauer, "Über Geschichte," *Die Welt als Wille und Vorstellung,* in *Arthur Schopenhauer Werke in zwei Bänden,* ed. Werner Brede (Munich: Hauser, 1977), 2: 44–53.

33. Jacob Burckhardt, *Historische Fragmente,* in *Gesamtausgabe,* ed. Albert Oeri and Emil Dürr (Stuttgart: Deutsche Verlags-Anstalt, 1929), 7: 225, 426–27; and *Weltgeschichtliche Betrachtungen,* in ibid., 7: 4; and *The Letters of Jacob Burckhardt,* ed. and trans. Alexander Dru (London: Routledge, 1955), 97.

34. In Geoffrey G. Field, *Evangelist of Race: The Germanic Vision of Houston Stewart Chamberlain* (New York: Columbia University Press, 1981), 177, 262.

35. In Klaus Dockhorn, *Der deutsche Historismus in England* (Göttingen: Vandenhoeck, 1950), 217.

36. James C. McClelland, *Autocrats and Academics: Education, Culture, and Society in Tsarist Russia* (Chicago: University of Chicago Press, 1979), 61–62.

37. J. Franklin Jameson, "The American Historical Review, 1895–1920," *American Historical Review* 26 (1920): 2. On the German influence on French historians, see Georg G. Iggers, *New Directions in European Historiography* (Middletown, Conn.: Wesleyan University Press, 1975), 44–45; and Claude Di-

geon, *La Crise allemande de la pensée française (1870–1914)* (Paris: Presses Universitaires de France, 1959), 374.

38. Guglielmo Ferrero, *Europe's Fateful Hour* (New York: Dodd, Mead, 1918), 55.

39. Irvin S. Cobb, *Paths of Glory: Impressions of War Written At or Near the Front* (New York: George H. Doran, 1915), 177–78.

40. Letter of Walter Harich, in Philipp Witkop, ed., *Kriegsbriefe deutscher Studenten* (Gotha, 1916), 70.

41. R. H. Tawney, cited in Fritz Stern, "Historians and the Great War: Private Experience and Public Explication," *Yale Review* 82, no. 1 (January 1994): 40.

42. Ernst von Salomon, *The Outlaws*, trans. Ian F. D. Morrow (London: Cape, 1931), 84–85. D'Annunzio's Fiume adventure was awash with similar urges and contradictions: Michael A. Ledeen, *The First Duce: D'Annunzio at Fiume* (Baltimore: Johns Hopkins University Press, 1977).

43. Lt.-Gen. du Parquet, *L'Aventure allemande en Lettonie* (Paris, 1926), 38, quoted in Hannsjoachim W. Koch, *Der deutsche Bürgerkrieg: Eine Geschichte der deutschen und österreichischen Freikorps, 1918–1923* (Berlin: Ullstein, 1978), 146.

44. T. S. Eliot, *Collected Poems: 1909–1962* (London: 1963), 194.

45. W. H. Auden, *The Double Man* (New York: Random House, 1941), 22.

46. See the works of Karl Heinz Bohrer, *Die Ästhetik des Schreckens: Die pessimistische Romantik und Ernst Jüngers Frühwerk* (Munich: Carl Hanser Verlag, 1978) and *Plötzlichkeit: Zum Augenblick des ästhetischen Scheins* (Frankfurt a.M.: Suhrkamp, 1981).

47. Emmanuel Berl, *Interrogatoire* (Paris: Gallimard, 1976), 137–99.

48. The literature on this change in temper is now substantial. Among the most distinguished studies are Paul Fussell, *The Great War and Modern Memory* (New York: Oxford University Press, 1975); Eric Leed, *No Man's Land: Combat and Identity in World War I* (New York: Cambridge University Press, 1979); George L. Mosse, *Fallen Soldiers: Reshaping the Memory of the World Wars* (New York: Oxford University Press, 1990); and the works by Robert Wohl and Samuel Hynes cited above. Jay Winter presents a different interpretation in his *Sites of Memory, Sites of Mourning: The Great War in European Cultural History* (Cambridge: Cambridge University Press, 1995.

49. H. M. Tomlinson, *Waiting for Daylight* (New York: Knopf, 1922), 108.

50. Fussell, *Great War and Modern Memory,* 320.

51. Frederick Karl, *Franz Kafka: Representative Man* (New York: Ticknor & Fields, 1991).

52. Robert G. L. Waite, *The Psychopathic God: Adolf Hitler* (New York: Basic Books, 1977), 45. Dorothy Thompson, after meeting Hitler, said of him: "He is inconsequent and voluble, ill poised and insecure. He is the very prototype of the little man." In "Good Bye to Germany," *Harper's Magazine,* December 1934, 12–14, quoted in Walter C. Langer, *The Mind of Adolf Hitler* (New York: Basic Books, 1972), 52.

53. Carroll Carstairs, *A Generation Missing* (London: Heinemann, 1930), 208.

54. Richard Cobb, *French and Germans, Germans and French: A Personal Interpretation of France Under Two Occupations, 1914–1918/1940–1944* (Hanover, N.H.: University Press of New England, 1983), xv.

55. Ernst Troeltsch, "Über die Maßstäbe zur Beurteilung historischer Dinge," *Historische Zeitschrift* 116 (1916): 1–47. Troeltsch continued to develop these ideas until his death in 1923. See his *Der Historismus und seine Probleme* (Tübingen: Mohr, 1922), and his essay "Das Wesen des modernen Geistes," in *Aufsätze zur Geistesgeschichte und Religionssoziologie,* ed. Hans Baron (Tübingen: Mohr, 1925), 297–337. In a set of lectures he presented in England in March 1923, Troeltsch did remark that historical relativism was "less intensively at work" in Britain "than it is amongst us on the Continent": *Christian Thought: Its History and Application,* trans. Ernest Barker et al. (London: University of London Press, 1923), 43.

56. Peter Novick, *That Noble Dream: The Objectivity Question and the American Historical Profession* (Cambridge: Cambridge University Press, 1988); also Jacques Revel and Lynn Hunt, eds., *Histories: French Reconstructions of the Past,* trans. Arthur Goldhammer et al. (New York: New Press, 1995).

Index